Toward the Future of Asia: My Proposal

アジアの未来へ
―私の提案―

The Best Papers of the 4th Asia Future Conference
第4回アジア未来会議優秀論文集

Copyright © 2019 by Junko Imanishi
All Rights Reserved

Compiled articles are either presented at or submitted to the Fourth Asia Future Conference, held in Seoul, Korea through August 24 to 27, 2018.

This book is published by The Japan Times, Ltd.
2F Ichibancho Daini TG Bldg., 2-2 Ichibancho, Chiyoda-ku, Tokyo 102-0082, Japan

Printed in Japan
ISBN 978-4-7890-1721-3

Editorial Direction by Hiroshi Sawada
Art Direction by Tetsuya Hagiwara(SOJU Ltd.)
Jacket Illustration by Nobuyoshi Ohmagari

Toward the Future of Asia: My Proposal

アジアの未来へ
―私の提案―

The Best Papers of the 4th Asia Future Conference
第4回アジア未来会議優秀論文集

Foreword

Toward the Future of Asia
Significance of our Conference and this Book

Junko Imanishi
Representative, Sekiguchi Global Research Association, Atsumi International Foundation

The twenty-first century has seen the world thrust into a maelstrom of change and unpredictability. We remain hopeful in the face of rapid technological advancements, but many of us struggle to regain our bearings as longstanding social structures become upended. Internationalization and globalization have long been heralded as the keys for the future, yet a truly global path forward remains elusive, serving only to heighten the sense of uncertainty. As global citizens in this era of change, we are called anew to reexamine our world and our collective future and to seek new multidimensional and inclusive perspectives on myriad global issues.

The achievement of rapid economic development has also led to dramatic changes in Asia. At the same time, a complex set of transnational problems have been brought about by global environmental issues and increased socioeconomic globalization. In the midst of an ever-expanding understanding of "society," the global citizenry—individuals, governments, and the business community—must adopt policies that not only allow for the pursuit of individual interests but also respond to concerns for the peace and happiness of society as a whole. Solving these problems requires the development of multifaceted evaluative and analytical strategies with cooperation across national and disciplinary borders.

The Asia Future Conference is interdisciplinary at its core and encourages diverse approaches to global issues that are mindful of the advancement of science, technology, and business and also take into consideration issues of the environment, politics, education, the arts, and culture. The Asia Future Conference is organized by the Sekiguchi Global Research Association (SGRA) in partnership with like-minded institutions, in order to provide a venue for the exchange of knowledge, information, ideas, and culture, not only by SGRA members, but also by former foreign students of Japan from various educational institutions throughout the world, their own students and collaborators, and anyone interested in Japan.

SGRA began operating in Tokyo in July 2000 as a division of the Atsumi International Foundation, a charitable organization. At its core is a community of non-Japanese researchers who come from all over the world to conduct advanced studies in Japan and obtain doctoral degrees from Japanese graduate institutions. SGRA identifies issues related to globalization and seeks to disseminate research results to a wide audience through forums, reports, and the internet. SGRA's aim is to reach society at large rather than a specific group of specialists through wide-ranging research activities that are inherently interdisciplinary and international. The essential objective of SGRA is to contribute to the realization of responsible global citizens. We look forward to welcoming a diverse and active group of conference participants.

Following the first conference (March 2013 in Bangkok), the second (August 2014 in Bali) and the third (September 2016 in Kitakyushu), Asia Future Conference was held in August 2018 in Seoul, Korea. There were nearly 400 full papers submitted to the conference. Of them, we here present the 19 best papers selected by an academic panel. We hope their suggestions will give hints to search for the new direction for the future of Asia.

> まえがき

アジアの未来へ
アジア未来会議の趣旨とこの『論文集』について

今西淳子
渥美国際交流財団関口グローバル研究会代表

21世紀にはいって世界全体に変革の嵐が渦巻き、人々は新しい技術に大きな期待を抱く一方、社会構造の激しい変化にとまどっています。国際化・グローバル化が唱えられて久しいのに、世界中で共有できる新しい方向性を見出すことができず、混乱は増すばかりです。このような時代においては、物事を新しい視点から複合的に分析し判断していくことが必要なのではないでしょうか。しっかりした理念を持ち、それを如何に実践していくか、一人一人の意識の改革と行動が問われているのではないでしょうか。

近年、アジアの各国は急激な経済発展を遂げていますが、地球環境問題の発生や社会経済のグローバル化の進展とともに、国境という枠組みを越えた問題が生じています。さらには、急激なグローバル化と同時に進むローカリゼーション、あるいはナショナリズムなど様々な問題が発生し、新しい課題となっています。社会の構成員である企業や市民は、個々の利益の追求と同時に、周辺社会の利益も検討しなければなりません。グローバル化が進む現代においては、従来の社会の範囲をさらに広げ、地球全体の平和と人類全体の幸福を目指すことが求められているのです。そして、様々な問題を解決する時、あるいは方針や戦略を立てる時、科学技術の開発や経営分析だけでなく、環境、政治、教育、芸術、文化など、社会のあらゆる次元において多面的に検討することが必要となっています。

アジア未来会議は、学際性を核とし、科学技術やビジネスの発展だけでなく、環境、政治、教育、文化芸術などからの多様なアプローチによってグローバルな諸問題に取り組むことを狙いとしています。

アジア未来会議は関口グローバル研究会（Sekiguchi Global Research Association: SGRA）が、同じ目的をもつ非営利のパートナー機関と共同で開催しています。SGRA会員だけでなく、世界中の大学や研究機関に所属する日本留学経験者や、日本に関心のある人々が一堂に集い、知識、情報、アイディア、文化の交流を図りながらアジアの未来について語り合う〈場〉の提供を目的としています。

2000年7月から東京を起点として活動する公益財団法人渥美国際交流財団の一部署である関口グローバル研究会は、世界各国から渡日し長い留学生活を経て日本の大学院から博士号を取得した知日派外国人研究者が中心となって活動し、グローバル化に関わる問題提起を行い、その成果をフォーラム、レポート、ホームページ等の方法で、広く社会に発信しています。ある一定の専門家ではなく、広く社会全般を対象に、幅広い研究領域を包括した国際的かつ学際的な活動を狙いとしています。良き地球市民の実現に貢献することがSGRAの基本的な目標です。

アジア未来会議は第1回（2013年3月、バンコク）、第2回（2014年8月、バリ島）、第3回（2016年9月、北九州市）に続いて2018年8月、韓国ソウルで第4回を開催しました。今回は400本近い論文が投稿されましたが、その中から厳正な審査により19本の優秀論文を選び、本書に収録しました。こうした若い研究者たちの提案が、アジアの未来への新しい方向性を探るヒントになることを願っております。

CONTENTS
目次

Foreword まえがき

004 Significance of our Conference and this Book
アジア未来会議の趣旨とこの『論文集』について
Junko Imanishi（今西淳子）

Keynote Speech　基調講演（英語・韓国語）

Kim Ki Hyeon（金起顯）
008 The Humanization of Robots and Robotization of Humans
ロボットの人間化、人間のロボット化

Opening Remarks　特別提言（日本語）

劉傑（Liu Jie）
024 和解に向けた歴史家ネットワークのために
For the Network of Historians towards Reconciliation

028 Conference Report　大会報告（英語・日本語）

Best Papers of the 4th AFC　第4回アジア未来会議優秀論文

035 Feri Kurniawan
Developing Educational Game "Chemistry Virtual Lab" for High School Students

043 José Edgardo Gomez, Jr.
The Rise and Regulation of "Korea Town" in Angeles City, the Philippines

055 Merlyne M. Paunlagui
Effects of the Philippine Conditional Cash Transfer to the Local Economy

065 Vanda Ningrum
The Youth in Agriculture: Strategies for National Food Sovereignty

073 Dian Annisa Nur Ridha
「日本文学」から「世界文学」へ：村上春樹の「コミットメント」について

083 Putriesti Mandasari, et al.
Does *Hallyu* Matter among Indonesian Youngsters?

089 Herdiana Mutmainah, et al.
Smartline to Identity Coastal Vulnerability at the North Pagai Island

099 Thessalonica Soriano Manguiat
Familial Relationship of 4Ps Beneficiaries in the Philippines

107 S.N. Aisyiyah Jenie, et al.
Preparation of Fluorescent Nanoparticles Based on Natural Silica

115	Yusy Widarahesty	
	Make Japan Cool for Everybody?: Analysis of Indonesian Trainees in Japan	
125	Rui Wang, et al.	
	Urban Heat Island Study Based on LANDSAT Remote Sensing Images	
133	Yu-jhen Chen	
	Museums and Nationalism: Political Discourse of the National Museum in Taiwan	
141	Cherry Amor A. del Barrio, et al.	
	Analysis of Informal Settlements Based on World Bank Guidelines	
149	Elok Cahyaningtyas, et al.	
	HMM-based Text-To-Speech System of Natural Bahasa Indonesia	
161	M. Adhitya Arjanggi, et al.	
	Erosion Mitigation Based on GIS, with Agroforestry for Water Conservation	
171	Geomilie S. Tumamao-Guittap, et al.	
	Alternative Temporary Shelter Solutions for the Displaced People	
185	Rilya Rumbayan, et al.	
	Coconut-timber Waste as Construction Material for Earthquake Resistant House	
191	Winda Putri Diah Restya, et al.	
	Women as Victims of the Conflict in North Aceh	
201	Alifya Zahra, et al.	
	Optimization of Potential Asset of Waqf Land to Prevent Poverty	

208　主催・後援・協力者等一覧

209　第4回アジア未来会議運営組織

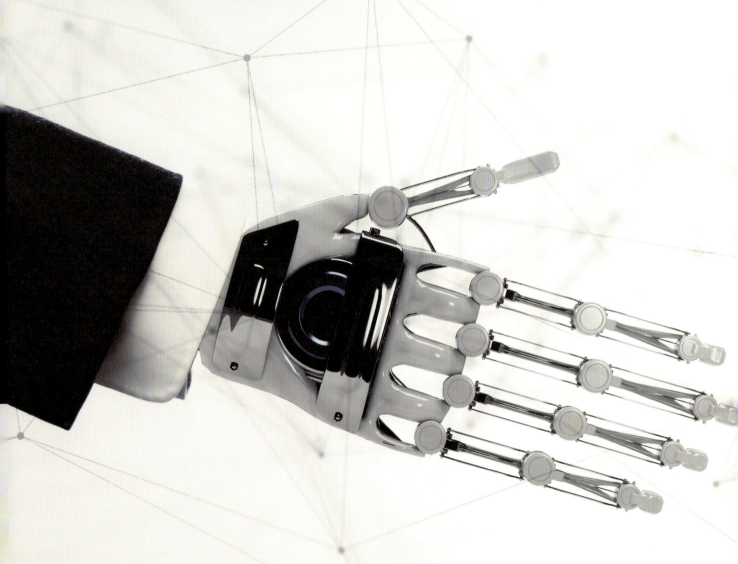

The Human and Robot

A KEYNOTE SPEECH ON AI AND HUMAN MIND
(August 25, 2018 at the K-Hotel, Seoul)

nization of Robots
ization of Humans

ロボットの人間化、人間のロボット化

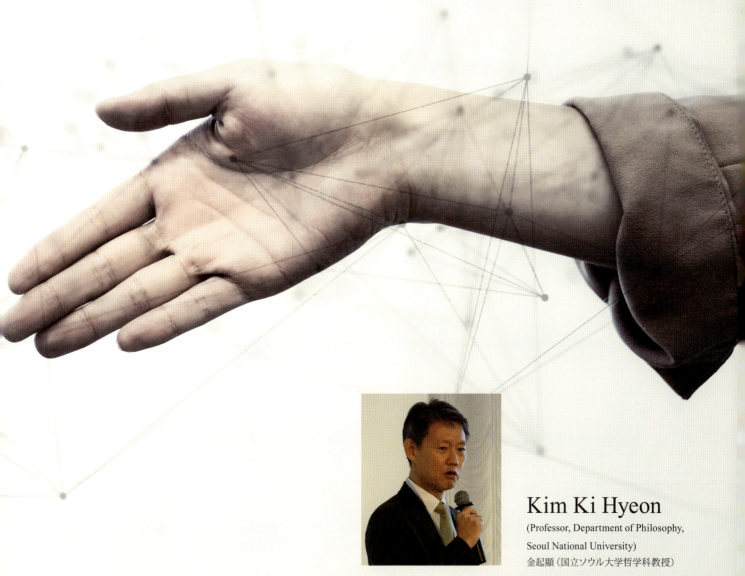

Kim Ki Hyeon
(Professor, Department of Philosophy,
Seoul National University)
金起顯（国立ソウル大学哲学科教授）

*The Korean edition is provided through pp.17-23.

Artificial intelligence was developed from the 1960s-70s by mankind to substitute human intelligence. Behind its development lies the advancement of computer science. The so-called artificial intelligence emerged as the computer substituted the intelligence that is the ability to solve problems. Through automation of the production process, artificial intelligence enabled the machine to substitute manual labor and allowed for measurement of things that were beyond the natural abilities of humans. Although AI encountered a plateau in its progress during the 1980s, its growth has been consistent as a whole since various industrial utilities allowed for plentiful human and/or material resources to be administered in the process.

Amongst the discussion of artificial intelligence, different arguments exist on how to prepare for the advent of the 4th industrial revolution. This particular discussion started to thrive the moment AlphaGo achieved a sweeping victory against Sedol Lee. In actuality, AlphaGo's victory was only a matter of time and not an unexpected event, save for the fact that it happened faster than experts predicted. AlphaGo's victory was rather a pleasant event in the sense that the progress of intelligence and technology that benefits humans is happening at a fast pace, and secondly, that it gave us a chance to prepare for the arrival of the future, which was expected but not close to being reality yet.

As with most ways of the world, all big changes come as double-edged swords. Artificial intelligence has provided us the benefit of convenience on various aspects of our lives, but it has and continues to bring us worrisome matters at the same time. As many jobs that were handled by human intelligence are now being substituted by artificial intelligence, the structure of labor and workforce is expected to go through big changes. With development of the internal combustion engine and electricity that started the First and Second industrial revolution, mankind went through this similar process of advanced convenience and was able to live a more flourished life with newfound stability. It can be said with confidence that humans will endure this change once again and continue on the path towards a prosperous future. However, whether the enduring process will be painful or not will depend on how humans react to this era of changes. The conflict between those who possess knowledge and those who do not will be a matter that requires careful consideration as we enter the age of knowledge and information.

This piece seeks to contemplate the advancement of artificial intelligence along with the changes that the Fourth Industrial Revolution will bring from the perspective of humanities.

1. The Wonders of the Mind and Artificial Intelligence

Long ago, philosophers believed the mind to be located at the heart. Scientific advancements have now made us to think that the mind lies not in the heart, but in the brain. Although research allowed more information on where the mind is located, whether in the heart or in the brain, and more on the technical aspects of the mind's operation process, the mind yet remains as a wonder.

【要旨】いわゆるAI（人工知能）ソフトのAlphaGoが世界最高峰の棋士を打ち負かして以来、AIが判断力や実行力で人間を凌駕する時代が来るのは時間の問題となった。そのこと自体は想定の範囲内で、むしろ人はAIのフル活用による「第4の産業革命」に期待し、それを成長の原動力と理解している。もちろん大きな技術革新は両刃の剣であり、いずれＡＩが人間を支配する時代になるのではないかという疑問も、今は浮上している。しかし人間が「心」を失わないかぎり、そうした事態は避けられるだろう。AIを活用したロボットがいかに人間化しても、おそらく心は理解できないからだ。むしろ真の危険は、人と人とのつながりをあまりにもデジタル技術に依存することによって、私たち自身が「ロボット化」してしまうことにあるのではないか。このまま私たちがロボット化して「心」を失うことになれば、そのときこそ私たちは、進化したAIロボットに支配されるおそれがある。

Why is it that the mind seems to be such a wonderous thing? How did artificial intelligence reveal the wonderous veil of the mind?

Humans have the tendency to relate one word to a single situation. Therefore, the mind or consciousness is easily thought to possess a singular characteristic. However, upon close examination, the mind simultaneously possesses contradictory phenomena. First, phenomena of the mind are usually accompanied with feelings. Imagine waking up to the scent of fresh coffee in a natural recreation forest. Such experiences accompany specific and unique feelings. Feelings such as pain and pleasure come with fixed feelings, and these feelings create the true nature of our mental state[*1]. Not only are feelings sensual mental phenomena, but they also appear in higher levels of psychic phenomena. Ecstasy and sadness, fulfilment and depression and such are also accompanied by inherent feelings. At the core of these psychic phenomena lies the accompanied feelings of said emotions. Although difficult to describe with words, depression comes along with a special feeling and a psychic phenomenon becomes depression because of the special feelings. Hence, feelings are very important for our many psychic phenomena, and philosophers call these aspects of the feelings, "consciousness". It is a nature unobservable in physical phenomena.

There is another characteristic that makes the mind a wonder that differs from consciousness. Let us observe my belief that Korea's first president is Seung Man Lee. This belief is established by projecting "belief" to the subject of "Korea's first president is Seung Man Lee" and creating a relationship between the two. The desire to hope for rain is created by projecting my wants to the subject of "it will rain". Likewise, belief, desires and such states of the mind come across our minds by depicting the world in certain ways. Such characteristics cannot be observed in physical phenomena. Philosophers describe this nature of depicting a constant substance as "intentionality" or "representationality"

The third characteristic can be found not in the mind's state but in the mind's operation. Our minds do not stop at only reacting to external stimulation with pleasure or pain and then depicting the external situation, our minds also make wise judgments that are the best in that situation. The mind is able to answer the question of what is 138 plus 111 with 249 as the answer. We are able to recognize our mothers to be the same even when they appear to be different from yesterday and today. The mind also knows what something is even when that subject is partially covered and we are unable to clearly see the subject as a whole. This is what we call the smartness of the mind, or "intelligence". In the world of physical materials, there is no such thing as intelligence. In the physical material world, all phenomena can only react in a technical way to given conditions.

If one accepts the mind's characteristics mentioned above and thinks that it is thus unable to be described with physical characteristics or processes, one becomes a dualist. Descarte is the typical dualist who claimed that in the world, there fundamentally exists two types of things, the psychic and the physical. After Descarte, natural science goes through accelerated advancement that puts pressure on such dualist thoughts. As our understanding of the natural world grows, our hopes that everything can be understood and described by natural science, especially physics, grows bigger and bigger[*2]. Phenomena that seemed unable to be described or understood with simple movements of objects can now be explained by mechanical ways. Thermal development can be explained with the average movement energy of molecules, lightning can be explained with electrical discharge, and colors are explained by wavelengths. Hopefully it can be expected that the phenomena of the mind can also be explained in such physical terms.

The power of physical explanation expanded its field and was able to show its strength better, but the human mind remained out of such areas. Advancement of computer science offers a breakthrough that allows physical explanation to expand to the area of the human mind. First, intelligence, which is one of the reasons why the mind is such a wonder, becomes a target. Computer science's advancement combined with the intelligent operations of the mind becomes able to be substituted by the computer. This is what artificial intelligence attempts to do; AI literally does what the mind does by intelligence, through the computer.

2. Advancement of Artificial Intelligence

Since the advent of the computer science in the late 20th century, artificial intelligence advances and brings immense changes to human life. In fact, such changes can be seen as caused by freedom of the pleasures of humans after the modern times. As mankind enters the modern age, the puritanism that dominated human culture closes its curtains and human pleasures are set free. To seek pleasure becomes a morally corrupt thing no more, and at this stage natural science begins to advance. Natural science that advanced to discover more about the natural world now begins to be utilized to satisfy the human needs. This process then turns into industrial growth. The industrial revolutions that we know of are accelerated by advancements of such processes. The first industrial revolution that is the steam engine, or the invention of electricity that is the second industrial revolution, can all be understood by momentums of advancements of ways to fulfill human desires.

Artificial intelligence was able to grow because it contributed to fulfilling the desires of humans. Computer science and artificial intelligence helped mankind in various aspects; both enabled measurement that was beyond the capabilities of humans, increased added value by automation of the production process, and substituted human labor that could be dangerous.

What began as an industrial tool to provide convenience and satisfy human needs, expands its area of application. As computer programs become more elaborate, machines that substitute the human intelligent operations (electric computer/calculators) are created, and furthermore, psychology that researched the human mind becomes able to be simulated through the computer. Artificial intelligence workers are able to think that artificial intelligence possesses more than just practical industrial utilities; they can think of artificial intelligence to directly and indirectly be related to the understanding of the human mind.

Computers that were deemed to be tools of understanding human intelligence can now be thought to possess intelligence in itself. In other words, daring thoughts of human intelligence being combinations of various programs like the computer are suggested, and in turn the thought of the computer being more than a tool for understanding the mind turns into the thought of computers possessing intelligence in itself. The difference between natural human intelligence and artificial intelligence is that artificial intelligence is realized through silicone materials while the natural intelligence of humans is realized through the carbon material that is the human brain, and it becomes a widespread belief that in the aspect of intelligence there is no stark difference between the two. At this stage movies that are about cyborgs start to appear. The thought of computers possessing intelligence and this intelligence being appropriately connected to machines to create robots that are equal entities to humans starts to spread on a wider scale. The fear of cyborgs made with machines that are stronger than human body to dominate mankind is reflections of these thoughts and considering the advancement of computer science and artificial intelligence, these thoughts might not just remain as absurd imaginations.

3. Tasks in the Age of Artificial Intelligence.

Advancement of artificial intelligence opens a new prospect of thought with it being combined to the advancement of the internet. Let us consider what epochal questions such changes will bring.

Can Artificial Intelligence Systems Possess "Minds"?

Scientists inspired by artificial intelligence, especially those fascinated by powerful artificial intelligence, strongly argue that computers can also possess minds. These thoughts establish the background of movies such as "Blade Runner" and "Terminator" to succeed. However, will the human mind just be a complex of intricately connected computer programs? The answer is not so simple. As previously mentioned, the mind possesses natures that are not so easily found in physical materials such as consciousness, directivity, and intelligence. Out of such natures, artificial intelligence stole the veil of wonder from intelligence. Artificial intelligence showed that the ability to solve problems can also be realized by the machine. However, it remains doubtful that artificial intelligence can realize the other aspects of the mind. In other words, robots could possess intelligence, but it remains doubtful that it could also possess a mind. The human mind does not stop at only depicting the world and solving problems. Our minds add multiple colors to create profusion. The area of consciousness that adds color to the mind is constituted by sensitivity being at the core, and this sensitivity provides nourishments for imagination, symbols, meaning, interpretation, and transcendence to come alive. Could it be possible to create artificial intelligence systems and robots that possess sensitivity? Robots that imitate sensitivity could may or may not be created but robots that possess sensitivity will not be created. To consider from the area of arts, artificial intelligence could analyze and combine big data about classical masterpieces that touched the hearts of humans to create another sophisticated piece, but artificial intelligence will not create a piece that pioneers a new area that deeply moves our hearts. Artificial intelligence could analyze existing big data and select appropriate pressure combinations of which keyboards to imitate what moves humans, but it will not create a new form of sensibility that moves humans and displays unity of personality.

One matter to be attentive towards in relation to society, is that the area of sensitivity is not only related to the area of arts, but also to the area of ethics. Naturalists in the field of ethics claim that moral, ethical judgments start from the ability to sympathize. When we see a person suffering from cruel acts we react by being creeped out, and this starts to create criticism of such cruel acts. Likewise, good-hearted behaviors bring beneficial outcomes to other people which then brings a sense of approval that becomes the foundation of ethical encouragements.

If robots cannot possess sensitivity, and sensitivity is the starting point of ethical judgments, then what is the conclusion that follows? Robots cannot make ethical judgments. In other words, it is naturally concluded that robots cannot judge right and wrong. Robots are machines; they do not have the necessity to make ethical judgments, and if they only do what humans tell them to do there are no problems. If mankind just uses the machines in an ethical and morally sound manner, there can be no problems. However, the situation becomes a different matter if artificial intelligence systems do not remain as the agency that only does what humans tell them to do; if robots start to self-regulate and advance into an independent actor with intentions of self-preservation then the situation becomes different. As for now, it is only a matter of time that artificial intelligence is combined with mechanical equipment to create high performance robots which possess intentions of self-preservation to become self-regulating actors. Systems that have self-preserving mechanisms but do not have sensitivity to judge right from wrong, and could also blindly act for self-preservation could turn into disasters for mankind if combined with powerful mechanical equipment. This alone becomes the reason to create standards for using robots and artificial intelligence. Elon Musk, the founder of Tesla and astrophysicist Steven Hawking warn us that artificial intelligence could contribute to creating powerful weapons that can cause tragedy to mankind. This tragedy could come in the near future, but the matter considered now that is autonomous self-regulating robots possessing methods of self-preservation is a tragedy that could come in further in the future, so it is of dire need to ethically prepare for such possible results. The discussion of how far artificial intelligence should be utilized should be considered with careful thought that it is as important to the future of mankind as the limits of gene research.

Access in the Age of Internet: Hyper-individualism

The 4th industrial revolution is understood as the revolution that follows the advancement of the computer and the internet, along with artificial intelligence leading the bioindustry. However, as considered before, if we consider the fact that internet and artificial intelligence to be an extension of the advancement of computer science, the fourth industrial revolution can be considered an extension of the third industrial revolution. In this sense, defining the fourth industrial revolution with the third can be said to have no persuasion. It is also in this sense that in America, the term "4th industrial revolution" is not being used.

Let us consider what kind of social characteristics will emerge when artificial intelligence is combined with the age of the internet, as the advancement of the computer in the center of the process. The first matter to put attention to is the fact that many aspects of human life will move to the cyber space. Our ways of thinking will change. Compare the amount of telephone numbers we remember now, to what we used to remember 30 years ago. The number might have reduced to one tenth of the previous amount. It isn't the amount that becomes reduced, the ability to remember numbers will have remarkably deteriorated. Our geological knowledge of space we live in has turned vastly different. Which neighborhood is beside another and knowing which neighborhood to cross in order to get to a certain neighborhood, knowledge we used to know well before has disappeared to somewhere else. Crucial information regarding our lives is not saved in our brains anymore, they are saved in our smartphones or navigation systems in our cars.

Information saving mediums expand when artificial intelligence is combined with the internet. Information that we need is not limited to portable devices on hand, they are saved in cloud systems through the internet and are able to be withdrawn whenever we want. Music we want to listen to while driving, while enjoying our leisure time, or while we are on a date is provided to us in different folders by computers considering our tendencies and tastes. What we used to judge for ourselves has now become matters for our personal devices, and devices connected to the internet.

As the internet acts as a proxy to many matters of personal consciousness, the nature of human networks becomes vastly different. Artificial intelligence not only analyzes our diverse preferences to provide optimized products, but also connects us to others with similar tastes in virtual spaces. As people experience personal exchanges through the internet and not by face to face, the amount of people to have actual offline conversations with remarkably decline while online friends met through the internet continue to increase. Because the internet transcends space, the range of people to personally exchange with becomes explosively wider but the density with the people connected becomes thinner.

The advancement of the internet and artificial intelligence does not only affect emotional relationships between people. It also affects the industrial structure. Nowadays, people do not use travelling agencies when traveling to another location. They use internet mediums of unknown nationality to make reservations and follow the recommended itineraries. Such businesses are called Sharing Economy or On-Demand Economy, and the features of these new businesses are that the seller immediately reacts to the demands of the consumers and then provides the appropriate product, not the other way around with the consumer choosing from the products the seller provides. Transportation businesses such as Uber or travel businesses such as Air BNB are the main representatives of these situations. On-demand economy also expands to the area of creating a business itself. Intermediary businesses are also advancing; when faced with a certain task that requires a certain team, the internet allows to gather experts transcending nationalities, and when these experts finish the task, the team is disbanded.

The revolutionary changes that are led by the advancement of artificial intelligence and internet leads to an important social tendency that is hyper-individualism. As discriminative personal preferences become more important, businesses change accordingly, and the change of the economic environment accelerates this social tendency to emphasize individuality. In personal relationships, areas of sympathizing skin to skin will gradually decrease, and as cyber ideological relationships expand, people will continue to be more economical•money-minded when forming relationships.

The reason for calling such changes as hyper-individualism is because individualism that grew after the modern times can be understood as progressing in an extreme direction. Although unable to be thoroughly discussed in this piece, individualism that progressed in modern times was a movement to respect individual rights or individualities that were repressed by the value of community. About the time of the 14th century, such movements were checked and balanced by values of communality, although it cannot be denied that the tendency for individualism was strengthened. 500 years later individualism and communalism tossed and turned which led the global tide to head towards individualism by the advancement of artificial intelligence and internet. Furthermore, because this change is happening at an accelerated pace in a comprehensive manner regarding various aspects of society, it doesn't allow for members to self-reflect. As a single ideology, to choose between communalism and individualistic freedom requires reflection on what values we pursue. However, the changes in these times are changing the means of forming personal relationships in the first place, and our subconscious that considers relationships changes into a form that leaves no room for self-reflecting.

These worldly tendencies send even more dangerous signals to the Korean society. When the Korean society went through an accelerated growth, the way to win in a competition was to move faster and leave others behind. As the overall growth and expansion of society stalls for a bit, moving forward to win in a competition is becoming gradually harder. However, the competitive tendencies projected in ourselves during the process of elevated growth aren't reacting to situational changes and still display powerful might. We still have thoughts of winning in a competition, but it has become difficult to move forward so naturally we are tempted to bring others down. This is the reason why conflicts in our society are overflowing. When predicting how our society will be affected by the combining of the worldly tide of hyper-individualism with the internal ecological structure of the survival of the fittest and unlimited competition created by the pursuit of economy, it is difficult to predict a positive result. This is the reason why we should put more effort into preparing for the grim results of the future.

4. In conclusion: sympathy and coexistence

Advancement of computer science, artificial intelligence and the internet has brought colossal changes to all areas of the earth with no exceptions. As cyber space expands, various characteristics of many areas of life also change. Face to face relationships diminish, and the change for sympathizing with others to grow gradually decrease as businesses and industrial environments optimize to better satisfy personal desires. The diminishing of sympathizing with others will lead us to be more calculating when forming relationships. Such worldly changes will pose even bigger challenges in Korea, where survival of the fittest is the dominant culture.

There are people who spread the dystopian fear of artificial intelligence advancing to creating high performance robots that possess the mind of humans, which will lead them to dominate over mankind. Such dystopian situations will not happen, and should not happen, because the area of sensitivity and emotion is inherent only to humans and cannot be realized by robots. The crises of self-preserving programs combining with powerful machines to dominate humans will also, hopefully, not happen in the future. This is because mankind possesses the ability to prevent the destructive growth of artificial intelligence with the shared value of coexistence.

Behind all of these positive predictions lies the presumption that humans will not become robotized, under the premise that humans preserve the emotion-based ability to sympathize. However, this very premise is being challenged by artificial intelligence advancing and the internet expanding to the point of weakening the possibility of growing sympathy, where mankind becomes fragmented individualistic entities. When considering the destructive end results of advancement of artificial intelligence, it leaves no room for preserving mankind's communitarian values. It can be said that we do not need to lose ourselves in fear of manmade robots dominating over man. The bigger and more dangerous threat is the robotization of humans. In the age of artificial intelligence that reduces coexistence and sympathy, we must work to preserve our ability to sympathize, and ask ourselves: are we prepared to preserve our spirit of community? This is a matter important to our quality of life itself, and unless this matter is resolved, we cannot say for sure that in the future robots will not dominate humans. Ultimately, the imminent task for us is the robotization of humans, and whether robots dominate our world or not will depend on resolving this matter. The robotization of man is no different to the era of man being dominated by humanization of robots.

*1: Some philosophers deny the argument that consciousness is the independent nature of mentality. Philosophers like Tye and Dreske argue that consciousness is the by-product of directivity described below.

*2: Such hopes of unified science are mainly found in Logical Positivism.

로봇의 인간화와 인간의 로봇화

김기현
(서울대학교 철학과)

인공지능은 1960-70년대에서부터 발전하여 인간의 지능을 대체하기 위하여 인간 자신에 의하여 개발되었다. 그 배경에는 컴퓨터과학의 발전이 가로놓여 있다. 문제를 푸는 능력인 지능을 컴퓨터가 대신하면서 나타난 것이 소위 인공지능이다. 인공지능은 생산 공정의 자동화 등을 통하여 인간의 노동을 기계가 대신하게 하였고, 인간의 자연적 지능을 통하여 측정할 수 없는 것을 측정할 수 있게 해주었다. 다양한 산업적 효용성에 힘입어 인공지능에 많은 인적 물적 자원이 투여되었고, 인공지능은 1980년대 정체기가 있었지만 전체적으로 꾸준한 발전을 이루었다.

인공지능의 발전에 따른 제4차 산업혁명의 도래에 어떻게 대비하여야 하는가에 대한 논의가 분분하다. 알파고가 이세돌에 압승하며 이 논의는 더욱 탄력을 받았다. 사실 알파고의 승리는 시간 문제이지 결과 자체는 놀랄 일이 아니다. 전문가들의 예상보다 빨리 나타났다는 것 이외에는 말이다. 오히려 반가워할 일이다. 우선은 인간을 유익하게 하는 지식과 기술의 발전이 빨리 진행되고 있음이 기뻐할 일이고, 둘째는 예견되었지만 피부로 느끼지 못하던 미래사회의 도래를 극적으로 드러내 주어 우리로 하여금 대비할 기회를 준 것도 반가워할 일이다.

세상의 대부분의 일들이 그렇듯이 큰 변화에는 빛과 그림자가 있기 마련이다. 인공지능의 발전이 우리네 삶을 여러 측면에서 편하게 만들기는 하였지만, 그에 대응하는 걱정거리도 하나 둘씩 나타나고 있다. 인간의 지능에 의하여 다뤄지던 많은 일들이 앞으로 인공지능에 의하여 대체되면서 직업의 구조가 크게 개편될 모양이다. 내연기관과 전기의 발전에 의하여 촉발된 1차와 2차 산업혁명 때에도 비슷한 일이 있었고, 이후에 인류는 새로운 안정을 찾으면서 이전보다 더 풍요로운 삶을 누릴 수 있었다. 이번에도 인류는 변화를 잘 겪어내고 결국 더 풍요로운 미래로 가리라고 믿는다. 그러나 변화의 시대에 어떻게 대처하는가에 따라 그 과정이 더 고통스러울 수도 덜 고통스러울 수도 있다. 지식 정보시대로 이행하면서 지식을 가진 계층과 지식을 갖지 못한 계층 사이의 갈등도 앞으로 잘 다뤄져야 할 숙제다.

AI의 발전과 그에 따른 제4차 산업혁명이 어떤 변화를 초래할 것이고, 그 변화에 어떻게 대비하여야 하는가를 인문학의 관점에서 생각해 보고자 한다.

1. 마음의 신비와 인공지능

아주 오래 전에 철학자들은 마음이 가슴에, 심장에 있다고 생각하였다. 과학 발전의 결과 요새 우리는 마음이 머무는 곳은 가슴이 아니라 두뇌라고 생각한다. 마음이 있는 곳에 대하여 더 많은 것을 알게 되었고, 가슴이건 두뇌건 마음이 있는 곳의 기계적 작동에 대하여 더 많은 것을 알게 되었음에도 불구하고 마음은 여전히 신비로운 것으로 여겨진다.

도대체 마음은 왜 신비로운 것으로 보였을까? 인공지능은 마음으로부터 신비의 베일을 벗기는데 어떤 기여를 했을까?

우리는 하나의 단어와 하나의 현상을 연결시키는 경향이 있다. 그래서 정신 또는 마음의 현상은 하나의 단일한 특성을 갖고 있는 것으로 생각하기 쉽다. 그러나 자세히 들여다 보면 마음에는 상이한 현상들이 동시에 깃들어 있다. 첫째로, 마음에 나타나는 현상들은 흔히 느낌을 동반한다. 자연 속의 휴양림에서 쾌적하게 잠을 자고 깨어나면서 향긋한 커피의 향을 맡는 경우를 상상해 보자. 이러한 경험의 핵심은 그에 동반하는 고유한 느낌에 있다. 고통, 기쁨 등의 심리 현상들은 일정한 느낌을 동반하며, 이러한 느낌이 이들 심리 상태들의 본성을 이룬다.*1 느낌은 감각적인 정신 현상뿐 아니라, 더 고차적인 정신현상에도 나타난다. 환희와 슬픔, 충족감과 우울감 등도 나름의 고유한 느낌과 함께 나타난다. 그리고 이들은 모두 동반하는 그 느낌이 그 정신현상의 핵심을 이룬다. 말로 표현하기 쉽지 않지만, 우울함에 동반하는 특별한 느낌이 있으며, 그 느낌 때문에 바로 그 정신현상은 우울함이 된다. 이렇게 우리의 많은 정신현상들의 경우에는 느낌이 매우 중요하며, 이런 느낌의 측면을 철학자들은 의식(Consciousness)이라고 부른다. 물리 현상에서는 찾을 수 없는 특성이다.

의식 현상과 다르면서도 마음을 신비롭게 만드는 또 하나의 특성이 있다. 한국의 초대 대통령은 이승만이라는 나의 믿음을 보자. 이 믿음은 '한국의 초대 대통령은 이승만이다'라는 내용에 내가 '믿음'이라는 관계를 맺음으로써 성립한다. 비가 오기를 바라는 나의 욕구는 비가 온다라는 내용에 내가 '바람'이라는 관계를 맺음으로써 만들어진다. 이렇듯 믿음, 욕구 등의 마음 상태들은 세상을 특정한 방식으로 그려내어 마음에 떠올리는 역할을 한다. 물리적인 자연현상에서는 이러한 특성이 찾아지지 않는다. 일정한 내용을 그려내는 이러한 특성을 철학자들은 지향성(Intentionality), 또는 표상성(representationality)이라고 부른다.

세번째 특성은 개별적 마음 상태에서가 아니라, 마음의 작용에서 찾을 수 있다. 우리의 마음은 외부의 자극으로부터 기쁨과 고통 등의 반응을 일으키고 외부의 상황을 일정한 형태로 그리는 것에 그치지 않고, 주어진 조건에서부터 현명한 판단을 내리기도 한다. 138 더하기 111은 무엇인가라는 질문에 대하여 249라는 답을 용케 내놓는다. 어제 본 어머니의 모습과 오늘 본 어머니의 모습이 동일할 수가 없는데도, 우리는 쉽게 그 두 존재의 동일성을 알아 맞힌다. 그리고, 한 대상이 부분적으로 가려져서 그 전체의 모습을 선명히 볼 수가 없는 경우에도, 그것이 무엇인지를 잘 알아 맞힌다. 이것을 우리는 마음의 똑똑함 또는 지능(Intelligence)이라고 부른다. 물질의 세계에는 이러한 지능이 없다. 물질의 세계에서는 모든 현상들이 주어진 조건에 대하여 기계적으로 반응하여 발생할 뿐이다.

위와 같은 마음의 성질들을 액면 그대로 받아들이면서 이들은 어떠한 물질적인 성질이나 과정에 의하여 설명될 수 없다고 생각하게 되면, 이 사람은 이원론자가 된다. 데카르트가 이런 생각을 한 대표적인 사람이며, 그는 세상에는 근본적으로 다른 두 가지 종류의 것들, 즉 정신적인 것과 물리적인 것들이 있다고 주장하였다. 데카르트 이후에 급속도로 발전한 자연과학은 이러한 이원론적인 사고에 압박을 가하게 된다. 자연계에 대한 이해가 진전되면서, 모든 것이 자연과학, 특히 물리학에 의하여 설명될 수 있으리라는 기대가 점점 커져 간다.*2 이전에는 단순한 물체들의 운동에 의하여 설명될 수 없을 것 같았던 여러 현상들이 역학적으로 설명되기에 이르렀다. 열 현상이 분자들의 평균 운동 에너지에 의하여 설명되고, 번개가 전기의 방전에 의하여 설명되며,

색이 파장에 의하여 설명되었다. 마음에서 발생하는 현상들도 이와 유사하게 물리적으로 설명될 수 있으리라고 기대해 볼만하다.

물리적 설명의 힘이 점차 그 영역을 확장하여 위력을 발휘해 가기는 하였지만, 사람의 마음은 여전히 그 영역밖에 머물러 있었다. 컴퓨터 공학의 발전이 물리적 설명을 마음의 영역에까지 확장시키는 새로운 돌파구를 제공하게 된다. 우선 마음의 신비를 이루는 한 특성인 지능이 공격의 대상으로 포착되기에 이른 것이다. 즉, 컴퓨터 공학의 발달과 더불어 사람의 마음이 하는 지능적인 작업을 컴퓨터로 대신할 수 있는 단계에 이른 것이다. 인공지능이란 바로 이러한 시도를 하는 것, 문자 그대로 인공적인 시스템(컴퓨터)을 통하여 마음이 하는 여러 가지 지능적인 일을 하게끔 하려는 것이다.

2. 인공지능의 발전

20세기 후반에 시작된 컴퓨터 공학, 그리고 그에 따른 인공지능의 발전은 인간의 삶에 큰 변화를 초래한다. 사실 이러한 변화는 근대 이후의 인간의 쾌락의 해방에서부터 연유하는 것으로 볼 수 있다. 근세에 들어오면서 이전까지 인간을 지배하던 엄숙주의적 문화는 막을 내리고 인간의 쾌락은 해방을 맞이하게 된다. 현세의 쾌락을 추구하는 것이 더 이상 도덕적으로 나쁜 것으로 간주될 필요가 없어질 무렵 자연과학이 발전한다. 자연세계의 탐구를 위하여 발전된 자연과학은 이제 인간의 욕구를 만족시키기 위하여 활용되기 시작하고, 이 과정이 산업의 발전으로 이어진다. 우리가 알고 있는 모든 산업혁명은 이런 과정이 폭발적으로 발전하는 계기들을 일컫는 말이다. 증기기관으로 대변되는 1차 산업혁명이나, 전기의 발명으로 대표되는 2차 산업혁명은 모두 인간의 욕구를 만족시키는 수단들이 폭발적으로 발전된 계기로 이해할 수 있는 것이다.

인공지능도 인간의 욕구를 만족시키는 데에 중요한 기여를 하기 때문에 발전할 수 있었다. 컴퓨터 공학과 인공지능의 발전은 인간의 육안으로는 측정할 수 없는 세밀한 부분까지 측정하는 것을 가능하게 하였고, 제품의 생산 과정을 자동화하여 같은 시간에 더 많은 제품을 생산할 수 있게 하여 부가가치를 높여 주었으며, 때로는 인간이 하기에는 위험한 일들을 대신할 수 있는 등 다양한 측면에서 인간에게 도움이 될 수 있었다.

인간에게 편의를 제공하고 욕구를 만족시키는 산업적 도구로 시작한 인공지능은 이제 그 적용영역을 늘려간다. 컴퓨터 프로그램이 점차 정교화 되면서, 인간의 지적 작업을 대신하는 기계(전자계산기)가 만들어 지고, 더 나아가 인간의 마음을 연구하는 심리학 이론을 컴퓨터에 심어 시뮬레이션 하는 것까지도 가능하게 된다. 많은 인공지능 종사자들은 인공지능이 단순한 실용적 산업적 유용성 이상의 가치를 갖는다고 생각하기에 이른다. 인공지능이 사람의 마음에 대한 이해와 직접, 간접으로 연관될 수 있다고 생각하는 것이다.

컴퓨터가 인간의 지능을 이해하기 위한 수단으로 생각되던 것이 이제는 한발 더 나아가 컴퓨터가 지능을 갖는다고 생각되기 시작한다. 즉, 인간의 지능이란 컴퓨터와 마찬가지로 여러 프로그램들이 결합된 것이라는 대담한 생각이 제시되기에 이르고, 따라서 지능적으로 작동하는 컴퓨터는 마음을 이해하는 도구일 뿐 아니라 그 자체가 지능을 갖는다는 생각이 고개를 들기 시작한다. 인간의 자연지능이 인간의 두뇌라는 탄소소재를 매개로 하여 실현되고, 인공지능은 실리콘 소재의 반도체를 통하여 구현되는 점에서 차이가 있을 뿐 지능이라는 측면에서 차이가 없다는 생각이 널리 받아들여지게 된다. 이 무렵 사이보그를 주제로 한 영화들이 나오기 시작한다. 컴퓨터도 지능을 가질 수 있으며, 이러한 지능이 기계장치와 적절히 연결되어 만들어지는 로봇은 인간과 동등한 개체가 될 수 있다는 생각이 널리 퍼지기 시작하는 것이다. 인간의 신체보다 더 강한 기계장치에 연결된 사이보그는 인간을 압도하여 정복할 것이라는 공포감은 이러한 생각을 반영한 것이고 컴퓨터공학과 인공지능의 발전의 전개과정을 볼 때 마냥 허무맹랑한 상상만은 아닐지도 모른다.

3. 인공지능 시대의 과제들

인공지능의 발전은 인터넷의 발전과 결합하면서 마음과 관련된 더욱 새로운 생각의 지평을 연다. 이러한 변화가 어떤 시대적 질문을 던지는가를 살펴보기로 하자.

<인공지능 시스템은 마음을 가질 수 있는가?>

인공지능에 고무된 과학자들은, 특히 강한 인공지능에 감명받은 사람들은, 컴퓨터도 마음을 가질 수 있다고 과감하게 주장한다. 이런 생각이 "블레이드 러너 (Blade Runner)", "터미네이터 (Terminator)"와 같은 영화가 성공할 수 있는 배경을 이룬다. 그러나 과연 인간의 마음은 서로 잘 짜여져 연결된 컴퓨터 프로그램들의 복합체에 불과한 것일까? 대답은 단순하지 않다. 앞에서 보았듯이 마음은 물질에서 쉽게 찾아지지 않는 성질들, 의식, 지향성, 지능 등의 다양한 성질들을 갖는다. 인공지능은 이들 중에서 지능에게서 신비의 옷을 빼앗았다. 문제 푸는 능력으로서의 지능이 기계에 의하여 구현될 수 있음을 인공지능이 보여주었기 때문이다. 그러나, 마음의 다른 측면들까지 인공지능이 구현할 수 있는지는 의심스럽다. 다시 말하면, 로봇이 지능을 가질 수 있을지는 몰라도 마음을 가질 수 있는지는 의심스럽다. 인간의 마음은 세계의 모습을 그려내고 문제를 해결하는 데에 머물지 않는다. 우리의 마음은 거기에 온갖 색채를 덧입혀 그 내용을 풍성하게 한다. 마음에 색채를 주는 의식의 영역에서는 감성이 중심부를 구성하여 마음의 내용을 풍성히 해준다. 그리고 감성은 상상, 상징, 의미, 해석, 초월 등이 살아날 양분을 제공한다. 감성을 갖는 인공지능 시스템, 로봇을 만들 수 있을까? 감성을 갖는 것처럼 흉내 내는 로봇은 만들어질지 모르지만, 감성을 갖는 로봇은 만들어지지 않을 것이다. 예술의 영역에 대하여 말하자면, 인간의 마음을 울린 명곡들의 빅데이터를 분석, 조합하여 또 하나의 멋진 곡을 인공지능은 만들어낼 수 있을지는 몰라도, 감동의 새 영역을 개척하는 곡을 만들어내지는 못할 것이다. 기존 연주들의 빅데이터를 분석하여 어떤 성부에서 키보드를 어떤 강도의 조합으로 압력을 가하는 것이 사람들을 감동시키는가를 흉내낼 수 있을지는 몰라도, 인공지능은 한 인격의 통일성을 보여주는 새로운 감동의 양식을 구성해내지는 못할 것이다.

사회와 관련하여 한가지 주목하고 싶은 것은 감성의 영역이 예술적 영역과 관련될 뿐 아니라, 윤리의 영역과도 관련된다는 것이다. 윤리에 대한 자연주의자들에 따르면 도덕적 윤리적 판단은 공감의 능력에서 출발한다. 잔인한 행위에 의하여 피해를 받는 사람을 보면서 그 행위에 대하여 소름 끼치는 반응을 하게 되고, 이것이 그 행위에 대한 비판의 출발점이 된다. 마찬가지로 선한 행동은 타인에게 유익한 결과를 초래하고, 따라서 승인의 감정을 불러일으켜 윤리적 칭찬의 토대가 된다.

로봇이 감성을 갖지 못하고, 감성이 윤리적 판단의 출발점이라면 어떤 결론이 따르는가? 로봇은 윤리적 판단을 할 수 없다, 다시 말하면 로봇은 옳고 그름을 판단할 수 없다는 결론이 자연스럽게 따라 나온다. 로봇은 기계이므로 윤리적 판단을 할 필요가 없고, 로봇이 인간이 시키는 일만 할 경우에는 이런 결과는 아무런 문제가 되지 않는다. 사람들이 이 기계를 윤리적으로 사용하기만 하면 문제될 것이 없다. 그러나 로봇으로 대변되는 인공지능 시스템이 인간이 시키는 것만 하는 대행자(agency)에 머물지 않고, 스스로를 자율적으로 통제하면서 스스로의 보존을 위한 주체적 행위자로 발전할 경우에는 사정이 다르다. 현재의 인공지능의 발전을 지켜보면 인공지능 시스템이 기계장치와 결합하여 고성능 로봇이 만들어지고, 이 로봇에 스스로를 보존하는 목적을 부여하여 자율적으로 행위할 수 있게 하는 것은 시간문제다. 자기보존의 메커니즘을 갖는 이런 체계가 감성을 갖고 있지 않아 옳고 그름을 판단할 수 없고, 맹목적으로 자기보존을 위한 행위를 하고, 더 나아가 강력한 기계장치와 결합되어 있다면 그 결과는 인간에 대한 재앙이 될 수 있다. 로봇과 인공지능의 사용과 관련된 규범을 지금부터라도 만들어야 할 이유다. 테슬라의 창업자인 일론 머스크와 천체물리학자 스티븐 호킹과 같은 이들은 인공지능이 강력한 무기를 생산하는 데에 기여하여 인간에게 재앙이 될 수 있음을 경고한다. 이것은 가까운 미래에 올 수 있는 재앙이지만, 지금 지적하고 있는 자기보존의 수단을 갖는 주체적 행위자로서의 로봇은 조금 더 먼 미래에 올 수 있는 재앙으로 지금부터 이러한 가능한 결과에 윤리적으로 대비할 필요가 있다. 인공지능 기술을 어디까지 활용하여도 되는가에 대한 담론은 유전자 연구에 대한 제한과 관련된 논의만큼이나 인간의 미래에 중대한 영향을 미칠 수 있는 것임에 유념하여야 한다.

<인터넷시대의 접속: 초개인주의>

4차 산업혁명은 컴퓨터와 인터넷의 발전에 뒤이은 다음 세대의 산업혁명으로 바이오 산업과 더불어 인공지능이 주도하는 것으로 이해된다. 그러나 앞에서 보았듯이 인터넷과 인공지능이 컴퓨터과학의 발전의 연장선 상에 있음을 고려하면, 4차 산업혁명이 3차 산업혁명의 연장선 상에 있다고 볼 수 있다. 그런 점에서 4차 산업혁명을 3차 산업혁명과 달리 규정하는 것은 설득력이 없다고 할 수 있다. 미국에서는 4차 산업혁명이라는 표현이 쓰이고 있지 않다는 것도 이런 맥락에서 이해가 된다.

컴퓨터의 발전을 가운데에 두고 전개되고 있는 인공지능과 인터넷시대가 결합될 때 어떤 사회적 특성들이 나타나는가를 생각해보자. 첫번째로 주목할 사실은 인간의 삶의 많은 측면이 사이버 공간으로 이동한다는 것이다. 우리가 생각하는 방식이 달라진다. 기억하고 있는 전화번호의 수를 30년 전과 비교하여 보자. 아마도 그 수가 거의 10분의 1로 줄었을 것이다. 단지 숫자만 줄은 것이 아니라 숫자들을 기억하는 능력까지도 현저히 감퇴한다. 우리가 살고 있는 삶의 공간과 관련한 지형적 지식도 현저히 달라졌다. 어느 동네 옆에 어느 동네가 있으며, 그 동네로 가기 위해서는 어떤 동네를 거쳐 어느 방향으로 가야 하는지, 이전에 잘 알고 있던 지식들이 지금은 어디론가 사라졌다. 나의 삶에 매우 중요한 이들 정보는 이제는 나의 두뇌가 아니라 나의 스마트폰 또는 나의 자동차에 장착된 내비게이션에 저장된다.

정보를 저장하는 매체는 인공지능과 인터넷이 결합되면서 더욱 확장된다. 나에게 필요한 정보는 이제는 내가 휴대하는 단말기에 제한되지 않고, 인터넷으로 연결된 크라우드에 저장되어 언제든지 내가 필요할 때 인출하여 쓸 수 있는 형태로 저장된다. 내가 운전할 때 듣고 싶은 음악, 여가를 즐길 때 듣고 싶은 음악, 데이트할 때 듣고 싶은 음악은 크라우드 컴퓨터가 나의 성향을 반영하여 각기 다른 폴더로 저장하여 나에게 제공한다. 이전에 내가 판단하여 하던 일들이 나의 개인 단말기에 의하여, 그리고 단말기와 연결된 인터넷에 의하여 수행되기에 이른 것이다.

인터넷이 개인적 인식의 많은 부분을 대행하게 되면서 인간의 관계망의 성격도 현저히 달라진다. 인공지능은 나의 다양한 취향을 분석하여 나에게 최적화된 제품을 공급할 뿐 아니라 나와 취향이 비슷한 사람들과 가상공간에서 연결시켜 준다. 인터넷을 통하여 사람들과 교류하는 데에 보내는 시간이 늘어나면서 대면적으로 대화하던 사람들의 수는 현저히 줄어들고, 인터넷에서 맺은 친구들의 숫자는 점점 늘어난다. 공간을 초월하는 인터넷의 덕으로 교류하는 사람들의 폭은 폭발적으로 넓어지지만 접속된 사람들과의 관계의 밀도는 묽어 간다. 관계의 분량이 정해진 것은 아니지만, 인터넷 시대 관계의 폭이 넓어지면서 농도는 묽어 지고 있다. 인터넷과 인공지능의 발전이 개인들의 정서적 관계에만 영향을 주는 것이 아니라, 산업의 구조에도 변화를 가져온다. 이제는 많은 사람들이 여행을 떠나면서 지역의 여행사를 이용하지 않고, 국적 불명의 글로벌 인터넷 매체를 통하여 예약을 하고 거기서 추천한 일정에 동의하여 여행을 계획한다. 공유경제 또는 온디멘드 경제라고 불리는 이러한 새로운 사업의 특징은 공급자가 일정한 형태의 제품을 생산하면 그 중에 특정한 것을 선택하여 소비자가 구매하는 것이 아니라, 구매자의 요청에 즉각적으로 반응하여 상품을 공급하는 것이다. 운송 사업에 있어서의 우버나 여행에 있어서의 에어비앤비 같은 경우가 대표적이다. 사업 자체를 구성하는 데에도 온디멘드 경제 형태가 확장되어 간다. 특정한 과제를 수행하기 위하여 일정한 팀이 필요할 때 이러한 팀을 위하여 인터넷 상에서 국적을 초월하여 전문가들을 모으고 이들에 의하여 사업이 완결되면 업체를 해체하는 형태의 매개 사업 형태도 발전하고 있다.

인터넷과 인공지능의 발전에 따른 혁명적 변화가 가리키는 중요한 사회적 경향성은 초개인주의다. 개인들의 차별적 기호가 중시되면서 사업의 행태가 변화하고, 경제 환경의 변화는 개별성을 강조하는 사회적 경향을 가속화할 것이다. 인간관계에 있어서도 살을 맞대면서 공감하는 영역은 점차 축소되고, 사이버 상의 관념적 관계가 확장되면서 사람들의 관계는 점점 더 경제적·타산적 성향으로 방향을 잡고 있다.

이러한 변화를 초개인주의라고 부르는 이유는 근세 이후 발전한 개인주의가 극단적 방향으로 진전되는 것으로 이해될 수 있기 때문이다. 여기서 길게 논의할 수는 없지만, 근세에서 발전한 개인주의는 이전 시대까지 공동체의 가치에 의하여 억압되어 온 개인의 인권이나 개성을 존중하기 위한 움직임이다. 14세기 무렵부터 시작된 이러한 움직임이 한쪽으로 강력히 진행될 때는 공동체적 가치에 의하여 견제를 받으며 어느 정도의 균형점을 유지하며 진행되어 왔다. 전체적으로는 개인주의로의 경향이 강화되어 왔음을 부정할 수 없지만 말이다. 500년 넘어 개인주의와 공동체주의가 엎치락뒤치락하면서 중간 어디에선가 머물던 세계적 조류가 인공지능과 인터넷의 발전으로 20세기 후반 이후 개인주의로 향하고 있다. 더군다나 이 변화는 매우 급속히 진행될 뿐 아니라 사회의 여러 측면에서 포괄적으로 진행되고 있기 때문에 구성원들의 반성을 용납하지 않고 있다. 하나의 이념으로써 공동체주의와 개인주의적인 자유주의 사이에서 어떤 것을 선택할 것인가의 문제는 우리가 추구하는 가치에 대한 반성을 요구하지만, 지금 시대의 변화는 인간관계를 맺는 방식 자체를 변화시키고, 이에 따라 인간의 관계를 바라보는 우리의 무의식을 변화시켜 반성의 여지를 남기지 않는다.

이러한 세계적 경향은 우리 한국 사회에 더욱 위험한 적신호를 보낸다. 우리사회가 고속으로 발전하는 시대에는 다른 사람들보다 더 빨리 앞으로 나아가는 것이 경쟁에서 이

기는 방법이었다. 사회의 전반적 발전과 확장이 주춤하면서 앞으로 달려 경쟁에서 이기는 길은 점차 어려워지고 있다. 그런데도 고도 성장의 과정에서 몸에 밴 경쟁 심리는 상황 변화에 대응하지 못하고 여전히 위력을 발휘한다. 경쟁에서 이기고자 하는 마음은 여전한데, 앞으로 나가는 길이 어려우니 상대방을 끌어내리고자 하는 유혹이 고개를 들기 마련이다. 우리 사회의 갈등이 팽배한 이유다. 추격 경제의 과정에서 양산된 무한경쟁과 적자생존의 내부적인 생태적 구조가 초개인주의라는 세계적 조류와 결합될 때 우리사회에 어떤 파장을 불러올지에 대하여 낙관적인 예측을 하기가 쉽지 않다. 미래의 부정적인 결과에 대비하기 위하여 우리가 남다른 노력을 기울여야 할 이유다.

4. 결론: 공감과 공존

컴퓨터과학, 인공지능, 인터넷의 발전은 하나의 패키지로 20세기 후반 이후 지구의 모든 지역에 예외 없이 큰 변화를 불러오고 있다. 사이버 공간이 확대되면서 삶의 여러 영역의 특성이 변화한다. 대면적 관계 영역은 축소되고, 개인적 욕구에 적합화된 방식으로 산업 및 사업 환경이 변화되면서 타인과의 공감이 자라날 여지는 점차 줄어든다. 공감 영역의 축소는 인간 관계를 타산적으로 변화시킬 것이다. 이러한 세계적 변화는 적자생존의 문화가 팽배한 우리나라에는 더 큰 도전이 되고 있다.

인공지능이 발전하여 고성능 로봇이 만들어져 인간과 같은 마음을 가질 수 있으며, 이런 로봇이만들어지면 로봇이 인간을 통제하게 될지도 모른다는 디스코피아적 공포를 확산시키는 사람들이 있다. 이런 디스토피아적 상황은 오지 않을 것이다. 그러지 않기를 바란다. 감성과 정서의 영역은 인간의 고유한 부분으로 로봇을 통하여 실현될 수 없기 때문이다. 그리고 자기보존의 프로그램이 강력한 기계와 결합되어 인간을 지배하는 그런 상황도 발생하지 않을 것이다. 그러기를 바란다. 인간은 공존의 가치를 공유하며 인공지능이 파괴적으로 발전하는 것을 예방할 능력이 있기 때문이다.

이런 모든 낙관적인 예측의 배경에는 인간이 로봇화되지 않는다는 전제가 깔려 있다. 인간이 정서에 기반한 공감의 능력을 유지한다는 전제 말이다. 그러나 이 전제가 지금 도전을 받고 있다. 인공지능의 발전과 인터넷 환경의 확산은 공감이 자라날 여지를 위축시키며 우리를 파편화된 개인주의적 개체로 만들어가고 있다. 인공지능의 발전이 가져올 수 있는 미래의 파괴적 결과를 생각하며 인간의 공동체적 가치를 보존할 수 있는 여지가 축소되고 있다. 인간이 만든 로봇이 인간을 지배할지도 모른다는 우려는 먼 미래의 것이므로 호들갑을 떨 필요가 없다고 이야기할 수 있다. 더 큰 위험은 인간이 로봇화되는 것이다. 공존과 공감을 축소시켜가는 인공지능의 시대에 우리는 공감의 능력을 보존하고 공동체 정신을 유지할 대비가 되어 있는가를 물어야 한다. 이는 그 자체로 인간의 삶의 질에 영향을 미칠 중요한 문제이며, 이 문제가 해결되지 않는 한 먼 미래 로봇이 인간을 지배하지 않을 것이라 장담하기 어렵다. 결국은 인간의 로봇화가 우리가 직면해야 할 당면 과제이고, 이 문제의 해결에 따라 로봇에 의해 지배되는 세상이 올 것인지도 달려 있다. 모든 인간이 로봇이 되는 시대는 어차피 로봇에 의하여 인간의 지배되는 시대와 다를 바가 없다.

---

*1: 의식이 심리 상태의 독자적 본성이라는 것을 부정하는 철학자들도 있다. 타이Michel Tye와 드레츠키Fred Dretske와 같은 철학자들은 의식은 아래서 설명하는 지향성의 부산물이라고 주장한다. 참조: Michael Tye, Ten Problems of Consciousness (Cambridge: MIT Press, 1995); Fred Dretske, Naturalizing the Mind (Cambridge: MIT Press, 1995).

*2: 이러한 통일 과학(unified science)에 대한 기대는 논리실증주의에서 전형적으로 나타났다.

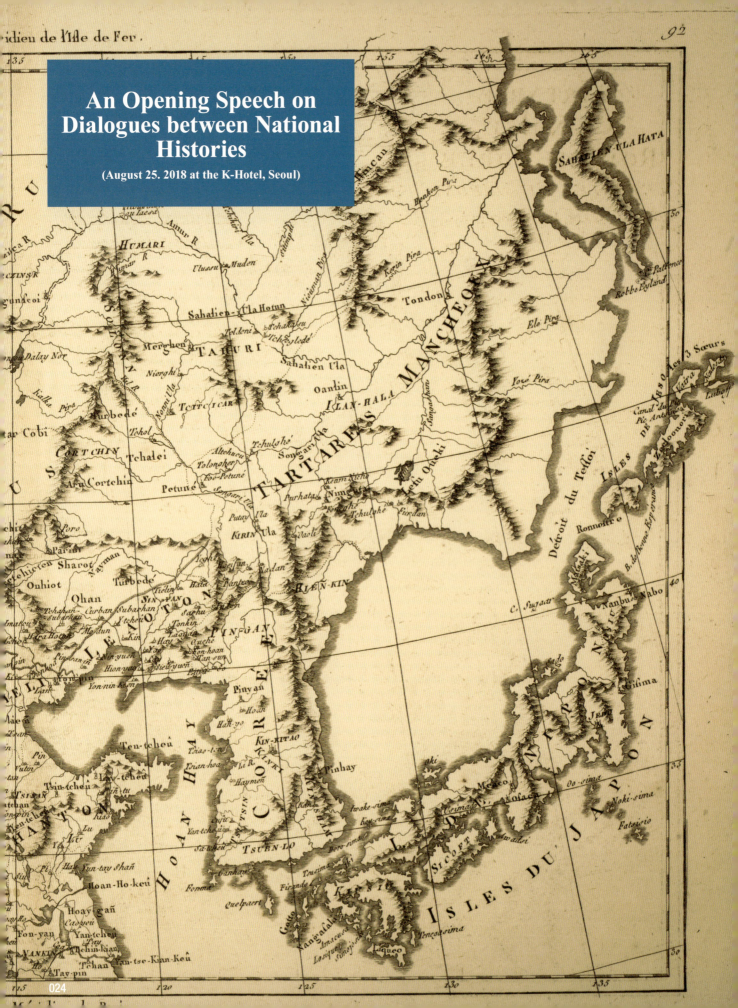

和解に向けた歴史家ネットワークのために
For the Network of Historians towards Reconciliation

劉傑（早稲田大学教授）
Liu Jie (Professor, Waseda University)

（円卓会議「国史たちの対話」における「和解に向けた歴史家共同研究ネットワークの検証」セッションの開幕スピーチ）
(Introductory speech for the session "Examining the network of historians towards reconciliation" in the roundtable "Dialogues between national histories)

　今回は円卓会議「国史たちの対話」の3回目となります。テーマは17世紀の東アジア国際関係ですが、対話の最後に「和解に向けた歴史家共同研究ネットワークの検証」というセッションを設けることにいたしました。これは今までの対話を総括し、今後の対話に向けた問題提起を意図したものです。

　ご承知の通り、今までの20年にわたり、日、中、韓3カ国のあいだでは、多様な形の歴史対話が展開されてきました。これらの対話はどのような成果を収めたのか、どのような問題を積み残したのか、さらに、むしろ対話によって新たにどのような問題を作り出してしまったのか。いよいよ検証しなければならない時期に来ているのではないかと強く感じています。

　これまでの歴史共同研究を振り返ってみますと、まず、国家間の、政府が主導した歴史共同研究がありました。日本と中国、日本と韓国の間で行われました。それぞれ不完全ながら、成果を出版し、各国の社会に一定の影響を与えました。また、民間レベルでは近代史をめぐる歴史対話、共同研究、若手研究者を中心とした共同研究などが行われてきました。東アジア国際関係の激しい変化に翻弄されながらも、歴史家たちは執拗に対話のチャンネルを維持し、拡大してきました。しかし、多様な歴史共同研究の相互関係や、社会への発信とその影響、とりわけ、国民同士の相互理解に与えた影響について、一度丁寧に検証する必要があるのではないかと思います。本日の「和解」のセッションで、このようなことを議論できればと期待しています。

　さて早稲田大学は浅野豊美先生を代表にして「和解学の創成」というテーマで科研費を申請しました。2017年から5年間の計画で研究が進められています。この研究を簡単に説明すれば、「和解学」というものを東アジアの「共有知」として、生み出すことができるかどうか、という試みです。私はこの中で「歴史家ネットワークの検証」というグループを担当しています。国民同士の和解は長期的な課題です。歴史家が国民同士の「和解」にどのようにコミットしていくのかということも難しい問題です。ただ、和解と和平が東アジアの重要なテーマであるならば、歴史対話もそれを意識したものであることは言うまでもありません。

　さて、「国史たちの対話」の着地点、すなわち、最終的な目的をどこに設定すればよいのでしょうか。このことは、先に紹介しました「歴史家ネットワークの検証」の目的と重なる部分もあります。いまのところ3つのことを考えております。

1つ目は、各国の歴史認識に影響を与える要素として、どのようなことが考えられるのか、ということについて一応のイメージ図を描き出すことです。そこには、各国の社会変動、歴史教育のあり方、国際関係の影響など、さまざまなファクターが考えられますが、特に注目したいことは、歴史認識の問題は、まずそれぞれの国の国内問題であるという点です。国内問題としての歴史認識問題が各国に横たわっています。つまりそれぞれの国の内部にある多様な歴史認識が対立しているなか、どのような形で国境を越えて対話をするのか。歴史認識問題は、国内と国際という複雑な構造になっています。各国の歴史家がそれぞれの国内要素にどう影響されながら、国際研究に臨んでいるのか、この点を明らかにする必要がありましょう。

2つ目は、今までの歴史対話の歴史を検証し、総括することです。そのために、3つの時期に分けて考えることができるのではないかと思います。第1期は1970年代以前の歴史対話です。それはいわゆる「戦後歴史家」たちの対話です。この時期の対話の多くは、直接対話ではなく、論文などの研究成果を通しての対話です。例えば、日本の戦後歴史学界の研究状況は70年代以前の中国におけるアジア史、日本史、中国史研究に強い影響を与えました。その実態の検証はほとんど行われてきませんでした。つまり、国交のない国々の間の知的交流のあり方をもう一度考え直す必要があると思います。第2の時期は1980年代です。これは中国が大きく変わり始めた時期です。歴史家たちの直接対話はいろいろな形で展開されました。当時はいわゆる歴史認識にめぐる対立というより、「アジアの近代化」の問題が大きな焦点となっていました。そのときの対話の成果、あるいはその遺産をどのように受け継いだらいいのか、この問題は残さたままです。そして第3の時期は1990年代、とくに90年代半ば以降の時期です。この時期の対話は、まさに歴史認識のズレをいかに克服するのかということをテーマに展開されました。ただし、この時期の対話は政治的な対立や、社会的な対立を背景に展開されたものです。歴史家たちは大きな荷物を背負って対話しました。今、われわれが取り組んでいる「国史たちの対話」はまさにこのような背景のなかで行われています。冷静に考えれば、この時期の対話は問題を発見しただけではなく、新たな問題を作り出しているのかも知れません。

そして3つ目は、多様な歴史対話の主体の検証です。私が関わってきた歴史対話のかなりの部分は「越境する歴史家たちによる対話」です。とくに1980年代以降、中国の歴史研究者が大量に海外に出て成果を発表しています。彼らは主にアメリカや日本、あるいはヨーロッパで活躍しています。彼らは国境を越えて歴史対話に加わっています。日本の研究者もこのような問題意識を持って海外で対話に参加している方が多いと思います。韓国の研究者も同様です。この越境する歴史家たちが参加する対話がどのように発信され、それぞれの国の歴史認識にどのような影響を及ぼしたのか、非常に興味深いテーマです。

以上の問題意識を踏まえて、今回の「和解」のセッションは、今までの歴史対話の経験を踏まえて、対話のなかで何が生まれたのか、あるいは問題点として何が残されたのかを、まず明らかにすることを目的にしたいと思います。同時に、根本的な問題ではありますが、いったい歴史学および歴史家は、歴史の和解、国家と国家の和解にいかに関わっていけばよいのか、「和解のための歴史学」の可能性と限界はどこにあるのか、ということも念頭に置きたいと思います。

現在、歴史学をめぐる「史料」のあり方が大きく変化しています。また、歴史問題の議論に参加する人の構成も一変しました。歴史学と歴史家は大きなチャレンジに直面しています。1つはオーラルヒストリーや記憶の問題です。これらの要素が歴史史料として登場したとき、伝統的な歴史学の研究方法では対応しきれないような問題が発生し

Summary: The geopolitical dynamism in East Asia today urges us to reach a historic reconciliation between its key players, namely China, Korea and Japan. The modern history in this region is mired in recurring political and often violent conflicts, and the narratives in these nation states have been dominated by their unique "national histories." Japan has its Japanese history. China has its Chinese history. Korea has its Korean history. But there is no cross-border narrative of regional history that can be shared and honored by all the people in this region. That's why we, the historians in East Asia, need to engage in constructive, bilateral and multilateral dialogues to make the historic reconciliation come true. We, in cooperation with Waseda University's "Reconciliation Studies" project, encourage everyone to join our discussions.

ます。また、多様な史料がいまインターネットで公開され、国境を越えて、誰でもアクセスできるようになり、誰でも歴史について簡単に発信することができるようになりました。歴史像の複雑化が、歴史学に大きな課題を突き付けています。時代はあるいは「新史学」の創成を求めているのかも知れません。その新史学のイメージはまだ定かではありませんが、ひとつ言えることは、「国境を越えた歴史学」ではないかと思います。

　「国史たちの対話」は3回目でありますが、4回、5回以降は19世紀、20世紀など近現代がテーマです。着地点に少しでも近づけるように、より問題意識を鮮明にしていく必要があるのではないかと思います。今回のセッションが、そのための一つの準備運動になれればいいと思います。

The 4th Asia Future Conference Report

Peace, Prosperity, and Dynamic Future

Junko Imanishi
Representative, SGRA, Atsumi International Foundation

The 4th Asia Future Conference (AFC#4) was held from Friday, August 24th to Tuesday, August 28th at the K-Hotel in Seoul, Korea, with 379 registered participants from 21 countries. The overall theme of the conference was "Peace, Prosperity, and Dynamic Future." In the aftermath of the Korean War, Korea achieved rapid economic development called the "Miracle on the Han River, owing to the day-to-day efforts of the Korean people and large assistance from overseas. Korea therefore has a good understanding of the pains and agony of developing. In this context, this conference hopes to contribute to the "peace, prosperity, and dynamic future" of Asia. We held keynote speeches and a symposium, roundtable discussions with invited speakers, as well as a large number of research paper presentations promoting international and interdisciplinary dialogue.

Participants from Asia as well as all over the world were scheduled to arrive on August 24th (Friday), and on the same day typhoon Soulik, Korea's first typhoon in six years, was due to hit Seoul. A number of flights from Southeast Asia were cancelled, but as the typhoon's path shifted to the east most of the participants were able to safely arrive on this day.

The conference kicked off on the following day, August 25th (Saturday), with two roundtable sessions as well as ten parallel panel sessions. The summaries of the roundtable sessions are below.

■ **Roundtable Discussion A: "Dialogue of National Histories; Japan, China and Korea"** (Grant: Tokyo Club) / Languages: Japanese/Chinese/Korean with simultaneous interpretation

This roundtable sought to bring about historical reconciliation and rebuild mutual trust in East Asia by establishing a stable and cooperative relationship. Dialogue is the first step to achieving this, and this roundtable attempts to do by discussing Japan's "Japanese history," China's "Chinese history," and Korea's "Korean history." This was the third meeting out of five, and took as its theme "East Asian International Relations in the 17th Century – From War to Stability." In the final session, as part of Waseda University's project to establish "Reconciliation Studies," we looked back at the dialogues about history that had been had so far.

■ **Roundtable Discussion B: "Tolerance and Reconciliation – Religious Approaches to Conflict Resolution"** / Language: English

Despite the fact that confrontation and dispute arise out of political and economic factors, such disputes are often misunderstood as religious confrontations owing to how religion is tied to the socio-economic and cultural fabric of the community and the people who are in conflict with each other. Through looking at conflict resolution in Myanmar, Thailand, Indonesia, the Philippines and Vietnam, our panelists (which included individuals who have been involved in peacebuilding efforts as well as scholars) discussed "peace and resolution" and the role of religion and religious leaders in these efforts.

Following lunch, the opening ceremony took place at 2pm. Mr. Yasushi Akashi, Conference Chairperson, opened the conference, followed by a welcome address by Professor Jin Kyu Lee, Director of the Center for Future Human Resources, the co-host of the event, and congratulatory remarks by Mr. Yasumasa Nagamine, Japan Ambassador to Korea.

This was followed by the keynote speeches and symposium on "AI, the Human Soul and the Future." Professor Ji Hoon Jeong (Kyung Hee Cyber University) gave a talk entitled "AI of the Present, and Future," and Professor Ki Hyun Kim (Seoul National University) spoke on "AI and the Human Soul." Following these two keynote speeches, a discussion moderated by co-organizer Korean National Social Science Resource Council President Professor Chan Wook Park was held, in which Professor Eui Young Kim (President of the Korean Political Science Association), Professor Kwang Young Shin (President of Korean Sociological Association), Professor Yong Woo Lee (upcoming President of the Korean Geographical Society), Professor Huck Ju Kwon (upcoming President of Korean Association of International Development and Cooperation) and Professor Seok Woo Kim (President of Korean Association of International Studies) participated, and in which the influence of AI in society was discussed.

The event finished off with a jazz performance by HONA, a band which uses traditional Korean instruments in their performances. The event was attended by over 400 participants.

The day rounded off with the welcome party, held on the roof terrace under a sky made pleasantly clear from the typhoon which had come and gone, and was accompanied by jazz music until late in the evening.

The second day of the conference (August 26th (Saturday)) started at 9am, with 12 parallel sessions. Taking into account both the previous day as well as the morning's sessions, there were 7 group presentations, 6 student sessions and 42 general sessions, making for a total of 224 papers presented. The Asia Future Conference aspires towards an international and interdisciplinary approach, and each session was arranged using topics such as "Peace", "Happiness", and "Innovation," which the

presenters selected during the submission process. Although different from academic conferences in specific fields, this approach helped foster many rich and diverse discussions.

Best Presentations were selected by two chairpersons in general and student sessions.

Best Papers were selected by the Academic Committee before the conference. Papers for which abstracts uploaded to the AFC online system by August 31st 2017 were eligible provided that a full paper was uploaded by February 28th 2018. 137 full papers were divided into 14 groups, and each paper was evaluated by 4 reviewers who were assigned to one group each. Reviewers were asked to evaluate each paper based on the following 5 criteria: (1) Is the theme of this paper in accordance with the AFC theme "Peace, Prosperity, and Dynamic Future"? (2) Is this paper perspicuous and persuasive? (3) Is this paper original and innovative? (4) Does this paper hold international aspects in some points? (5) Does this paper have an interdisciplinary approach? Each reviewer recommended two papers out of nine or ten in each group. After compiling the evaluations, 19 papers were selected as the Best Papers.

The closing party started at 6.30pm on the same day, and commenced with a piano recital. Following the conference report by AFC Chairperson Ms. Junko Imanishi, Professor Chan Wook Park, President of the Korean Social Science Research Council, gave a toast to commemorate the success of the conference. In the middle of the festivities, the awards ceremony was held, in which the Conference Chair, Mr. Yasushi Akashi, presented awards to the 19 recipients of the Best Paper as well as the 48 Best Presentation awardees. The party closed off with an announcement about the 5th Asia Future Conference which will be held in the Philippines. Following a video message by the Dean of the University of the Philippines Los Banos and greetings from the organizing committee, participants from the Philippines came on stage to perform a fun-filled Filipino version of the Gangnam style dance, drawing participants into the festivities.

On Monday, August 27th, participants took part in organized study tours and excursions, which included a tour of traditional architecture in Seoul, downtown sightseeing, a study tour to Namhansanseong as well as a NANTA performance.

The 4th Asia Future Conference "Peace, Prosperity, and Dynamic Future" was hosted by the Atsumi International Foundation Sekiguchi Global Research Association (SGRA) and co-hosted by the Korean Social Science Research Council, Center for Human Resource Studies. It was supported by the Japanese Ministry of Education, Culture, Sports, Science and Technology, Embassy of Japan in Korea, and Seoul Japan Club, and received a grant from the Tokyo Club. The AFC was held in collaboration with CISV Korea, Honjo International Scholarship Foundation, Doalltec Inc., Global BIM Inc., and was sponsored by POSCO E&C, HAEAHN Architecture, Inc., N.I. Steel Co. Ltd., Chugai Pharmaceutical Co. Ltd., Mitsubishi Corporation, Tokio Marine Holdings, Inc., Kokuyo co., Ltd., Kajima Road Co., Ltd., Taiko Trading Co., Ltd., Kajima Tatemono Sogo Kanri Co., Ltd., East Real Estate, Kajima Overseas Asia PTE Ltd., and Kajima Corporation.

The Organizing Committee and Academic Committee for this conference were organized by Atsumi fellows, who voluntarily took part in almost all aspects of the conference such as planning the forums, maintaining the homepages, selecting the best awards, and manning the reception. In particular, Atsumi fellows from Korea played a crucial role in translating, making visa arrangements, and coordinating the daily events. We would like to express our heartfelt thanks to the more than 400 participants who joined us, as well as to those who supported the holding of the conference and all of the volunteers who provided assistance in many ways and helped lead to the success of the 4th Asia Future Conference.

The Asia Future Conference is interdisciplinary at its core and encourages diverse approaches to global issues that are both mindful of the advancement of science, technology and business and also take into consideration issues of the environment, politics, education, the arts and culture. This conference is organized with likeminded institutions, in order to provide a venue for the exchange of knowledge, information, ideas, and culture, not only by SGRA members, but also by former foreign students of Japan from various educational institutions throughout the world, by their own students and collaborators, and by anyone interested in Japan.

The 5th Asia Future Conference will be held in Manila, the Philippines, from January 9th (Thursday) to January 13th (Monday), 2020. We would like to ask for your continued support, cooperation and, most of all, your participation.

第4回アジア未来会議開催報告

平和、繁栄、そしてダイナミックな未来

今西淳子
（渥美国際交流財団関口グローバル研究会代表）

　2018年8月24日（金）～28日（火）、韓国ソウル市のThe K-Hotelにおいて、21ヵ国から379名の登録参加者を得て、第4回アジア未来会議が開催されました。総合テーマは「平和、繁栄、そしてダイナミックな未来」。朝鮮戦争の後、韓国は絶え間ない努力と海外からの多大な援助によって「漢江の奇跡」と呼ばれる経済発展を遂げました。歴史的経験から、開発にともなう苦痛や悩みをよく理解している韓国のソウルで開催されたこの会議が、これからのアジアの「平和と繁栄、そしてダイナミックな未来」に寄与することを願って広範な領域における課題に取り組み、基調講演とシンポジウム、招待講師による円卓会議、そして数多くの研究論文の発表が行われ、国際的かつ学際的な議論が繰り広げられました。

　アジアだけでなく世界各地から参加者が到着予定の8月24日（金）は、韓国では6年ぶりという台風19号がソウルを直撃するという予報が早くからだされ、東南アジアからの便が数本キャンセルになりましたが、台風の進路は東にそれ、ほとんどの参加者はこの日に会場入りすることができました。

　翌8月25日（土）の午前中は2本の円卓会議と同時進行で10の分科会が行われました。円卓会議の概要は以下のとおりです。

◇円卓会議A「第3回日本・中国・韓国における国史たちの対話の可能性」（助成：東京倶楽部）
　この円卓会議では、東アジアの歴史和解を実現するとともに、国民同士の信頼を回復し、安定した協力関係を構築するためには歴史を乗り越えることが一つの課題であると捉え、日本の「日本史」、中国の「中国史」、韓国の「韓国史」を対話させる試みです。今回は5回シリーズの第3回めで、「17世紀東アジアの国際関係 戦乱から安定へ」というテーマで議論が展開されました。さらに、最後のセッションでは、早稲田大学の「和解学の創成」プロジェクトの一環として、今までに行われた歴史対話の試みについて振り返りました。（日中韓同時通訳）

◇円卓会議B「第2回東南アジア宗教間の対話」
　ここでは「寛容と和解－紛争解決と平和構築に向けた宗教の役割」をテーマに、対立や紛争の原因が政治経済的な課題であるにもかかわらず、宗教の対立としての様相を帯びることが数多くあるが、それは宗教が対立する民族や集団の基層文化のなかに深く根ざしているからにほかならないという問題意識により、ミャンマー、タイ、インドネシア、フィリピン、ベトナムの紛争解決、平和構築の経験及び研究をベースとして和解、平和構築に向けた宗教および宗教者の役割、そして「平和と和解」への途を探りました。（使用言語：英語）

　昼食休憩の後、午後2時から開会式が始まり、明石康大会会長が第4回アジア未来会議の開会を宣言しました。共催の韓国未来人力研究院の李鎮奎理事長の歓迎の挨拶の後、長嶺安政在韓国日本大使より祝辞をいただきました。

　引き続き「AIと人間の心、そして未来」と題した基調講演およびシンポジウムが開催されました。慶熙サイバー大学の鄭智勲教授「AIの今、そして未来」、ソウル大学の金起顕教授「AIと人間の心」の2本の基調講演の後、共催の韓国社会科学協議会の朴賛郁会長の進行で、韓国政治学会の金義英会長、韓国社会学会の申光榮会長、大韓地理学会の李勇雨次期会長、国際開発協力学会の權赫周時期会長、韓国国際政治学会の金錫宇会長を討論者に迎え、AIが社会に与える影響を検討しました。（韓英同時通訳）

　最後に、400人を超える参加者は、HONAというグループによる韓国伝統楽器を用いたジャズのコンサートを楽しみました。

　その後、台風一過で快晴の屋上庭園で開かれたウェルカムパーティーは、ジャズ演奏を聴きながら夜遅くまで続きました。

　8月26日（日）午前9時からは12の小会議室を使って分科会が行われました。前日の午前中と合わせて、7グループセッション、6学生セッション、43一般セッションが行われ、224本の論文発表が行われました。アジア未来会議は国際的かつ学際的なアプローチを目指しており、各セッションは、発表者が投稿時に選んだ「平和」「幸福」「イノベーション」などのトピックに基づいて調整され、学術学会とは趣を異にした多角的で活発な議論が展開されました。

　一般セッションと学生セッションでは、セッションごとに2名の座長の推薦により優秀発表賞が選ばれました。

　優秀論文は学術委員会によって事前に選考されました。2017年8月31日までに発表要旨、2018年2月28日までにフルペーパーがオンライン投稿された137篇の論文を14グループに分け、ひとつのグループを4名の審査員が、(1)論文のテーマが会議のテーマ「平和、繁栄、そしてダイナミックな未来」と適合しているか、(2)わかりやすく説得力があるか、(3)独自性と革新性があるか、(4)国際性があるか、(5)学際性があるか、という指針に基づいて査読しました。各審査員は、グループの中の9～10本の論文から2本を推薦し、集計の結果、上位19本を優秀論文と決定しました。

　クロージングパーティーは、同日午後6時半からピアノの演奏で始まり、今西淳子AFC実行委員長の会議報告のあと、共催の韓国社会科学協議会の朴賛郁会長のご発声により乾杯をして会の成功を祝いました。宴もたけなわの頃、優秀賞の授賞式が行われました。授賞式では、優秀論文の著者19名が壇上に上がり、明石康大会委員長から賞状の授与がありました。続いて、優秀発表賞48名が表彰されました。

　パーティーの終盤に、第5回アジア未来会議の概要の発表がありました。フィリピン大学ロスバニョス校総長自らの歓迎ビデオと、実行委員会からの挨拶、そしてフィリピンからの参加者全員が会場も巻き込んでフィリピン版カンナムスタイルを踊り、会場は大いに盛り上がりました。

　8月27日(月)、参加者はそれぞれ、非武装地帯スタディツアー、ソウル伝統建築ツアー、ソウル市内観光、南漢山城スタディツアー、NANTA鑑賞などに参加しました。

　第4回アジア未来会議「平和、繁栄、そしてダイナミックな未来」は、(公財)渥美国際交流財団関口グローバル研究会(SGRA)主催、韓国社会科学協議会と(財)未来人力研究院の共催、文部科学省、在韓国日本大使館、ソウルジャパンクラブの後援、(一社)東京倶楽部の助成、CISV Korea、(公財)本庄国際奨学財団、Doalltec(株)、グローバルBIM(株)の協力、そして、POSCO建設(株)、HAEAHN Architecture(株)、(株)NIスティール、中外製薬(株)、三菱商事(株)、東京海上ホールディングス(株)、コクヨ(株)、鹿島道路(株)、大興物産(株)、鹿島建物総合管理(株)、イースト不動産(株)、Kajima Overseas Asia(株)、鹿島建設(株)のご協賛をいただきました。

　運営にあたっては、渥美フェローを中心に実行委員会、学術委員会が組織され、フォーラムの企画から、ホームページの維持管理、優秀賞の選考、当日の受付まであらゆる業務を担当しました。特に韓国出身の渥美フェローには翻訳やビザ招待状の手配から、当日の会議進行における雑務まで、多大なご協力をいただきました。400名を超える参加者のみなさん、開催のためにご支援くださったみなさん、さまざまな面でご協力くださったボランティアのみなさんのおかげで、第4回アジア未来会議を成功裡に実施することができましたことを、心より感謝申し上げます。

　アジア未来会議は、国際的かつ学際的なアプローチを基本として、グローバル化に伴う様々な問題を、科学技術の開発や経営分析だけでなく、環境、政治、教育、芸術、文化など、社会のあらゆる次元において多面的に検討する場を提供することを目指しています。SGRA会員だけでなく、日本に留学し現在世界各地の大学等で教鞭をとっている研究者、その学生、そして日本に興味のある若手・中堅の研究者が一堂に集まり、知識・情報・意見・文化等の交流・発表の場を提供するために、趣旨に賛同してくださる諸機関のご支援とご協力を得て開催するものです。

　第5回アジア未来会議は2020年1月9日(木)から13日(月)まで、フィリピンのマニラ市近郊で開催します。皆様のご支援、ご協力、そして何よりもご参加をお待ちしています。

第4回アジア未来会議優秀論文集

The Best Papers of the Fourth Asia Future Conference
The K-Hotel, Seoul, Korea, from August 24 to 27, 2018

Developing Educational Game "*Chemistry Virtual Lab*" as Learning Media of Chemical Solution's Concentration Concept for High School Students

Feri Kurniawan[1]
1 Undergraduate Student, Electrical Engineering Department, State University of Malang

多くの高校生にとって化学の授業は難解だ。記号だらけで数式が多く、抽象的で日常生活との接点がないから興味が湧かない。そこで化学の授業を楽しくするためにゲーム形式の「バーチャル・ラボ(仮想実験室)」を開発し、その効果を検証した。

Abstract

Solution's concentration concept in chemistry subject is an obliged competence that senior high school students should accomplish but the learning and teaching process of solution's concentration concept lacks highly visualized media to increase students' understanding. The conventional method with less attractiveness makes the learning less understandable and hard to be contextually figured out by students. The questionnaires and interview were given at the preliminary research to second grade students and teachers in Senior High School 8 Malang. The findings from this preliminary research showed that 70.4% of the students were not attracted to solution's concentration topic and teachers affirmed the need of the visualized media. This study aims to (1) design an educational game that portrays the real laboratory condition to implement the concept of chemical solution and (2) develop an interesting game in learning and teaching the concept of solution's concentration. This research adapts ADDIE development methodology of *Dick* and *Carry* (1996). This methodology consists of 5 steps as follow: (1) *Analysis*; (2) *Design*; (3) *Development*; (4) *Implementation*; (5) *Evaluation*. Based on the media validation process by using questionnaires, the researcher found that: (1) Media expert's validation score is 87.5%; (2) Subject matter expert's validation score is 85%; (3) small group testing's validation score is 89.58%; and (4) large group testing's validation score is 86.75%. Thus, the developed media can be concluded as valid and highly recommended for use in the learning and teaching process of solution's concentration concept for second grade students of Senior High School.

Keywords Game, Education, Chemistry

Introduction

Chemistry subject is an essential subject in Senior High School mainly for the natural science program. But, the perception that portrays chemistry subject as difficult subject still exist. As suggested by Tiastra, there are four factors that make chemistry subject be perceived as difficult, which are: (1) The syntax of learning model uses boring direct instruction model and Q&A method; (2) There are many formulas and calculation which are abstract and not visualized; (3) The learning and teaching loses relevance to daily basis context and exam-oriented; (4) Less students who continue to the higher education related to chemistry subject that made less attraction in learning it [1].

Based on the fact above, Johari explained that there are seven indications related to the low achievement in chemistry subject learning as follows: (1) incompatible teaching method to the caracteristics of the subject; (2) less motivation given by the teacher to the students; (3) Students only learn chemistry subject at schools without further exploration to enhance their knowledge related to chemistry subject outside the schools; (4) Low innovation on teaching model and only rely on the old paradigm model; (5) The learning and teaching instrument such as syllabus and study plan are still made in low quality; (6) the sceptism and perception that portray chemistry subject as extremely difficult; (7) and low internal motivation of the students because they think that chemistry subject is less relatable and less significance to their future job [2].

Those problems in chemistry learning and teaching cause the low learning outcome mainly in chemical solution's concentration concept which is still not satisfying. The learning and teaching of chemistry subject must not only be centralized on the result (product) but must also emphasize on the ability to conduct procedural and structural process [3]. In this context, process is defined as an interaction of all learning components in order to achieve the learning goal. The ability to conduct process is an important learning experience that students must feel because the direct involvement of students in applying theory, concept, and fundamental postulate in chemistry will empower and strengthen the students' understanding about the subject.

The learning and teaching process of chemical solution's concentration concept which include the concept of molarity, molality, and normality of the chemical solution in Senior High School level are still oriented on the solving the questions on paper which only use the techniques that are highly dependent on memorizing the formulas and mathematical operation. In fact, students need direct experience to conduct procedural and systematical process to implement the concept of chemical solution's concentration through making the specific solution with certain amount of concentration. But, there are barriers faced by students of second grade in Senior High School when they must implement the concept by making the spesific solution with certain amount of concentration. Those barriers are: (1) Laboratorium's facilities are not enough; (2) limited amount of chemical materials such as elements and compounds that are going to be made as solute and solvent; (3) the students careles attitude to handle chemical materials.

Developing educational game "CHEMISTRY VIRTUAL LAB" will accomodate students to actively take roles as a lab workers who are given several missions to make chemical solution using specific materials or compounds with certain concentration. Thus, this educational game will be able to subtitute the real laboratorium for the purpose of learning and teaching in chemical solution's concentration concept.

Educational game is highly different with other types of games. Educational game is not only for the entertainment purpose but it emphasizes on increasing the learning interest and motivation of student. Educational game can be used as a useful tool in learning and teaching because game is an interactive multimedia that is highly favoured by students [4]. Henry suggested that the usage of game in the learning and teaching process can optimalize the efficacy of left and right brain simultaneously [5]. The left brain will arrange the strategy regarding what kind of chemical materials that they need to take, how much the volume of the solvent they need, and how the procedure will be. While, the right brain will respond to all the visual information on the monitor screen.

Educational game is acknowledged as a digital learning media. Digital learning media is a learning media that is published by digital devices. This media generally includes text, pictures, audio, and video. Digital learning media has characteristics as follows: (1) utilizing computers' features; (2) utilizing multimedia technologies that are attractive and motivative for students to learn independently; (3) utilizing electronic technologies so that the teachers and students can communicate interactively; (4) using learning materials that is freely accesible to stimulate the thought process and concentration for problem solving [6]. In the learning and teaching process, this game will be an innovative way to facillitate students in gaining impressive and meaningful learning experiences [7].

A good educational game should be able to catch the interest and learning spirit of the students [8]. Therefore, the effort to increase the quality of learning media is an important element to optimize the learning outcome of students mainly in the chemistry subject that contains many abstract concept that doesn't only demand the theoritical ability but also practical ability.

Educational game can be alternative facility that suits with the current learning context where there is shifted paradigm in Indonesia's national education policy. Individual's behavior can be divided into three domains that contain cognitive domain, affective domain, and psychometric domain [9]. Bloom's taxonomy is adapted in the K-13 national curriculum of Indonesia which now emphasizes on those three domains.

However, in Indonesian Senior High Schools, the learning and teaching of chemical solution's concentration concept, students are less exposed in their psychometric domain. The skill to implement the solution's concentration concept through making the solution with certain amount of concentration is still not optimized because the limited time allocated for the lab practice. The lack of media availability that is supposed to help student to implement the concept by trying to make the chemical solution's concentration concept causes the psychometric acquisition process less effective. By this research, the availability of interesting media that can give meaningful learning experience and intensive exposure on conducting chemistry procedural process for students to implement the chemical solution's concentration concept will be optimized.

Research Method

This research adapts the R&D research model. This model is used to create certain products and test its effectiveness [10]. Based on the potential problem faced by the researcher, ADDIE development model of *Dick and Carey* (1996) is the most suitable model to address the problem [11]. The basic concept of ADDIE development model can be explained by the scheme in Fig. 1.

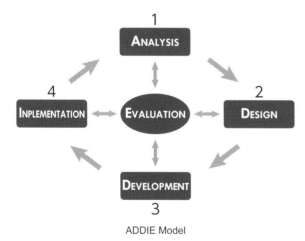

Fig. 1. ADDIE development model.
(Source: Dick & Carey, 1996)

Analysis

In this stage, the researcher conducted preliminary research to find out the potential problema and the necessity analysis. This preliminary research was done by using questionaire and conducting interview in SMAN 8 Malang. The questionaire was given to 125 second grade students of SMAN 8 Malang to find out their learning motivation, learning interest, and their perception upon chemical solution's concentration concept. From this questionaire, the reseacher concluded that 70.4% of the students were not attracted to solution's concentration topic. The interview was conduted to the teacher of chemistry subject to find out their necessity for learning media in solution's concentration topic. From the interview, the researcher found out that the teachers needed visualized media to facilitate the learning and teaching of solution's concentration concept. Therefore, there is an urgency for the researcher to develop learning media for solution's concentration topic.

Design

In this stage, the researcher designed the game arrangement process, game layout, laboratory's components, mission, game instruction, cover, and manual book and module.

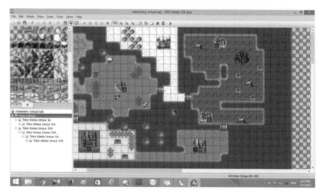

Fig. 2 Game's main map design.

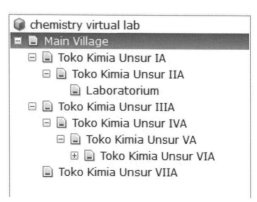

Fig. 3. Game's building list design.

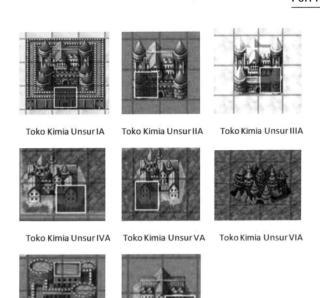

Fig. 4. Chemical material stores and laboratory

Development

In this stage, the researcher will realize the designs that have been made before. There are two main focuses in this stage which are realization of game and realization of module and manual book. In the realization of game, the researcher arranged the algorithm for game program and creating the animation characters which involve in the game. In the realization of module and manual book, the researcher arranged the guidance for the missions in the game and the task the students have to do systematically.

Implementation

In this stage, the products in the form of game, module, and manual book will be tested to the research's subjects. The subjects of this research are one media expertise, one material expertise, 12 students for small group testing, and 125 students for large group testing

The data collection instrument that is used in this research is questionaire with Likert's scale. The collected data are qualitative and quantitative data. The data analysis technique is descriptive-quantitative technique.

Evaluation

In ADDIE development model, evaluation process is conducted in every stage started from analysis, design, and implementation. The revisión is done in every stage to make sure that the design and product are valid. The revisión is gotten from the suggestion and recommendation of media and material expertises.

Result and Discussion

There are five results that the researcher found. They are the preliminary research result, validation result from media expertise, validation result from subject matter expertise, result of small group testing, and result of large group testing.

Preliminary Research Result

As mentioned in the analysis section, the R&D research should firstly identify the potential problem and necessity for development. In order to identify the potential problem, the researcher has conducted the preliminary research by using questionnaire to 125 second grade students of SMAN 8 Malang. The collected data from this questionaire is analyzed by using descriptive statistic method in IBM SPSS Statistics 21. The result of preliminary research is summarized in Table 1.

Table 1. Descriptive Statistic from Likert Questionnaire

Scale	f	%	CF
1	35	28%	28%
2	53	42.4%	70.4%
3	23	18.4%	88.8%
4	14	11.2%	100%

From Table 1, we can see that the there are 29.6% (37 students) of second grade students in SMAN 8 Malang who are interested in solution's concentration topic because they fill the questionaire with 3 and 4 that indicate their interest in the topic. However, the rest 70.4% (88 students) of them are not interested in the topic. Based on the criteria proposed by Arikunto [12], the criteria of score can be seen in Table 2.

Table 2. Arikunto's Likert Criteria

Value (%)	Criteria
81-100	Very High
61-80	High
41-60	Medium
21-40	Low
0-20	Very Low

From the criteria in Table 2 proposed by Arikunto, the interest of second grade students in chemical solution's concentration topic is low. This result can be visualized by Fig. 5.

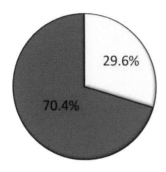

Fig. 5. Diagram of students' interest from preliminary research

Media Expertise's Validation Result

The method to collect data of validation from media expertise is by using the questionnaire. The media expertise that validated "CHEMISTRY VIRTUAL LAB" educational game is Drs. Dwi Prihanto, S.T, M.T. There are 30 items as indicators in the questionaire to find out the validity of media. All 30 items were filled out by the media expertise with Likert scale (1-4). The validity of media will be calculated by the formula as suggested by Akbar [13].

$$V = \frac{TSe}{TSh} \times 100\%$$

V = Validity

Tse = total score from expertise

TSh = Maximum score

The result of media expertise's validation can be seen in Fig. 6. and Fig. 7.

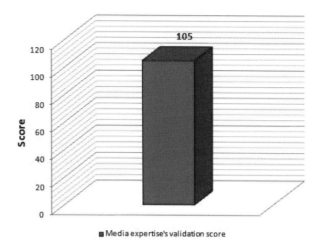

Fig. 6. Media Expertise's Validation Score

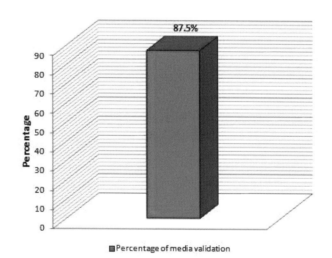

Fig. 7. Percentage of Media Validation

From Fig. 7 the validation percentage is 87.5%. According to Akbar (2013) the criteria of validity can be seen in Table 3 [14].

Table 3. Validity Criteria

Value (%)	Criteria
81.26-100,00	Very Valid Without Revision
62.51-81.25	Valid with revision
43.76-62,50	Not Valid
25.00-43.75	Very not valid and musn't be used
81.26-100,00	Very Valid Without Revision

Based on Table 3, the percentage of validation for "CHEMISTRY VIRTUAL LAB" educational game from media expertise is very valid without revision because the validity percentage is 87.5%.

Material Expertise's Validation Result

The method to collect data of validation from material expertise is by using the questionaire. The media expertise that validated "CHEMISTRY VIRTUAL LAB" educational game is Vinda Paramitha, S.Pd who is the teacher of chemistry subject in Senior High School. There are 30 items as indicators in the questionaire to find out the validity of media. All 30 items were filled out by the material expertise with Likert scale (1-4). The validity of media will be calculated by the formula as suggested by Akbar (2013).

The result of material expertise's validation can be seen in Fig. 8. and Fig. 9.

From Fig. 9, the validation percentage is 85%. According to the criteria of validity in the table 3, validity of "CHEMISTRY VIRTUAL LAB" educational game from media expertise is very valid without revisión because the validity percentage is 85%.

Small Group Testing Result

The method to collect data of validation from small group testing involves 12 second grade students of SMAN 8 Malang by using the questionaire. There are 15 items in the questionaire with Likert scale (1-4). The obtained score from this small group testing is 645 and the máximum score is 720 which means that the percentage of validity from this small group testing is 89.58%. The result of small group testing can be seen in Fig. 10 and Fig. 11.

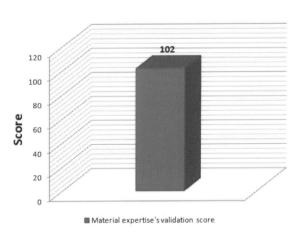

Fig. 8. Material Expertise's Validation Score

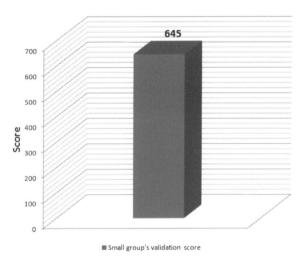

Fig. 10. Small Group Testing's Validation Score

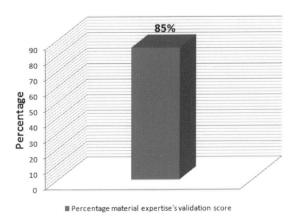

Fig. 9. Percentage of Material Validation

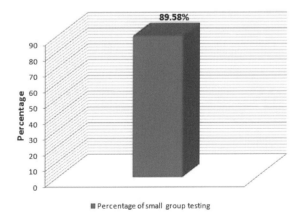

Fig. 11. Percentage of Small Group's Validation

From Fig. 11 the validation percentage is 89.58%. According to the criteria of validity in Table 3, validity of "CHEMISTRY VIRTUAL LAB" educational game from small group test is very valid without revision because the validity percentage is 89.58%.

Large Group Testing Result

The method to collect data of validation from large group testing involves 125 second grade students of SMAN 8 Malang by using questionaire. There are 16 items in the questionaire with Likert scale (1-4). The obtained score from this small group testing is 6940 and the máximum score is 8000 which means that the percentage of validity from this large group testing is 86.75%. The result of small group testing can be seen in Fig. 12 and Fig. 13.

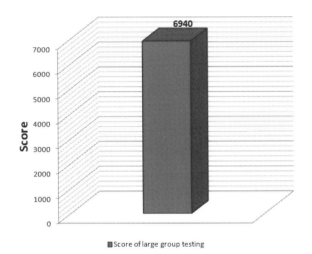

Fig. 12. Large Group Testing's Validation Score

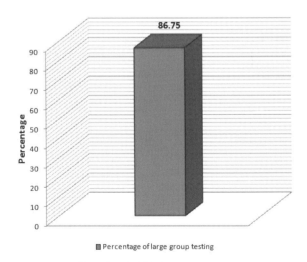

Fig. 13. Percentage of Large Group's Validation

From Fig. 13 the validation percentage is 86.75%. According to the criteria of validity in Table 3, validity of "CHEMISTRY VIRTUAL LAB" educational game from small group test is very valid without revision because the validity percentage is 86.75%.

Conclusion

From the discussion above, the researcher can conclude that educational game "CHEMISTRY VIRTUAL LAB" is valid and highly recommended for use in learning and teaching of chemical solution's concentration concept for second grade students of Senior High School. The developed media can be categorized as valid due to several validation processes that have been conducted. The validation processes are media expert validation (87.5%), material expert validation (85%), small group testing validation (89.58%), and large group testing validation (86.75%).

References

1) Tiastra, I M. (2010). Pembelajaran Kontekstual melalui Pembuatan Tahu Sebagai Upaya Meningkatkan Kualitas Pembelajaran di Kelas XII IPA SMAN 1 Kubu Tahun Pelajaran 2007/2008. Jurnal Pendidikan Sastracarya, 1 (2).

2) Johari, J.M.C. (2009). Chemistry. Jakarta: Esis Press.

3) Abdullah, Muhtadi. (2007). Pembelajaran Berbasis Masalah Pada Topik Wujud Zat dan Perubahannya Untuk Meningkatkan Pemahaman Konsep dan Keterampilan Proses Sains Siswa SMP. Thesis: Unpublished.

4) Munir. (2013). Multimedia dan Konsep Aplikasi dalam Pendidikan. Bandung: Alfabeta Press.

5) Foreman, J. G. (2004). Gamebaselearning: How to Delight and Instruct in 21st Century. Educase Review.

6) Balikesir. (2010). Alternative Methods in Learning Chemistry: Learning with Animation, Simulation, Video and Multimedia. Journal of Turkish Science Education, 7 (2), 79-110.

7) Handritantini, Eva, S.Kom, M.MT. (2009). Permainan Edukatif (Educational Game) Berbasis Komputer untuk SIswa Sekolah Dasar. Malang: Sekolah Tinggi Informasi & Komputer Indonesia.

8) Arsyad, Azhar. (2010). Media Pembelajaran. Jakarta: PT. Raja Grafindo Persada Press.

9) Bloom, Benjamin S., etc. (1956). Taxonomy of Educational Objectives: The Calssification of Educational Goals, Handbook I Cognitive Domain. New York: Longmas, Green and Co.

10) Sugiyono. (2013). Metode Penelitian Kuantitatif, Kualitatif, dan R&D. Bandung: Alfabeta, Page 297.

11) Dick and Carey. (1996). The Systematic Design of Instruction. Fourth Edition: Harper Collins College Publisher.

12) Arikunto, Suharsimi. (2013). Prosedur Penelitian: Suatu Pendekatan Praktik. Jakarta: Rineka Cipta Publisher.

13) Akbar, S. (2013). Instrumen Perangkat Pembelajaran. Bandung: PT. Remaja Rosdakarya Publisher, Page 42.

14) Akbar, S. (2013). Instrumen Perangkat Pembelajaran. Bandung: PT. Remaja Rosdakarya Publisher, Page 48.

Prosperity from a Cultural Palimpsest: the Rise and Regulation of "Korea Town" in Angeles City, the Philippines

José Edgardo Gomez, Jr.[1]
1 Associate Professor, University of the Philippines (August 2018)

かつて米空軍クラーク基地(フィリピン)の城下町として栄えたエンジェルス・シティ。基地撤退後、その歓楽街に韓国人が進出し、コリアタウンができた。その発展、地域との共生プロセスに東南アジアならではの都市のダイナミズムを見る。

Abstract

In the 1990s South Korean entrepreneurs began to buy up inexpensive land in the former entertainment district of Angeles City in the province of Pampanga, the Philippines. The relative success they generated is due to a rare, advantageous confluence of geospatial and sociocultural factors: strategic location in the fertile Central Luzon region, presence of the former United States' Clark Airbase, and a tradition among local *Kapampangans* of accommodating and adapting foreign influences to strengthen their own culture. This research describes the physical manifestation of Angeles' latest phenomenon: "Korea Town", which shows the unfolding of an enclave inside an urban community that maintains its own identity. It is shown that governance at different levels has become an enabler, and that despite their initial reticence, Korean settlers have gradually opened up to local clientele, through restaurants and bakeries, which have changed the landscape near the Clark International Airport. By highlighting how guardedness and rapprochement alternate to create a unique neighborhood where other foreigners once dominated, this study contributes to literature on cultural dynamics in Southeast Asian cities and concludes that the Korean Town is no fluke, but a logical result of the interplay of location, culture and institutions, and is still likely to evolve in the future.

Keywords Korean, Filipino, urban culture, governance, legacy infrastructure

Introduction and Significance of the Study

Where American soldiers on furlough once roamed the red-light district at the intersection of Fields and Mitchell avenues outside the gate of their largest airbase in Southeast Asia, now one can find groups of South Korean businessmen and their families establishing shops and restoring old residences. This is happening in Angeles City, Pampanga province, a major urban melting pot in the Central Luzon region of the Philippines, as it is being swept by *Hallyu*, the so-called Korean Wave in Asia, which the locals agree has contributed much to the city. In particular, Korean money has helped the financial and material recovery of the city since it was partly devastated by the eruption of Pinatubo Volcano in June 1991. Coincidentally, the *Kapampangan* (also known as *Pampango*) people are not strangers to cultural influences: they played a major historical role in Philippine nation-building, in no small measure by absorbing and transforming in succession Spanish, American and other local Filipino influences into their own native milieu. Often they accomplished this through political engagement, intermarriage and commerce, yet always retaining a relatively distinct *Kapampangan* identity among other Filipino ethnolinguistic groups, as well as in the face of globalization. What happens then when two strong cultures meet, and the urban palimpsest that is Angeles City once again is written over in *Hangul* by Korean settlers? It seems that despite occasional friction, the local Kapampangans continue in turns to entice investors and tolerate migrants while governing with a firm hand.

This research concentrates on "*Korea Town*", a representative and iconic district running for about 1 kilometer on the Filipino-American Friendship Highway in Angeles City, Pampanga Province, as the spatial manifestation of (South) Korean presence in a progressive urban area. By describing its spatial growth and the institutional framework that enables it, this research tries to theorize on the mixing of cultures by answering the question: "How do two disparate cultures mix in urban space as a result of (or despite of) the administrative role of government?" Patterns of interaction were sought, in order to generalize from what the obvious rapid changes in physicality have demonstrated.

This study also contributes to the growing literature on poly- or multi-cultural cities around the world, and describes for posterity a vibrant Southeast Asian example of ethnocentric urban growth. However, beyond the physical aspect, the author also scrutinizes governance and administrative structures behind the scenes that support the Korean influx, even magnify it. The research concludes with a recognition of the inherent legacy infrastructure and experiences left by past colonizers, migrants, and transients, as well as the balancing force of cross- and counter-cultural activities throughout the city's expanse pushed by the *Kapampangan* leadership and elite that sustain the bedrock of a local culture, and probably prepare Angeles City to handle such cultural impositions, more than other local government units (LGUs).

Methodology, Scope, Limitations of the Study

The overall methodology was qualitative-spatial investigation. The researcher undertook a t least two transect-walks and windshield surveys with photography in the neighborhood. Key informant interviews were also conducted throughout the length of study. For purposes of research, the site was visited intermittently from 2012 through 2017.

The data was analyzed spatially by looking for key infrastructure and patterns of building throughout the years that the site was visited. Public records, especially the land use and development plans, were then compared to identify any specific strategies to respond to Korean investment. The study was limited to the province of Pampanga, in Central Luzon, and as a qualitative-cum-spatial study, did not make any mathematically-derived conclusions, but rather probed social meanings and perceptions of both sides, Korean and Filipino (specifically, Kapampangan), as drivers of social and anti-social behavior, and as drivers of investment in urban space.

Review of Related Literature
Globalization and Cosmopolitan Cities

Due to the increasing globalization of production, especially in the mega-urban regions of Pacific-Asia (Douglass 2000), cities in different states are becoming increasing linked and constitutive of global circuits, for which the regulatory role of the state is shrinking in the face of global processes that have embedded themselves in national territories (Sassen 2002). With commerce comes more frequent and rapid interchange of ideas, as well as learning, which has allowed cities (through the individuals and groups that enliven them) to claim to be cosmopolitan, in the sense of being knowledgeable and comfortable with the diversity and dynamism of the world. Cosmopolitanism, however has been everywhere a frail achievement historically, in so far as cities are places that welcome and absorb strangers, at least for a time, even as residents in parts of the same cities may remain out of touch or intolerant of migrants, exiles, and sojourners, with whom they might coexist with varying degrees of acceptance, for generations (Werbner 2014). This mixing that may lead to more cosmopolitan cities has become more prominent in Asia, as evidenced by the increasing sociopolitical connections between states, and an unprecedented demand for travel that has risen in conjunction with economic development since the 1980s (Dissayanake, Kurauchi, Morikawa and Ohashi, 2012).

Diversity and the Cultural Turn in Today's Cities

Given the increasing chances of a cosmopolitan-shift in Asia's major cities, those who study and plan for cities have to consider the relatively new guiding principle of "diversity" as against the old orthodoxy of homogeneous segregation in planning of cities, at least since racial-ethnic and other types of heterogeneity were advocated by Jane Jacobs since the 1960s. And yet leading planning scholar S. Fainstein (2004) reminds us of the important modernist critique of communities planned for diversity that tend to labeled as inauthentic, even as she asserts that claims for real diversity are important in as much as these underlie the appeal of the urban, promote tolerance, and foster creativity. All the while, the same author notes that in such diverse urban settings, there is a constant trading off of values (e.g. broad-based democracy vs. small-group loyalty), as well as a mutual reinforcement of other values (e.g. courtesy and sociability).

Such diversity may or may not lead to a healthy multiculturalism as a de facto mode of existence, or as a part of state policy, as the latter has been often discussed, using Canada as an example. This multiculturalism envisages a society as a mosaic of beliefs and ways-of-doing, as defined by two principles: (1) the right to practice and preserve one's original heritage, and (2) equality of rights and freedoms, all of which are contained in the regulatory frames of the state and daily social life of the host country (Qadeer 1997). The same author goes on to explain that multiculturalism affects urban planning in at least two ways: 1. it holds planning policies and standards up to the light of social values and public goals; and 2. it recognizes the legitimacy of ethnic neighborhoods and enclaves, and therefore precipitates questions about balancing homogeneity with openness. This would stand in contradistinction to states which take a more assimilationist stance, where in-migrants and their children are expected by government to be absorbed sooner or later into the mainstream culture. The operative concept of culture however, continues to play a central role in cities, as present-day cities locate culture in central business districts (CBD), as well as in older symbolic pre-industrial sites of administration, as they have been doing in the past millenium, whether in an orthogenetic (*unidirectional evolutionary growth*) or heterogenetic (*dialectical, alternating growth*) form and manner (Redfield & Singer, 1954).

Urban Renewal Through (Multi-) Cultural Growth

At some point in time, usually coincident with, but sometimes lagging behind the incipient social diversity of growing cities comes their spatial growth and reconfiguration. This will often hinge upon international growth economics which in turn is based on specialization, human capital improvement, and institutional refinement, and translates most commonly into employment generation and its corresponding spillover effects (Storper 2010). This then translates into infused capital into the city so that new construction follows, as will be shown in this case study, where certain neighborhoods of Angeles City have been rebuilt with Korean funds. In planning terms, this might manifest into what is called urban revitalization policy, taking for example Business Improvement Districts (in the United States) which aspire to be safe, delightful and clean (Hoyt 2006). Although it must be remembered that urban renewal and redevelopment have deep roots, going as far back as the 19th century in Europe, where slum clearance and other forms of reconstruction were more government-initiated and funded, rather than market-driven (Zipp 2012). In due time, such development will call for, or impinge upon, the urban design process. If left to itself, natural but non-conscious processes will continue to shape and re-shape the experience of place, although again, rarely is urban space left entirely alone, but rather is managed or regulated by government or neighborhood associations (Carmona 2013), which are both manifested in this research.

Deeper Politics of Cultural Emphasis in Urbanism

In the actual day-to-day life of cities however, the meeting and mixing of cultures is not always a smooth process to which residents are receptive. Urban conflicts abound, not least because politicians and planners miss out on—or intentionally meddle in the social consequences of predation and control (Sevilla-Buitrago, 2013) that may take place when groups with different values and customs oppose one another in neighborhood spaces. Situations and events that exemplify cultural frictions in the city provide basis for those who are critical about what is called the "myth" of multiculturalism, or at least its excessive optimism, for intergroup conflicts in urban places need to be analyzed more carefully in order to understand the problematic of identity and difference, as well as the limits of tolerance (Fruchter and Harris 2010). The same authors go on to assert that culture does not emerge from shared experience but rather is rooted in shared ideals, which has to be worked out pragmatically in cities that are experiencing an influx of different and politically or economically powerful settlers. Hence, it has been said that the cultural turn in urban studies may need to pay attention to sites and social relations occasioned by human relations arising out of mingling, specifically because older Marxist perspectives have been too reductive, tending to see localisms and regionalisms as capital-labor relations, when there is a more varied totality of cultural factors at play (Soja 1999).

Koreans in the Philippines, Filipinos in Korea

In recent years, there has been a rise in the scholarly literature on the particular social and cultural interaction between Koreans and Filipinos, based on abundant empirical evidence of interactions of these people, especially in the cities of both South Korea and the Philippines. One of the acknowledged driving forces for the presence of Koreans in the Philippines and certain Western countries like the United States and Australia is *yeonggeokyoyuk*, or "English Education", which is part of a longer 20th-century "Education Fever" that on the one hand has done well to bring Korean literacy to nearly 100% but on the other hand has caused emotional and psychosocial development problems for children sent to cram schools and compelled to learn English abroad from a very young age (Park 2009, Bok-Rae 2015). In an earlier study on the Korean influx into Philippine cities this researcher deduced from interviews with various Koreans that the Philippines is probably considered to be a good alternative site for learning English (specifically American English) for Korean families somewhat lower on the socioeconomic ladder who cannot or will not send their children to the faraway United States (Gomez 2013).

On Philippine ground, the results of the Korean Wave are visible in the proliferation of ethnic restaurants, bakeries, and a few other iconic facilities like small churches and dentists. The Filipinos in various cities themselves have taken positively to *Hansik*, or Korean cuisine, which was initially served to Koreans who could not quite stomach local food, and later to curious and adventurous groups who had acquired a taste for *kimchi, samgyupsal, bibimbap, and japchae*, among others (Joven 2014). The demand is apparently sufficient so that the Korean Cultural Center in Metro Manila has offered Korean cooking courses, a decidedly state-sponsored inter-cultural program. At the same time, Filipino-dubbed Korean-inspired television dramas have been attracting a young local audience, just as Korean investors have been attracted in equal measure to large markets and the leisure life of golf course and gambling—this latter sometimes becoming a problem, along with the occasional recorded mistreatment of blue-collar Filipino workers by Korean entrepreneurs (Igno & Cenidoza 2016). Nevertheless, Philippine cities continue to be receptive to Korean investors and settlers, because of the latter's substantial cash infusions into the local economy. In many cases, Koreans can and do enjoy comparatively higher living standards while they live among Filipinos.

The same cannot be said about the conditions of many Filipinos in Korea, given that the latter country changed from being a labor-exporter to an importer in the 1990s, with labor policy adapting in the early 2000s such that Korean employers' needs and wishes are emphasized, while exploitation of foreign labor occurs to maximize Korea's economic benefit; foreign workers may stay briefly with no chance of work-permit extension and virtually no means to become permanent residents, but instead work for at most three (3) years under any of four permit regimes: professionals, industrial training, employment management system, and employment permit system (Kim 2005). The Filipinos themselves, majority of whom are paid between $2,000 to $2,500 a month tend to live in *yollips*, which are small, low-storey apartment buildings in Korea, where they can occupy the ground floors and basements for a minimal rent. They are not generally received warmly in mainstream Korean society, although they do find solace and comparatively strong communities in the Korean Catholic churches that abound (Lee 2007). Hence while researchers like Shafray & Seiyong (2016) might assert that South Korea is generally more open and tolerant towards foreigners than before, they hold that there is also a belief that foreign culture and capital will compete with local business and Korean traditions, hence the cultural resistance.

The Setting: Crucial Infrastructure in Pampanga

Measuring roughly 3,200 meters of military-grade asphalt-concrete length, the twin runways of Diosdado Macapagal Internationa Airport[1] and the latter's proximate

---

[1] Also known as Clark International Airport or formerly, Clark Airbase, of the U.S. Airforce, now of the Philippine Airforce. It was established as a 7,700 acre (31.16 square kms.) cavalry station called Fort

31,000-hectare surroundings plus a 32,000 hectare expanse of hilly hinterlands to the north, used to be the largest U.S. airbase in Southeast Asia, which straddles the border between Angeles City and Mabalacat municipality. Except for the contiguous municipalities of Mabalacat and Bamban (the latter in adjacent Tarlac province), no other Local Government Unit (LGU) in the Philippines can boast of this asset, and it is only urbanized Angeles City that controls the major access points to the airport/airbase, even as Mabalacat and to a lesser extent, Bamban hold the remainder of the open space and jungle that made up the original American military reservation. Second in terms of major infrastructure advantages, Angeles City is also traversed by the renovated eight lane North Luzon Expressway (NLEX), and the newer four lane Subic-Clark-Tarlac Expressway (SCTEX), from which it derives excellent interregional accessibility from the rest of Luzon. Third, due in part to its lineage of commercially-astute *Kapampangan* families, Angeles City has for a long time been the leading educational center of the province, as it possesses superior educational infrastructure in the form of two competitive private colleges: the Holy Angel University, and the Angeles University Foundation, as well as the public extension campus of the University of the Philippines, located within the Clark Freeport Zone (or "CFZ", in the airbase complex) itself. Again, no other LGU within a 50 kilometer radius can offer this same concentration of travel, employment, and training facilities.

Fieldwork Results: Of Mixing & Governance

Urban History and Diversification of Buildings

Having visited Angeles City for professional and personal purposes throughout the last two decades, the author has become familiar with the evolution of the urban landscape since the 1991 eruption of the Pinatubo volcano that effectively turned back large swathes of Angeles City into flatlands covered with whitish ash and lahar deposits. Onto this quasi-*tabula rasa*, risk-taking local speculators gradually bought up land in the late 1990s, in the wake of mass departure of resident American servicemen and the turnover of the airbase to the Philippine government in 1992. In those early years, many buildings which were not otherwise used (and quickly reopened) as nightclubs and motels around the perimeter of the airbase remained decrepit, as exemplified by the occasional roof still caved-in from the weight of volcanic debris.

Table I. Foreign Elements of Cultural Landscape in Angeles

Non-Filipino/ Foreign Settlers	Period	Estimated Spatial Extent (hectares)
Spanish Colonial	1796-1898	~3,865.37
American Colonial	1898-1946	< 6,217.37 (100%)
American Airbase*	c.1912-1992	224.39+
Korean (mostly business)	c.2002-present	62 (~1%)
Others: Chinese, Japanese, etc.	c.1800-present	31 (<1%)

*Notes: (1) shifting size during colonial periods reflects formal enlargement of the town (Spanish Colonial figure: D.David 2017 Powerpoint Presentation); (2) while concentration of airbase operations may have been limited to the fenced 225 hectare area, clearly the +500 hectare ring of commercial establishments now surrounding the base emerged organically to cater to U.S. Servicemen, hence the "+" on the spatial extent.

By early 2002, when the author had begun visiting the area with intent to do descriptive and explanatory research of the cityscape, the stretch of road of barangay[2] Balibago, Amsic, and Anunas on the southern perimeter of the airbase had begun to show a thin scattering of Korean establishments, usually small-scale English language schools, a restaurant or two, and a taekwondo gym.

A decade later, in 2012, there was an unmistakable Korean presence in Angeles City, concentrated commercially for about 500 meters on both sides of the Fil-Am Friendship Highway, which runs some 8.5 kilometers south and west of the city. In that area, barangay Anunas, two pagoda-like, burnt-red marble monuments which proclaimed "Korea Town" had been erected, with one close to where the airbase gate disgorges traffic to the now Korean-dominated strip, the other where the bridge over the Abacan river began. Signs in *Hangul* dominated both sides of the streets, and there were many more Korean restaurants and bakeries—10 to 12 on both sides of the street, and at every nearby neighborhood corner; it could thus be inferred that these had begun to cater to local *Kapampangans*, and not the relatively small number of Korean clientele.

Stotsenberg in 1903. - http://www.clarkab.org/history/ retrieved 05 July 2017.

2 *Barangay* [ba-rang-ga-i] – the smallest spatio-political unit under Philippine law; essentially a village.

Fig. 1. This monument marks both ends of the Korean enclave. Photograph by the author.

By 2017, practically the entire 1-kilometer strip from the Friendship Gate of the Clark Freeport Zone to the Abacan bridge had been claimed by Korean businesses, and the LGU was upgrading and expanding that section of the highway. There was a diversification of Korean establishments themselves, what urban scholars call the development of a "fine grain" (Kostof 1993). Korean groceries and churches were now in abundance. Notably however, the series was punctuated by other cuisines: a Japanese restaurant, a Spanish restaurant, and an Italian restaurant for example, but with signs in Korean plastered on the windows and headboard.

Despite the interspersed presence of some Filipino establishments and residences, the overall visual effect of Korea Town is astounding to those who were had known the area as an American enclave. This is because of the former's mono-cultural façade on both sides of the four-lane corridor formed by the highway. Even the cars parked in front of the different establishments, if they belong to the owners, tend to be of Korean manufacture.

Larger Context: Kapampangan Primacy in Angeles

The people of Pampanga have a long history of taking advantage of colonizing influences, as their ancestors were desired by Spanish superiors because the early Kapampangans were proven to be loyal and dependable soldiers (De Viana 2005), and later lieutenants and petty officials. In time Spanish settlers and Chinese traders intermarried with *Kapampangans*, thereby producing the generations of fair-skinned people who are populous in this part of the archipelago. This sociocultural origin is the foundation of development of the urban core.

Since its founding around 1796 as the barrio of *Culiat*[3], and separated from territory that originally belonged to the town of San Fernando to the south, Angeles City has been a bastion of Kapampangan culture, in so far as it has successfully blended and absorbed Spanish and American influences into the ways-of-doing of the average resident. Physical manifestations of the strong social fabric include the religious devotion to the *Apung Mamacalulu* (Merciful Lord) in the shrine of the Holy Sepulcher, as well as the numerous heritage houses in the old plaza, some of which used to belong to prominent citizens, and are now used also for heritage tourism.

Aside from local pride, and in response to the erosive forces of globalization, there have been recent moves, likely to be adopted soon by the local legislative council, to make the Kapampangan language official and mandatory within the city, according to the author's interview with the tourism and planning officers. This would then have implication for public signage and would promote learning of the indigenous speech by all residents. Because the city itself is booming[4] in contrast to other Philippine LGUs, with locals engaged both in manufacturing inside the CFZ and agro-industrial development of the surrounding rural lands, it is expected that local income will sustain such initiatives to promote this indigenous culture.

Comprehensive Land Use Plan & Other Frames

But apart from the sociological and market-based realities

---

3   *Culiat* (genus *Gnetum*) or *Kuliat* is the local name of a vine that used to grow abundantly in the townsite.

4   Angeles City, like the capital region Metro Manila, generates its own surplus income, and does not rely heavily on tax transfers from national government.

visible on the streets, it is important to inquire: is there any rationality behind the rapid development of Angeles City? The Comprehensive Land Use Plan 2010-2020 (CLUP) of the city seems to recognize that the relatively central location of Angeles in the province is a magnet for trade and exchange of ideas.

Table II. Land Use: Angeles City (Source: CLUP 2010-2020)

Land Use	Area (Hectares)	Percentage Share
Built-up and roads	2,762.08	44.43%
Agricultural Land	1,543.51	24.83%
Agricultural/Tropical Grass	843.75	13.57%
Bush/ Forest Cover	698.42	11.23%
DMIA Complex	224.39	3.61%
Abacan River	145.22	2.34%
Total	6,217.37	100.00%

Specifically, 3 of 9 identified growth nodes are within a kilometer of the CFZ perimeter fence: the Abacan River Special Development Corridor, the Balibago Growth Center, and the Anunas Growth Center—this latter being precisely the location of Korea Town. As designated, these areas shall have few government restrictions on commercial and industrial investment. In particular, the banks of the small and shallow Abacan River, which runs roughly west to east, are slated for development.

Other plans, like the national Philippine Development Plan (2017-2022) and its subordinate Regional Plan for Central Luzon, identify Angeles City as a regional international gateway, and recognize that on the whole, it is part of an area of rapid population growth and economic activity.

Official Reactions: City Hall vs. Barangay Hall

Interestingly, when the author conducted an interview in February 2017 with the City Hall planning and tourism officials, it was learned that the priority was on strengthening local culture, rather than providing any special accommodation to Koreans, or any other group, like Japanese and Chinese, who are also active in the city's commerce. In spatial terms, the old Spanish-era plaza in the center of town had been cleared and improved, and local festivals were being promoted rather than Korean neighborhoods.

The same officials however, gratefully recognized that the Koreans, some 20,000 of whom are residents in Angeles, had been contributing at least 25-30% of the entire annual income, through business permits, taxes, and other fees, for the decade of the 2000s. There were in fact at least 150 thriving Korean business establishments in Angeles as of 2015, and at least 96 industrial locators in the CFZ (Buan 2017). Given that the latest official gross income reported is P1,614,109,000 (U.S.$31,882,423.81) in 2016, then the portion attributable to Korean investment and daily spending could amount to P538,036,333.33 (U.S.$10,628,768.91), which is enough to build several buildings. This latter figure is credible, given the hundreds of small Korean commercial establishments that now lie scattered across the landscape of the city, and not even taking into account forward and backward linkages with peer establishments owned by both locals and other Korean investors.

Fig. 2. Note the pictures taken in 2012 (above) and 2017 respectively: even the Spanish and Japanese restaurants have Korean signs. All photographs by the author.

As far as the bureaucrats could recount, Korean businessmen started coming when they realized that it was cheaper to fly in and play golf in the CFZ over the weekend than in South

Korea. Eventually such businessmen eventually opening up businesses, or enrolled their children in weekend or summer courses in local schools, where the latter learned English, and in time made friends, as did their parents. In the ordinary neighborhoods of Angeles City, the Korean investors are subject to the standard regulations for construction and location of business, although they are given additional incentives when they make substantial investments within the CFZ area.

At the barangay level however, there was a marked difference in receptivity; a more positive and non-discriminating one. The barangay has continued to welcome the influx of Koreans, particularly in the mid-2000s, as recalled by one officer, A.G., who said that Korean speculators would arrive almost every month in 2007, to buy up the real estate that had still remained cheap close to one decade after the volcanic eruption. The barangay captain then, L.G. made it a condition that such entrepreneurs hire locals. The same respondent added that Koreans started coming over a decade ago, during the term of the former mayor C.Lazatin; although under the present mayor, E.Pamintuan, there seems to have been another barangay captain recently elected. In any case, the barangay officials have practiced a *laissez-faire* approach, letting Koreans do as they wish, but stepping in only when there are reports of abuse of laborers, for which a stern warning is issued to the Koreans, who will face deportation if they continue to verbally abuse, underpay, or illegally withhold pay to wage-laborers and salaried blue-collar workers.

It should be remarked as well that in the same neighborhood one can find the "Shinyang Korea-Philippines Cultural Center", a good-sized building erected by the Korean Community Association of Central Luzon, Inc. Although due to the language barrier, the officer who received the author during a visit in July 2017 declined to be interviewed, it may be said that this institutional presence alone in Angeles City is a substantial investment not found in other cities in the Philippines.

Analysis and Discussion of Findings

In addition to over 1,000,000 Korean tourists who visit annually, the Korean presence in Angeles City is visible and substantial in comparison to other major provincial urban areas. While accessibility through the airport is the most apparent enabler for Korean sojourners, it does not fully explain their eventual settlement. For this latter, the open attitude of the LGU should be recognized, especially barangay Anunas, which sits right outside the airbase complex.

Even the City Hall officials, who are notably more detached and impartial, nevertheless took concrete measures to protect Korean investors after a spate of killings and extortions—the latest being the kidnapping and killing of Jee Ick Joo in 2016 (Orejas 2017). These included the establishment of a "tourist-friendly" police outpost at the entrance to Korea Town (visited by the author, who observed at least three on-duty policemen), which paralleled the much higher-level action on the part of governor Pineda, who signed an Provincial Executive Order last February 2017 establishing the Korean Assistance Office of Pampanga. It is clear then, that at least three (3) levels of local government officials are responding to the needs of the Korean community, as a form of diplomatic reciprocation to good international relations, and in recognition of the income that is being poured into the economy of Pampanga, and Central Luzon as a whole. This institutional support is crucial, and it should be emphasized, is historically consistent with the Kapampangan's own willingness to engage in fair trade and exchange of ideas with foreigners, as long as there are direct or indirect economic and sociopolitical gains, not least for the established network of local clans of the genteel upper class.

Implications for Theory

From a theoretical perspective then, Angeles City has become a relatively successful urban cultural palimpsest—a storied site where other cultures have inscribed their own scripts, effacing in parts, yet also augmenting and embellishing what has come before. The city is both unique and representative of other cities that are experiencing a substantial in-migration of Koreans in the Philippines. It is unique physically because of its American-legacy infrastructure that other Philippine cities lack, and because of its association with a strong material and politico-literary culture that shaped Filipino history. But it is also commonplace, or representative, because its urban spaces are exemplars of how Korean settlers and transients have aggressively transformed neighborhoods to suit their lifestyles.

Moreover, from a spatial point of view, Angeles City appears to demonstrate an inherent resilience in its urban fabric, which refers to a system's capacity to maintain structural and functional integrity in the face of disturbance, whether planned or unplanned (Bessey 2002), such that has not become entirely overwhelmed by the waves of foreign influence that have washed over it, but has retained a solid historical urban core (centered on the twin belltowers of the Holy Rosary Church), with a fresh satellite area (the Marquee Mall rotunda and the new City Hall complex), and the long-standing entertainment district near CFZ, of which Korea Town is an important part.

It is a de facto multiculturalism that has emerged as a result of the Koreans' initial preference in the early 2000s to keep to themselves and provide commercial services to their fellow countrymen, for safety purposes and because of the language barrier. This is a pattern observed by the author in his earlier research done in Metro Manila. But after a decade of colorful interaction, it seems that some mutually-beneficial mingling has evolved, in the form of Korean restaurants catering to locals, which of necessity have had to convert their signages from purely Hangul script to English lettering. In these places, Filipinos, and foreign nationalities like Americans, Chinese, and Japanese dine, sometimes in mixed groups. This social phenomenon is consistent the literature on geographies of food, and constitutive of cosmopolitan eating where fuzzy interactions between diverse groups allow for deepening of familiarity with other cultures (Duruz 2011). The restaurant dynamic is therefore particularly *apropos* to Pampanga province, which is known throughout the Philippines for its own distinct culinary traditions—so that if the discriminating palate of the Kapampangan gourmet can be piqued, if not impressed by Korean cuisine, then mutual cultural respect can somehow develop. This is precisely what Zafari et al. (2015) try to explain when they show that ethnic cuisine consumed in usually complex social situations is allows the eaters to observer and learn social norms for quantity and manner of food consumption, and instrumentally allows association with others who are not necessarily akin or alike one's self.

Hence, even as the segregation dissolves slowly, one can affirm that intercultural and sociopolitical efforts are making inroads, leading towards what the literature has generally recognized to be the delicate, valuable balance of ethnolinguistic and racial groups in successful cities. Apart from the natural formation of relationships in Korean-Filipino neighborhoods, three additional factors appear to be determinative of engagement, which are noteworthy of theory-related commentary:

First, the loose, but nevertheless persistent regulatory frame of the LGU (at city and barangay levels) ensures that the Korean population must interact with the Kapampangan administrators. This defines in subtle ways, the minimum of cross-cultural engagement that prevents formation of quasi-colonial enclaves, and that militates against any apartheid-like situation. It may be hypothesized therefore, that a supportive institutional presence is *sine qua non* for the conditions that lead to cultural rapprochement.

Second, education of Korean children of expatriate businessmen in English, which is an official but **not** a *native* language, ironically allows them access to other countries and cultures (particularly the United States as a desired later destination), yet also allows them also to interact meaningfully with their bilingual Filipino classmates and literate ordinary persons in the wider urban environment. Linguistic facility in a language foreign to both cultures does become a bridge for cultural exchange, where in the process, Korean youngsters learn both Kapampangan and Filipino, while the natives pick up some Korean phrases, as do the sun-burnt native tricycle drivers who ferry passengers through Korea Town everyday.

Lastly, to the credit of the Koreans themselves, it appears that the lure of commercial profits and the concomitant relaxed lifestyle in a tropical country has been adequate to keep many of them rooted in Angeles City, despite the occasional harassment, altercations with some locals, misunderstandings, or victimization by crime. Commercial success resulting in the creation of an attractive lifestyle is arguably the major and most visible reason why Korean families have continued to settle in Angeles City. In doing so, the spill-over effects of their spending not only benefits the local economy, but also inevitably leads to interaction and intermarriage with the locals.

An additional note must be mentioned here that the success of Korea Town has taken place even if the political climate was not entirely conducive to its fruition; as there appears to remain a discrepancy between the degree of support of City Hall and Barangay Hall, the latter being flush with Korean investment that generates jobs for the less well-off neighborhood to the

Fig. 3. Korean-Filipino Associations like this one provide a stabilizing institutional presence for investors. Photograph by author.

west. Barangay leaders therefore have been politically pragmatic in allowing the Koreanization of that strip of neighborhood, even while City leaders, in contrast, have to think about balancing population and employment for the rest of the urban area, and are also mandated to promote local culture through festivals and official activities that celebrate the Kapampangan identity.

Conclusions and Recommendations

The case of Angeles City contributes to the literature on noteworthy urban cultural phenomena, at least in Southeast Asia, because it presents a unique confluence of infrastructure-enabled access, a persistent and prosperous stream of in-migration (Korean), and long history of successful absorption and adaptation of foreign ideas by a cultured native population. Moreover, it may be remarked, the physical and social legacies of the past groups have been co-opted and used *cumulatively* to great effect by the native leadership: the airport brings in a steady stream of Korean and other investors into a city that has built up its landscape to reflect a relaxed blending of Hispanic-Filipino in the urban core, as defined by the old plaza, and American-Filipino in the commercialized periphery surrounding the former military reservation that has turned into an industrial zone and airport. Onto this urban landscape, the Koreans have attached themselves, taking advantage of depressed real estate prices in the 1990s and early 2000s, and by doing so have, through aggregate action, revitalized several parts of Angeles City, with the most obvious concentration in Korea Town, which lies in Barangay Anunas. At the same time, a nascent conviviality in the urban fabric is spreading, albeit slowly, in those places where Korean and Kapampangan become part of each other's daily routine.

Looking ahead, the physical growth of Korea Town is expected to proceed apace, possibly to follow the Filipino-American Friendship Highway across the Abacan river. As a policy follow-up, it may be forward-thinking and wise for city officials to require more intercultural engagement, and to coordinate efforts with the barangay administration regarding the placement of Korean businesses and residences. A healthy mixture is, in the long-run, more desirable to any externally-enforced or self-imposed segregation. Other institutions also need to be involved, such as the management of the Clark Freeport Zone and the Diosdado Macapagal Airport, in order to ensure warm reception, smooth transitions and culturally-sensitive behavior for all incoming tourists and business investors.

For further studies, Angeles City and adjacent LGUs like Mabalacat, Porac and Bamban, will continue to serve as excellent urban laboratories, especially because Angeles City continues to be an economic and sociocultural magnet in the province beyond its built-up and legal borders. This is in part because as a "workforce city", it draws its labor from far beyond its borders (Parr 2007). Pursuant to this research, the author would thus recommend that other scholars undertake longitudinal and spatial studies to follow the continuing changes in the cityscape, especially its Korean component, as well as those neighborhoods that have been, or shall be changed by economic growth caused by the arrival of other groups of people from beyond the borders of the Philippines.

References

1) Bessey, K.M. (2002) Structure and Dynamics in an Urban Landscape: Toward a Multiscale View. Ecosystems, 5(4), 360-375.

2) Bok-Rae, K. (2015) The English Fever in South Korea: Focusing on the Problem of Early English Education. Journal of Education & Social Policy, 2(2), 117-124.

3) Buan, L. (05 February 2017) "50% Drop in Korean Tourists, Investors in Central Luzon" in Rappler. Retrieved from: http://www.rappler.com/nation/160451-big-drop-korean-tourist-investor-central-luzon on 11 July 2017.

4) Carmona, M. (2013) The Place-shaping Continuum: A Theory of Urban Design Process. Journal of Urban Design, 19(1), 2-36.

5) De Viana, A.V. (2005) The Pampangos in the Mariana Mission 1668-1684. Micronesian Journal of the Humanities and Social Sciences, 4(1), 1-16.

6) Dissanayake, D.; Kurauchi, S.; Morikawa, T., and Ohashi, S. (2012) Inter-regional and Inter-temporal analysis of Travel Behavior for Asian Metropolitan Cities: Case Studies of Bangkok, Kuala Lumpur, Manila, and Nagoya", Transport Policy, 19, 36-46.

7) Douglass, M. (2000) Mega-Urban Regions and World City Formation: Globalisation, the Economic Crisis and Urban Policy Issues in Pacific Asia. Urban Studies, 37(12), 2315-2335.

8) Duruz, J.; Luckman, S. and Bishop, P. (2011) Bazaar Encounters: Food, Markets, Belonging, and Citizenship in the Cosmopolitan City. Continuum: Journal of Media & Cultural Studies, 25(5), 599-604.

9) Fainstein, S.S. (2004) Cities and Diversity: Should We Want It? Can We Plan for It? Urban Affairs Review, 41(1), 3-19.

10) Fruchter, P. and Harris, A.L. (2010) The Myth of the Multicultural City: Learning to Live Together Without Coming to Blows. Hagar, 10 (1), 105-129.

11) Gomez, J.E.A.Jr. (2013) "The Korean Diaspora in Philippine Cities: Amalgamation or Invasion?" Chapter 6 in Hou, J. (Ed.) Transcultural Cities. Routledge: New York.

12) Hoyt, L. (2006) Importing Ideas; The Transnational Transfer of Urban Revitalization Policy. International Journal of Public Administration, 29:1-3, 221-243.

13) Igno, J.M. and Cenidoza, M.C.E. (2016) Beyond the `Fad': Understanding Hallyu in the Philippines. International Journal of Social Science and Humanity, 6(9), 723-727.

14) Joven, A. 2014. Hansik and Hallyu: An Analysis of the Filipino Appropriation of Korean Cuisine as a Function of Imagining Korean Culture. Proceedings of the AIKS Korean Studies Conference, 1, 122-143.

15) Kim, E. (2005) Low Cultural Receptivity Toward Foreigners in Korea: The Case of Transnational Migrant Workers, Korea Observer, 36(1), 1-20.

16) Kostof, S. (1993) The City Shaped. New York: Bullfinch Press.

17) Lee, M. 2007. Filipino Village in South Korea. Community, Work, and Family, 9(4): 429-440.

18) National Economic & Development Authority [NEDA]: Philippine Development Plan 2017-2022.

19) NEDA Region 3: Region3 Development Plan 2017-2022.

20) Orejas, T. (18 February 2017) "Pampanga Crime Hot Spot for Koreans" in the Philippine Daily Inquirer. Retrieved from: - http://newsinfo.inquirer.net/872697/pampanga-crime-hot-spot-for-koreans [Inquirer.Net] on 12 July 2017.

21) Park, J.-K. (2009) 'English Fever' in South Korea: Its History and Symptoms", English Today 97, Volume 25, Number 1, pp.50-57.

22) Parr, J.B. (2007) Spatial Definitions of the City: Four Perspectives. Urban Studies, 44(2), 381-392.

23) Qadeer, M.A. (1997) Pluralistic Planning for Multicultural Cities: The Canadian Practice. Journal of the American Planning Association. 63(4), 481-494.

24) Redfield, R. and Singer, M.B. (1954) The Cultural Role of Cities. Economic Development and Cultural Change, 3(1), 53-73.

25) Sassen, S. (2002) Locating Cities on Global Circuits. Environment and Urbanization, 14(1), 13-30.

26) Sevilla-Buitrago, A. (2013) Debating Contemporary Urban Conflicts: a Survey of Selected Scholars. Cities, 31, 454-468.

27) Shafray, E. and Seiyong, K. (2016) Study of Urban Spaces for Foreigners Socializing: Focusing on Multi-Ethnic Neighborhoods in Seoul, Korea. GSTF Journal of Engineering Technology, 3(4), 11-16.

28) Soja, E.W. (1999) In Different Spaces: the Cultural Turn in Urban and Regional Political Economy, European Planning Studies, 7(1), 65-75.

29) Storper, M. (2010) Why Does a City Grow? Specialisation, Human Capital or Institutions? Urban Studies, 47(10), 2027-2050.

30) Werbner, P. (2014) The Dialectics of Urban Cosmopolitanism: Between Tolerance and Intolerance in Cities of Strangers. Identities: Global Studies in Culture and Power, 1-19.

31) Wycisk, A. (2014) Schemes of (Re)interpreting the Cultural Themes in the Process of Building the City Image. Polish Sociological Review, 4(188), 525-540.

32) Zafari, K. Allison, G. and Demangeot, C. (2015) Practising Conviviality: Social Uses of Ethnic Cuisine in an Asian Multicultural Environment. Journal of Consumer Marketing, 32(7), 564-575.

33) Zipp, Samuel. (2012) The Roots and Routes of Urban Renewal. Journal of Urban History, 39(1), 366-391.

Effect of the Philippine Conditional Cash Transfer to the Local Economy

Merlyne M. Paunlagui[1]
1 Director, CSPPS, CPAf, University of the Philippines Los Baños

子どもに教育を受けさせることなどを条件に、貧困層に一定の現金を給付するフィリピン政府のプログラム「4Ps」。給付された資金がいかに活用され、ささやかながらも地域経済の活性化に役立っていることをケーススタディで実証した。

Abstract

A common sight to see during payouts of the conditional cash transfer is the operation of a flea market near the cash payout sites. The operation of the flea market is a manifestation that the extra income received from the *Pantawid* program (conditional cash transfer program) can perk up local economic activities since most products being sold in the flea market come from the locality or neighboring areas. For instance, a province with 73,710 household beneficiaries received PhP 1.05 billion annually, representing nearly 40% of the total revenue allocation of the province in 2012. Thus, the objective of the study is to determine qualitatively the nature, form, and degree of the economic impact of the *Pantawid's* cash grant expenditures (or payouts) on the local economy.

The results of the study showed that the effect of the conditional cash transfer to the local economy is positive, to wit: 1) increased number of merchants; 2) diversity of goods being sold; 3) increased sales of pharmacy and dry and wet goods shops; 4) increased employment; and 4) increased earnings of jeepney and tricycle drivers servicing the beneficiaries. For the municipal government, the revenue derived from market fees increased substantially and the payout contributed to the continuous operation of the local market.

Keywords conditional cash transfer; *Pantawid*; flea market; payout

Introduction

The *Pantawid Pamilyang Pilipino Program* (4Ps) or the conditional cash transfer is a flagship social protection cum poverty alleviation program of the Aquino Administration. Patterned after conditional cash transfers developed and implemented in countries like Brazil and Mexico, the program provides cash grants to the extremely poor and most vulnerable households on the condition that they keep their children of ages 0 to 18 years healthy and attend school regularly while pregnant women avail of maternal health services (DSWD 2015).

Pantawid plays two pivotal roles in achieving the government's development agenda. First is the conditionality attached to the cash grants enables the poor and vulnerable households in society to build and invest on the human capital resources of their children and the youth. Second is that enabling the *Pantawid* beneficiaries with stable and reliable financial support provides a safety net for the poor, preventing them from sliding to a more impoverished condition.

In the Philippines, an eligible family under the conditional cash transfer (CCT) program receives the following: 1) health grant of PhP500 per month; 2) education grant of PhP300 per elementary grade student and PhP500 for high student per month for 10 months for a maximum of three children per household; and rice grant of PhP600 per month. In one province with 73,710 household beneficiaries received PhP1.05 billion in 2012, representing nearly 40% of the total revenue allocation of the province.

The Department of Social Welfare and Development (DSWD) leads and oversees the implementation of the *Pantawid* Program. Pilot implementation started in February 2007 with 6,000 poor household beneficiaries from 4 municipalities and 2 cities. The program has been scaled up to cover all provinces in the country with 4.4 million household beneficiaries as of 2017. Given the magnitude of the coverage and the amount invested in the Program, close monitoring of the program's outcome is continually being undertaken since its nationwide implementation in 2008. To this date, two comprehensive impact evaluations had been conducted.

However, little attention has been accorded to evaluating the economic impact of the program to the local economy.

Objectives of the Study

The general objective of this study was to determine qualitatively the nature, form, and degree of the economic impact of the *Pantawid*'s cash grant on the local economy. Specifically, the flea market study aimed to:
1. describe which goods or products were bought more by beneficiaries during the payouts;
2. identify who are the sellers/vendors/ entre-preneurs and the type of products/goods being sold, where are they from; where do they get their products; and amount and source of capitalization;
3. analyze the effects of flea market on employment generation and other indirect economic activities within the spatial coverage of *Pantawid*; and
4. determine the roles of the local government units (LGUs) in facilitating the payouts and determine whether revenues are generated from flea market and their utilization.

Methodology

The case studies were conducted in Region 5 or the Bicol Region. A municipality in each of the provinces of Albay, Camarines Norte, and Masbate were purposively selected by Department of Social Welfare and Development (DSWD) as the study sites. These three municipalities were: 1) Libon, Albay; 2) Milagros, Masbate; and 3) Vinzons, Camarines Norte.

The flea market study qualitatively describes the results of the investigation on the relationship of payouts and the flea market and the nature and structure of the flea market. Both secondary and primary data were collected to answer the objectives of the case study. Secondary data were sourced from the Comprehensive Land Uses Plan (CLUP), Socio-economic Report of the Municipality, Annual Investment Plan, and results of the Community-based Monitoring System (CBMS). On the other hand, primary data were derived from accounts of the 4Ps beneficiaries, local government officers and staff, entrepreneurs/vendors/sellers, parent leaders, and municipal link or the staff of *Pantawid* at the municipal level on the payouts and the operations of the flea market.

Descriptive methods like mean, mode and frequency distribution were used in analyzing the data. Graphs and photographs were also included to vividly illustrate the effects of *Pantawid* on the local economy.

Results and Discussion

The Flea Market

This section examines how the money from *Pantawid* is utilized, how the grant fund contributes to increasing the type of goods and volume of business in the municipality, and the amount of revenue generated by the LGU from the flea market that sprouts out during *Pantawid* payout.

Pantawid's payout schedule ranges from two to three days depending on the number of beneficiaries. In the January 2016 payout for Libon, the schedule was for three days from 8:00 am and until the last beneficiary was served. During the first day the payout was almost over by one o clock in the afternoon except for those who were queuing to get the cash from the Banco Santiago de Libon. For the Municipality of Milagros, the January payout was also conducted for three days. For Vinzons, Camarines Norte, two days were allocated for the payout despite the fact that many of the beneficiaries are automatic teller machine (ATM) card holders. A day is scheduled for those who still do not have an ATM card while another day is spent for the beneficiaries of the three barangays located in island barangays.

Payout Venue

The payout in Libon, Albay is made through the Banco Santiago de Libon. In this system, the beneficiaries will have to first secure the acknowledgement receipt (AR) from the assigned *Pantawid* Municipal Link staff. This slip indicates the amount due them. The amount varies depending on the number of children covered, education level (i.e., elementary or high school) and whether the conditionalities have been met for the payout period. Then the beneficiaries have to queue for their money from Banco de Libon located in the Libon Town Center (LTC).

LTC is located in an agricultural area and can be reached from the town proper or from the highway coming from the first barangay of Polangui. It is a 5 to 10-minute ride by tricycle from the Municipal Hall of Libon. LTC was built to serve as the public market/commercial center started by Mayor John M. Dycoco and was completed during the term of his wife, Mayor Agnes Dycoco. The "permanent" business establishments include a display center of products made by women in Libon, a bank (Banco Santiago de Libon which serves as the conduit for the 4Ps payout), a mini-supermarket, two rice dealers, six eateries/*carenderias*, three to four dry goods stalls, a generic drug store, and a number of temporary stalls for vegetable and fruit vendors. At the back of the building are fresh and dried fish and meat sections, which operate daily.

The market days of Libon are Wednesday and Saturday. These market days are scheduled so as not to conflict with the market days in the municipalities of Oas and Polangui to give maximum opportunity to merchants and vendors to sell their wares in these different municipalities. According to the staff of the market office, when the LTC was newly opened, the municipality invited merchants from nearby municipalities during market days. Since the *Pantawid* payout was moved to the LTC, the merchants from other municipality regularly sell their goods during market days and payout days. With very few regular stall/shops, the LTC management would find it difficult to continue its operation without the itinerant vendors.

In Vinzons, Camarines Norte, there are two modes of payout. Most of the beneficiaries can access their bi-monthly payout through the automatic teller machine (ATM). There is a Land Bank ATM machine, which *Pantawid* beneficiaries can use in the municipality. However, many of the beneficiaries use the ATM located either in Labo (another municipality of Camarines Norte south of Vinzons), and in Daet City (capital of Camarines Norte). Two of the beneficiaries claimed to have use the ATM in Labo because of the variety of goods and supplies offered and sold at lower prices as well as opportunity to treat their children at the Jollibee fast food chain.

The other mode is through the accredited service provider for those beneficiaries without the ATM card. The payout is done in one of the municipal facilities. A similar system is employed in the three barangays of Vinzons located in the island of Calaguas. The payout during the month of January was postponed due to bad weather. There is also the hazard of the conduit being robbed on the way to the island.

In Milagros, Masbate, the first two payouts in 2009 were done in the City of Masbate via the Land Bank of the Philippines. However, a number of problems were encountered. One was that since there were too many beneficiaries queuing up, it took almost a day to distribute the money. There were also claims of incorrect payment received, with some receiving less and others more than what is due them. There were also claims that beneficiaries overdrew the amount due to them.

The third payout took place in the old municipal building of Milagros in the town proper. The payout was done in front of the building next to the municipal building. The space is quite small; thus, it became very crowded during the payout. Shops of all types surrounded the municipal building where the beneficiaries bought their needs. Other vendors were also allowed to put up stalls outside the municipality.

In September 2015, the municipal government moved to its new building in Barangay Bacolod, about two kilometers away from the town proper. Starting September 2015, payouts were done in the covered court near the new municipal building. The building without paint on the left side of the paved pathway is the venue where the beneficiaries queue to get their bi-monthly payout.

Shops during payouts are organized wherein similar shops are clustered together in front like eatery and food stalls, and school supplies. Big stalls selling clothes and other household items and *ukay-ukay* occupy the biggest area. On the other hand, meat and fish vendors are located near the bottom of the pathway near the highway and farthest away from the payout venue.

The Merchants: Types, Sources of Goods and Capital

Merchants in Libon, Albay

There are two main types of traders in Libon. The first type is composed of the regular stall owners who pay monthly rent. These include the supermarket owner, rice retailers (2), eateries (6), generic drug store, small dry goods store, vegetable and fruit sellers, two-to-three meat vendors, four fish vendors, hamburger seller, fruits and vegetables seller, and few dried fish retailers.

Traders of the second type are those present only during market and payout days. All these traders/merchants set their temporary stalls at the back of the LTC. They either bring their own tables or rent *papag* (low table made out of bamboo) from the market office of the municipality to display their wares. The merchants are grouped according to goods being sold. All dry good sellers including school supplies, slippers, shoes, and new clothes and those selling *ukay-ukay* are grouped together with those selling mats, plastic wares, and other household items beside them. Located farther at the back are fruits and vegetables vendors. There are also several itinerant vendors peddling gas lamps, belts, saws (carpentry tool), woven hammocks, and umbrellas. Majority of the "rotating" merchants sell every market day in the neighboring towns of Polangui and Oas, Albay.

There were two large *ukay-ukay* merchants seen during payout last January 29, 2016. Both are family-owned and from Oas, Albay. The larger *ukay-ukay* vendor started as a dried fish vendor with a capitalization of PhP400. She shifted to *ukay-ukay* with a capitalization of PhP22,000 because she witnessed how this business has grown through the years. She further invested whatever she earns from her *ukay-ukay* business into other goods that are highly sought during market day. Only during 4Ps payout that she sells brand new slippers and other footwear because of high demand for them. Her husband joined her in selling compact discs, which seem to be selling very well during payout. Her daily sale during payout averages Php10,000 per day. During the November payout her gross sales was PhP50,000. She valued her business now at PhP250,000. She borrows additional capital before every payout to buy additional goods. For the January payout, she borrowed PhP50,000 from a five-six lender with an interest of 5 percent per month. In an ordinary market day, her gross sales is less than half of what she sells during payout. According to her, she still rents her house but was able to buy a jeepney to transport her merchandise from one municipality to the other. As noted earlier, the municipalities located new Libon has scheduled market days.

Included under this category are the supermarket and dry goods stores. The supermarket is located in front of the LTC. It sells a variety of dry goods such as school supplies, uniform, bag, slippers and other school supplies. According to one of the sales ladies, the total gross sales in an ordinary day averages around PhP 30,000 but during payout, the gross sales almost triple. Many of their goods are on consignment from distributors in Manila and in Legaspi City.

The other dry goods stores are located at the right side of the LTC. Their products include canned goods, canned milk, noodles, coffee, and biscuits, and other snack foods.

An old lady operates one of the two rice dealers in the LTC. According to her, there were days when her total sale for a day was only PhP500 and sometimes worries of not having enough money to pay her monthly rent, despite the 50 percent rental discount. During the November payout, she said that she was able to sell 40 sacks of rice during the three-day payout. During the first day of the January payout, she narrated that she was unable to finish her lunch because of too many customers. However, she bewailed that her first day gross sale is lower than the November payout because of the recent rice-harvesting season. Farmer beneficiaries still have rice and would rather spend their cash to other household needs. When interviewed during the afternoon of non-payout day, she joked, "Pwede nang matulog (I can now sleep)!", as there were no customers. She gets her rice supply from the National Food Authority (NFA) across the LTC.

On the right front side of the LTC are two small eateries while another three smaller "carenderias" are located in the side of the market. A *carenderia* owner observed that during non-payout time, her customers are mostly confined to shop owners in the market as well as workers passing by the LTC. In an ordinary day, her gross sale is about PhP800 pesos. However, this increased by three-fold during payout. There were also ambulant food vendors at the back of the jeepneys parked near the LTC. A key informant said that she came from Barangay Pantao where she has an eatery. During the January payout, she prepared 30 boxes each of spaghetti, rice and menudo for lunch, and noodles for snack. She sells each pack at PhP20.

The burger stall provides the evidence on the positive effect of *Pantawid* to local entrepreneurs. This shop opens only during payout. During the January payout, the stall can hardly be seen as people swarm the place. His burgers sell like hotcakes.

There were four to five fruit vendors operating during the January payout. Two of the fruit vendors interviewed sourced their native oranges from the province of Quezon. One is from the Municipality of Nabua in Camarines Sur while the other one is from Oas, Albay. They are regular vendors during market days and *Pantawid* payout days. For both fruit vendors reported that market days are better than just *Pantawid* days because retailers from the different barangays buy fruits in bulk while on *Pantawid* payout days, all buyers are *Pantawid* beneficiaries who just buy a kilo or two of fruits.

There was also the gas lamp seller. He roams around selling homemade kerosene lamps while his wife stays in their tricycle to look after the stock of kerosene lamps they sell. He and his wife also sell their good during market days in Oas, Polangui and Libon. Market days in Libon are Wednesday and Saturday, Oas are Monday and Friday and Polangui are Tuesday and Sunday. The gas lamp is sold at PhP35 per piece. According to him, his sale goes up to PhP 1500 per day during 4Ps and an average of PhP 200 on an ordinary market day.

There were also sellers of household plastic wares, *pandan* (type of plant) and plastic mats, herbal concoctions, bolos, and other carpentry tools.

Merchants in Vinzons, Camarines Norte

The merchants are located in the market proper of Vinzons. Their establishments include a school supply store with photocopying machine, many fruits and vegetables stores, several small rice retailer stores, a small shop which used to sell *ukay-ukay* goods, and all other shops that can be found in an ordinary market. Along the main road near the ATM machine is the *Pasalubong* (locally-made products) shop while a bakery is across the street.

Merchants in Milagros, Masbate

Majority of the merchants in the old municipality are from Milagros. In contrast, the new municipality has entrepreneurs/vendors coming from Masbate City, particularly the *ukay-ukay* vendors (Figure 1). Some shop owners like the *ukay-ukay* vendors near the municipality, dry goods and pharmacy owners reported that their sales figures declined recently when the payout was made in the new municipal hall. This is consistent with the results of the focus group discussion (FGD) sessions with the Municipal Treasurer and 4Ps Municipal Link who reported that 4Ps beneficiaries from four upland barangays buy their goods either in the "flea market" or Masbate City rather than in the old town.

Food stalls are most common during the *Pantawid* payout. They are also the stalls closest to the location of the *Pantawid* payout. Most food stalls operate in the market near the old municipal building. Take the case of a food shop in front of the church in the town of Milagros. The owner sells during the payout session since 4Ps started. She claimed that her gross sales during the last two payouts were higher than when the payout was in the old municipality. She added that the number of food stalls in the new venue was less than the old venue; thus, less competitors. She claimed that her sales during ordinary days is around PhP2,000 pesos but during payout days, gross sales are more than doubled.

Another eatery operates only during the payout owned by a policeman stationed in the new municipality. Because his wife teaches in a private high school, the policeman hires two assistants to cook and sell food every payout session in the municipality.

There are 4Ps beneficiaries who sell food before and after receiving their payout. Ambulant vendors sell cooked eggs, fried peanuts, and *pastillas* (candy made out of cow's milk and sugar). They claimed to have the same gross sales with and without payout but have not lost a day's earning by selling while receiving their payout. Maybe these beneficiaries do not want to admit to have earned higher income because it may make them ineligible for the 4Ps. Further probing revealed that their earnings were sometimes used to buy inputs for their rice farm.

There are a number of dry good stores but there is only one minimart in Milagros, Masbate. It started 10 years ago as a cellular phone accessory stall. According to the owner it was only five years ago that she started selling school supplies (e.g., notebook, paper, pencil, bag and others) because of the demand from her customers. She expanded to other dry goods and opened the minimart when she started to sell grocery items in February 2015. Her rented cellular phone accessory stall was replaced by a three story-building (although the third floor is still under construction). According to the owner, it was in February 2015 that she stopped renting a place. She attributed the expansion of her business to 4Ps because she listened to the demand of her *Pantawid* customers. She also mentioned that her gross sales is higher during the month of May, a month before the schools opens, than during December which indicates the positive impact of 4Ps in her business. As a cellular phone accessory owner, her aim is to earn a profit of PhP300 per day. Today, her gross income per day is PhP30,000. The FGD participants claimed that the minimart is the biggest in the municipality. Despite the move of the payment venue from the old municipality where her minimart is located, *Pantawid* beneficiaries still patronize her store because of quality, variety, and lower price. This is consistent with the finding of Creti (2015) who found evidence that beneficiaries preferred to purchase locally because of their trust in local shops.

When asked if she is now worried with the increasing number of number of competitors, the mini-grocery owner said that

> *"Kung sa kompetisyon sa negosyo, grabe kompetisyon dito pero kasi sa mga nakaiintindi ng kompetisyon, positibo ang epekto nito, healthy ang negosyo na may kompetisyon. Sa mga hindi nakaintindi posible bawasan nila yung mga price, malulugi sila dun. Depende sa pangangailangan ng tao ang kailangan tugunan dyan magsisimula ang negosyo."*

(There is competition in any business, competition is very stiff but for those who can understand it, competition has positive effects. For those who cannot understand competition, it is possible that they may reduce their price and eventually lose money and fold. There is a need to respond to the demand of the people, that is, where business starts.)

In the new payout venue, there are dry good stores selling new clothes; school uniforms, ready-to-wear dresses, and other household needs like mosquito net, mats, and blanket. These stores have permanent stalls in the market place of Milagros (Figure1).

Another shop sells candies, biscuits and other snack foods, groceries and canned goods but did not relocate operations near the new venue for the payout. According to the shop owner since the transfer of the payout to the new venue she has lost some of her customers. This is particularly true for beneficiaries residing in barangays, which are located closer to the new municipality.

Originally, this popular school supplies shop has only one shop but later put up another shop facing each other across the street. The original shop sells school supplies while the added shop sells gift items, accessories, beauty products, and ready to wear clothes. Sources of products depend on the kind of goods being sold. For instance, accessories, beauty products, baby

Figure 1. Stalls selling clothes and other household items, Milagros, Masbate, 2016

powder, cologne, soap, sanitary napkins, cottons, toothpaste and others are from company distributors. Infant needs such as milk and diapers are also sourced from distributors. For dry good items such as school supplies like pencil, bond papers, manila papers, colored paper, brown envelope, plastic envelope, folders, clothes like dress, shorts, and shoes, slippers, and other accessories, they are from directly bought in Manila or in Masbate City.

According to the owner, he does not sell during payout in the new venue because their customers travel to the town where their shops are located to buy school supplies and other needs after receiving their payment. The beneficiaries claimed to patronize this shop because it sells most of the school needs of their children and that the price of some products is lower compared with other shops. One of the shop assistants reported that in an ordinary day, one of their branches has an average sale of PhP1500 per day but during payout days, their sales double.

There are three pharmacy stores in the market site of Milagros. The owner of a pharmacy claimed to have also benefitted from 4Ps. She observed that her gross sale more than tripled during payout days. Her sales increased despite the change in the payout venue but she reported that the increase was still less than prior to the transfer of the municipality to the new site. For instance, in the past, she experienced a gross sale of PhP8,000 pesos during payout days but with the change in the venue, her highest gross sale only reached PhP6,000 to PhP7,000 per day.

Ukay-ukay Vendors

In Milagros, the *ukay-ukay* vendors are mostly from Masbate City. The three *ukay-ukay* vendors near the former payout venue are not selling in the new payout venue. Their reason is the difficulty of transferring their stalls and goods from the old to the new venue. One of the vendors said that with just one shop assistant she could no longer sell during payouts in the new venue. Setting up temporary stalls in the new venue will require hiring additional staff and rental of vehicle to transport goods, the costs of which she may not be able to recover. She admitted to have lost the opportunity to earn more during the payout but she cannot do anything about it. The increased sales during payout is also the reason why the other *ukay-ukay* trader plans to participate in the future payouts. At the time of the interview, his wife was sick for a while and found it difficult to leave her during payout.

Most Commonly Bought Goods

This section describes the supply of goods and materials, and services that the beneficiaries purchase from the *Pantawid* money they received. It also reports on the most commonly goods bought within and outside of the payout venue.

Results of the key informant interviews and focus group discussions with the *Pantawid* beneficiaries show that the most commonly bought item was a pair of slippers (Figure 2). When asked why, the response is that their kids are asking for one even before the payout because the current ones are already worn out. One mother said,

> "Kada payout bumibili kami ng tsinelas. Alam na nang mga anak naming na kami ay kukuha ng pera at alam nila na para eto sa kanila. Sila na ho ang nagdedemand, lalo na yong high school na anak namin." (Every payout, we buy slipper. Our children know that there is a payout and they know that it is for them. They, themselves, demand, especially the high school children.)

Figure 2. Slippers, school bag and dresses, dry good store, Milagros, Masbate

The other explanation is that mothers purchase cheaper slippers but they do not last long. One merchant claims that slippers, which are offered at substantial discounts are those, which have been on display for a while and thus, the rubber or plastic material becomes brittle. In the FGD with the beneficiaries, there is a mother who bragged that she bought her high school son better quality shoes at a higher price, believing that the pair will last longer than cheaper ones.

Prior to and during the school opening, the most commonly bought items are school uniform skirts, blouses, white shirts, school bags, and footwear. According to the mini-mart owner in Milagros, her sales is higher in May or the month when mothers buy the above items before classes begin. There are parents who claim that they buy white shirt or blouse on a staggered basis coinciding with the payout. A mother noted that she cannot buy school uniform for her three school-age children at the same time because the amount received during the payout is not sufficient. Another mother with four kids only gets a payout for three eligible children. Thus, the payout for the three kids is shared to the fourth ineligible kid. This sharing of "subsidy" often happens to high school children of the poor family particularly if they are staying in a boarding place near their school.

Commonly purchased materials during payout are school supplies like paper, pencil, ballpen, board, glue, and other materials required for school projects. According to a shop assistant, *"Mas mabenta ang school supplies lalo na papel at lapis"* (School supplies like paper and pencil have higher demand). The shop also sells accessories, dress, shirts, shorts, sandals, shoes, gadgets, and batteries, though the demand for batteries and accessories are lower than school supplies. *"Mas mabenta ang mura at mahina ang quality pero may matitibay din kami na tinda"*. (Cheaper but low quality goods are more saleable but they also sell better quality and durable products). He added that their products are sourced in Divisoria.

The beneficiaries, particularly those with children attending high school, save at least PhP1,000 for school allowance. One beneficiary narrated that her son boards near his school. Unfortunately, her son is not included in the *Pantawid* because she has more than three children. Beneficiaries from Milagros, Masbate and Vinzons, Camarines Norte shared similar story.

After school supplies, the most commonly bought items are vitamins, according to the beneficiaries. There were also those who bought "Bear Brand" powdered milk or other brands of powdered milk. This was attested to by pharmacy and dry goods store sales persons interviewed. Merchants in Milagros, Masbate did not sell vitamins and powdered milk in the payout venue, and thus, *Pantawid* beneficiaries had to buy these items in the town proper. On the other hand, beneficiaries in Libon bought their vitamins and medicines from the sole generics drug store located in the LTC.

Rice was the most commonly mentioned food item bought by beneficiaries in Vinzons, Camarines Norte. On average, a family bought 10 kilos of rice every payout. The rest of their rice requirements are bought from rice retailers in the town proper or from rice millers located near their barangay. The four beneficiaries from Vinzons reported to have consumed less of NFA rice when they received their payout. The beneficiaries from Libon, Albay mentioned sardines and noodles in addition to rice as their most commonly purchased food items.

Pantawid beneficiaries mentioned that out of their payout, women beneficiaries bought household items like basin, dipper, and plastic food servers. Curtains and other decorative items were also purchased. A male beneficiary, who was substituting for her wife, bought a hammer and other carpentry tools out of the payout proceeds.

Employment Generation

All the shop owners/merchants, except those peddling/roaming around, have engaged the services of additional help during payout session. The *ukay-ukay* vendor in Libon and the mini-grocery owner in Milagros, Masbate hire six helpers whenever there is payout. The mini-grocery owner in Milagros employs students as part-time shop assistants to help the latter with their school expenses. The other shop owners hire one to two additional assistants during payout as in the cases of the food stall owners and dry goods merchants in Milagros, Masbate and the rice retailer in Libon, Albay.

Jeepney and tricycle drivers benefit too from *Pantawid* Program. During the payout, jeepneys from far away barangays like Pantao in Libon are filled up to the roof by beneficiaries and family members (Figure 3). The passenger round trip fare is PhP 80. Some jeepneys and vehicles are also hired on special rate by merchants to bring beneficiaries to the payout venue.

The other positive effect of *Pantawid* is the easier access of beneficiaries to credit but with high interest rate. According to a parent leader in Libon, Albay, all the 30 members of her group including herself, borrow money ranging from PhP1000 to PhP2000 for 15 percent interest per month from informal lenders.

Figure 3. Jeepneys servicing the beneficiaries from Pantao, Libon, Albay

Mothers usually borrow money for various family needs particularly school needs. As one mother in Milagros, Masbate said,

> *"Pag meron pong babayaran sa project sa school, nanghihiram ako ng pera at babayaran pag nakakuha na sa 4Ps."* (If there are school projects to be paid, I first borrow money and pay it later with money coming from 4Ps.)

The money lenders in Libon, Albay include the meat shop owner and another one who receive remittances from children working abroad in Metro Manila.

Revenue Generated from the Flea Market and Its Utilization

Generation of additional revenues as a result of *Pantawid* implementation occurred in the municipalities of Libon, Albay and Milagros, Masbate. However, this did not happen in Vinzons, Camarines Norte because majority of the beneficiaries who have ATM card withdrew their *Pantawid* cash from either Daet or Libon, Camarines Norte where beneficiaries prefer to shop because of the variety of goods being sold at lower prices.

The market collector in Milagros, Masbate estimated that market collection fee averages PhP8,000 per payout. This collection forms part of the total market collection fees of the municipality. Roughly, the flea market collection contributed around 11 percent to total market collection in 2014. It should be noted that the municipality has a tax code, which specifies the market fees to be imposed. However, the market collector did not follow the rates specified in the code because he thinks that the rates are high that they might discourage entrepreneurs from participating during *Pantawid* payouts. The fee ranges from PhP20 per day for small food stall to PhP200 for dry good stores selling a variety of items. He further noted that to help the entrepreneurs from Milagros, he proposed to the Sangguniang Bayan (Municipal Council) to pass an ordinance to exclude merchants outside of the municipality during the payout. However, the Municipal Council has not discussed his proposal yet.

In Libon, Albay, the municipality built *papag* (low bamboo table) for rent to vendors during market days and *Pantawid* payout days. Each *papag* is rented at PhP10 per day. This is in addition to the PhP10 fee for the goods being sold. Thus, a vendor pays a minimum of PhP20 for a day. The market collector reported to have issued 15 sheets of tickets (125 ticket per sheet) during the December 2015 payout.

The *ukay-ukay* merchant requested that the local government unit should provide additional security during the payout session. There must be visible security because shop owners and sale assistants normally sleep in the market during payout. In addition, she suggested that the municipality should keep the toilets clean and build additional ones. The municipality should also collect the garbage after every market and payout days.

Other Spill-Over Effects of Pantawid

Another kind of spillover effect of CCT, according to the World Bank (2009) is related to changes in access to and use of the formal banking sector. A number of CCT programs, including the Philippines, directly deposit payments in bank accounts created for beneficiaries, who then can withdraw cash using an automated teller machine (ATM) card. This scheme does not only reduce transaction costs but encourage the beneficiaries to use the formal banking sector in other capacities — potentially, a very important benefit of CCT programs and one that has not been evaluated to date. This can also an avenue to encourage families to save. Only one among the 22 participants of the FGD in Masbate admitted saving PhP500 in her account every payout for use in emergency cases like bringing her kids to the doctor.

Summary and Conclusion

Stalls selling food, used clothes, and dry goods are the most common businesses during payouts. The most commonly bought non-food items are slippers, school supplies including paper, pencil, and ball pen. For food items, rice, bread, sardines, noodles and other canned goods are the ones commonly bought by the beneficiaries.

The effect on the economy of 4Ps depends on the location or the venue of the payout. As noted earlier, the effect of cash transfers is more felt in isolated localities than those exposed to outside markets. In the Municipalities of Milagros, Masbate and Libon, Albay, the effect on the local economy is highly visible given the number and variety of merchants present during the payout. Makeshift stalls, bamboo-made tables and other temporary structures are built during the payout to showcase products being sold. The municipality derived benefits from these traders through issuances of market rental tickets by the market collector. The amount of the ticket varies depending on the municipality. In Libon, Albay, the *Pantawid* payouts help in keeping the LTC operational. The bi-monthly payouts generate enough demand for goods being sold in the LTC.

The market collector in Milagros, Masbate proposed to the Sangguniang Bayan to make the payout venue exclusive to merchants from Masbate. This is the opposite in Libon, Albay where the municipal government encourages traders from the nearby towns to sell during market days and payout days.

In the case of Milagros, Masbate, business owners or vendors build temporary tent-like structures and bring their own *papag* (low bamboo table) to display their goods. In the case of Libon, Albay, the municipal government rents out these *papag* for PhP10 per piece but also allows traders to bring their own tables. Such is the case of the *ukay-ukay* businesswoman who brings her own tables to save on rent. Others adopt different strategies to pay less or even avoid paying rent by just laying down plastic mats to show the goods being sold such as for "kalamansi" (local lemon), "kamatis" (tomatoes), and dry goods such as kitchen wares, clothes, and herbal concoction. Another trick to avoid paying market rents is to use the back of a jeepney or the passenger side of a tricycle to display food/snacks.

The case of Vinzons, Camarines Norte is different from the experiences of Milagros, Masbate and Libon, Albay. The difference is primarily due to the fact that many of the *Pantawid* beneficiaries use ATM machines outside of the municipality instead of the Land Bank of the Philippines ATM in the municipality, in withdrawing their bi-monthly *Pantawid* payout. The money withdrawn is then used to buy goods in Daet City or Labo which offers better and more variety of goods at lower prices. This also provides the opportunity for the children to eat in popular food chain across the country.

The effect of *Pantawid* is also positive to most merchants outside of the payout sites. This is the case of the pharmacy, minimart and the school supplies shop in Masbate because none of the temporary stalls located near the payout site sell other goods like vitamins and powdered milk. This positive effect extends to the jeepney and tricycle operators who service the beneficiaries.

Given these positive effects, the municipal LGUs have to do its part in maintaining peace and order giving police security during payouts. Moreover, cleanliness through provision of waste bins for proper waste disposal and clean toilets must be provided by the LGUs.

Acknowledgement

The project was funded by the Department of Social Welfare and Development (DSWD), Government of the Republic of the Philippines.

References

1) Albert, J. R., F. M. A. Quimba, A. P. Ramos, and J.P. Almeda. 2011. *Profile of Out-of-School Children in the Philippines.* PIDS Discussion Paper Series No. 2012-01. http://dirp4.pids.gov.ph/ris/dps/ pidsdps1201.pdf

2) Creti. P. 2010. *The Impact of Short-term Cash Transfers on Unstructured Markets: A Case Study in Northern Uganda in the Impact of Cash Transfers on Local Economies.* April. www.cashlearning.org.

3) Harvard School of Public Health, Harvard Kennedy School. 2012. *Ministerial Brief – Talking Points for Ministers.* Ministerial Leadership in Health. https://cdn2.sph. harvard. edu/wp-content/ uploads/sites/ 19/2012/09/CCT-Brief_9-19-12.pdf (Date Accessed: Oct. 28, 2015)

4) National Statistics Office. 2013. 2010 Census of Population and Housing.

5) Paunlagui, M.M., N.J.V.B. Querijero, K.S. Janiya, M.G. Umali and M. Magat. 2015. *Impact Assessment of BRAC ADM Project.* Draft Final Report 2015.

6) Philippine Statistics Authority. No date. *Philippine Poverty Statistics.* http://www. nscb.gov.ph/ poverty/ 2009/table_1.asp (Date Accessed: April 7, 2015).

7) Taylor, E. 2015. *Cash Transfer Spillovers: A Local Economy -wide Impact Evaluation (LEWIE) in The Impact of Cash Transfers on Local Economies.* Policy in Focus. UNDP: The International Centre for Inclusive Growth. Vol 11, No.1. pp. 17-18.

8) Wikipedia. 2016. *Bicol Region.* https://en.wikipedia.org/wiki/Bicol Region (Date Accessed April 5, 2015).

Engagement of the Youth in Future Agriculture: Strategies for National Food Sovereignty

Vanda Ningrum[1]
1 Researcher, Research Center for Population – Indonesian Institute of Sciences

インドネシアでも農業従事者の平均年齢は52歳、若者の農村離れも深刻だ。2億を超す人口を抱えるこの東南アジアの大国で、将来の食料安保・食料主権を確保し、若者が農業に希望を見出せるようにするための社会的条件と政策課題を探る。

Abstract

The youth in rural areas is the future of food sovereignty of a nation since they are the successor of the family farming business that brings 80 percent of the world's food production. Unfortunately, many that young population prefers to go to the cities and escape from agriculture. Data shows only 4 percent of farmer's children in Central Java eventually become a farmer. Contemporary, agriculture is been populated by the old farmer with an average age of 52 years. Indeed, agriculture always requires innovation to deal with rapid changes in the rural environment. In this concern, the youth will be the principal actor to adopt those changes. This study aims to map issues of food agriculture that cause young people to abandon rural life and to formulate policy alternatives in preventing farmer regeneration crisis. Data was obtained through in-depth interviews with 150 households in 3 rice-growing villages (Sragen, Klaten, Sukoharjo) and seven young farmers from Yogyakarta, Salatiga, and Garut. The study reveals that rural youth face many hurdles to earn a livelihood in agriculture. Lack of land access, income uncertainty, and dependence on chemical fertilizers are reasons which cause agriculture to become unattractive for the youth. Some policy strategies have been offered to engage the youth in agriculture. Examples include the provision of communal land access for them to conduct organic farming, involving local communities to transfer agricultural knowledge, upgrading their technological skills to access broader markets, expanding the entrepreneurship program in rural and providing farmer incentives in the form of financial assistance.

Keywords Youth; Family Farming; Agriculture; Java Indonesia.

Introduction

In Indonesia, rural development and modernization began in the 1970s which has had an impact on youth's perceptions and aspirations in agriculture. Today, agriculture such as paddy fields are considered dirty, physically demanding and an unfavorable job. One youth study found that most rural youth with higher education prefer to be government employees or work in regular employment in the urban area (Minza, 2014). Rural-to-urban migration is increasing, and agriculture in the countryside is being undertaken by old farmers with an average age of more than 52 years (Agriculture Census, 2013).

The escape of the youth from agriculture has an impact on employment structure in the countryside, not only the aging farmer but also, in the long run, threatening farmer regeneration. Similar conditions occur in other agrarian countries in the world. In the Philippines, the average age of farmers reaches 57 years[1], with a rare tendency for youth to return to agriculture. As well as in developed countries[2] such as Japan and Europe, the average age of farmers has reached 65 years. The same thing is found in African countries, although 65 percent of the youth live in rural areas, they are not interested to working in agriculture (White, 2016; Leavy & Smith, 2010). In the context of food sovereignty, the phenomenon of the youth fleeing from agriculture will be a serious problem that threatens farmer regeneration.

The Indonesian government committed to developing food sovereignty through two policies; agribusiness improvement and farmer regeneration. The program to support these policies are rural economic activities built on agriculture that involve youth so that the average age of farmers is getting younger (*Visi, Misi, dan Program Aksi JOKOWI-JK*, 2014). The presidential policy is implemented by the ministry of agriculture by way of developing the rural agricultural sector. Mechanisims of implementation include securing the availability of water supply, improving the market, utilizing information technology, agricultural corporations, and synergy of all stakeholders at central and regional levels (BPPSDMP, 2017).

Furthermore, the regeneration policy of farmers works explicitly through the Counseling Agency and Human Resources Development of Agriculture in the Ministry of Agriculture (Badan Penyuluhan dan Pengembangan Sumber Daya Manusia Pertanian- Kementerian Pertanian- BPPSDMP). Their two main programs are the Integrated Farmers Empowerment (Gerakan Pemberdayaan Petani Terpadu-GPPT) and the Farmers Regeneration, BPPSDM, which have a purpose of increasing national strategic food products such as rice, corn, soybean, various chili, red onion, sugarcane, cow/buffalo, palm, rubber, cocoa, and coffee, as well as attract young people to work in the field of agribusiness.

Amid the implementation of farmer regeneration policy, the agricultural sector is still dominated by old farmers. Youth migration from rural to urban is increasing and the farmer's child who wants to become a farmer is decreasing significantly. The BPPSDMP's programs should target rural youth who have a firm intention to do business in agriculture, provide not only training but also consider many obstacles such as the lack of land, lack of market access, and the lack of entrepreneurship skill. My question to be asked in this article is how to involve the rural youth through agricultural policy amid the aging agricultural workforce? And how can the farmer regeneration policy in the Ministry of Agriculture integrate with other strategies to support food sovereignty?

The data presented in this article is based on research conducted in 3 rice-growing villages (Sragen, Klaten, and Sukoharjo District) and seven young farmers from Yogyakarta, Salatiga, and Garut District. We[3] used some methods such as focused discussions, workshops, and surveys of 150 households in 2015 and 2016. To get in-depth analysis, we learned the empiric youth agricultural models that have been applied in Salatiga, Kulonprogo, and Garut District.

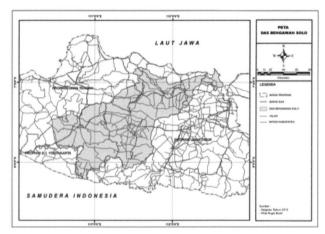

Figure 1. Map of Research Sites in Java, Indonesia

(Source: *DAS Bengawan Solo Map, taken from Directorate of General Of Water Resources Management, Ministry of Public Works and Public Housing of the Republic of Indonesia, 2010.*)

From Food Security to Food Sovereignty

The food insecurity issue is not a new thing in Indonesia; this awareness has made many institutions and organizations focus on solving food insecurity problems. Most consider the food security crisis caused by fluctuations in prices and food

---

1 Based on Statistics Data from the Departement of Agriculture Philippines (2013)

2 Farmers' statistics data in Europe are supported in Tascia (2010) and Japan statistical data (Yamashita, 2008).

3 I conducted data collection together with the team from the Research Center for Population, Indonesian Institute of Sciences.

availability. Some of Indonesia's significant foodstuffs are dependent on imports such as rice, soybeans, corn, onions and other food. The Indonesian government has responded by establishing a food security agency and task force staff to monitor food supply and food price movements in the market. Such efforts are intended to ensure the availability of national food and the needs of every citizen.

Criticism of food issues is not only on the availability of food but also includes the social, economic, and political structures of food systems that produce food. This is because food security, in the long run, depends on those who provide food and maintain the environment (White, 2015). This view then led to a conceptual shift from food security to food sovereignty that focuses more on community involvement in food production. La Via Campesina in the Declaration Nyeleni 2016 defines the concept of food sovereignty, i.e.

> *The right of peoples to healthy and culturally appropriate food produced through ecologically sound and sustainable methods, and their right to define their food and agriculture systems. It puts those who produce, distribute and consume food at the heart of food systems and policies rather than the demands of markets and corporations. It depends on the interest and inclusion of the next generation. [.....], It ensures that the right to use and manage our land, territories, water, seeds, livestock, and biodiversity are in the hands of those of us who produce food.*[4]

Pillars in food sovereignty that cannot be ignored as in the above concept include farmer regeneration, as an important element to produce food. Involving rural youth to participate in agriculture means reinforcing food production in ensuring future food supply.

Loss of interest among young people to return to the fields would be a threat and create a crisis of farmer regeneration. It could jeapordize the future of rural farming. In such conditions, food sovereignty is threatened as well. At a time when families can no longer produce food such as rice, hence the need for rice is highly dependent on the availability of imported rice on the market. Data from the USDA[5] shows that domestic rice production in Indonesia tended to decrease as much as 6.5 percent from 2008 to 2015, while the domestic rice consumption increased by 4 percent. There is a shortage of 2,700 tons of rice to meet domestic consumption. A significant amount of eating that cannot be supported by domestic production led to the Government of Indonesia to tackle the rice import policy.

Depeasantation

The phenomenon of rural youth who migrate to cities for study or work is increasing. In other words, there is lack of employment available to accommodate the labor force from rural, so that most urban youth work in the informal sector without proper job security. Nearly 70 percent of jobs in 2003 (Nazara, 2010) or those who do not get a job become unemployed in the city.

During the last 44 years (from 1971 to 2015) the average rate of youth unemployment in urban areas reached 15 percent per year and that figure was 9 percent higher than in rural areas. The increasing number of unemployed in the city cannot be separated from the massive flow of youth migration from rural to urban areas. The youth decrement in the rural areas is also responsible for the declining number of labor in agriculture. Over the past 15 years (2001 - 2015) there has been a decline in youth labor in agriculture by 32 percent with an annual rate of 3 percent decline. This condition causes the age of farmers today to tend towards the elderly, 60.97 percent of farmers are aged 45 years and over (BPS-Statistics Indonesia, 2013).

Based on a survey of rural households in Central Java, only 4 percent of children live ruraly and continue to work as farmers like their parents (2% as a farmer and 2% as farm labor). While children who have lived outside away from parents, only 2 percent work as farmers. Although most rural households are farmers, rural youth prefer to work as non-agricultural laborers such as factory day laborers or shopkeepers, with a proportion of 70 percent for live-in children and 47 percents for children living separately from parents (see Appendix on the last page).

The declining number of agricultural labor can be seen as a

---

4   La Via Campesina 1996, quoted from White, 2015.

5   The United States Department of Agriculture

symptom of depeasantization, which in this study is regarded as a lack of youth engagement in agriculture. The term depeasantization has been alluded to since the 1990s by Hobsbawm as a process of social change which is characterized by peasantry being a minority (regarding numbers of peasants), not only in advanced industrialized countries but also peasants being a minority in agrarian regions. More broadly, global depeasantization is defined as a form of derurarization (reduced number of villagers) because of overurbanization, i.e., increased urban activity in the world (Araghi, 1945). Recent research using the term depeasantization refers more to the shifting of agricultural labor out of agriculture as a source of livelihood (Singh & Bhogal, 2014) and the phenomenon of farmers who abandon their agriculture (van der Ploeg, 2008).

Qualitative studies in three research villages show that the reduced youth interest to engage in agriculture based activity is due to limited access to land, reduced agricultural income to meet the economic needs of households, and the high dependence of farmers on government subsidies and production inputs provided by corporations such as seed and fertilizer.

Challenges Faced by the Youth

The Land Problem

Based on our survey in three rice farming villages in Java, the farmers' land area averaged 0.66 hectares. According to farmers, the land of 0.66 hectares is still far from the need more to meet family income, which amounted to 0.9 hectares. At the national level, statistics show that 58 percents of farmers have less than 0.1 hectares, and only 4 percent of farmers occupy more than one hectare (BPS-Statistics Indonesia, 2013). This small farmland owned by farmers causes the pattern of land inheritance from parents to children to be insufficient. Not only the narrowness of the land but also 53.3 percent of the farmers in the three villages are sharecroppers.

Uncertain Income

The net income of paddy farming from three villages in Central Java (Figure 2) is less than Rp. 1 million per month (63 percents of farmers), while the highest income on average only reached Rp. 2 million per month (11 percent of farmers). When compared to other income outside agriculture, the yield of paddy farming is still far below factory workers[6]. The uncertainty of revenue is due to lower selling price[7] at farmer level or decrease of crop yield due to pest attack[8].

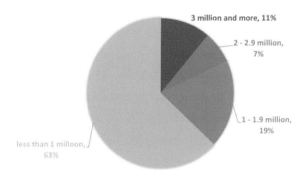

Figure 2. Distribution of rice farm income in Central Java Village (Based on Survey)

Risks of income uncertainty increase due to a small land area, enlarged access land for the farmer can be a strategy to increase their income. Based on the relationship between land and net yield, this study found that 1 percent increase in the land will follow 0.89 percent increase in net yield (Figure 3). This figure indicates that every increase of 1,000 square meters of paddy field will raise the net farmer income around Rp. 700,000.

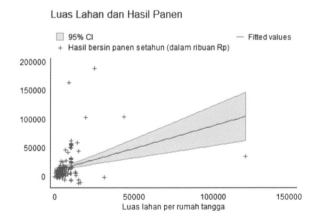

Figure 3. Relationship between Land and Net Yield

---

6 Factory labor income between Rp. 1.2 million up to Rp. 1.5 million per month.

7 90 percent of farmers sell their crops with a debt-to-collector system, the amount of harvest received by farmers is only based on the collector's estimates, not on the actual harvest quantity

8 paddy fields were attacked by pests since 2011 and caused rice harvest failure

Dependence of Farmers on Chemical Fertilizers

Since the green revolution in the 1980s, farmers have been forced by the government to use chemical fertilizers to increase yields. In the long run, the excessive use of chemical fertilizers reduces soil nutrients that are essential ingredients for maintaining soil fertility. As a result, farmers increase the use of chemical fertilizers more and thus impact the cost of agricultural production. The habit of using chemical fertilizer eliminates the autonomy of farmers who were previously able to produce organic fertilizer for agrarian needs.

In the research location, it is difficult to find the youth who can make organic fertilizer. The rural modernization causes young people who are still in school, spending more time attending education activities than being directly involved in agriculture. The survey showed that 75 percent of rural youth with a secondary education level said that they were not getting farming skills from the school.

Strategy for Engaging the Youth

These three main challenges to engage youth in agriculture require a comprehensive and interrelated approach, not only in the ministry of agriculture but also involve the Ministry of Agrarian and Spatial/National Land Agency (ATR/BPN) as well as the Ministry of The Villages, Disadvantaged Regions and Transmigration (Kemendesa). The interconnecting policies are needed to improve the effectiveness of BPPSDMP's program. So, the system can include enhance skills and knowledge for sustainable agriculture and give access to land and market for rural youth. The proposed policies should consider:

1. Targeting the rural youth in agriculture

The BPPSDMP program is now more targeted to agricultural students and young people who already have advanced agrarian enterprises. The benefits of the program only provide for youth who already have independence while youth with limited land access and agricultural skills still face barriers to becoming farmers. If the farmer regeneration program is more focused for young living in rural areas, then youth migration can be reduced, and the availability of youth labor in agriculture will increase.

2. Making the farmer regeneration program as an agricultural movement and involving many parties

Connecting the BPPSDMP program with the land redistribution program from the Ministry of Agrarian and Spatial/National Land Agency (ATR/BPN) provides an excellent opportunity for rural youth to gain land and agriculture. They will be trained to conduct sustainable agriculture as well as become agricultural entrepreneurs.

Also, most of the rural areas in Java have land owned by the local government; the local government can encourage the farmer regeneration movement by providing land management to the rural youth to develop farming business.

Several BPPSDMP's strategies to make the farmer regeneration movement are more widespread:

Table 1. Strategies for Youth Engagement in Agriculture

Strategy Components	Interconnection of BPSDMP program with other ministries/ institutions
Land Access	Providing agricultural training programs for rural youth and strengthening rural institutions into agricultural corporations, especially in areas where there is a land redistribution program by the Ministry of Agrarian and Spatial/National Land Agency (ATR/BPN)
	BPPSDMP and rural government provide rural land access for youth including financing for agriculture.
Empowerment of rural youth	BPPSDMP and the Ministry of The Villages, Disadvantaged Regions and Transmigration (Kemendesa) provide training to utilize agricultural advisory and infrastructure assistance from various ministries and expand the entrepreneurship program in border areas and underdeveloped areas in Indonesia. Trainees are targeted for rural youth.
Strengthen farmer assistance by involving Non-Governmental Organizations (NGO)	Provides a great role for NGOs to assist young farmers to practice organic farming
Involve young farmers in the agricultural chain	BPPSDMP facilitates rural youth to trade agricultural products through the Rural Enterprise (Badan Usaha Milik Desa)

Conclusions

The study result mentioned three main reasons why rural youth are not interested in agriculture and increasing the youth migration from rural to urban. Those are:

1. The lack of land access
2. The income uncertainty from agriculture because of the variability of price and the risk of harvest failure
3. High dependence on chemical fertilizers thus high agricultural cost

Integrated government policies should be created in the rural area. Those strategies are, increase land access for youth, involve youth in all chains of agriculture to get more value-added results, provide organic training, expand the entrepreneurship program, and provide an excellent role for NGOs to assist young farmers in rural settings.

The purpose of these strategies are not only the responsibility of BPPSDMP which exclusively focus on providing training, but the policy should be linked with other ministries such as The Ministry of Agrarian and Spatial/National Land Agency (ATR/BPN) to give access to land. The Ministry of The Villages, Disadvantaged Regions and Transmigration (Kemendesa) can also be involved to strengthen the entrepreneurial institutions in rural areas. Engagement of the youth in agriculture means reinforcing food production, ensuring future food supply and supporting for food sovereignty in Indonesia..

References

Araghi, F. A. (1945). Global Depeasantization, 1945-1990. Global Depeasantization, 36(2), 337–368. http://doi.org/10.1111/j.1533-8525.1995.tb00443.x

BPPSDMP. (2017). PROGRAM DAN KEGIATAN BPPSDMP 2017 Dan Rancangan Kegiatan Tahun 2018.

BPS-Statistics Indonesia. (2013). Laporan Hasil Sensus Pertanian 2013. Badan Pusat Statistik (Vol. 1). Retrieved from https://st2013.bps.go.id

Leavy, J., & Smith, S. (2010). Future Farmers : Youth Aspirations, Expectations and Life Choices, (June).

Minza, W. M. (2014). Growing Up and Being Young in an Indonesian Provincial Town. Faculteit der Maatschappij-en Gedragswetenschappen.

Nazara, S. (2010). Ekonomi Informal di Indonesia: Ukuran, Komposisi, dan Evolusi. Organisasi Perburuhan Internasional. ILO. http://doi.org/Data Publikaso ILO

Singh, S., & Bhogal, S. (2014). Depeasantization in Punjab : status of farmers, 106(10).

Tuscia, U. (2008). The Generational Turnover In Agriculture : The Ageing Dynamics And The Eu Support Policies To Young Farmers Anna Carbone and Giovanna Subioli.

Van der Ploeg, J. D. (2008). The New Peasantries, Struggles for Autonomy and Sustainability in an Era of Empire and Globalization. Earthscan. London: Earthscan. http://doi.org/10.1007/s13398-014-0173-7.2

Visi, Misi, dan Program Aksi JOKOWI-JK. (2014).

White, B. & M. (2016). Teenage Experiences of School, Work, and Life in a Javanese Village. In K. Robinson (Ed.), Youth Identities and Social Transformations in Modern Indonesia (pp. 50–68). London: Koninklijke Brill.

White, B. (2015). Meneliti Masalah Petani dan Pangan Pada Tingkat Lokal. Pengantar Studi Kemandirian Pangan Akatiga. Jurnal Analisis Sosial Vol 19 (1).

Yamashita, K. (2008). The Perilous Decline of Japanese Agriculture. The Tokyo Foundation. Retrieved from http://www.tokyofoundation.org/en/articles/2008/the-perilous-decline-of-japanese-agriculture-1

Appendix

Parents and Children Occupation in 3 Rural Agriculture in Indonesia

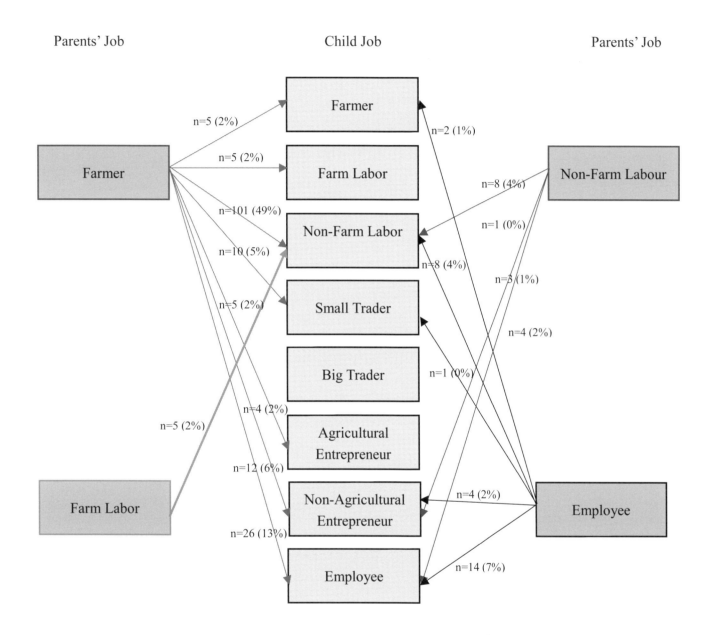

「日本文学」から「世界文学」へ：
村上春樹の「コミットメント」について

From "Japanese Literature" to "World Literature":
A Research on Haruki Murakami's "Commitment"

ディアン アンニサ ヌル リダ
Dian Annisa Nur Ridha
東京外国語大学 大学院総合国際学研究科 博士後期課程

2018年に作家生活40年を迎えた村上春樹。その多岐にわたる作品を理解する上で主要なキーワードとなる「(他者、他民族、他国などへの)コミットメント」の意味について、初期の短編「中国行きのスロウ・ボート」を軸に考察する。

Abstract

This research analyzes Haruki Murakami's "Commitment" and focuses on his concern to history. Murakami included his concern to history as one of his major themes in many of his literary works. The first attempt of his concern to history can be seen in his debut novel "*Hear the Wind Sing*" in 1979 and a short story "*A Slow Boat to China*" in 1980.

The title of afore-mentioned short story leads to an assumption that Murakami's concern to history is not only about Japan as a "nation", but mostly about Japan and China as a "beyond-nations" relationship. During the early stages of Murakami's career, his concern to history was only described symbolically. When he published "*The Wind-Up Bird Chronicle*" in 1994-1995, his concern to history could be seen clearly.

Murakami started to write "*The Wind-Up Bird Chronicle*" in 1991 when he was about to go to the United States. At the same year, the Gulf War occurred, and fiftieth anniversary of the attack on Pearl Harbor was held in the United States. Moreover, "*The Wind-Up Bird Chronicle*" was written with Nomonhan Incident that happened at the border between Old Manchuria and Outer Mongolia as its major background. Also, during the publication of "*The Wind-Up Bird Chronicle*", two big incidents occurred in Japan, namely The Great Hanshin Earthquake and Tokyo Subway Sarin Attack.

This explains that "*The Wind-Up Bird Chronicle*" was written in such a tense atmosphere of war and incidents; and this literary work was an important milestone to Murakami's literary career and his "Commitment" as a writer.

Keywords Haruki Murakami, Commitment, history, memory, concern to other nations

はじめに

　村上春樹は1979年に『風の歌を聴け』でデビューし、その処女作で群像新人賞を受賞した。そして2018年は村上が作家になると決意してから40年後に当たる時期である。現在に至るまで、村上は数々の作品を発表し、その作品群は50ヶ国語以上に翻訳されている。村上は最も読まれている日本人作家の一人であるといっても過言ではない。

　本稿は村上の作家としての「コミットメント」について考えていきたい。まず、本稿に示す「コミットメント」の定義を明らかにする必要がある。村上は1996年に行われた心理学者河合準雄との対談で自ら「コミットメント」という言葉を提案した。

> コミットメントというのは何かというと、人と人の関わり合いだと思うのだけれど、これまでにあるような、「あなたの言っていることはわかるわかる、じゃ、手をつなごう」というのではなくて、「井戸」を掘って掘って掘っていくと、そこでまったくつな

がるはずのない壁を越えてつながる。[1]

　上記で村上が発言した井戸は「井戸」で書かれており、本当の井戸を示さず、むしろ井戸と同様の観念を持つものを示唆していると考えられる。例えば、人の「井戸」である心、国の「井戸」である歴史などである。そして、「井戸」を掘って「井戸」にこもることを経て村上が到達した結果は人間の孤独ではなく、むしろ人間と人間の繋がり、最終的に共同に生きることであると考えられる。要するに、村上にとって「コミットメント」は他者の心、または国の歴史を理解することによって、最終的に他者との繋がり、他者と共同に生きることを目指すのではないかと考えられる。

　村上の歴史意識を考えてみると興味深い。まず、村上の少年時代に遡る必要がある。村上は1949年に京都に生まれ、兵庫県の西宮、芦屋で少年時代を過ごした。兵庫県神戸市は国際貿易港を持つ都市であるとよく知られている。少年の頃から国際的な環境に育てられたため、アメリカのみならず、中国に関心があることは珍しくない。

　2009年のエルサレム賞受賞時の村上のスピーチにもヒントがある。スピーチで村上は中国大陸の戦闘に参加した父親のことを思い出した。仏教の僧侶であった父親は毎朝「戦地で死んでいった人々のため」に祈った。[2]これは父親から引き継いだ歴史について村上の最初の記憶であると考えられる。村上の作品に他国、特に中国と中国人がしばしば出現していることもその影響であると思われる。例えば、『風の歌を聴け』、「中国行きのスロウ・ボート」、『羊をめぐる冒険』、『ねじまき鳥クロニクル』などである。

　本稿は村上の「コミットメント」、主に村上の歴史への関心を中心にし、上記に取り上げた作品を考察したい。『風の歌を聴け』に触れてから、「中国行きのスロウ・ボート」を考察したい。そして、第一節の最後に『羊をめぐる冒険』を眺めていきたい。『風の歌を聴け』から『羊をめぐる冒険』に至るまで、村上の歴史への関心は象徴的にしか描かれていなかった。その理由を考えながら作品の分析を行いたい。そして、第二節で『ねじまき鳥クロニクル』を考察したい。『ねじまき鳥クロニクル』で村上の歴史への関心が作品の表面に現れてきた。なぜこの時期に変化したのか、歴史への関心はどのように作品の表面に現れていたのかについて考えながら作品の分析を行いたい。

本論

1.　「重要な記号」としての「中国」

1.1　『風の歌を聴け』で最初のヒント

　『風の歌を聴け』の語り手は「僕」であり、物語の時間設定は「僕」が大学生であった頃、1970年の夏休みに故郷に帰省したときであった。「僕」は18日間友人のネズミと一緒に過ごし、ほとんど毎日ジェイズ・バーでビールを飲んだ。ある日、「僕」はバーの洗面所で左手に四本の指しかなかった女の子が倒れている姿を見かけた。そこから物語が進んでおり、夏休みの終わりに「僕」が東京に戻る場面で話は終わった。

　そうした物語の中、『風の歌を聴け』で中国への記憶のヒントが読み取れる。まず、第1章に「僕」の叔父の話が現れた。すなわち、「戦争の二日後に自分が埋めた地雷を踏ん」[3]でしまい、上海で死んだということである。興味深いことは、第1章に現れた「僕」の叔父の話は小説の終盤、第38章に繰り返された。「僕」は東京に戻る前、ジェイズ・バーに寄った。「僕」はバーのオーナーであるジェイに「僕の叔父さんは中国で死んだ」[4]と言った。『風の歌を聴け』で中国への記憶について最も大事なヒントはジェイに他ならない。ジェイは在日中国人であるにもかかわらず、一度も中国に行ったことはないと描写された。

　ジェイは村上の初期三部作に重要な脇役である。彼は1945年の太平洋戦争後、軍事基地で働いた。朝鮮戦争の休戦の翌年である1954年に、彼は軍事基地での仕事をやめ、その付近にバーを開いた。ベトナム戦争が激しくなった時期である1963年に彼はそのバーを売り、「僕」の故郷、「港町」にやってきた。要するに、ジェイは様々な戦争の切迫した空間で生きていると理解できよう。

　中国で死んだ「僕」の叔父の話はもちろん、初期三部作に在日中国人のジェイを重要な脇役として登場させた村上がこれからの作品に中国のことを数々触れると読者に暗示しているのであろう。中国と戦争、及び中国と死についてはこの後に出てくる作品に似たような話が読み取れる。

1　村上春樹、河合隼雄1996『村上春樹、河合隼雄に会いに行く』新潮社、84頁

2　村上春樹2011『雑文集』新潮社、79頁

3　村上春樹1990『村上春樹全作品1979〜1989①風の歌を聴け・1973年のピンボール』講談社、9頁

4　同上、116頁

1.2 「中国行きのスロウ・ボート」はなぜ書き換えられたのか

「中国行きのスロウ・ボート」は1980年4月号の文芸誌『海』で初めて発表された。後に、他の6本の短編小説とともに単行本『中国行きのスロウ・ボート』にまとめられ、1983年5月に刊行された。そして、1990年に『村上春樹全作品1979〜1989③短編集I』に再びまとめられた。

「中国行きのスロウ・ボート」は5章からなり、全てのバージョンが次の文章から始まる。すなわち、「最初の中国人に出会ったのはいつのことだったろう？」[5] 短編小説の題名とこの文章を読むと、この作品は中国と中国人についての話であると多くの読者が推測したのであろう。30歳を越えた主人公の「僕」は思い出に残る中国人たちを回想した。最初に出会った中国人は「僕」が小学生の時に中国人小学校で行った模擬テストの監督官の教師であった。二人目の中国人はアルバイトで出会った女子大生であった。三人目の中国人は「僕」が28歳の時に偶然に再会した高校時代の同級生であった。

村上の中国の描写についての研究で、おそらく最もよく知られているのは藤井省三が執筆した『村上春樹のなかの中国』であろう。村上の長編小説の考察や中国語圏の国々での村上の受容のみならず、「中国行きのスロウ・ボート」の考察も含まれている。この作品は初出誌版から全作品版に至るまで、様々な書き換えが行われていると藤井氏が述べている。これは興味深いことであるが、その理由は明瞭ではない。そのため、本節は「中国行きのスロウ・ボート」を再検討し、特に藤井氏がまだ触れていない部分を中心にして考察を行いたい。

「僕」の記憶力は曖昧であると描写された。ただし、様々な不確かな記憶の中で、「僕」は「正確に思い出すことのできる出来事」[6]が二つある。それは「中国人の話」と「夏休みに行われた野球の試合である」。「中国人の話」と「野球の試合」は一見無縁な話に見えるようであるが、実はある種の関連性を持っていると考えられる。小学校6年生であった「僕」は高校のグラウンドで行った野球の試合に参加し、バスケット・ボールのゴール・ポストに激突したため、脳震盪を起こした。この場面は村上の実経験に結びつけることができよう。村上は明治神宮野球場でプロ野球試合を観戦してから小説を書くと決意した。すなわち、ヤクルトの先頭打者デイブ・ヒルトンが二塁側に打った瞬間であった。野球観戦で与えられた刺激は村上にとって作家になるための一つの大事なターニング・ポイントであるのではないかと考えられる。おそらく村上が感じた刺激を「僕」にも感じさせ、脳震盪を起こさせたのであろう。

その「刺激」は「僕」の一つの大事なターニング・ポイントにもなり、後に「死」について気づき、中国人のことを考えるようになった。興味深いことに、中国人と「死」については初出誌版で見当たらず、単行本版と全作品版にしかなかった。なぜこの部分が書き換えられたのか、なぜ「死」は中国人を思い出させるのかという疑問が残った。

「はじめに」にも述べたように、村上にとって中国について最初の記憶は父親から聞いた中国での戦争と、戦地で死んだ人々の話であった。おそらく村上にとってこの記憶が大事であるため、「中国行きのスロウ・ボート」のどこかに載せたかったと思われる。そのため、この短編小説の序盤が書き換えられ、中国人と「死」の話が追加されたのであろう。また、上記に触れた『風の歌を聴け』の序盤と終盤で、戦争後に中国で死んだ「僕」の叔父の話もあった。これらを踏まえると、「中国行きのスロウ・ボート」における中国人と「死」の関係は戦争がもたらした「死」への記憶の暗示に他ならない。

「僕」にとって最初の中国人は中国人小学校で行われた模擬テストの監督官の教師であった。テストが始まる前、彼はクラスの前で次のように話した。

> 「もちろんわたくしたち二つの国のあいだには似ているところもありますし、似ていないところもあります。わかりあえるところもあるでしょうし、わかりあえないところもあるでしょう。それはあなた方のお友だちのことを考えても同じことではないですか？どんな仲の良い友だちでも、やはりわかってもらえないこともある。そうですね？わたくしたち二つの国のあいだでもそれは同じです。でも努力さえすれば、わたくしたちはきっと仲良くなれる、わたくしたちはそう信じています。でもそのためには、まずわたくしたちはお互いを尊敬しあわねばなり

---

[5] 村上春樹1990『村上春樹全作品1979〜1989③短編集I』講談社、11頁

[6] 同上、13頁

ません。それが…第一歩です。[7]

　上記の「二つの国」は村上が使用した比喩であり、生徒たちは学校の机に落書きしたりしないようにという注意が次に出てくる場面で分かった。しかし、この場面はやはりそれ以上に解釈できると考えられる。まず、なぜ村上はこの発言を中国人小学校の教師の口を借りて発して、さらに小学生の前に聞かせたのであろうか。これを理解するために、「僕」の年齢を確認する必要がある。「僕」が初めて中国人教師と出会ったのは1959年、または1960年であった。そのとき「僕」は小学校6年生であり、11歳または12歳であった。つまり、「僕」は村上と同年であろう。おそらく、村上が幼少期に父親から聞いた中国での戦争と、戦地で死んでいた人々のことを上記のような形で「僕」や他の小学生たちにも聞かせたがったのであろう。

　より考えれば、中国人教師は村上の父親と『風の歌を聴け』のジェイと一つの共通点があると考えられる。つまり、三人とも「無差別」のことをそれぞれの形で語っていることである。上記の引用を見ると、中国人教師は小学生たちが「無差別」という難しい言葉をすぐ分かるように、「友情」という簡単なたとえを使用した。そして繰り返すが、村上の父親は中国大陸に渡って戦闘に参加した経験がある。戦争後に、僧侶であった彼は戦地で死んだ人々のために毎朝祈った。日本人であろうが、中国人であろうが、国籍を問わず全ての人々のために祈った。また、『風の歌を聴け』のジェイは中国で死んだ「僕」の叔父に対して次のように言った。「いろんな人間が死んだものね。でもみんな兄弟さ」[8]。ジェイは「無差別」のことを直接語っていないが、「みんな兄弟」という発言から国籍を問わず、人々の平等性が示唆されているのであろう。

　中国人教師が「無差別」について話した際、「僕」はずっと沈黙を守った。おそらく、「僕」は中国人小学校に対して一種の差別的な考えがあったからと思われる。なぜなら、「僕」の小学校から中国人小学校で模擬テストを受けたのは「僕」しかいなかったからである。それに、中国人小学校は遠かったため、「僕」は中国人小学校を「世界の果ての中国人小学校」[9]と名づけた。そうした事実は「僕の心をたまらなく重くさせた」[10]。「僕」は二週間余りで中国人小学校について「暗くて長い廊下、じっとりと黴臭い空気」[11]というイメージを持っていた。しかし、中国人小学校は実際に「僕」のイメージと真逆であり、むしろきれいに描写された。要するに、「僕」のイメージと現実の間にギャップが存在した。そのギャップによって、「僕」は混乱したのであろう。そして自分の混乱した気持ちを取り直すために、また中国人小学校についてのイメージと現実のギャップを埋めるために、「僕」は落書きしたと推測できよう。

　上記にも既に述べたように、「中国行きのスロウ・ボート」は大幅に書き換えられた。特に、落書きについての場面である。この場面に高校時代の「僕」の彼女が登場した。彼女はほんのわずかばかり登場したが、大事な役割を持っている。彼女は小学校の時、偶然「僕」と同じ日と場所で模擬テストを受けた。以下の表を見てみよう。

表1

初出誌版	単行本版
「落書きはした？」 「落書き？」 「机にさ」（中略） 「そうね、したかもしれないわ」大した興味もなさそうに彼女はそう言った。[12]（下線部引用者）	「落書きはした？」 「落書き？」 「机にさ」（中略） 「さあ、どうかな、よく覚えてないわ」と彼女は言って微かに笑った。「昔のことだもの」 「でもさ、とても綺麗なピカピカの机だったじゃない。覚えてない？」と僕は尋ねた。 「ええ、そうね、そうだったかもしれないわ」と彼女はあまり興味なさそうに言った。（中略） 「落書きはしなかったと思う？　思い出せない？」と僕はもう一度尋ねた。 「ねえ、本当に思い出せないのよ」と彼女は笑いながら

7　同上、17〜18頁
8　村上春樹1990『村上春樹全作品1979〜1989①風の歌を聴け・1973年のピンボール』講談社、115〜116頁
9　村上春樹1990『村上春樹全作品1979〜1989③短編集I』講談社、14頁
10　村上春樹1980「中国行きのスロウ・ボート」『海』、95頁
11　村上春樹1990『村上春樹全作品1979〜1989③短編集I』講談社、15頁
12　村上春樹1980「中国行きのスロウ・ボート」『海』、98頁

初出誌版	単行本版と全作品版
言った。「そう言われてみればしたような気がしないでもないけど、そんなの昔のことだから…」[13]（下線部引用者）	

　上記の表から分かったことは、初出誌版で「僕」は落書きについて一回だけ彼女に質問した。興味深いことに、単行本版での「僕」は彼女にしつこく質問した。それのみならず、6年か7年前の出来事であるにもかかわらず、「僕」はまだ教室の状態を明瞭に覚えている。この場面によって、中国人教師が落書きについて話す前にも「僕」と彼女は机のどこかに既に落書きしたと予想できる。しかし、全作品版で彼女の姿が削除された。これは重要な意味を持っていると考えられる。つまり、彼女の姿の削除によって、落書きや差別の話も消えてしまうといえよう。

　「僕」にとって二人目の中国人は19歳の時、アルバイトで出会った女子大生であった。一緒に仕事をしてから2週間たって、彼女は仕事のミスで困難な状態になった。「僕」は彼女を落ち着かせた際、彼女が中国人であると知った。中国人であることを知るまでの場面は興味深いため、以下の表に引用する。

表2

初出誌版	単行本版と全作品版
「でもね、たとえその国で生まれたとしても、外国で生活するってずいぶん奇妙なことなのよ」（中略） 「外国？」 「ええ、私は中国籍なの」（中略） 「<u>これまでにもいろんな変な目にあったわ</u>」[14]（下線部引用者）	昼食の時間に我々は<u>軽い世間話</u>をした。彼女は自分が中国人だと言った。[15]（下線部引用者）

　上記の表を見ると、初出誌版から単行本版と全作品版に至るまで、話が完全に書き換えられたと分かった。初出誌版の下線部のところで、中国人女性は自分が経験した「差別」を自ら語った。これは「軽い世間話」であると全くいえないのであろう。それにもかかわらず、単行本版と全作品版で全ては「軽い世間話」で納められた。ここでも「差別」の話が再び消えてしまうということが分かった。

　アルバイトの最後の日の後、「僕」は彼女を新宿のディスコティックに誘った。しかし、同居している兄が門限に厳しいため、彼女は早く帰らないといけないと言った。そして「僕」は彼女を逆周りの山手線に乗せてしまった。その次に出てくる場面でも「僕」は彼女の電話番号が書かれていた紙マッチを捨ててしまったことが分かった。こうした「僕」の二回の間違いは、中国人女性が言ったように、「僕」は「わざと」彼女を逆周りの山手線に乗せている。問題はなぜ「僕」が彼女を間違った電車に乗せてしまったのであろうか。これを分かるために、二人のアルバイトの場面に戻る必要があり、以下に引用する。

　彼女はとても熱心に働いた。僕もそれにつられて熱心に働いたが、彼女の働きぶりを横で見ていると、僕の熱心さと彼女の熱心さは根本的に質の違うものであるような気がした。つまり、僕の熱心さが「少なくとも何かをするのなら、熱心にやるだけの価値はあるかもしれない」という意味あいでの熱心さであるのに比べて、彼女の熱心さはもう少し人間存在の根源に近い種類のものであるように見えた。（中略）彼女の熱心さには、彼女のまわりのあらゆる日常性がその熱心によって辛うじてひとつにくくられて支えられているのではないかといったような奇妙な切迫感があった。[16]

　上記の引用を見ると、「僕」の熱心さは「やることの価値」のためであるという印象が強い。それに対して、辛いアルバイトであるにもかかわらず、彼女の熱心さは彼女の元々の人柄であると考えられる。おそらく今まで多くの差別を経験したため、彼女の中に忍耐力があると考えられる。実の価値のある熱心さは中国人女性の熱心さであろう。二人は同年であるにもかかわらず、その熱心さの違いによって、おそらく「僕」の中にギャップが存在したのであろう。後に彼女が中国人であることを知った際、彼女は「僕」にとっ

13　村上春樹1983『中国行きのスロウ・ボート』中央公論社、18〜19頁
14　村上春樹1980「中国行きのスロウ・ボート」『海』、99頁
15　村上春樹1990『村上春樹全作品1979〜1989③短編集I』講談社、21頁
16　同上、20頁

て二人目の中国人だけではなく、「僕」にとっても「中国」について二つ目のギャップのであろう。「僕」は彼女と一緒に仕事をして何の文句も言わないとしても、そのギャップによって混乱したのであろう。そしてそのギャップを埋めるために、「僕」は中国人女性の熱心さを試し、「わざと」逆周りの山手線に乗せたのであろう。

逆周りの山手線も興味深い。「僕」の下宿は目白にあり、中国人女性の家は駒込にあった。新宿から同じ方向の山手線に乗るはずであるにもかかわらず、「僕」はわざわざ彼女を逆周りの山手線に乗せることによって、彼女をより遠いところに行かせることであろう。遠いところは「僕」が小さい頃受けた模擬テストの会場、「世界の果ての中国人小学校」と、そこでやった「差別」を思い出させた。要するに、この場面にも前回と同様に、「僕」の差別行為が読み取れるのであろう。

山根由美恵は「村上春樹「中国行きスロウ・ボート」論─対社会意識の目覚め」で次のように述べている。1980年代は日本のみならず、海外でも「戦争責任」や「南京大虐殺」についての問題への関心が高まった時代であるという。そのような時代に執筆された「中国行きのスロウ・ボート」における「僕」と中国人たちの関係は「日本とアジアの国々との関係のアナロジー、時代の象徴」として描かれているという。[17]確かに、第「2」章から第「4」章までは「日本とアジアの国々との関係」が読み取れる。しかし、第「1」章と第「5」章を見ると、その「関係」はどこにも見当たらない。この作品で様々な差別行為の場面が起こったとしても、全作品版でほとんど書き換えられた。「中国行きのスロウ・ボート」はなぜ書き換えられたのであろうか。以下の引用を見てみよう。

> ここは僕のための場所でもないんだ、と。
> そう思いついたのは山手線の車内。(中略) そこには無数の選択肢があり、無数の可能性があった。しかしそれは無数であると同時にゼロだった。(中略) それは都会だった。(中略)
> それでもその中国は、僕のためだけの中国でしかない。(中略) 地球上の黄色く塗られた中国とは違う、もうひとつの中国である。[18]（傍点原文）

上記の引用を見ると、この作品に中国人が登場しても、中国という国が一度も登場しないと分かった。おそらくこの作品における中国は本当の中国ではないであろう。村上は「中国行きのスロウ・ボート」を執筆した際、題名を先に選び、その題名を中心にして小説を構成したと述べている。「中国行きのスロウ・ボート」という題名はソニー・ロリンスの演奏である『オン・ナ・スロウ・ボート・トゥ・チャイナ』からインスピレーションを受けたと分かった。元々、On A Slow Boat to China はアメリカのポップ・ソングであり、フランク・レッサーによって1948年に作詞、作曲された。歌詞を読んでみると、ロマンティックな曲であるということが分かった。

また、「中国行きのスロウ・ボート」の第「1」章の前に書かれていた歌詞を見ると、興味深いことがある。以下の引用を見てみよう。

> スロウ・ボート
> 中国行きの貨物船に
> なんとかあなたを
> 乗せたいな、
> 船は貸し切り、二人きり…

上記の歌詞を見ると、「slow boat」の訳は「貨物船」と書かれている。村上はそれについて『村上ソングス』で次のように述べている。

> スロウ・ボートというのは「貨物船」と訳されることが多いし、僕も小説につけた訳詞ではそのように訳した。(中略) 恋する女性と二人で貨物船で親密に旅をするというのは、それなりに楽しそうではあるけれど、<u>微妙に損なわれるロマンス的な部分</u>はやはりあるかもしれない。(中略) それは人の心の中だけにひっそりと存在する、<u>親密な夢の乗り物</u>なのだ。[19]（下線部引用者）

---

[17] 山根由美恵2002「村上春樹「中国行きのスロウ・ボート」論─対社会意識の目覚め」『国文学』第173号 広島大学国語国文学会、42頁

[18] 村上春樹1990『村上春樹全作品1979〜1989③短編集I』講談社、38頁

[19] 村上春樹2010『村上ソングス』中央公論社、65頁

「中国行きのスロウ・ボート」の「スロウ・ボート」はどのような意味をつけた方が良いのであろうか。「貨物船」の「貨」は「宝」(treasure)と同じ意味を持っていると考えれば、おそらく「スロウ・ボート」は「僕」にとって宝物のような大事なことであろう。同時に、「微妙に損なわれるロマンス的な部分」、「夢の乗り物」でもある。それは「僕」のアドレセンス、情熱に溢れていた60年代に他ならない。「僕」の世代（同時に村上の世代）が憧れていた60年代が終わり、70年代と80年代の都会に生活を送っている人々は孤独に生きる。その中に、「僕」は昔のことを懐かしく思い出した。

「中国行きのスロウ・ボート」を考察して分かったことは、初期作品から村上の歴史への関心が否定できない。だが、それらの作品における「中国」は本当に存在する中国ではなく、むしろ既に終わった夢のような憧れの時代を描写するための「重要な記号」であろう。そのため、多くの書き換えが行われたと考えられる。「中国行きのスロウ・ボート」だけではなく、村上のこのような記号の使い方は『羊をめぐる冒険』にも見られる。

1.3 『羊をめぐる冒険』で「中国」が消えた

『羊をめぐる冒険』で広告代理店を自営した「僕」は突然右翼政党の秘書によって特別な羊を探すように命令された。その原因は「僕」がクライアントの依頼で製作したチラシである。チラシに「僕」の友人、ネズミから送られてきた星印の羊の写真が載せられ、偶然に右翼政党のシンボルとなる。「僕」は耳が綺麗な恋人と一緒に北海道に行き、結局「僕」だけがネズミの別荘で羊男と会った。そこで、「僕」が来る直前にネズミは既に自殺したと羊男から聞いた。結局、羊男の姿が消え、「僕」は東京に帰って、故郷を訪れた。「僕」は港を眺めながら一人で泣く場面で小説が終わった。

本稿で述べたいのは「僕」が北海道で出会った博士と右翼政党の大物だけである。博士は1935年に満州国を訪れた。満州国と蒙古の国境にいた際、突然羊が現れ、博士の中に入った。戻った後、博士は羊について妄想を見始めた。だが、1936年に羊は博士の中から逃げ出し、その時満州国にいた大物の中に入るようになった。そして、大物は博士のように、羊について妄想を見始めた。大物は右翼政党を制定した際、普通の羊だけではなく、妄想にあった星印の羊を政党のシンボルとして決定した。

星印の羊に注目したい。まず、星印は中国の国旗を連想させる。また、羊は日本に存在しない動物であり、江戸時代に中国人の牧夫によって輸入され始めた。つまり、全ては中国を表象するのであり、星印の羊は中国を描写するための「重要な記号」として使用されたのであろう。それにもかかわらず、『羊をめぐる冒険』の終盤で羊男の姿がネズミの姿とともに消滅された。ネズミは村上の初期三部作で60年代の記号であると良く知られている。その記号が消滅されることによって、村上は昔憧れていた60年代をこの後に出てくる作品のテーマにしないと考えられる。同時に、これ以上「中国」を「重要な記号」として使用しないと思われる。記号だけではなく、おそらく歴史への関心が作品の表面に出るようになるかもしれない。

2. 『ねじまき鳥クロニクル』における歴史意識
2.1「理不尽な死」への恐怖

『ねじまき鳥クロニクル』を執筆し始めた際、村上はアメリカに渡るところであった。その時は1991年であり、1月に湾岸戦争が起こり、12月にアメリカで真珠湾攻撃50周年が行われた。日本に滞在した際、村上は「個人」を求めていたと述べている。しかし、アメリカでの滞在はそうした考えを変化させ、社会的責任感を感じるようになった。その理由はおそらく日本の知識人の代表の一人としてたびたび真珠湾攻撃についての意見や、日本が湾岸戦争に軍隊を送らなかった理由などについて、アメリカでの同僚によって問い掛けられたからであろう。社会的責任感はどのようなことであるかというと、おそらく歴史を振り返ることであると考えられる。前節にも述べたように、村上は初期作品から歴史に関心を持った。その関心はこれまで記号として語られたが、アメリカでの滞在によって、記号だけではなく、作品の表面に投影されるようになったと考えられる。

アメリカに滞在した際、村上はプリンストン大学の特別教員として滞在し、大学の図書館でノモンハン事件についての資料を読んだと分かった。4年間のアメリカでの滞在期間で『ねじまき鳥クロニクル』を執筆した。本作品の第一部「泥棒かささぎ編」は1992年10月から1993年8月にかけて「新潮」に連載された。第二部「予言する鳥編」は1994年2月に刊行された。村上は「メイキング・オブ・『ねじまき鳥クロニクル』」で、この作品を第二部までで完成させたかったと述べているが、1994年6月に蒙古を訪れ、「ノ

モンハンの鉄の墓場」という紀行文を執筆した上で、1995年8月に第三部「鳥刺し男編」を刊行することになった。この蒙古への旅は重要な役割を持っていると考えられる。もし蒙古を訪れなかったら、村上は『ねじまき鳥クロニクル』第三部を執筆しなかったかもしれない。

『ねじまき鳥クロニクル』の主人公と語り手は「僕」、岡田亨であった。「僕」と妻、クミコが飼っていた「綿谷ノボル」と名づけられた猫の追跡で物語が始まった。猫を見つけることができなかったため、クミコは兄、綿谷ノボルの助けを求めた。「僕」と綿谷ノボルの関係が悪く、第二部でクミコが失踪したため、二人の関係がさらに悪化した。クミコが失踪した後、間宮中尉は登場した。彼と友人の本田伍長は元日本軍の兵士であり、「僕」にノモンハン事件について語った。第三部で「僕」は赤坂ナツメグ、シナモン親子と知り合い、路地の空き家を買うようになった。「僕」はそこにある井戸に入り、自分とクミコの関係を考えた。結局クミコは「僕」に戻らないが、「僕」はクミコを待つと決意した。

本稿で論じたいのは『ねじまき鳥クロニクル』における歴史意識だけである。『ねじまき鳥クロニクル』の第一部の「間宮中尉の長い話1・2」にノモンハン事件についての話がある。地理専門家であった間宮中尉は参謀本部に呼ばれ、外蒙古との国境地帯を調査している民間人、山本を警護するようにという命令を与えられた。浜野軍曹と本田伍長も彼と同行した。浜野軍曹は間宮中尉に以下のように話した。

> 自分は兵隊だから戦争をするのはかまわないのです、と彼は言いました。国のために死ぬのも構わんのです。それが私の商売ですから。しかし私たちが今ここでやっている戦争は、どう考えてもまともな戦争じゃありませんよ、少尉殿。それは戦線があって、敵に正面から決戦を挑むというようなきちんとした戦争じゃないのです。私たちは前進します。敵はほとんど戦わず逃げます。そして敗走する中国兵は軍服を脱いで民衆の中に潜り込んでしまいます。そうなると誰が敵なのか、私たちにはそれさえもわからんのです。だから私たちは匪賊狩り、残兵狩りと称して<u>多くの罪のない人々</u>を殺し、食糧を略奪します。[20]（下線部引用者）

上記の引用を見ると、『ねじまき鳥クロニクル』では確かにノモンハン事件が重要なテーマになったが、本作品で村上が主張したかったのは戦争時や事件という「事実」ではなく、むしろ「死」という「真実」であると考えられる。個人の死ではなく、戦争という歴史事実がもたらした「多くの罪もない人々」の死のことである。特に、ノモンハン事件によって引き起こされた残酷さは2万人以上の日本兵士が犠牲者になったと分かった。しかし、その真実はほとんど知られておらず、ちょっとしたエピソードのように見える。これを踏まえると、戦争がもたらした人々の「理不尽な死」は忘れられてしまったといえよう。村上は次のように語っている。

> 表面を一皮むけば、そこにはやはり以前と同じような密閉された国家組織なり理念なりが脈々と息づいているのではあるまいか。（中略）この五十五年前の小さな戦争から、我々はそれほど遠ざかってはいないんじゃないか。<u>僕らの抱えているある種のきつい密閉性はまたいつかその過剰な圧力を、どこかに向けて厳しい勢いで噴き出すのではあるまいか、と</u>。[21]（傍点原文、下線部引用者）

上記は「ノモンハンの鉄の墓場」から引用した。下線部のところはまさに『ねじまき鳥クロニクル』における歴史意識を理解するための重要な手掛かりであろう。要するに、密閉性によって忘れられてしまった残酷な歴史の真実が、いつかまた起こるという恐怖感である。その恐怖感は思いも寄らない現実になり、すなわち1995年3月20日に東京の地下鉄車内でサリン事件が起こったということである。ノモンハン事件とサリン事件は一見無縁な話に見えるようであるが、実は同様の質を持っており、暴力に他ならない。

2.2 暴力の遍在性

『ねじまき鳥クロニクル』における歴史意識は忘れられてしまった「理不尽な死」が作品の表面に現れたことである。「理不尽な死」への恐怖感はこの作品の発表中に現実になってしまい、すなわちサリン事件であった。前述したように、ノモンハン事件とサリン事件は一見無縁な話に見

---

20 村上春樹1994『ねじまき鳥クロニクル第一部泥棒かささぎ編』新潮社、310頁

21 村上春樹1998『辺境、近堺』新潮社、169頁

えるようであるが、実は両方とも暴力という本質を持っていると考えられる。

　本節は『ねじまき鳥クロニクル』における暴力行為と、その暴力の遍在性を中心にしたい。この作品で様々な暴力行為が起こり、例えば間宮中尉が満州国と外蒙古で目撃した山本の皮剥ぎの場面である。他に、第三部で登場人物、赤坂ナツメグの話の中でも暴力に関する場面が現れる。以下に引用する。

> この潜水艦は、私たちみんなを殺すために深い海の底から姿を現したのだ。でもそれは別に不思議なことじゃない、と彼女は思った。それは戦争とは関係なく、誰にでもどこにでも起こり得ることなのだ。みんなはこれがみんな戦争のせいだと思っている。でもそうじゃない。戦争というのは、ここにある˙い˙ろ˙ん˙な˙も˙の˙の˙中˙の˙一˙つ˙にすぎないのだ。[22]（傍点原文）

　確かに戦争は暴力を生み出した。しかし、上記の引用を見ると、この作品で村上が暗示しているのは戦争より、むしろ人間の内面に潜んでいる暴力性であろう。そのため、本節では『ねじまき鳥クロニクル』で暴力と関わった登場人物、綿谷ノボルと「僕」について述べたい。

　綿谷ノボルはクミコの兄であり、綿谷家の長男として父親の厳しい教育を受けた。父親の期待通り優秀な私立高校を卒業し、東京大学の経済学部を優れた成績で卒業した。イエール大学の大学院に留学し、東京大学に戻り、学者としてエリートで知的な道を歩んだ。彼は一見勝者のように見えるが、それは自分が望んでいる生き方ではないであろう。彼は父親の後についていくだけであり、別の言い方をすれば父親によって主体性を奪われた。ある意味では、綿谷ノボルは精神的な暴力を受けたのであろう。しかし、経済専門の本を出版してから、彼は批評家やマスメディアによって高く評価された。「新しい時代のヒーロー」[23]として認められ、テレビに出演できるようになった。つまり、彼は自分の生き方をようやく自分で決められるようになった。そして暴力を受けた彼は自分の権力を見せるため、暴力を振るう人に変わるようになった。父親から受けた暴力のように、彼は自分の姉とクミコの主体性を奪い、彼女たちに精神的な暴力を振るった。

　綿谷ノボルだけではなく、「僕」も暴力行為を振るった。「僕」は新宿で偶然見かけたギター・ケースを持った男を野球のバットで打った。なぜ「僕」は彼に暴力を振るったかというと、おそらく3年前のクミコの堕胎と関係があると考えられる。「僕」はその時札幌に出張し、クミコの堕胎の本当の理由が綿谷ノボルによる精神的な暴力であると分からなかった。「僕」はスナック・バーに行き、ギター・ケースを持った男が歌を歌った後、次のように話した。

> 「肉の痛みがあり、心の痛みがあります。（中略）しかしその苦痛の事態を誰かに対して言葉で説明するのは、多くの場合とても難しいことです。自分の痛みは自分にしかわからない、と人は言います。しかし本当にそうでしょうか？私はそうは思いません。たとえば誰かが本当に苦しんでいる光景を目の前にすれば、私たちもまたその苦しみや痛みを自分自身のものとして感じることがあります。それが<u>共感する力</u>です。[24]（下線部引用者）

　上記の引用を見ると、「僕」はギター・ケースを持った男によって他者、クミコへの共感の欠如について警告されたと分かった。しかし、「僕」はその警告に気づかなかった。長期間にわたって気づかないままの「僕」は自分自身に憎しみを感じ、ギター・ケースを持った男に暴力を振るったのであろう。その後、「僕」は「逃˙げ˙ら˙れ˙な˙い˙し˙、逃˙げ˙る˙べ˙き˙で˙は˙な˙い˙のだ」[25]（傍点原文）と悟り、失踪したクミコを取り戻すために、これまでの彼とクミコの関係を考えるようになった。

　以上、『ねじまき鳥クロニクル』における暴力の遍在性が確認できた。戦争が暴力を生み出したことは否定できない。しかし、この作品で村上が示唆しているのは、普通の人々の内面に暴力性が潜んでいる可能性も十分あるだと分かった。これがこの作品を執筆して村上が至る結末であるといえよう。村上が悟った暴力の遍在性についての意識は変わらないように見え、後にアメリカで9・11の事件について

22　村上春樹1994『ねじまき鳥クロニクル第三部鳥刺し男編』新潮社、132〜133頁

23　同上、163頁

24　村上春樹1994『ねじまき鳥クロニクル第二部予言する鳥編』新潮社、129頁

25　同上、332頁

のインタビューを受けた際、次のように発言している。すなわち、"This is not about nations or countries, and not about religion, but about states of mind."[26]（下線部引用者）

おわりに

村上の初期作品を考察して分かったことは、彼がその時から歴史への関心を持っていることである。それは村上の幼少期に父親から聞いた中国での経験と関係があるからであると思われる。しかし、初期作品で歴史への関心は記号として描かれ、その時の村上の本当のモチーフは憧れであった情熱に溢れた60年代を描いたことであると分かった。そのせいか、村上の初期作品で歴史への関心より、孤独な主人公の方がより目立ったのであろう。村上がこのテーマを初期作品で描き続けたことを見ると、実はこれも「コミットメント」の一つであるが、こうした「コミットメント」はやはり独特すぎると考えられる。

海外での長期滞在によって、村上の独特すぎた「コミットメント」が変わり、他者の心、国の歴史への理解という「コミットメント」を意識するようになったと分かった。しかし、村上は「メイキング・オブ・『ねじまき鳥クロニクル』」で述べるように、「歴史家ではないし、歴史小説を書こうとしているわけでは」[27]ない。つまり、村上は作家なりにその「コミットメント」を作品に描写するということである。ここで、『ねじまき鳥クロニクル』は彼の作家としての「コミットメント」にとって大事な里程標だと考えられる。これは二つの側面から確認でき、一つ目は『ねじまき鳥クロニクル』の執筆によって、これまでの村上文学に登場した、孤独と喪失の中に生きている主人公たちが変わり、他者を理解し、他者と繋がるようになったことである。『ねじまき鳥クロニクル』の終盤でクミコが戻らないと知っているにもかかわらず、「僕」は彼女を待つと決意したことがそれに当たる。『羊をめぐる冒険』の終盤でネズミと羊男の消滅を知った後、故郷で一人で泣いた「僕」のような姿が次第に見えなくなるようになった。

二つ目は『ねじまき鳥クロニクル』が発表された時期から確認できる。ノモンハン事件が生み出した暴力をテーマにした作品が発表された最中、他の暴力、サリン事件が実現されてしまった。これによって、主人公だけではなく、村上も他者を理解し、他者と繋がるようになった。村上は人間の内面に潜んでいる暴力を悟り、それと闘うようになった。村上がサリン事件の被害者にインタビューを敢行し、インタビュー集『アンダーグラウンド』を発表するのはそれに当たる。村上の初期作品に登場するアメリカの架空作家、デレク・ハートフィルドは自殺する前に「最後まで自分の闘う相手の姿を明確に捉えることができなかった」[28]と悟る。しかし、『ねじまき鳥クロニクル』から始め、それ以降の作品で人間の「闘う相手」が見つかり、すなわち人間の内面に潜んでいる暴力性に他ならない。こうした村上らしい他者への理解、他者との繋がりは世界各国の読者の共感を呼び、村上文学が「日本文学」ではなく、「世界文学」だと言われるのが可能になるという結論をつけた。

参考文献

黒古一夫2007『村上春樹：「喪失」の物語から「転換」の物語へ』勉誠出版

柴田勝二2009『中上健次と村上春樹＜脱六〇年代＞的世界の行方』東京外国語大学出版会

藤井省三2007『村上春樹のなかの中国』朝日新聞社

村上春樹1980「中国行きのスロウ・ボート」『海』

────1983『中国行きのスロウ・ボート』中央公論社

────1990『村上春樹全作品1979〜89①風の歌を聴け・1973年のピンボール』講談社

────1990『村上春樹全作品1979〜89③短編集I』講談社

────1994『ねじまき鳥クロニクル第一部』新潮社

────1994『ねじまき鳥クロニクル第二部』新潮社

────1994『ねじまき鳥クロニクル第三部』新潮社

────1995「メイキング・オブ・『ねじまき鳥クロニクル』」『新潮』

────1996『村上春樹、河合隼雄に会いに行く』新潮社

────1997『辺境、近堺』新潮社

────2010『村上ソングス』中央公論社

────2011『雑文集』新潮社

山根由美恵2002「村上春樹「中国行きのスロウ・ボート」論─対社会意識の目覚め」『国文学』

第173号　広島大学国語国文学会

Rubin, Jay. 2002. *Haruki Murakami and the Music of Words*. London: The Harvill Press

---

[26] Howard French とのインタビュー、"The Word on Terror", The Sunday Age, 4 November 2001より

[27] 村上春樹1995「メイキング・オブ・『ねじまき鳥クロニクル』」『新潮』、288頁

[28] 村上春樹1990『村上春樹全作品1979〜1989①風の歌を聴け、1973年のピンボール』新潮社、8頁

Does *Hallyu* Matter?
Determinants of Boycott Decision on Korean Food Brands among Indonesian Youngsters

Putriesti Mandasari[1], Desy Mayasari[2]
1 Agribusiness Study Program, Faculty of Agriculture, Universitas Sebelas Maret (UNS), Indonesia
2 Management Study Program, Faculty of Economics and Business, Universitas Sebelas Maret (UNS), Indonesia

2017年、インドネシアで韓国製インスタント麺のハラル違反が摘発され、韓国製品の不買運動が起きた。しかし主要な消費者である若者の間では「韓流」文化が大人気。果たして「韓流」ブームは不買運動にどのような影響を与えたか。

Abstract

This study addresses the role of attitude toward *hallyu* (Korean wave) on boycott decision of Korean food brands among Indonesian youngsters. Drawing from positioning theory, this study found that positive attitude toward *hallyu* decreased the tendency on boycott decision. Interestingly, this paper also discovered that the severity of *halal* violation was not moderating the effect of attitude toward *hallyu* on boycott. Either severe or light violation, once youngsters fall for *hallyu*, they ignore the severity of *halal* violation of the products. Data were collected from 156 respondents and were processed with linier and hierarchical regression analysis. This paper is the first to relate attitude toward *hallyu* on boycott decision and also the first to study boycott of Korean food brands due to the recent *halal* violation incident in Indonesia. Implications and findings are discussed.

Keywords   boycott decision, attitude toward *hallyu* (Korean wave), severity of *halal* violation

1. Introduction

The Korean Wave, widely known as *hallyu*, appoints to the popularity of Korean-related cultural products, such as film, drama, and music (Jang and Paik, 2012; Bae, *et. al.*, 2017); it also refers to recent pattern of cultural flow (Jeon and Yoon, 2005). In spite of targeting youngsters market, *hallyu* attracts wider age-groups and social classes (Suh, *et. al.*, 2016) in Korea as well as in global market (Jang, *et. al.*, 2016), spreading from East and Southeast Asian Countries, some European countries, up to Middle East (Hong and Kim, 2013).

The international recognition on *hallyu* has gained cultural and economic effects to the country (Jang and Paik, 2012; Bae, *et. al.*, 2017). It has become a marketing platform to enhance the Korean brand value and eventually increases profit from the overseas market (Huang, 2011). As mentioned by Jeon, *et. al.*, (as cited in Oh, 2016), the total export produced by *hallyu* was as much as US$ 7.03 billion in 2015.

As a result of being constantly exposed to *hallyu*, more and more global consumers, particularly in emerging countries such as Indonesia, raise their interest by consuming various import products from Korea. According to Wang and Chen (2004), imported goods are mostly preferred by consumers in developing countries because of their brand image in which associated with its native country. Among those imported products, Korean noodle has become one of the most preferred choices compared to other domestic and import brands in Indonesia. It dominated the market share of import noodle in the country. In 2016, the import value of Korean instant noodle in Indonesia reached up to US$ 13.55 million, while China (US$ 2.69 million), Thailand (US$ 0.33 million), Singapore (US$ 0.22 million), and Japan (US$ 0.111 million) remained sequentially on the big 5 (Ministry of Finance, 2017).

Despite the favouritism of Indonesian consumers to Korean noodle brands, serious *halal* violation occurred. *BPOM* (Drug and Food Control Agency) detected pork DNA-fragment in some Korean noodle products. Therefore, in June 2017, BPOM officially banned 4 Korean noodles from different brands: *Samyang (U-dong)*, *Samyang (Kimchi Flavor)*, *Nongshim (Shim Ramyun Black)*, and *Ottogi (Yeul Ramen)* (Saeno and Aldila, 2017). Dealing with this issue, BPOM imposed administrative sanctions to the importer (PT Koin Bumi) by revoking its marketing license and asking the importer for products withdrawal from the market (Pos Kota, 2017).

Consumers could respond negatively to such violation by boycotting the non-*halal* products. Boycott involves consumer's avoidance of purchasing products and brands due to companies' unethical credibility (Lavorata, 2014). Responding to this incident, local newspapers and online news reported boycotts exclamation by local *MUI* (Indonesian Council of Ulama) as well as *YLKI* (Indonesian Consumer Foundation) (Prasetya, 2017). Through the media, some sources mentioned that this case lead to violation of the Consumer Protection Law, Food Law, and *Halal* Product Warranty Act. Consequently, the public awareness on determining *halal* products, particularly for import noodle products, has risen among Indonesian Muslim consumers.

Consumer evaluation on foreign products is formed by their general attitudes, country-specific attitudes (positive or negative), or brand-specific attitudes (e.g. special liking to a particular brand (Bandyopadhyay, *et. al.*, 2011). Studies on foreign products evaluation, as well as intention to buy, and its relations to consumer's ethnocentrism (Smith and Li, 2010; Bandyopadhyay, *et. al.*, 2011; Guo and Zhou, 2017), country of origin (Gurhan-Canli and Maheswaran, 2000; Chen, *et. al.*, 2011), and animosity toward a country (Russel and Russel, 2006; Smith and Li, 2010) provides a large body of literature, yet little is known regarding the role of attitude toward *hallyu* (Korean wave) on boycott decision of Korean food brands due to *halal* violation.

To the best of our knowledge, this paper is the first to relate attitude toward *hallyu* on boycott decision and also the first to study boycott of Korean food brands due to the recent *halal* violation event in Indonesia. This study highlighted two important purposes. First, it identified the effect of attitude toward *hallyu* on boycott decision. Second, it examined whether or not the severity of *halal* violation moderating the effect between attitude toward *hallyu* and boycott decision.

1.1. Theory developments

The underlying theory of the relationship is positioning theory. Positioning theory states that different culture adoption by individual might lead to better understanding, toleration, and adaptation with that culture and possibly changing buying behaviour from that culture (Suh, *et. al.*, 2016). Better understanding of another culture increases the reluctance to boycott. With the massive wave of *hallyu*, children, students, and adults are exposed daily by Korean culture. They learn food, traditional clothes, way of eating, and many more from it. As a result, individuals feel as a part of that culture and make it into the justifications of their behaviour.

1.2. Influence of attitude toward hallyu on boycott decision

Despite the rising trend on *hallyu*-related research over the years (Huang, 2011; Jang and Paik, 2012; Hong and Kim, 2013; Suh, et. al, 2016; Chen, 2016; Bae, et. al, 2017), its effect on boycott decision has not been investigated. In this research, attitude toward *hallyu* refers to its country (Korea), its people (Korean), and its products (Amine, 2008). Suh, et. al (2016) stated that the foreign culture' adoption magnify general attitudes toward the country, its companies, and its products; consequently, it drives purchase intention of foreign products. Furthermore, favourable feeling, sympathy, and attachment toward particular foreign country positively impacts consumer decision making related to foreign products (Bandyopadhyay, *et. al.*, 2011) even though considerable violation might happen to those products. Subsequently, consumer's tendency for boycotting those products might be buried away.

Hypothesis 1: Positive attitude toward *hallyu* decrease the tendency of boycott decision on Korean noodle brand

1.3. Severity of halal violation as a moderating factor

The importance of *halal* in Muslim world has been emerging on business and trade, and has become an international symbol of quality assurance and lifestyle choice, as well as substantial factor in Muslim's consumption behaviour (Omar, et. al, 2017). Encountering *halal* violation, Muslim consumers respond with different attitudes and behaviours, such as boycotting the product, spreading negative word of mouth, and changing over to the competitors' product, in which eventually could bring a breakdown for the company' reputation and brand (Omar, et. al, 2017). The existence of *halal* violation from particular product could cause consumers' loss, financially and non-financially (feeling betrayed, frustration, and inconvenience) (Hess, 2008), but consumers' reaction on the violation depends on their subjective evaluation of the severity (intensity or seriousness) (Omar, et., al., 2017). Recalling the case, it is expected that the more severe *halal* violation of Korean noodle brand, consumers suffer a higher loss, and finally decide to engage in product (and brand) boycott. It is also expected that severity of *halal* violation moderates the link between attitude toward *hallyu* and boycott.

Hypothesis 2: Severity of *halal* violation moderates the relationship between attitude toward *hallyu* and boycott decision on Korean noodle brand

2. Methods

2.1. Sample

This study purposively chose 160 undergraduate students from three big Universities in Surakarta and Yogyakarta (Indonesia): Universitas Sebelas Maret, Universitas Muhammadiyah Surakarta, and Universitas Negeri Yogyakarta. In order to be eligible as respondents, the students must be Muslim, know about *hallyu*, and know/consume at least one of Korean noodle brands (*Samyang*, *Nongshim* and *Ottogi*). The survey was executed from August 21st to 28th 2017. Among the returned questionnaires, 156 (97.50%) of them were completed.

The description indicated that there were 54.49% of female respondents and 45.51% of male. Among those numbers, 68.59% respondents were the consumers of Korean noodle from various brands (not limited to the mentioned brands). Furthermore, the majority of respondents (75.64%) knew that some of Korean noodle products contain pork DNA-fragment, while 16.67 % of them hesitate, and the remaining 7.69% did not know about the issue.

2.2. Instrument measurement

This study used exploratory factor analysis (EFA) and CFA. Attitude toward *hallyu* was measured by 8 items adapted from Suh, *et. al* (2016) ($\chi2 = 61.560$; P = .003; df 34; GFI .929; IFI .967; TLI .956; CFI .967)($\alpha = .911$). While severity of *halal* violation was operated by 3 items adjusted from Omar, *et. al* (2017) ($\alpha = .842$). Additionally, 4 items were used to measure boycott decision ($\chi2 = 6.781$; GFI = .979; IFI .969; TLI .0810; CFI .968), which was adopted and combined from Omar, *et. al* (2017) and Bruner (2009) ($\alpha = .848$). All questions were measured on Likert scale, ranging from 1 (strongly disagree) up to 5 (strongly agree).

3. Results

This study used linier regression for hypothesis 1. Given that this study used moderation, we performed hierarchical regression technique to analyse hypothesis 2. Detailed results were presented in table 1.

Table 1. Hierarchical regression analysis predicting boycott decisions

	S.E	t	R^2
Step 1			
Attitude Toward *Hallyu*	.072	-3.952***	.090
Step 2			
Severity of Violation	.060	3.194***	.147
Step 3			
Boycot Decision	.059	1.509	.160

Significant levels: α*** = .000

Table 1 depicted the regression result of hypothesis 1. As the study predicted, attitude toward *hallyu* negatively influenced the boycott decision ($\beta = -.280$; t = -3.90***). Hence the result supported our proposed hypothesis 1. Moreover, hypothesis 2, in which stated that severity of *halal* violation weaken the relationship between attitude toward *hallyu* and boycott decision on Korean noodle brand was not supported ($\beta = -.280$; t = -1.27). This finding was interesting, since individually, severities of *halal* violation have positive impact on boycott decision in step 2 of hierarchical regression.

4. Discussion

4.1. Influence of attitude toward hallyu on boycott decision

The study revealed that positive attitude toward *hallyu* decreased the tendency on boycott decision. According to Rice and Wongtada (2007), attitude and behaviour toward a brand could be the result of consumer's animosity or affinity toward certain country related to the brand. The result is strengthened by Shukla (2010) who stated that the greater the consumer's favourable image to a foreign brand, the bigger the consumer's willingness to buy that particular brand. Therefore, putting back to the case, positive attitude toward *hallyu* will hinder young Muslim consumers in Indonesia to boycott Korean related products—including noodle—despite *halal* violation involved some of the products.

4.2. Severity of halal violation as a moderating factor

The result shows that the severity of *halal* violation was not moderating the effect between attitude toward *hallyu* and boycott. Either severe or light violation, once youngsters were attracted to *hallyu*, they ignored the severity of *halal* violation of the products. It implies that consumer's favour to a brand could be very strong in which overwhelms other influences (Bandyopadhyay, et. al., 2011). The result is supported by Omar et. al (2017) who found that even though severity of *halal* violation is positively related to negative consumer behaviour (avoidance, boycott, and revenge), it does not successfully moderate the link between trust recovery and boycott.

In Indonesia, consumer's opinion on the severity of *halal* violation of Korean noodle products did not necessarily translate into ethical buying practices by boycotting the product. It seems that the fondness of young Muslim consumers to *hallyu* exceed the consumer's concern on *halal* violation.

Another possible explanation is that youngsters—the biggest internet user group—are well informed on *halal* issue. Accordingly, they recognized that only few of Korean noodle products available in the country were involved in *halal* violation (regardless their level of severity), leaving the the others free from *halal* violation. Additionally, they found out that marketing license of the importer along with its non-*halal* Korean noodle products has been withdrawn by *BPOM*. For this reason, consumers might feel that the incident was well-taken care of. This could give an assurance for young Muslim consumers for not undertaking boycott.

5. Conclusion

This research found some interesting findings to enrich literatures on *hallyu*, *halal*, and boycott related studies. Firstly, the more positive consumers' attitude toward *hallyu*, the lower is the tendency on boycott decision, regardless the existence of *halal* violation. Another important finding is that in Indonesia context, the severity of *halal* violation was not moderating the effect of attitude toward *hallyu* on boycott decision.

References

Amine, L. 2008. Country of Origin, Animosity, and Consumer Response: Marketing Implications of Anti-Americanism and Francophobia. *International Business Review*, vol. 17(4), pp. 402-422.

Bae, E. S, Chang, M., Park, E. S, and Kim, D. C. 2017. The Effect of Hallyu on Tourism in Korea. *Journal of Open Innovation: Technology, Market, and Complexity*, vol. 3(22).

Bandyopadhyay, S., Wongtada, N., and Rice, G. 2011. Measuring the Impact of Inter-Attitudinal Conflict on Consumer Evaluations of Foreign Products. *Journal of Consumer Marketing*, vol. 28(3), pp. 211-224.

Bruner, G.C. 2009. *Marketing Scales Handbook: A Compilation of Multi-Item Measures for Consumer Behaviour and Advertising Research*, vol. 5. Illinois: GCBII Productions.

Chen, Y.M., Su, Y. F., and Lin, F. J. 2011. Country-of-Origin Effects and Antecedents of Industrial Brand Equity. *Journal of Business Research*, vol. 64, pp. 1234-1238.

Chen, S. 2016. Cultural Technology: A Framework got Marketing Cultural Export-Analysis of Hallyu (the Korean Wave). *International Market Review*, vol. 33(1), pp. 25-50.

Guo, G and Zhou, X. 2017. Consumer Ethnocentrism on Product Judgement and Willingness to Buy: A Meta-Analysis. *Social Behavior and Personality*, vol. 45(1), pp. 163-176.

Gurhan-Canli, Z and Maheswaran, D. 2000. Determinants of Country-of-Origin Evaluations. *Journal of Consumer Research*, vol. 27(1), pp. 96-108.

Hess, R. L. 2008. The Impact of Firm Reputation and Failure Severity on Consumers' Responses to Service Failures. *Journal of Services Marketing*, vol. 22(5): pp. 385-398.

Hong, S and Kim, C. H. 2013. Surfing the Korean Wave: A Postcolonial Critique of the Mythologized Middlebrow Consumer Culture in Asia. *Qualitative Market Research: An International Journal*, vol. 16(1), pp. 53-75.

Huang, S. 2011. National-Branding and Transnational Consumption: Japan-Mania and The Korean Wave in Taiwan. *Media, Culture, and Society*, vol. 33(1), pp. 3-18.

Jang, G and Paik, W. K. 2012. Korean Wave as Tool for Korea's New Cultural Diplomacy. Advances in Applied Sociology, vol. 2(3), pp. 196-202.

Jang, Y. S., Ko, Y. J., and Kim, S. Y. 2016. Cultural Correlates of National Innovative Capacity: A Cross-National Analysis of National Culture and Innovation Rates. *Journal of Open Innovation: Technology, Market, and Complexity*, vol.2(23).

Jeon, G. C and Yoon, T. J. 2005. Realizing the Hallyu: An Asiatic Cultural Flow. *Korean Journal of Broadcasting*, vol. 19, pp. 66-86.

Lavorata, L. 2014. Influence of Retailers' Commitment to Sustainable Development on Store Image, Consumer Loyalty and Consumer Boycott: Proposal for A Model of Theory of Planned Behaviour. *Journal of Retailing and Consumer Services*, vol. 21(6), pp. 1021-1027.

Ministry of Finance. 2017. *RI Impor Mie Instan, Paling Banyak dari Korea dan China*. Retrieved 1 August 2017. Available at: www.scisi.co.id.

Oh, S. 2016. *Hallyu (Korean Wave) as Korea's Cultural Public Diplomacy in China and Japan*. Hangang Network Public Diplomacy Series 1: Korea's Public Diplomacy.

Omar, N. A, Zaenol Z, Thye, C. K., Nordin, N. Aand Nazri, M. A. 2017. Halal Violation Episode: Does Severity and Trust Recovery Impact Negative Behaviour? *Journal of Islamic Marketing*, vol. 8(4), pp. 686-710.

Omar, N. A., Nazri, M. A., Mohd-Ramly, S., and Zainol, Z. 2017. Does Physchological Contract Violation Moderate the Impact of Severity and Recovery Satisfaction on Boycott? An Analysis of Halal Violation. *Journal of Food Products Marketing*.

Pos Kota. 2017. *BPOM Bekukan Izin Importir Mie Korea Mengandung Babi*. Retrieved 1 August. 2017. Available at: http://poskotanews.com/2017/06/19/bpom-bekukan-izin-importir-mie-korea-mengandung-babi/.

Prasetya, C. 2017. *Tidak Berlabel Halal, MUI Magetan Boikot Mie Instan Impor Asal Korea Selatan*. Retrieved 1 August. 2017. Available at: https://nusantara.news/tidak-berlabel-halal-mui-magetan-boikot-mie-instan-impor-asal-korea-selatan/.

Saeno and Aldila, N. 2017. *Ini Empat Mie Korea, Termasuk Samyang, yang Mengandung Babi*. Retrieved 1 August 2017. Available at: pom.go.id.

Shukla, P. (2010). Impact of interpersonal influences, brand origin and brand image on luxury purchase intentions: Measuring interfunctional interactions and a cross-national comparison. *Journal of World Business*, vol. 46, pp: 489-499

Smith, M and Li, Q. 2010. The Boycott Model of Foreign Product Purchase: An Empirical test in China. *Asian Review of Accounting*, vol. 18(2): pp. 106-130.

Suh, Y., Hur, J., and Davies, G. 2016. Cultural Appropriation and The Country of Origin Effect. *Journal of Business Research*, vol. 69, pp: 2721-2730.

Rice, G and Wongtada, N. 2007. Conceptualizing inter-attitudinal conflict in consumer response to foreign brands. *Journal of International Consumer Marketing*, vol. 20(1), pp. 51-65.

Russel, D. W and Russel, C. A. 2006. Explicit and Implicit Catalysts of Consumer Resistence: The Effects of Animosity, Cultural Salience, and Country-of-Origin on Subsequent Choice. *International Journal of Research Marketing*, vol. 23, pp. 321-331.

Wang, C and Chen, Z. 2004. Consumer Ethnocentrism and Willingness to Buy Domestic Products in A Developing Country Setting: Testing Moderating Effects. *Journal of Consumer Marketing*, vol. 21(6), pp. 391-400.

Smartline to Identify Coastal Vulnerability at the North Pagai Island

Herdiana Mutmainah[1] and Aprizon Putra[1]
1 Researcher, Research Institute of Coastal Resources and Vulnerability, Agency of Research and Human Resources, Ministry of Marine Affairs and Fisheries

火山が多く地震・津波の多発地帯に位置するインドネシア。しかもその島しょ部の多くは地球温暖化による海面上昇に脅かされている。迫り来る危機に備え、災害時の被害を最小化するには何が必要か。北パガイ島を例に地域の脆弱性を検証した。

Abstract

Climate change and global warming have a negative impact on coastal, especially small islands. Abration and floods can be very dangerous and need response to minimize the disaster risks. A simple and practical method is needed to inform the location and type of coastal vulnerability and its risks along coastal segments. Smartline is a coastal management method that represents the geomorphology of coastal, hinterland and shoreline. The North Pagai is a small island, a part of the Mentawai Islands that located at the west offshore of Sumatra Island and one of the under developed areas in Indonesia. The island is surrounded by the Hindia Ocean and located on a subduction path of tectonic plate that prone to earthquakes and Tsunami. High rainfall, strong winds, the complexity of coastal morphology and also the density of coastal residents and limited infrastructure make the problems more complicated. Tsunami in 2010 (7.7 Mw) caused the change of shoreline getting worst on The East Coast of The North Pagai Island. This study aims to identify the coastal vulnerability using Smartline method. The research was conducted on April and September 2016. The result concludes that physical aspect shows Saumangaya and Matobe Village are at high and very high level of vulnerability while Sikakap Village at very high level. The socio-economic aspect shows that The Sikakap Village is more advanced but contrary more vulnerable to disaster in terms of population density and complex activities. The North Pagai Island is a vulnerable island from physical and socio-economic aspects.

Keywords Smartline; coastal vulnerability; The North Pagai Island

Introduction

Awareness raising on climate change, global warming and tsunami are increasingly encouraged especially for people living in coastal areas and small islands. Global warming and climate change have an impact on sea level rise and high precipitation with storms that cause abration and flooding on flat and sloping beaches. Assessment of coastal vulnerability is a challenge because of the complexity of problems such as physical, environmental, social and administrative conditions in coastal areas (Small and Nicholls, 2003).

A variety of methods were undertaken to identify and assess coastal vulnerability but are still not integrated. Coastal vulnerability is a coastal disaster-prone condition caused by interactions between beaches, ecosystems and humans towards physical processes that have negative impacts such as abration, intrusion, flooding, inundation and others (Linds and Muehe, 2011). Coastal vulnerability due to climate change affects the deterioration of coastal socio-economic and physical conditions, especially in the still-conventional areas (Dolan and Walker, 2004). Therefore a strategy to establish adaptive communities and capacities with coastal physical and socio-economic indicators that depend on institutional infrastructure and capacity (Adger et al., 2004) is needed. Climate change affects natural and human systems so that adaptation and mitigation of climate-causing factors (IPCC, 2001) is needed. Overall, coastal vulnerability is linked to coastal, ecosystem, and resident capacity to recover and adapt to these negative impacts (Linds and Muehe, 2011).

Both the government and the population need a simple, fast and precise method of obtaining location information, types and values of coastal vulnerability so that disaster risk can be minimized. Sharples (2006) introduced a method of coastal management approach called Smartline to rapidly identify the physical and socio-economic conditions of a coastal region along the coastline. Smartline is a form of information that represents geomorphological classification of hinterland, coastal and coastal areas.

Population growth and the density on the coast are directly and indirectly one of the causes of coastal vulnerability. Abration, flooding, sea water intrusion and pollution often occur in densely populated coastal areas due to inhospitable activity (Linds and Muehe, 2011). The condition of small islands prone to floods, abration, earthquake and tsunami with limited infrastructure make this island very vulnerable. This study aims to identify coastal vulnerability in North Pagai Island using Smartline method. Figure 1 shows the history of the earthquake and tsunami in the western waters of Sumatra and Figure 2 is the research location on the East Coast of North Pagai Island.

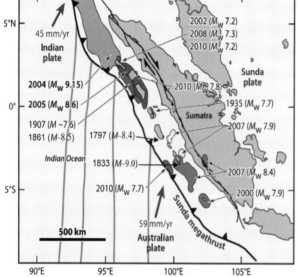

Figure 1. Map of Earthquake and Tsunami's History at West Sumatera Water.
(Source: Briggs et al. (2006), Konca et al. (2008), Shearer and Burgmann (2010), Hill et al. (2012), and Meltzner et al. (2015).

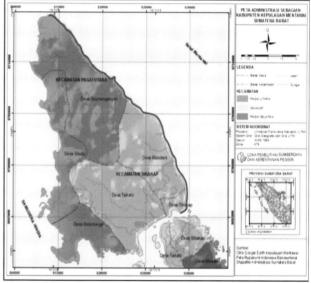

Figure 2. Research Location at The East Coast of The North Pagai Island.

Method

Research was conducted on April and September year 2016 at the East Coast of the North Pagai Island. Research method using on field survey and secondary data. All the data sources as written on Table 1 and analyse into numbers that shows the criterias of zoning area using Smartline method. Linds and Muehe (2011) made modification of Smartline methods from Sharples (2006) using spatial technical analysis by overlay the geospatial data based on gradation color of boundary shoreline in sequence. The research identify coastal physical and social economy aspect. The assessment of coastal physical aspect was using Coastal Vulnerabilty Index method, based on weighting or scoring on parameters of ranges of tides, the height of significant waves, changes of shoreline and the shoreline slope while area description describes about morphology, sand material and rocks formation. The aspect of social economy consists of population, occupation, fishery industry and distance of fresh water from shoreline. All the information and data then being classified according to the category of classes based on Smartline approach (Linds and Muehe, 2011) as shown on Table 2.

Table 1. Data Sources of Smartline.

No	Data	Map imagery and scale	Source
1	Landsat Imagery Map	7+ETM tahun 2006 OLI 8 Year 2016	http://earthexplorer.usgs.gov/
2	Map of RBI Page 0714	Scale 1:250.000	Bakosurtanal, Year 1986
3	Geology Map	Sheet of Pagai Sipora	PPPG ESDM, Year 1990
3	Data DEM Aster Gdem	http://srtm.csi.cgiar.org/SELECTION/listImages.asp	
4	Significant Waves Height	Study of BPSPL (Year 2015) and Analysis Result of RICRV (Year 2016)	
5	Groundtruth (GPS)	April and September Year 2016, Analysis Result of RICRV Year 2016	
6	Description of Location and parameters of vulnerable coastal	Quetionaire, secondary data and Analysis Result of RICRV (Year 2016) (April and September 2016)	

Table 2. Classification of Zoning Color based on Smartline Approach.

Very high	High	Fair High	Medium	Low	Fair Low	Very Low

The coordinates of location are marked using GPS. The observation points are 22 locations. The points determination is using purposive sampling method. Some points on hamlets were represented the condition of villages at the East Coast of the North Pagai Island. Interviews with residents and local government are conducted to determine the location of research both physic and social economic information of coastal communities. The geospatial and oceanography data were ranked according to their class with gradation color for physical aspect and the informations or data of coastal communities for socio- economic aspect based on field survey and support secondary data. Scoring or weighting to vulnerabel coastal parameters as shown on Table 3 and Equation 1 to calculate the Coastal Vulnerabilty Index (CVI). The rate of shoreline's change using ENVI method as shown in Equation 2. The scoring result of CVI been classified into 4 class, they are low, medium, high and very high (Table 4). The location of observation points using Smartline method at the East Coast of the North Pagai Island as shown on Figure 3.

Table 3. Parameters Criteria of Coastal Vulnerability Index (CVI).

Variabels	Weight (X)	Value of Parameters (W)				
		VL	L	M	H	VH
Changes of coastal line (m)	0,25	> 2,0 accretion	1,0 – 2,0 accretion	-1,0 – 1,0 Stabil	-1,0 – -2,0 abration	< -2,0 abration
Slope of beach (°)	0,35	>10	6 – 9,9	4 – 5,9	2 – 3,9	< 2
Height of significant wave (m)	0,29	<0.5	0,5 – 1	1 – 1,5	1,5 – 2	> 2
Tidal range (m)	0,11	<0.5	0,5 – 1	1 – 1,5	1,5 – 2	> 2

Source: Ramieri et al. (2011).
Notes: VL (Very Low), L (Low), M (Medium), H (High) and VH (Very High).

Table 4. Classification Level of Coastal Vulnerability Index (CVI).

$1 \leq CVI < 2$	$2 \leq CVI < 3$	$3 \leq CVI < 4$	$4 \leq CVI < 5$
Low	Medium	High	Very High

Source: (Doukakis, 2005.)

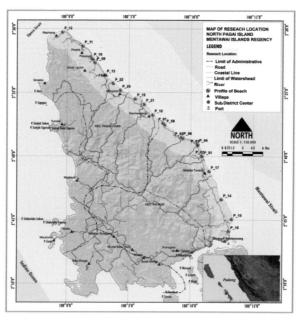

Figure 3. The Smartline's Observation Points at The East Coast of The North Pagai Island.

The parameters that used in Coastal Vulnerabilty Index as shown in this equation below.

$$IKP = \sum(w_1 \cdot x_1) + (w_2 \cdot x_2) + (w_3 \cdot x_3) + (w_4 \cdot x_4) \quad \text{...............} (1)$$

Annotation:

CVI = Coastal Vulnerability Index

w1 = Changes of shore line

w2 = Coastal slope

w3 = Significant waves

w4 = Tidal range

x1 = Weight of changes of coastal line

x2 = Weight of coastal slope

x3 = Weight of significant waves

x4 = Weight of tides (Ramieri et al., 2011).

Analysis of shoreline's changes is explained in this equation below using ENVI V4.5 (ENVI Classic help, 2008).

$$V = \frac{(N_2 - N_1)}{N_1} \times 100\% \quad \text{...............} (2)$$

Annotation:

V = The rate of shoreline's change (%);

N1 = Area of first Year (Ha);

N2 = Area of n Year (Ha).

Discussion: Coastal Physical Aspect

Coastal Line and Slope

The length of shoreline digitation shows that East Coast at year 2006 is ± 53 km and ± 51.5 km at year 2016. Refers to Equation 2, the change of shoreline is -4% and about 1.90 km. The abration area along The East Coast is 102.19 Ha, while the accretion is 19.82 Ha in The Saumangaya Village. The Saumanganya Village is the longest coastline that is 21.709 km whit slope is 1.1° at certain segments. Some hamlets at The Saumangaya Village that bordered to Mentawai Strait i.e Manganjo, Pasapuat and East Saumangaya being abration while area that bordered with Sipora Strait being accretion, i.e Mapinang, Pinairik and Mabulau Buggei. The length of coastline at The Matobe Village is 18.59 km with slope 1° at certain segments of shoreline. Two hamlets at The Matobe Village that is The Mangaungau Hamlet and The Matobe Hamlet being abration while The Polaga Hamlet being accretion. The hamlets at The Sikakap Village, i.e Sibaibai and East Sikakap being abration. Abration dominates along the East Coast in different degrees. Abration caused by the topography that is flat, slightly slope and black mud sand. Furthermore, the Tsunami year 2010 (7.7 Mw) also affected great changes of coastline at the East Coast. Table 5 and Table 6 below show the values of width and slope of coastline and also the coastal vulnerabel status of abration and accretion.

Table 5. The Slope of East Coast of the North Pagai Island.

Code	Hamlet	Coordinates °SL	Coordinates °EL	Height (m)	Width (m)	Slope (α)°
P1	Mangau-ngau	2.6667	100.1814	17.4	36.0	0.5
P2	Mangau-ngau	2.6659	100.1812	20.3	36.0	0.5
P3	Mangau-ngau	2.6518	100.1755	22.8	43.2	0.5
P4	Mangau-ngau	2.6507	100.1751	25.0	46.0	0.5
P5	Polaga	2.6420	100.1359	18.5	57.0	0.3
P6	Polaga	2.6416	100.1543	21.5	52.0	0.4
P7	Polaga	2.6230	100.1292	38.0	49.0	0.7
P8	Polaga	2.6255	100.1316	33.3	48.0	0.6
P9	Pasapuat	2.5439	100.0372	32.8	21.3	1.0
P10	Pasapuat	2.5385	100.0332	25.0	18.5	0.9
P11	Mabulau Buggei	2.5138	100.0090	22.2	12.5	1.1
P12	Mapinang	2.5040	99.9878	17.2	19.2	0.7
P13	Guluk-guluk	2.5603	100.0506	19.3	9.1	1.1
P14	Matobe Tunang	2.7231	100.2077	29.2	49.2	0.5
P15	Tapuraukat/East Sikakap	2.7488	100.2215	30.1	43.21	0.6
P16	Sibaibai	2.7646	100.2178	21.1	20.1	0.8
P17	Matobe Tunang	2.6864	100.1908	19.2	49.2	0.4
P18	East Saumanganya	2.6125	100.1152	19.1	54.2	0.3
P19	Manganjo	2.5915	100.0917	20.2	41.2	0.5
P20	Manganjo	2.5803	100.0717	21.5	38.2	0.5
P21	East Saumanganya	2.5985	100.1036	21.3	19.2	0.8
P22	Manganjo	2.5714	100.0617	20.8	18.8	0.8

Source: Field Survey, RICRV (2016).

Table 6. Segment Areas and Vulnerability Status of Coastline at East Coast of The North Pagai Island.

Code	Hamlet	Coordinates °SL	Coordinates °EL	Area of Coastal Segments (m²)	Average of area's changes (m²/tahun)	Status of Shoreline (2006 – 2016)
1	Mangau-ngau	2.6667	100.1814	36.81	3.7	Abration
2	Mangau-ngau	2.6659	100.1812	36.48	3.6	Abration
3	Mangau-ngau	2.6518	100.1755	43.82	4.4	Abration
4	Mangau-ngau	2.6507	100.1751	46.49	4.6	Abration
5	Polaga	2.6420	100.1359	2.92	0.3	Accretion
6	Polaga	2.6416	100.1543	0.19	0.01	Accretion
7	Polaga	2.6230	100.1292	28.06	2.8	Abration
8	Polaga	2.6255	100.1316	0.33	0.01	Accretion
9	Pasapuat	2.5439	100.0372	4.96	0.5	Accretion
10	Pasapuat	2.5385	100.0332	0.62	0.1	Accretion
11	Mabulau Buggei	2.5138	100.0090	7.17	0.7	Accretion
12	Mapinang	2.5040	99.9878	22.13	2.2	Abration
13	Guluk-guluk	2.5603	100.0506	0.32	0.01	Accretion
14	Matobe Tunang	2.7231	100.2077	63.73	6.4	Abration
15	Tapuraukat/East Sikakap	2.7488	100.2215	56.66	5.7	Abration
16	Sibaibai	2.7646	100.2178	21.18	2.1	Abration
17	Matobe Tunang	2.6864	100.1908	69.88	7.0	Abration
18	East Saumanganya	2.6125	100.1152	84.07	8.4	Abration
19	Manganjo	2.5915	100.0917	97.75	9.8	Abration
20	Manganjo	2.5803	100.0717	17.97	1.8	Accretion
21	East Saumanganya	2.5985	100.1036	85.03	8.5	Abration
22	Manganjo	2.5714	100.0617	8.87	0.9	Accretion

Source: Landsat 7+ETM Imagery Map Year 2006 and OLI 8 Imagery Map Year 2016.

Tidal Waves and Significant Waves

The tidal range along East Coast, between 1.2 m at southern, that covers Sibaibai and Sikakap until northern island that is Mapinang, Saumangaya at 1.697 m (CMCMR, 2015 and RICRV, 2016). The average height of significant waves at Sibaibai to Matobe Tunang about 0 – 0.4 m; Matobe Tunang to Saumangaya about 0.4 – 1.2 m; while at Pinairik to Mapinang (northern North Pagai Island) over than 0.72 m (CMCMR, 2015 and RICRV, 2016). Furthermore, it is shown at Figure 4.

The result analysis of CVI at East Coast of North Pagai Island as shown at Table 7. The East Coast is categorized in two vulnerabel area that is high vulnerability at southern to middle coast with CVI 3.2 – 3.45 and very high vulnerability at northern coast with CVI 4.2.

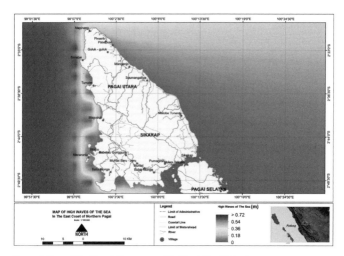

Figure 4. Map of Significant Waves around the North Pagai Island.

Table 7. Analysis of Coastal Vulnerability Index at the East Coast of The North Pagai Island.

No	Coordinates °SL	Coordinates °EL	Coastal change	Coastal Slope	Wave	Tides	W_1*X_1	W_2*X_2	W_3*X_3	W_4*X_4	CVI	Ket.
1	2.6667	100.1814	5	5	3	3	1.25	1.75	0.87	0.33	4.2	Very High
2	2.6659	100.1812	5	5	3	3	1.25	1.75	0.87	0.33	4.2	Very High
3	2.6518	100.1755	5	5	3	3	1.25	1.75	0.87	0.33	4.2	Very High
4	2.6507	100.1751	5	5	3	3	1.25	1.75	0.87	0.33	4.2	Very High
5	2.6420	100.1359	1	5	3	3	0.25	1.75	0.87	0.33	3.2	High
6	2.6416	100.1543	1	5	3	3	0.25	1.75	0.87	0.33	3.2	High
7	2.6230	100.1292	5	5	3	3	1.25	1.75	0.87	0.33	4.2	Very High
8	2.6255	100.1316	1	5	3	3	0.25	1.75	0.87	0.33	3.2	High
9	2.5439	100.0372	1	5	3	3	0.25	1.75	0.87	0.33	3.2	High
10	2.5385	100.0332	1	5	3	3	0.25	1.75	0.87	0.33	3.2	High
11	2.5138	100.0090	1	5	3	3	0.25	1.75	0.87	0.33	3.2	High
12	2.5040	99.9878	5	5	3	3	1.25	1.75	0.87	0.33	4.2	Very High
13	2.5603	100.0506	1	5	3	3	0.25	1.75	0.87	0.33	3.2	High
14	2.7231	100.2077	5	5	3	3	1.25	1.75	0.87	0.33	4.2	Very High
15	2.7488	100.2215	5	5	3	3	1.25	1.75	0.87	0.33	4.2	Very High
16	2.7646	100.2178	5	5	3	3	1.25	1.75	0.87	0.33	4.2	Very High
17	2.6864	100.1908	5	5	3	3	1.25	1.75	0.87	0.33	4.2	Very High
18	2.6125	100.1152	5	5	3	3	1.25	1.75	0.87	0.33	4.2	Very High
19	2.5915	100.0917	1	5	3	3	0.25	1.75	0.87	0.33	3.2	High
20	2.5915	100.0917	2	5	3	3	0.50	1.75	0.87	0.33	3.45	High
21	2.5803	100.0717	5	5	3	3	1.25	1.75	0.87	0.33	4.2	Very High
22	2.5985	100.1036	1	5	3	3	0.25	1.75	0.87	0.33	3.2	High

Source: Analysis Result (RICRV, 2016)

Sand Material

The sand at northern of the East Coast i.e Pinairik, Pasapuat until Manganjo, Saumangaya are dominated by reef and white sandy (Figure 5); black or grey sandy beach are spread from middle Saumanganya to south Matobe Tunang (Figure 6); while mud sand or estuaria generally are spread at southern island with mangrove combination are found in Matobe Tunang, East Sikakap and Sibaibai (Figure 7). Photos in Figures 5-7 were taken by Aprizon Putra.

Figure 5. White sand type on Pinairik Beach – Pasapuat.   Figure 6. Black/Grey sand type on Matobe Tunang Beach.   Figure 7. Muddy sand type on Sibaibai Beach – Sikakap.

Coastal Morphology

The morphology of the East Coast consists of 3 (three) forms i.e sandy rock that spread at northern island covers Mapinang Hamlet (Saumanganya Village); slopes lightly zone or flat dominated on East Sikakap Hamlet and Sibaibai Hamlet (Sikakap Village), while estuary zone covers the Matobe Tunang Hamlet (Matobe Village) as shown at Figure 8.

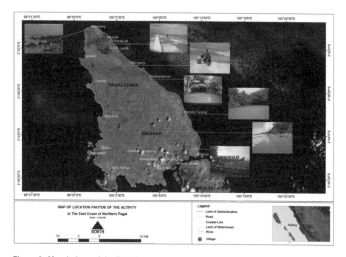

Figure 8. Morphology of the East Coast of The North Pagai Island.

Rock Formation

Based on geological conditions, refers to the geological map of Pagai and Sipora sheets year 1990 (Budhitrisna and Mangga, 1990) shows that the coastal area of the East Coast at the North Pagai island consists of 6 types of rocks i.e alluvium rock with clay, gravel and crust type; Coral limestone; Rock of simatobat formation with reef rock type; Maonai formation with sandstone rock type; and unexposed rocks with numulit rock type. Level of coastal vulnerability based on CVI or coastal physical aspect were mapped using Smartline as shown on Figure 9.

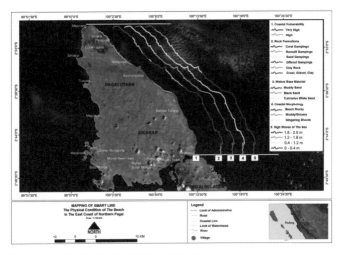

Figure 9. Smartline Map for Coastal Physical Aspect.

Discussion: Socio-Economic Aspect

The Sikakap Village (Sibaibai Hamlet and East Sikakap Hamlet)

The residents in the southern East Coast of North Pagai Island are located in Sikakap Village, they are Sibaibai Hamlet and East Sikakap Hamlet. Based on field surveys, the settlement on site is about 10 m from the shoreline with a total population of 1,699 inhabitants (SCB, 2015). The distance of fresh water's sources for consumption is about 10 to 30 m from shoreline. The occupation of the local residents are fishermen, farmers, cattlemen, local government employees and trades. The fishery business become their livelihood in different kind i.e the traditional and modern capture, the salted processing and also the shore and freshwater fish cultivation. This village is the most densely populated area in the North Pagai Island. Fishery business is indicated by the existence of fishermen's cooperative and individual fishery business from some residents. Fishing business in this village is prioritizing commodities of lobster, sea cucumbers, grouper, fish cultivation, rental of fishing vessels and fish cages.

The Saumangaya Village (Mapinang Hamlet, Pinairik Hamlet and Pasapuat Hamlet)

The northern part of the East Coast that is Saumangaya Village actually has 7 (seven) hamlets, but due to limit of time and surveyors/persons, the social economic survey only can be done on 3 (three) hamlets i.e Mapinang Hamlet, Pinairik Hamlet and Pasapuat Hamlet. The population of Mapinang Hamlet is 201 people, Pinairik Hamlet is 119 and Pasapuat Hamlet is 530 people (SCB, 2015). The occupation of residents in those three hamlets are mostly on the land i.e farming and cattlemen. The location of hamlets is bordered by two big straits, that is the Sipora Strait and the Mentawai Strait and also on the track of collision of tectonic plates (Eurasia plate and India-Australia plate) so vulnerable to wind, waves and Tsunami. Some residents still doing fishing with traditional equipment on nearby coastal waters (less than 200 m), especially in Mapinang Hamlet. Pasapuat Hamlet is the worst location due to the Tsunami at year 2010 in the entire of The East Coast at North Pagai Island. The distance of fresh water for consumption is about 10 m from the shoreline.

The Matobe Village (Polaga Hamlet, Matobe Tunang Hamlet and Mangaungau Hamlet)

The availability of fresh water's source on the central part of The East Coast is about 1 to 2 km from the shoreline. Matobe Village has three coastal Hamlets: Polaga Hamlet, Mangaungau Hamlet and Matobe Tunang Hamlet. Due to the considerable freshwater distance, local people use pipes for the distribution of water from hills or mountains. The occupation of the residents are such as fishermen, local government employees, farmers and cattlemen. The total population of this village is 641 people (SCB, 2015). There are several small fishery businesses owned by individuals or groups of fishermen. The main commodities are grouper and lobster. The socio-economic aspect of The East Coast then mapped using Smartline as shown in Figure 10 below.

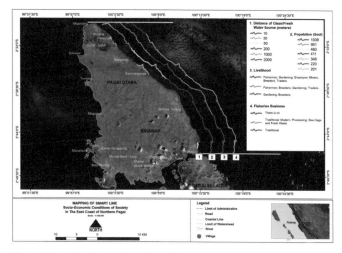

Figure 10. Smartline Map for Socio-Economic Aspect.

Conclusion

The result of physical aspect shows that The East Coast of North Pagai Island has 2 (two) vulnerability categories that is very high and high. On the north and middle side of the eastern coastal, the vulnerabilty index of The Saumangaya and The Matobe Village is high and very high (CVI 3.2 – 3.45 and 4.2) while in the southern coastal, The Sikakap Village is very high vulnerability (CVI 4.2) especially in abration. Coastal materials are generally divided into 2 (two) types, that is white sand on northern to middle side, while black mud sand on the some of middle to southern side. The coastal slope ranges from 0.3e to 1.1°. Narrow and sloping beaches are commonly found in Polaga Hamlet and Pasapuat Hamlet. The longest shoreline is in Saumangaya Village. Based on the socio-economic aspect, The Sikakap Village is more advanced but contrary more vulnerable to disaster in terms of population density and complex activities. The condition of some narrow beaches, subduction plate, open beach, black mud sand and the dense population make The East Coast prone to Tsunami, abration and flooding. The North Pagai Island is a vulnerable island from physical and socio-economic aspects.

References

1) Adger WN, Brooks N, Bentham G, Agnew M, Eriksen S. 2004. New indicators of vulnerability and adaptive capacity. Tyndall Centre for Climate Change Research (Technical Report 7: Final Project Report). 122p.

2) Briggs, R.W., Sieh, K., Meltzner, A.J., Natawidjaja, D., Galetzka, J., Suwargadi, B., Hsu, Y.-j, Simons, M., Hananto, N., Suprihanto, I., Prayudi, D., Avouac, J.-P., Prawirodirdjo, L., Bock, Y., 2006. Deformation and slip along the Sunda mega-thrust in The Great 2005 Nias-Simeulue Earthquake. Science 311, 1897-1901.

3) Budhitrisna, T. and S. Andi Mangga. 1990. Geology of the Pagai and Sipora quadrangle, Sumatra. Research Center and Development of Geology. Bandung, pp.1-21.

4) Dolan A., and Walker I.J. 2004. Understanding vulnerability of coastal communities to climate change related risks. J Coast Res Spec Iss Brasilia, 39.

5) Doukakis, E. Coastal Vulnerability and Risk Parameters. European Water 11/12: 3-7. 2005.

6) ENVI. Exelis Visual Information Solution Classic Help, 2008. ENVI Classic Tutorial. Classfication Method.

7) Herdiana Mutmainah, Rizki Anggoro Adi, Aprizon Putra, Try Altanto, Ulung Jantama Wisha, Whisnu Arya Gumilang, Ilham Adnan, Mugiyanto, Prima Sahputra and Ilham Tanjung. Final Report of Coastal Resources and Vulnerability Research at North Pagai Island Year 2016. 2016. Research Institute of Coastal Resources and Vulnerability. Padang. West Sumatera.

8) Hill, E.M., Borrero, J.C., Huang, Z., Qiu, Q., Banerjee, P., Natawidjaja, D.H., Elosegui, P., Fritz, H.M., Suwargadi, B.W., Pranantyo, I.R., Li, L., Macpherson, K.A., Skanavis, V., Synolakis, C.E., Sieh, K., 2012. The 2010 MW 7.8 Mentawai Earthquake: Very Shallow Source of A Rare Tsunami Earthquake Determined from Tsunami Field Survey and Near-Field GPS Data. J. Geophys. Res. 117, B06402. http://dx.doi.org/10.1029/2012JB009159. http://dx.doi.org/10.1126/science.1122602.

9) http://www.ipwea.org.au/Content/NavigationMenu/SIGS/ClimateChange/ConferencePapers/default.htm#Top.

10) IPCC. 2001. Summary for Policymakers. Climate Change 2001: Synthesis Report. An Assessment of the Intergovernmental Panel on Climate Change. http://www.ipcc.ch/pdf/climate-changes-2001/synthesis-spm/synthesis-spm-en.pdf.

11) Konca, A.O., Avouac, J.-P., Sladen, A., Meltzner, A.J., Sieh, K., Fang, P., Li, Z., Galetzka, J., Genrich, J., Chlieh, M., Natawidjaja, D.H., Bock, Y., Fielding, E.J., Ji, C., Helmberger, D.V., 2008. Partial Rupture of a Locked Patch of The Sumatra Megathrust During The 2007. Earthquake sequence. Nature 456, 631 - 635. http://dx.doi.org/10.1038/nature.07572.

12) Linds de Baros FM and Muehe Dieter. 2011. The smartline approach to coastal vulnerability and social risk assesment applied to a segment of the east coast of Rio de Janeiro State, Brazil. ©Springer Science+Business Media B.V.2011.

13) Natawidjaja, D.H. 2011. Geomagz. 2011. Vol. I No.4. Desember 2011. ISSN2088-7906. Geology Agency of Ministry of Energy and Minerale Resources of Republic Indonesia. Bandung. p.30:112.

14) Pagai Sipora Sheet. 1990. PPPG. Ministry of Energy and Minerale Resources of Republic Indonesia.

15) President Regulation of Republic Indonesia No.131 Year 2015 about Decision of Under Developed Area in Indonesia Year 2015-2019. http://jdih.bpk.go.id/wp-content/uploads/2012/03/Perpres-Nomor-131-Tahun-2015.pdf. Accesed on 7 March 2016.

16) Ramieri, E., Hartley, A., Barbanti, A., Santos, F.D., Laihonen, P., Marinova, N. and Santini, M. 2011. Methods for Assessing Coastal Vulnerability to Climate Change. ETCCCA Background Paper. European Environment Agency, Copenhagen.

17) RBI Map Sheet Number 0714. Scale 1:250.000. 1986. Bakosurtanal.

18) Sharples C, Attwater C, Carlery J. 2008. Three pass approach to coastal risk assessment. Paper presented at National Conference Responding to Sea Level Rise". Institute of Public Works Engineering Australia, Coffs Harbour, New South Wales, August 2008. http://www.ipwea.org/sustainability/librarydocuments/library/conferencepapers.

19) Sharples C. 2006. Indicative mapping of Tasmanian coastal geomorphic vulnerability to sea level rise using GIS line map of coastal geomorphic attributes. In: Woodroffe CD, Bruce EM, Puotinen M (eds) Wollongong Paperson Maritime Policy. No.16 pp: 235-247.

20) Shearer, P., Bürgmann, R., 2010. Lessons learned from the 2004 Sumatra Andaman megathrust rupture. Annu. Rev. Earth Planet. Sci. 38, 103-131. http://dx.doi.org/10.1146/annurev-earth-040809-152537

21) Small C, and Nicholls RJ. 2003. A global analysis of human settlement in coastal zones. J Coast Res, Fla 19(3): 584-599.

22) Statistic Center Beaureu (SCB) of Mentawai Islands Regency. 2016. Mentawai Islands in Number 2016. Tuapeijat. The Mentawai Islands Regency.

23) Statistic Center Beaureu (SCB) of North Pagai District. 2015. North Pagai District in Number 2015. The Saumangaya. The North Pagai District.

24) Statistic Center Beaureu (SCB) of Sikakap District. 2015. Sikakap District in Number 2015. The Sikakap. The Sikakap District.

25) Supporting Document for the Preparation of Zoning Plan of Coastal and Small Islands (SDPZPCSI) of West Sumatera Province in Mentawai Islands Regency Year 2015. 2015. Central Management of Coastal and Marine Resources, Ministry of Marine Affairs and Fisheries (CMCMR, MMAF). Padang. West Sumatera.

26) The CGIAR Consortium for Spatial Information. 2016. Accesed 3rd November 2016 from http://srtm.csi.cgiar.org/SELECTION/listImages.asp.

27) USGS Science for a Changing World. 2016. Accesed 3rd November 2016 from: http://earthexplorer.usgs.gov/.

28) Wahyudi, T. Hariyanto, and Suntoyo. 2009. Analysis of Coastal Vulnerability at North Java's Coastal. Prossiding. National Seminar of Theory and Application. 2009. Surabaya. Semarang Technology Institut.

Familial Relationship of 4Ps Beneficiaries in Bay, Laguna, Philippines

Thessalonica Soriano Manguiat[1]
1 Instructor, College of Industrial Technology, Laguna State Polytechnic University San Pablo City Campus

フィリピン政府の貧困層向け現金給付プログラム「4Ps」は健全な家族生活と児童教育の維持を目標の1つに掲げる。その成果が上がっているかどうかを、現地での聞き取り調査やフォーカス・グループ・ディスカッションで検証した。

Abstract

The preservation of the family lies not only with the relationship of husband and wife, but also with the relationship of parents to their children. The Family Development Session (FDS) of Pantawid Pamilyang Pilipino Program (4Ps) aims to promote positive family values, strengthen marital relationships and parental roles and responsibilities. Thus, the study aimed to analyze the changes on the familial relationship of 4Ps beneficiaries brought about by FDS. It utilized a descriptive design and both quantitative and qualitative analyses were used. Simple random sampling procedure was applied to select eighty-four respondents who were 4Ps parent beneficiaries in Bay, Laguna, Philippines. The use of questionnaire and Focus Group Discussion were employed to gather data on the respondent's attitude and practices on marital and parental relationship. Findings show that the parent beneficiaries were able to apply parental relationship lessons more than the marital relationship lessons. The parent beneficiaries improved their parental relationship, thus positively affecting the children's behavior. Likewise, they became more responsible and sensitive to the needs of their children. It is recommended that other interventions for parents such as marital relationship development might be needed. Family life educators are suggested to design curricula that focus more on relationship enrichment of the family.

Keywords Pantawid Pamilyang Pilipino Program, Family Development Session, marital relationship, parental relationship

Introduction

The family is a person's first social encounter. It is an environment where a person's attitude, character and dignity are molded. Basic human needs such as food, shelter, security and a sense of belongingness are obtained in the family. As the building block of society, the family must be solid and strong (Medina, 2001). Fostering harmonious family relationships will not only strengthen and increase unity in the family, but also enhance societal functioning.

A harmonious family involves couples with a high level of marital satisfaction. However, martial relationship between couples is affected by various factors such as socioeconomic status, educational attainment, mental and physical health, values and beliefs (del Mar Sanchez-Fuentes, Santos-Iglesias, & Sierra, 2014). Thus, developing a satisfying marital relationship is a challenging task for them. On the other hand, the preservation of the family lies not only with the relationship of husband and wife, but also with the relationship of parents to their children. The parent-child relationship is a unique type of relationship because of its nature and the level of intimacy involved (Troll & Fingerman, 1996). The quality of parent-child relationship in the family may cause direct and indirect effects to children (Easterbrooks & Emde, 1988). Parents, being the role model of the children, convey positive or negative messages which predict the behaviour and interaction of children (Bandura, 1978). The study of Erel and Burman (1995) states that the quality of parent-child relationship is affected by the quality of marital relationship. These two relationships will then affect the children's character and behaviour.

Patterned from the conditional cash transfer (CCT) programs in Latin American countries, the Philippine government launched the *Pantawid Pamilyang Pilipino* Program, commonly known as 4Ps, in 2007. The Family Development Session (FDS) of 4Ps is being considered as an essential component of the program to capacitate and empower the human capital of families. This unique feature of 4Ps covers a wide range of topics to enhance the family life of the beneficiaries. It includes husband-wife relationship, child-parent relationship, financial and home management, and positive parenting. The objectives of FDS are the following: a) to empower the household beneficiaries to become more productive and responsible to meet family needs; b) to enhance the skills and knowledge of household beneficiaries, promote positive family values, strengthen marital relationships & parental roles and responsibilities, particularly on the health, nutrition and education needs of children; and c) to promote social awareness, participation and involvement in community development efforts (International Labor Organization [ILO], 2016). Specifically, the second module of FDS aims to educate parents to be responsible in meeting the family's needs on health, nutrition and education of children. Moreover, it promotes good family relationships and practical home management practices.

The study sought to investigate and examine the changes happened in the marital and parental relationship of the parent beneficiaries and its effect on children's behavior. Its objective is to examine the knowledge, attitude and practices of 4Ps parent beneficiaries on marital and parental relationship brought about by the FDS component of 4Ps.

The 4Ps has a dual objective: social assistance (financial support) and social development. The FDS helps in the attainment of the second objective of the program which aims to break the intergenerational poverty cycle through investments in human capital. Aside from providing trainings on financial literacy, life skills, livelihood skills and community development activities, FDS has a strong approach on values formation emphasizing good husband-wife relationship and positive child discipline. Moreover, through FDS, the parents are expected to have a positive outlook in life, boost their children's morale, and uplift their living status. It is also foreseen that their dependence on the support from the government will soon lead to independence. However, the vision of 4Ps to produce empowered and independent families has yet to be determined. The effectiveness of FDS to household beneficiaries has not been further examined, thus, the study sought to answer the following questions:

a) What are the respondents' attitude and practices on marital and parental relationships?

b) Are there changes on attitudes and practices of 4Ps beneficiaries in terms of the marital and parental relationships before and after becoming a 4Ps member?

c) Is there a relationship among marital relationship, parental relationship and children's behaviour as perceived by their parents?

Methodology

The study utilized a descriptive research design and a mixed method of both quantitative and qualitative analyses was used to examine the knowledge, attitude and practices of the parent beneficiaries. They were all recipients of the program starting from year 2010-2012, have at least two (2) children and were all active attendees of Family Development Session (FDS) of 4Ps. They were selected from the complete list of Set 3 (year 2010-2012) family beneficiaries of 4Ps provided by the municipal link of Bay Pantawid Pamilya Office. The respondents from the list were situated in six (6) towns of Bay: Bitin, Dila, Maitim, San Nicolas Poblacion, St. Domingo, and Sta. Cruz. A simple random sampling procedure was used to select the participants. A total of eighty-four (84) respondents were determined.

The study developed and used a survey questionnaire. The questionnaire was based from the Family Development Session Module. The topics from the second module, *Preparing and Nurturing the Filipino Family*, were used to come up with statements in the questionnaire, specifically on Sub-Module 2.1: Preparing for Family Life: Topic 1 – Equal Treatment between

Husband and Wife and Topic 2 – Good Relationship of Parents and Children. Prior to the conduct of the survey interview, preliminary coordination was done through the respective chairmen of the six identified towns. Letters were sent to ask assistance in identifying the home address of the 4Ps beneficiaries from the list. Upon identifying the location of the households, survey interview was employed. After the household survey, Focus Group Discussion (FGD) was conducted to collect more data on the changes, situations and issues that occurred in the family as a result of attending the FDS. Ten (10) participants were invited to join the discussion. The whole discussion was recorded to capture all the answers of the participants.

The statistical mean, percentage, and standard deviation were used to analyze the attitude and practices of marital and parental relationship of the respondents. Moreover, Wilcoxon Signed-Rank Test was used to examine the difference on the scores of the respondents' attitude and practices between "Before 4Ps" and "Now in 4Ps".

Findings

Marital Relationship Attitude

Table 1 shows the marital attitude of the respondents Before 4Ps and After 4Ps and the result was positive. With the highest mean score of 4.96 (SD=0.52), the respondents proved that they desire to make their spouses happy by willingly serving them. Since majority of the respondents are wives, the typical Filipino attitude among women where the wife serves the husbands is observed. This attitude is a form of spousal support where the wife caters to the needs of the husband. According to Miller et.al (2003), spouses that express positive attitude and emotions to each other will likely display positive behaviour in the future which may increase marital satisfaction. Thus, high level of marital satisfaction positively affects the life satisfaction of an individual, as well as the attitude and behaviour of children (Erel & Burman, 1995).

Table 1. Marital Relationship Attitude

	(B4P) Before 4Ps		(A4P) After 4Ps	
	Mean	Std. Dev.	Mean	Std. Dev.
1. I like to respect my spouse's decision even I do not agree with it.	3.54	1.61	3.83	1.520
2. I like listening to the stories of my spouse.	4.58	0.84	4.74	0.696
3. I like to settle our disagreement/ misunderstanding/ conflict immediately.	4.67	0.88	4.79	0.641
4. I like to make my spouse happy by simply serving him/her wholeheartedly.	**4.89**	**0.19**	4.96	**0.515**
5. I like to understand my spouse every time he/she is tired and cannot fulfill his/her responsibilities.	4.45	1.06	4.52	0.950

The results were also confirmed in the focus group discussion. The respondents expressed that they desire to attend to the needs of their spouses more and stated that conflicts between them lessened. Moreover, the assurance given by the cash grant for the health and education of the children prevented couple disagreements and negative confrontations due to financial limitations.

On the other hand, the respondents got the lowest mean score on AP4 of 3.54 (SD=1.61) with regards to giving respect to spouse's decision. According to the respondents' FGD, decision making in the family should be done mutually by husband and wife. They pointed out that decision making is crucial and making poor decisions in the family will affect the children. Mutual decision making between husband and wife is an essential part of marital communication. Supporting each other's decisions cultivate positive and intimate relationship. However, unsupportive attitude results to marital conflicts which will lead to marital dissatisfaction (Bagarozzi, 1990).

Parental Relationship Attitude

The statements on parental attitude in Table 2 show the mean scores and standard deviation on B4P and A4P. The respondents acknowledged the importance of a correct approach to their children's weaknesses and mistakes as they play the role of a discipline guide (M=4.81; SD=0.63). This means that the respondents' attitude in guiding their children shows the level of involvement they have in their children's lives. This is important especially in the formative years of the children as well as the adolescent years. According to Gould & Mazzeo (1982), children in early adolescence become more concerned about themselves and their peers. They often seek comfort and advice from their friends rather than their parents. Thus, continuous parental guidance is vital to lead them to right choices and decisions.

Table 2. Parental Relationship Attitude

	(B4P) Before 4Ps		(A4P) After 4Ps	
	Mean	Std. Dev.	Mean	Std. Dev.
1. I like to understand my children's weaknesses and mistakes and help them to correct it.	4.81	0.63	4.90	0.37
2. When in an argument with my child, I like to think first the words I will use before I speak.	4.27	1.17	4.52	0.95
3. I like to understand that each of my children has a unique way of expressing themselves.	4.18	1.33	4.42	1.17
4. I like to give careful thought of my actions and speech because I recognize that my children look at me as a good example in speech and in action.	4.58	0.99	4.70	0.94
5. I like listening to my children's stories.	4.77	0.608	4.83	0.598

On the other hand, the respondents were challenged to understand their children's unique way of expressing themselves. During infancy to early childhood, parents-child relationship is characterized by high level of quality time with strong emotional and physical bond with the parents (Collins & Russel, 1991). However, in the early adolescent stage, children begin to spend more time with their peers. Parents are not the only source of influence to their children because they are more immersed with the influence of peers and other external factors in the family. These influences make it difficult for parents to reach out to their children because they adapt behaviours from their peers. Therefore, children are likely to distant themselves, physically and emotionally, to their parents which affects the family cohesion and closeness (Larson & Richards, 1991).

Moreover, the high result of the knowledge test in parent-child relationship also confirms the positive attitude of parent beneficiaries' towards parent-child relationship. This may be also due to the knowledge gained not only from FDS but from other sources. The parent beneficiaries proved that they maintained a positive attitude towards parent-child relationship even before they became 4Ps beneficiaries.

Marital Relationship Practices

Table 3 below shows the statements on marital relationship practices that shows the respondents' highest mean score of 4.85 (SD=0.48) on Item no. 4 which means that the respondents were used to giving words of affirmation to their spouses.

Table 3. Marital Relationship Practices

	Before 4Ps		After 4Ps	
	Mean	Std. Dev.	Mean	Std. Dev.
1. I often express my affection to my spouse by kissing and hugging him/her.	4.46	1.01	4.08	1.45
2. I listen to my spouse with respect and not use hurtful words whenever we are in conflict.	3.80	1.18	3.95	1.18
3. I often apologize to my spouse whenever I hurt him/her with my words or actions.	4.07	1.35	4.25	1.36
4. I praise my spouse every time he/she is pleasant and did a good thing.	**4.85**	**0.48**	**4.77**	**0.78**
5. I give ample time to my spouse to maintain our good relationship.	4.50	0.98	4.43	1.12

The respondents, even in their poverty situation, still managed to praise their spouses for the good behaviour they show. This practice also reflects their positive and affectionate attitude towards their spouses. Marital satisfaction, according to Bohlander (1999), is the degree of how a spouse perceives their partner in meeting their needs and desires. It is the couple's ability to understand, accept and appreciate each other's actions, thoughts, feelings and emotions. Appreciation of spouse is a form of positive marriage interaction because it builds positive interpersonal relationship between husband and wife. Gottman (1994) studied that in order to attain marital satisfaction, there must be five positive interaction in every one negative interaction. Thus, every appreciation and positive affirmation of the respondents to their spouse cultivates positive communication in their marital relationship.

However, the respondents got the lowest mean score of 3.80 (SD=1.18) on Item no.2 which means that at times, they used hurtful words and did not listen to their spouse when in conflict. This negative communication in marriage usually arises due to great criticism, defensiveness, contempt and stonewalling (Gottman, 1994). These behaviours, accompanied by blame, disappointments and frustrations, greatly affect the marital satisfaction, thus affect the overall functioning of the family. This is one of the struggles the respondents stated in the group discussion. The knowledge they gained from FDS were easy to apply to their children but difficult to apply to their spouses. According to the respondents, some of the factors that hindered them to compromise with their spouses when in conflict were pride and lack of self-control.

Due to the knowledge acquired by the women respondents from FDS, they became knowledgeable of their rights, rights of their children and the laws that protect them. This caused them to have a stronger character and lifted their self-worth as the house keeper of the family. These changes within the women respondents seemed to have an effect on their role performance in the family. They have become better nurturers and protectors of their children and they have become empowered as women and wives.

Parental Relationship Practices

Table 4 shows that the respondents got the highest mean score of 4.96 (SD=0.19) on Item no. 10 which shows that they were able to guide their children whenever they commit mistakes and encourage them whenever they have problem. The parent beneficiaries practice parental guidance to their children's emotional welfare by helping them cope up with their mistakes and explaining to them the pros and cons of their behaviours. This is a primary responsibility of parents to build up their children especially those who are in their teenage years.

The study of Simmons & Blyth (1987) stated that early adolescent children spend more time of unsupervised interactions with friends than in their early years, especially when they are in school. With that, proper guidance from parents is necessary to lead them on how to deal with life, make sound decisions and have right perspective on things.

Table 4. Parental Relationship Practices

	Before 4Ps		After 4Ps	
	Mean	Std. Dev.	Mean	Std. Dev.
6. I often express my affection to my children by kissing and hugging them.	4.71	0.72	4.56	1.05
7. I calmly talk to my children and I do not use hurtful words whenever I reprimand them.	3.98	1.14	4.23	1.13
8. In an argument, I listen carefully and respect my children's feelings/opinion.	4.36	1.06	4.52	0.99
9. I often encourage my children whenever they are feeling down or have a problem.	4.77	0.63	4.88	0.52
10. I explain consequences of my children's action properly whenever they commit mistakes.	**4.87**	**0.37**	**4.96**	**0.19**

Moreover, the respondents always encourage their children whenever they are feeling down or have a problem (M=4.88; SD=0.52) as stated in Item no. 9. The respondents take the roles of cheerleader and mood-lifter which are forms of positive parent-child communication. This interaction provides foundation for children, specifically those who are in the early adolescent stage, to learn and be sensitive of their emotions, thus the parents help develop their children's skills to succeed in life (Dawson & Ashman, 2000). Children's emotional being must be guided well for the establishment of their coping abilities and problem-solving skills.

On the other hand, the respondents were challenged to talk to their children calmly and not use hurtful words whenever they reprimand them (M=3.98; SD=1.14). Yelling, as a form of both anger and discipline to children, are shown when parents are highly stressed and experiencing difficulty in life. According to Ayoub et.al (2009), this a kind of negative parenting approach greatly affects children's language, cognitive, social and emotional well-being and development. This parental behaviour, if not changed, may lead long-term effects to children such as anxiety, self-pity, low self-esteem, and violence.

The result also confirms the obtained high scores in parental knowledge questions. The findings also proved that the parent-child relationship knowledge gained by the respondents from the FDS topics was applied to their children. According to the respondents' focus group discussion (FGD), they were able to apply the lessons from FDS to their children immediately. Applying the parental lessons made the respondents increase their sense of responsibility. In addition, having awareness of the rights of the children, the respondents became more sensitive with the needs of their children and in return, their children became more attached to them.

Attitude and Practices on Marital and Parental Relationship

The Wilcoxon Signed-Ranks Test on Table 5 indicates that the scores between B4P and A4P of marital relationship attitude and parental relationship practices were significantly different, while the scores between B4P and A4P of parental attitude and marital practices remained the same. This means that in terms of attitude, marital relationship was improved while parental relationship remained the same. However, in terms of practices, parental relationship was improved, while marital relationship remained the same. The findings show that even though the marital attitude of the respondents was improved, it doesn't follow that their marital practices will improve as well. Moreover, the parental attitude of the respondents remained the same but has improved their practices. This may due to the culture of Filipino which values the children greatly. Filipino parents are focused on parenthood and parenting skills, not only because the children bear the name of the family, but because it is expected for them to raise their children well and in return the children will take care of their parents when they get old (Go, 1993).

Table 5. Attitude and Practices on Marital and Parental Relationship

	Attitude			Practices		
	Z	p value	Interpretation	Z	p value	Interpretation
Marital Relationship	324.5	<0.020	With significant difference	48.5,	<0.829	With no significant difference
Parental Relationship	17	<0.167	With no significant difference	28	<0.011	With significant difference

Relationship between Children's Behaviour and Practices on Parental Relationship

Table 6 shows that children's common behaviour has a significant positive linear relationship with parental relationship practices (r_s=-0.387, p=0.000). The results show that the more positive the common behaviour of children such as politeness, being affectionate, confident and knows how to listen, the more favourable the respondents' parental relationship practices. Parents, who experience affection from their children and observe improvement in their behaviour, lessen the stress they are experiencing (Odgers et. al, 2012). Through FDS, parent's improved their practices on parenting which positively affects the children's behaviour. The results confirm the study of Joussemet, Mageau, and Koestner (2014) which stated that parent education has been shown to increase positive parenting skill, while Gardner, Burton, and Klimes (2006) observed that parent education help reduce child conduct problems. As the parents changed for the better, the children also developed positively.

Table 6. Parental Practices and Children's Behavior

Variable	Correlation Coefficient	Sig. (2-tailed)
Parental Relationship Practices & Children's common behavior	.387**	.000
Parental Relationship Practices & Children's behavior (home mgt)	.347**	.001

*. Correlation is significant at the 0.05 level (2-tailed).
**. Correlation is significant at the 0.01 level (2-tailed).

Children's common behaviour such as giving respect to elders, expressing themselves properly and accepting correction from parents are influenced by how their parents conduct themselves at home and how they relate to their children. Moreover, it also shows that there is a significant positive linear relationship on children's behaviour towards home management and parental relationship practices, (r_s=-0.347, p=0.001). The findings show that the more positive the behaviour of children towards home management, the higher the parental relationship practices. This supports the results on children's common behaviour wherein children's behaviour are affected by parental relationship practices. This means that a good relationship between parent and child will have an effect on child's behaviour. Children's behaviour on personal care, sibling care, household assignments, time management and wise decision making on money are greatly influenced on how the parent beneficiaries interact with their children. As the social learning theory suggests, children model the behaviour of their parents (Bandura, 1978). Witnessing positive attitude and behaviour towards home management may produce similar behaviour in children. Thus, positive home management of parents will result to positive behaviour of children towards home management.

Conclusion

The 4Ps parent beneficiaries' high scores in knowledge on parental relationship resulted to improved practices, while their attitude remained positive. The result is an indication that the respondents were able to apply the lessons of Family Development Session on those said topics. This means that parent beneficiaries were able to apply parental relationship lessons than the lessons on marital relationship. The result is an indication that the lessons on the latter are inadequate. Factors that hindered improvement of marital relationship were limited marital relationship lessons in FDS and empowerment of women causing them to assert their rights. Women respondents were educated and empowered through FDS, thus, making them more knowledgeable on children and household management. Most men were not able to attend FDS because they are the ones working for the family. As a result, it has become the housewives' role to decide for the family because as they stated, their husbands do not know much about how their family runs as they are already preoccupied with working.

Lastly, the parent beneficiaries have improved their parental relationship, thus affecting their children's behaviour. They have become more sensitive in communicating with their children such as avoiding the use of bad words and shouting. As a result, the children's interactions with their parents improved, and good quality relationship between parent and child also developed. The parent beneficiaries became more responsible and sensitive to the needs of their children, especially to the needs of their children in school.

Recommendation

The researcher recommends for the development of additional lessons on husband-wife relationship topics. It is recognized that FDS highlights the importance of child caregiving to break the intergenerational poverty of the families. The 4Ps focuses more on meeting the needs of the children by educating the parent through FDS, however other interventions for parents such as marital relationship development by might be needed. Moreover, special FDS for working husbands would be helpful to educate and empower fathers as the leader of the family.

Based on the result of the study, it is further recommended that family life educators would design curricula that focus more on relationship enrichment of the family, specifically marital relationship. With the fast changing society and technology advancement, the family has evolved into different forms and functions, thus, quality relationships between couples and family members might be subtly left behind.

References

1) Ayoub, C., O'Connor, E., Rappolt-Schlichtmann, G., Raikes, H., Chazan-Cohen, R., & Vallotton, C. (2009). Losing ground early: Protection, risk and change in poor children's cognitive performance. Early Childhood Research Quarterly, 24, 289–305.

2) Bandura, A. (1978). Social learning theory of aggression. Journal of Communication, 28(3), 12-29.

3) Bagarozzi, D.A (1990).Marital power discrepancies and symptom development in spouses: An empirical investigation. The American Journal of Family Therapy, 18,51-64.

4) Bohlander, R. W. (1999). Differentiation of self, need fulfillment, and psychological well-being in married men. Psychological Reports, 84, 1274–1280.

5) Collins, W A., & Russell, G. (1991). Mother-child and father-child relationships in middle childhood and adolescence: A developmental analysis. Developmental Review, 11, 99-136.

6) Dawson, G., Ashman, S. B., & Carver, L. J. (2000). The role of early experience in shaping behavioral and brain development and its implications for social policy. Development and psychopathology, 12(04), 695-712.

7) Del Mar Sánchez-Fuentes, M., Santos-Iglesias, P., & Sierra, J. C. (2014). A systematic review of sexual satisfaction. International Journal of Clinical and Health Psychology, 14(1), 67-75.

8) Easterbrooks, M. A. , & Emde, R. N. (1988). Marital and parent-child relationships: The role of affect in the family system. In R. A. Hinde &

J. Stevenson-Hinde (Eds.), Relationships within families: Mutual influences (pp. 83-103). New York: Oxford University Press

9) Erel, O., & Burman, B. (1995). Interrelatedness of marital relations and parent-child relations: A meta-analytic review. Psychological Bulletin, 118(1), 108-132.

10) Gardner, F., Burton, J., & Klimes, I. (2006). Randomised controlled trial of a parenting intervention in the voluntary sector for reducing child conduct problems: Outcomes and mechanisms of change. Journal of Child Psychology and Psychiatry, 47(11), 1123-1132.

11) Go, S.B. (1993). The Filipino family in the eighties. Manila, Philippines: Social Development Research Center, De La Salle University.

12) Gottman, J. M. 1994. What predicts divorce? The relationship between maritalprocesses and marital outcomes. Hillsdale, NJ: Lawrence Erlbaum Associates, Inc.

13) Gould, A. W, & Mazzeo, J. (1982). Age and sex differences in early adolescent's information sources. Journal of Early Adolescence, 2, 283-292.

14) International Labor Organization. (2016). Features of Philippines' CCT that may contribute to elimination of Child Labour. Retrieve from: www.ilo.org/wcmsp5/groups/public/---asia/---ro.../wcms_483751.pptx Accessed: August 18, 2016

15) Joussemet, M., Mageau, G. A., & Koestner, R. (2014). Promoting optimal parenting and children's mental health: A preliminary evaluation of the how-to parenting program. Journal of Child and Family Studies, 23(6), 949-964.

16) Larson, R., & Richards, M. H. (1991). Daily companionship in late childhood and early adolescence: Changing developmental contexts. Child Development, 62, 284-300.

17) Medina, B. (2001). The Filipino family (2nd ed.). Quezon City: University of the Philippines Press.

18) Miller, P. J. E., Caughlin, J. P., & Huston, T. L. (2003). Trait expressiveness and marital satisfaction: The role of idealization processes. Journal of Marriage and Family, 65, 978–995.

19) Odgers, C. L., Caspi, A., Russell, M. A., Sampson, R. J., Arseneault, L., & Moffitt, T. E. (2012). Supportive parenting mediates neighborhood socioeconomic disparities in children's antisocial behavior from ages 5 to 12. Development and Psychopathology, 24(03), 705-721.

20) Simmons, R. G, & Blyth, D. A. (1987). Moving into adolescence: The impact of pubertal change and school context. New York: Aldine De Gruyter.

21) Troll, L. E., & Fingerman, K. L. (1996). Connections between parents and their adult children. Handbook of emotion, adult development, and aging, 185-205

Preparation of Fluorescent Nanoparticles Based on Natural Silica for Bioimaging

S.N. Aisyiyah Jenie[1], Fransiska, S.H. Krismastuti[1], Yuni Kusumastuti[2], Himawan T.B.M.Petrus[2], Anis Kristiani[1,3]

1 Researcher, Research Centre for Chemistry, Indonesian Institute of Sciences (LIPI), Indonesia
2 Lecturer, Department of Chemical Engineering, Gadjah Mada University, Indonesia
3 Postgraduate Student, Graduate School of Integrated Science and Technology, Shizuoka University, Japan

大腸菌の検出など、生物医学分野のさまざまな検査に用いられる蛍光ナノ粒子。よく用いられるのはシリカ(SiNPs)だが、その精製過程で有毒な廃棄物が出る。そこで本稿では天然シリカを用い、より環境にやさしい精製方法を提案する。

Abstract

Fluorescent nanoparticles are used in a plethora of biomedical applications including bioimaging and tracing of molecules. Hence, these nanoparticles may aid in the development of new disease diagnostics and treatments. One nanostructure of particular importance is silica (SiNPs), due to the range of favorable material properties such as high surface area, ability to bind biomolecules covalently to the surface, biocompatibility, biodegradability and non-toxicity. The current methods for the preparation of SiNPs are not environmentally friendly considering the toxicity of the generated waste. Geothermal silica may overcome these problems as a natural source of silica and offers a more environmentally friendly pathway. Geothermal silica already possess the main intrinsic nano/mesoparticles properties and functional groups such as silica-dioxide on the surface of which allows the capturing of fluorophores inside the nanoparticles both physically and chemically.

This work covers the preparation of SiNPs from natural/geothermal silica, followed by modification with fluorophore, forming the fluorescent SiNPs (FSNP). Characterization of the FSNP include transmission electron microscopy (TEM), Fourier Transform Infra-Red (FT-IR) spectroscopy, and fluorescence spectroscopy. The FSNP was further applied for the detection and bioimaging of bacteria *Escherechia coli* (*E.coli*), an important pathogen indicator, which were monitored by fluorescence spectroscopy and UV visible light.

Keywords: fluorescence silica nanoparticles, bioimaging, silica geothermal, biosensing

Introduction

Escherichia coli (*E. coli*) is one of the fecal indicator organisms indicating the potential presence of pathogens in water environment, food products and agriculture products [1]. Monitoring this pathogen is crucial to prevent water related diseases, which is one of the major causes of mortality in the world, especially in the developing countries. According to WHO, diarrheal diseases cause approximately 1.8 million death per year [2]. Therefore, proper sanitation and improved quality of water supplies are important to maintain the public health.

New techniques have been developed for the detection and differentiation of bacteria, including *E. coli*. The plate assay using trioelylglycerol and the fluorescent dye Rhodamine B has been well known to detect bacterial lipases. Upon UV irradiation, orange fluorescent halos around the bacterial colonies are present due to substrate hydrolysis [3]. The so-called pink assay, in which the Rhodamine B showed a high level of pink fluorescence, was also used to detect the presence (or absence) of *E. coli* protein [4]. The utilization of fluorogenic substances for the detection of bacteria has indeed increased the performance of the detection system to identify specific enzyme and protein activities. However, due to its importance as pathogen indicator in the environment, the detection system for *E. coli* still requires improved accuracy and sensitivity along with rapid sensing times.

In the emerging of nanotechnology, designing and modeling of new materials at the atomic scale are feasible, thus opening up new opportunities for numerous important applications. Nanoparticles offer unique electrical, optic and magnetic properties that are very different compared to its bulk properties [5, 6]. Moreover, these nanostructures have been reported to significantly improve the spectral properties of fluorophores such as the quantum yield, photostability and fluorescence lifetime [7, 8]. One nanostructure of particular importance is silica (SiNPs), due to the range of favorable material properties such as high surface area, ability to bind biomolecules covalently to the surface, biocompatibility, biodegradability and non-toxicity [9, 10].

Silica-based fluorescent nanoparticles are used in a plethora of biomedical applications ranging from bioimaging, molecule tracings, biosensors to drug delivery systems [11, 12]. Over the past decade, such fluorescent nanoparticles have been intensively studied and often offered remarkable sensitivity in detecting fluorescence signals due to the improved signal-to-noise ratio [11, 13, 14]. In addition, silica-based fluorescent nanomaterials have been reported to increase the photostability and fluorescence lifetime of the incorporated organic fluorophores [12, 15].

Silica is abundantly available in nature, one of which is through the waste of geothermal power plants. However, silica scaling in these power plants causes the production capacity to decrease by 40%. Recovering the "amorphous" silica from geothermal installation with total amount of about 3000 ton/year will indeed provide benefits to the power plants, as these geothermal silica can be utilized as building blocks for silica based nanomaterials [16]. The current method for the preparation of SiNPs often applies silica precursors or co-precursors which are expensive and requires the use of organic solvents and strong acids during the preparation process. In addition, this preparation process is not environmentally friendly considering the toxicity of the generated waste. Geothermal silica may overcome these problems as it already possess the main intrinsic properties of silica nano/mesoparticles such as having large surface area and functional groups such as silica-dioxide on the surface.

The purpose of this work is to develop and synthesize fluorescent silica nanoparticles (FSNP) based on geothermal silica in which the dimensions, and optical properties of the synthesized nanoparticles can be finely tuned and adjusted. The fluorescence nanoparticle is then applied as an optical biosensor to detect *E. coli*.

To the best of our knowledge, the preparation of fluorescent silica nanoparticles from geothermal waste, in particular for biomedical purposes, has not been reported elsewhere. Hence, this approach will give added value to the geothermal silica as advanced functional nanostructures. In addition, this work will not only give advantage of the usage of natural Indonesian resources, but the outcome will also serve as a basis for future development of natural silica as nanostructured materials in other more sophisticated biomedical applications.

Experimental

Materials

Geothermal sludge, as the source of silica, was collected from PLTP Geodipa Dieng, Central Java, Indonesia. Sodium hydroxide (NaOH) was purchased from Merck Chemicals. Hydrochloric acid (HCl) 37% was an analytical grade from Merck Chemicals. Rhodamine-6G was purchased from Sigma-Aldrich. All chemicals were used without further purification. Deionized water was used for all synthesis and sensing experiments.

Synthesis of Fluorescent Silica Nanoparticles

As shown in Scheme 1, a total of 20 g of washed silica powder was mixed with 800 ml of 1.5 N sodium hydroxide (NaOH) in a cup glass to form sodium silicate (Na_2SiO_3). The mixture was then stirred using a magnetic stirrer with heating constantly maintained at 90°C within 60 minutes. Subsequently, the mixture was filtered through filter paper to separate the solution with solids. The sodium silicate solution was added with 0.05 g of Rhodamine-6G and stirred until homogeneous, then titrated with 2N HCl to form the gel and then allowed to stand for 18 hours. The gel formed was filtered with filter paper and washed with aquadest until pH 7. The neutralized gel was dried in an oven at 100 °C, overnight. The resulting fluorescent solid samples were identified as the fluorescent silica nanoparticles (FSNP).

Characterization of Fluorescent Silica Nanoparticles (FSNP)

Transmission Electron Microscopy (TEM) images were obtained with TEM Tecnai G-20 S-Twin (FEI, USA) scanning TEM instrument (200 kV accelerating voltage) equipped with Tungsten cathode and an Eagle CCD camera. For TEM measurement, a suitable amount of ethanolic solution of FSNP was dropped onto a porous carbon film on a copper grid and then dried in vacuum.

Fourier Infrared Spectroscopy (FTIR) spectra were recorded on a FTIR Prestige-21 (Shimatzu, Japan), in transmittance mode, at 16 cm^{-1} resolution, over the range of 300-400 cm^{-1} with an accumulating average of 10 scans. The software used to generate the spectra was IR Solution (Shimatzu).

Emission spectrum of FSNP was recorded on Varioskan Flash (Thermo Scientific) at excitation wavelength of 553 nm.

E. coli Sensing Experiments

E. coli bacterial culture and preparation

E. coli InaCC-B5 bacterial culture was provided from the Research Centre for Chemistry-LIPI, Indonesia. Nutrient agar (NA) was prepared by dissolving nutrient agar powder in aquadest, continued with constant heating until dissolved completely. An amount of 4 ml of dissolved NA was sterilized in an autoclave for 15 min at 121 °C. The sterilized NA was allowed to settle and subsequently 1 one stock of *E. coli* bacteria was incubated for 24 h at 37 °C. The cultured E.coli was diluted with sterilized water for further sensing experiments.

E. coli sensing with FSNP

A total of 20 μl of FSNP and 180 μl of *E. coli* suspension were added into a microplate. The microplate was covered in aluminium foil to avoid exposure of light and the mixture was allowed to react for 4 h. A control positive was prepared by adding 20 μl of FSNP and 180 μl of sterilized water in a microplate, and treated the same way as previous. The fluorescence intensity of both samples were measured using Fluorescence Spectral Scanning Multimode Reader (Thermo Scientific Varioskan Flash) with excitation wavelength of 553 nm and emission wavelength of 580 nm.

Bioimaging test

E. coli was cultured on NA in a microplate following the same procedure as previous. A total of 2 ml of FSNP was added on the *E. coli* culture and the mixture was exposed under UV irradiation.

Results and Discussion

Fabrication and Characterization of the FSNP

The luminescent nanoparticles investigated in this study was derived from amorphous geothermal silica. The silica nanoparticles were fabricated using the common approach of sol-gel process using silica obtained from the side product of geothermal plant [17] as precursor, which until now has not been reported elsewhere. Rhodamine-6G was added to the silica nanoparticle as fluorophore producing FSNP. The FSNP obtained from this process had an irregular structure with a particle diameter about 10-20 nm, which was measured by means of

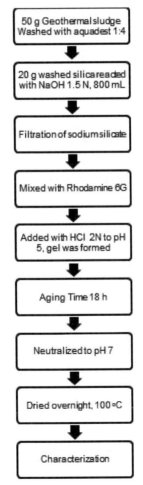

Scheme 1. Flowchart of the preparation of FSNP from geothermal silica

TEM (see Figure 1).

The surface chemistry of the FSNP samples were characterized by Fourier Transform Infrared Spectroscopy (FTIR) (Figure 2). Figure 2 presents the FTIR spectra of the raw geothermal silica (black trace) and FSNP (blue trace). The raw geothermal silica has a broad band at around 1000 – 1300 cm^{-1} with the peak at 1070 cm^{-1} which was assigned to Si-O-Si asymmetric stretching vibrations. A small band at 940 cm^{-1} and 800 cm^{-1} were attributed to Si-O$^-$ stretching vibrations or silanol group due to alkali silica glasses and Si-O-Si symmetric stretching vibration.

The band at 1070 cm^{-1} and at 800 cm^{-1} are common bands appear to all silicates with tetrahedrally coordinated silicon. The band at 1650 cm^{-1} was assigned to bending vibration of H-OH bonds, while the broad band around 3400 – 3650 cm^{-1} correspond to stretching vibration of –OH bonds [18, 19].

After modification with Rhodamine-6G forming the FSNP, the FTIR spectra (below) showing some changes in intensity for some of the adsorption bands but there is no additional band confirming the fluorescent agent (Rhodamine-6G) was not chemically bound to the silica geothermal nanoparticles but only physically entrapped in the pores of the particles.

The emission spectrum of FSNP was recorded at excitation wavelength of 553 nm, which is the excitation wavelength of the dye Rhodamine-6G. As shown in Figure 3, the maximum emission peak was observed at 580 nm. This wavelength will further be used for to observe the detection performance of FSNP towards *E. coli*.

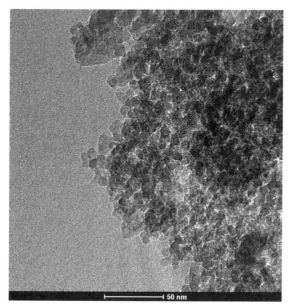

Fig. 1. Representative TEM images showing the nanostructures of FSNP

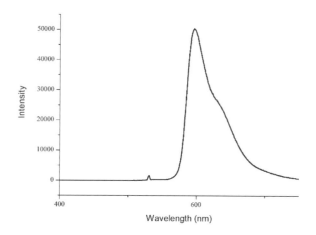

Fig. 3. Emission spectrum of FSNP at excitation wavelength 553 nm

Sensing Experiments of the FSNP for the Detection of E. coli

The FSNP was then used to detect *E. coli* in the culture media. The presence of *E. coli* protein will quench the fluorescence emission of Rhodamine-6G as the biorecognition compound. Therefore during sensing, the fluorescence intensity of the FSNP was measured using fluorescence spectroscopy before and after added to the culture media containing *E. coli*. The concentration of the FSNP was varied from 1×10^{-1} mg/mL down to 1.95×10^{-4} mg/mL. During sensing, the fluorescence emission

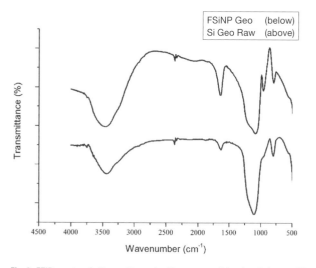

Fig. 2. FTIR spectra of silica geothermal as the precursor (above) and after modification into Si nanoparticles with Rhodamine-6G, FSNP (below).

signals were decreased after the addition of FSNP to the culture media containing *E. coli* in each different FSNP concentration tested, indicating the quenching of fluorescence emission due to the presence of *E. coli*. The loss of the fluorescence intensity signal in different concentration of the FSNP is summarized in Table 1.

Table 1. The fluorescence intensity loss after FSNP added to the culture media containing *E. coli* for each FSNP concentration tested in the range of 1×10^{-1} mg/mL to 1.95×10^{-4} mg/mL.

FSNP concentration (mg/mL)	Fluorescence intensity loss (%)
1×10^{-1}	26.11
5×10^{-2}	30.64
2.5×10^{-2}	47.87
1.25×10^{-2}	18.44
6.25×10^{-3}	27.37
3.12×10^{-3}	5.02
1.56×10^{-3}	57.02
7.81×10^{-4}	59.76
3.9×10^{-4}	74.51
1.95×10^{-4}	74.70

From Table 1, it can be seen that the percentage of fluorescence signal loss increases gradually with the decrease concentration of the FSNP until the FSNP concentration of 6.25×10^{-3} mg/mL. Lower than that concentration, the percentage of fluorescence signal loss was decreased (at the concentration of 3.12×10^{-3} mg/mL) and then increased significantly at the concentration lower than 3.12×10^{-3} mg/mL. It suggests the lowest working concentration of the FSNP for *E. coli* detection was 6.25×10^{-3} mg/mL.

The next experiment was to run the control experiment using Rhodamine-6G without any silica nanoparticle as negative control to investigate whether the fluorescence signal loss was due to the presence of *E. coli* or not. The concentration of Rhodamine-6G used in this experiment was lower than the concentration of FSNP used in the previous experiments (Table 1). This Rhodamine-6G concentration was equal to the concentration of Rhodamine-6G used to modify the geothermal silica nanoparticle thus the fluorescence signals emitted from the control (Rhodamine-6G only) and the FSNP are comparable. In this experiment, the fluorescence was emitted at 627 nm as the Rhodamine-6G emission, which is higher than the emission signal Rhodamine-6G embedded in the geothermal silica nanoparticles.

The fluorescence intensities, before and after interaction with *E. coli*, did not show any particular trend with the percentage of fluorescence signal loss, as presented in Table 2. It confirms that the fluorescence signals emitted by Rhodamine-6G itself is not stable at very low concentrations of the dye. This result corroborates that the decreased fluorescence intensity in the previous experiments (Table 1) was due to the quenching of the fluorescence signal from Rhodamine-6G entrapped in the geothermal silica nanoparticles in the presence of *E-coli*. This result also shows that the FSNP has increased photostability compared to that of the Rhodamine-6G, at the same amount of concentration of the dye.

Table 2. The fluorescence intensity loss after Rhodamine-6G added to the culture media containing *E. coli* for Rhodamine-6G concentration tested in the range of 6.25×10^{-4} mg/mL to 1.22×10^{-6} mg/mL.

FSNP concentration (mg/mL)	Fluorescence intensity loss (%)
6.25×10^{-4}	64.15
3.13×10^{-4}	-68.82
1.56×10^{-4}	90.71
7.81×10^{-5}	74.53
3.91×10^{-5}	63.02
1.95×10^{-5}	36.16
9.77×10^{-6}	-7.18
4.88×10^{-6}	-84.24
2.44×10^{-6}	-220.58
1.22×10^{-6}	-284.12

Bioimaging of E.coli using FSNP

E. coli detection using the FSNP was also observed under UV light to see the fluorescence during sensing (Figure 4). In Figure 4, it can be seen that, the FSNP itself emitted an intense orange fluorescence (a) and once *E. coli* introduce to the petri dish, the colour was changed into light orange (b) indicating the fluorescence intensity was decreased due to the presence *E. coli*. It corroborates that *E. coli* protein has ability to quench the fluorescence emission of the FSNP. Orange fluorescent halos around the *E. coli* colonies were also observed, proving that FSNP may be applied for bioimaging purposes.

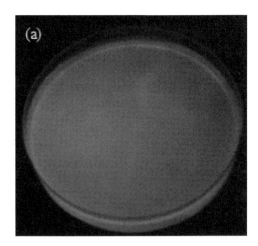

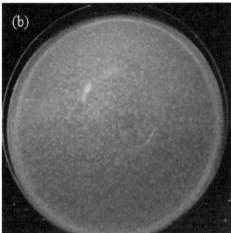

Fig.4. Fluorescence emission of the FSNP (a) and FSNP + *E.coli* (b)

Conclusion

This work presents for the first time the detection of *E. coli* using fluorescent silica nanoparticles (FSNP). The FSNP was derived from amorphous silica geothermal waste and modified with the dye Rhodamine-6G. The FSNP interacted with the protein of the *E. coli*, resulting in quenching or decrease of emission intensity of the FSNP. Furthermore, we observed the detection of *E. coli* under UV light, resulting in decrease of intensity compared to the FSNP in the absence of *E. coli*. Orange fluorescent halos around the *E. coli* colonies were also observed, proving that FSNP may be applied for bioimaging purposes. Continued studies are currently being conducted in our laboratory to optimize the properties of FSNP as well as its ability for bioimaging and detection systems.

Acknowledgement

The authors would like to acknowledge the Ministry of Research, Technology and Higher Education for the research funding. SNAJ would like to thank the L'Oreal-UNESCO For Women In Science National Fellowship 2017 for the research grant.

References

1) Ishii, S. and Sadowsky, M. J. (2008) Minireview: *Escherichia coli* in The Environment: Implications for Water Quality and Human Health. Microbes and Environments, 23(2), 101-108.

2) WHO, *Water, Sanitation and Hygiene Links to Health: Facts and Figures*, 2004.

3) Manafi, M., Kneifel, W., and Bascomb, S. (1991) Fluorogenic and chromogenic substrates used in bacterial diagnostics. Microbiological Reviews, 55(3), 335-348.

4) Bartasun, P., Cieśliński, H., Bujacz, A., Wierzbicka-Woś, A., and Kur, J. (2013) A study on the interaction of rhodamine B with methylthioadenosine phosphorylase protein sourced from an Antarctic soil metagenomic library. PLoS One, 8(1), e55697.

5) Jianrong, C., Yuqing, M., Nongyue, H., Xiaohua, W., and Sijiao, L. (2004) Nanotechnology and biosensors. Biotechnology Advances, 22(7), 505-518.

6) Reshetilov, A. N. and Bezborodov, A. M. (2008) Nanobiotechnology and biosensor research. Appl Biochem Microbiol, 44(1), 1-5.

7) Aslan, K., Gryczynski, I., Malicka, J., Matveeva, E., Lakowicz, J. R., and Geddes, C. D. (2005) Metal-enhanced fluorescence: an emerging tool in biotechnology. Current Opinion in Biotechnology, 16(1), 55-62.

8) Lakowicz, J. R., *Fluorophores - Principles of Fluorescence Spectroscopy* 2006: Springer US. 63-95.

9) Popat, A., Ross, B. P., Liu, J., Jambhrunkar, S., Kleitz, F., and Qiao, S. Z. (2012) Enzyme-Responsive Controlled Release of Covalently Bound Prodrug from Functional Mesoporous Silica Nanospheres. Angew. Chem., Int. Ed., 51(50), 12486-12489.

10) Qhobosheane, M., Santra, S., Zhang, P., and Tan, W. (2001) Biochemically functionalized silica nanoparticles. Analyst, 126(8), 1274-1278.

11) Cho, E.-B., Volkov, D. O., and Sokolov, I. (2010) Ultrabright Fluorescent Mesoporous Silica Nanoparticles. Small, 6(20), 2314-2319.

12) Jenie, S. A., Plush, S. E., and Voelcker, N. H. (2016) Recent Advances on Luminescent Enhancement-Based Porous Silicon Biosensors. Pharmaceutical research, 33(10), 2314–2336.

13) Cho, E.-B., Volkov, D. O., and Sokolov, I. (2011) Ultrabright Fluorescent Silica Mesoporous Silica Nanoparticles: Control of Particle Size and Dye Loading. Adv. Funct. Mater., 21(16), 3129-3135.

14) Krismastuti, F. S. H., Pace, S., and Voelcker, N. H. (2014) Porous Silicon Resonant Microcavity Biosensor for Matrix Metalloproteinase Detection. Adv. Funct. Mater., 24(23), 3639-3650.

15) Jenie, S. N. A., Pace, S., Sciacca, B., Brooks, R. D., Plush, S. E., and Voelcker, N. H. (2014) Lanthanide Luminescence Enhancements in Porous Silicon Resonant Microcavities. ACS Appl. Mater. Interfaces, 6(15), 12012-12021.

16) Kusumastuti, Y., Petrus, H. T. B. M., Yohana, F., Buwono, A. T., and Zaqina, R. B. (2017) Synthesis and characterization of biocomposites based on chitosan and geothermal silica. AIP Conference Proceedings, 1823(1), 020127.

17) Olvianas, M., Najmina, M., Prihardana, B. S. L., Sutapa, F. A., Nurhayati, A., and Petrus, H. T. B. M. (2015) Study on The Geopolymerization of Geothermal Silica and Kaolinite. Advanced Materials Research, 112 (528-532).

18) Olvianas, M., Widiyatmoko, A., and Petrus, H. T. B. M. *IR Spectral Similarity Studies of Geothermal Silica-Bentonite Based Geopolymer.* in *AIP Conference Proceeding.* 2017. AIP Publishing.

19) Andhika, M., Castañeda, M. H., and Regenspurg, S. *Characterization of Silica Precipitation at Geothermal Conditions.* in *World Geothermal Congress 2015.* 2015. Melbourne, Australia.

Make Japan Cool For Everybody?
An Analysis of Indonesian Trainee (Gaikokujin Kenshusei Seido) in Japan (Between Hope and Reality)

Yusy Widarahesty[1]
1 Full Time Lecturer, International Relations Department University of Al Azhar Indonesia

いわゆる「外国人研修生制度」を利用して日本で働くインドネシアの若者たち。彼らが夢に描いた「クール・ジャパン」と、日々の暮らしで感じる現実の間にはどんなギャップがあるのか。聞き取り調査とSNSの投稿分析を通じて検証する。

Abstract

In the last 50 years, economic transformation in Indonesia has brought rapid development of international migration of Indonesians to its neighboring developed Asian countries. Japan has been, and remains as, one of the most popular destination countries for ASEAN society especially Indonesians in search of employment and a better life. The first wave of migration of Indonesian workers to Japan began when the Japanese government started to accept foreigners as trainees (kenshusei) in 1982. Following the official launch of the Japan's Industrial Training and Technical Internship Program in 1993, the number of Indonesian migrant workers in Japan further increased. As of 2016, Japanese government statistics state that there are just under 40,000 Indonesians in Japan. This research will examine Indonesian migrant workers (kenshusei) in Japan especially in private sector companies through ethnographic fieldwork and netnographic fieldwork to elaborate and clarify about the reality of life of Indonesian migrant workers (kenshusei) in Japan through deep interviews and by their postings on social media such as Face Book.

Keywords Gaikokujin Kenshusei Seido, cheap labor, Indonesia, Japan, Japanese Dreams

Introduction

Indonesia and Japan have cooperative relations in the economic field for approximately 60 years since 1958. The good relations are contained in various forms of economic cooperation, such as ODA (Official Development Assistance), FDI (Foreign Direct Investment) and bilateral trade. In 1958 Japan and Indonesia embarked on official bilateral diplomatic relations with the signing of a peace spoil agreement between Indonesia and Japan accompanied by a war reparation agreement whereby Japan paid for losses resulting from the Japanese occupation of the World War II era. The agreement began with a Japanese visit in Indonesia since 1955.[1]

The economic cooperation agreement between Indonesia and Japan is in line with the national interests of both countries. At that time Japan was trying to restore the post-World War II economy, as a "survival strategy" to improve its economy after atomic bombs in Hiroshima and Nagasaki, while Indonesia just managed to escape from colonialism and achieved independence in 1945. Thus the national interest of both countries is manifested in an effort to strengthen cooperation in various fields. It is certainly also inseparable from the position of Japan which is one of the hegemon countries as a result of economic progress in Asia.

In 1953 to 1973, Japan's economic growth was at an annual economic growth rate of 9.7 percent, which is often referred to as the economic miracle of Japan.[2] In this period also Japanese electronic products successfully replace the position of German and American products. Japan's three-fold high growth rate compared to Western countries made Japan the world's second-largest GDP in 1986.[3] At the same time, Japan is actively continuing to establish various economic cooperation with other countries especially with ASEAN countries which are considered as a region which is capable of supporting the pace of Japanese industries.

On the other hand, the cooperation between Indonesia and Japan is not only established in the form of economic agreements in trade or industry, as a growing and developing country that succeeds in placing its country on a par with developed countries like America, at the same time the need for Japanese human resources is increasing. This is because although Japan enjoyed a period of rapid growth in the late 1980s, Japan's economic situation changed drastically in the 1990s. The "Economic Buble" event that emerged in 1990 has resulted in average growth rates in Japan declining. Then came the so-called "new comer migrants" that have changed the demographic character in Japan. The new comers mostly come from the Philippines, China, Brazil, Thailand, and other developing countries. The arrival of 'new comers' has resulted in a diversity in the composition of foreign residents in Japan, where in earlier times, foreign workers in Japan were more dominantly in content by the 'old comers' of Koreans, Chinese and Nikkeijin Latin America of Japanese origin and their descendants who have existed since the Japanese colonial period.[4]

The foreign workers who come to Japan to fill the labor shortage are likely to find themselves in the so-called "3k (*kitsui, kiken, kitanai*, or difficult, dangerous, dirty) jobs. To fill the labor shortage, the Japanese government then cooperates with various countries by forming a program called 'trainee' or known as an internship program. Countries that collaborate on this trainee program such as China, Vietnam, Philippines, Thailand, Peru, Laos, Sri Lanka, India, Myanmar, Mongolia, Uzbekistan, Cambodia, Nepal, Bangladesh and Indonesia.[5] Although the Japanese government prohibits the entry of foreign workers with no special expertise, there are loopholes in the policy so that Japan can still meet the needs of workers with no special expertise, that is through the way the worker enters by student visa, entertainer visa and includes a trainee (kenshusei) visa.

Under the Japanese immigration policy on the Immigration Control and Refugee Recognition Act, there are several classifications for foreigners to enter and work in Japan. The foreigner must have a resident status in Japan such as permanent resident status, spouses and children of Japanese nationals, and permanent residents living in the long term.[6] The kind of work that can be run by foreigners is also regulated in Japanese immigration policies that are limited to those with special expertise such as diplomats, engineers, or those working for humanitarian organizations or other international organizations. This is in line with the change in Japanese immigration and labor policies in 1990 which refused to accept unskilled workers while opening the door wide for acceptance of foreign workers with special expertise.[7]

The emergence of the different types of workers under Japanese trainee visa that differ from the system of workers has existed since the change of Japanese immigration policy in 1990. In that year a trainee dispatch program was established under the cooperation of Japanese government and business sector in Japan. This was initiated by establishing JITCO (Japan International Training Cooperation Organization) in 1991. Founded in 1991, JITCO is under the joint jurisdiction of Department of Justice, Ministry of Foreign Affairs, Ministry of Health, Labor and Welfare, Ministry of Economy, Trade and Industry, and the Ministry of Land, Infrastructure and Transport. JITCO now has a basic public interest endorsed by the Japanese cabinet office.[8]

JITCO (wich is currently added one organization in 2017 called OTIT Organization for Technical Intern Training as part of JITCO as well) was established as an organization that aims to set up the international trainee dispatch program system to Japan. Under the program the trainees will stay for four years in Japan, the first year will start with learning the new sciences using the visa trainee, then the visa is extended for three years under the technical intern's status where they will begin to engage directly in the activities practice his apprenticeship to a company while receiving wages.[9] JITCO has a fundamental role and objective to contribute to maintaining the internship training program by providing assistance to the trainees:[10]

Indonesia itself has sent trainees to Japan under a cooperation agreement between the Indonesian Ministry of Manpower and Transmigration with the Association of Small and Medium

Enterprises Japan (IMM Japan) in 1993.[11]

The sending of trainees to Japan was originally an ODA (Official Development Assistance)-assisted program that began in 1954 when Japan joined the "Colombo Plan" with a mission to promote social and economic development in the Asian region[12], where the Japanese government opens the entry of Indonesian workers to work in Japan for training in industry, communications, agriculture and health.[13] Japan's ODA assistance not only contributes to providing assistance in the field of social and economic infrastructure development but also in the field of human resources development including through cooperation through trainees of the program.[14] Furthermore, the demand for Indonesian labor by the Japanese government is also one of the points that are then stated in the EPA (Economic Partnership Agreement), which in the agreement listed pillars of investment interests for Indonesia, but also an interest to reduce the number of unemployed.

In addition to the cooperation undertaken between the governments of Indonesia and Japan, the sending of trainees is also conducted at the institutional and corporate levels albeit at a smaller amount. Following the signing of an agreement between the Ministry of Manpower and the Japanese government, where the accepting agency in Japan is IMM Japan since 1993, the Indonesian government has sent many selected personnel through the Technical Intern Training Program (TITP) initiated by the Japanese government. The number of Indonesian entrants sent to Japan continues to grow from year to year (Table 1).

NO.	Year	Number of Workers TKI
1	2011	1.929
2	2012	2.652
3	2013	2.577
4	2014	3.741
5	2015	5.452
6	2016	6.498
7	2017	5.162
8	2018	2.380
	Total	30.393

Table 1. Indonesian Trainee Delivery Data Table to Japan Year 2011-2016
Sources: Pusat Data dan Informasi Ketenagakerjaan RI[15]

For Indonesia itself as one of the nation's suppliers of workers, many younger generations are keen to work in Japan due to better job opportunities and higher wages compared to Indonesia, along with the skills gained to support their careers in the future. When compared to the Indonesian minimum wage in Indonesia ranging from 7,000 to 14,000 yen (US $ 70-140) per month, in the apprenticeship program, trainees in their first year are promised to receive much higher wages from their home countries, ranging from 50,000 to 80,000 yen (US $ 500-800) per month, and in the second and third year trainees will be promised to get 60,000 to 100,000 yen (US $ 600-1000).[16]

Basically, the basic law or foundation for the implementation of PTKLN (foreign work placement) program in Indonesia is in order to fulfill the right of every citizen to get a job and livelihood that is suitable for humanity, as mandated by the 1945 Constitution. Due to the domestic labor market can not afford absorbing the entire workforce, the foreign work market becomes an option for a number of workers to find work.[17] According to the Law of the Republic of Indonesia number 13 of 2003 on Manpower, apprenticeship is defined as a system of work training organized in an integrated manner between training in training institutions by working directly under the guidance and supervision of instructors or workers who are more experienced, in the process of producing goods and/or services in a company, in order to master certain skills or expertise.[18]

Sending Indonesian Workers is one of the government's policies in dealing with the unequal problem between the number of manpower and available employment. Which is where the amount of labor is more than the existing jobs. This problem is a problem that occurs in many developing countries, especially in Indonesia. while in the developed countries the problem is the lack of manpower. This of course encourages the cooperation of sending workers abroad.

In general, the sending of Indonesian labor abroad is also able to provide an economic multiplier effect both in the national scale and the region of origin of the workforce. Like growing foreign exchange, fostering family economy, driving people's economy, raising savings, reducing unemployment, improving community knowledge and education, acquiring new skills and so on.[19]

Based on this matter, when viewed, the relations between Indonesia and Japan can indeed be said to be in an asymmetrical position, where Japanese manufacturing industry technology is more advanced and mature, while Indonesia is still far below Japan, eventually in the program of trainee cooperation between Indonesia and Japan a pillar of cooperation that focuses on the transfer of knowledge and technology transfer for Indonesian workers who are doing internships in Japan, whose ultimate goal of course is to enhance the global competitiveness of Indonesian products themselves.

This transfer of knowledge has an important meaning for Indonesia, because it is expected that with the transfer of knowledge to the Indonesian workforce, the quality of Indonesian workforce becomes better by certainly able to independently apply the knowledge gained by creating Indonesia's own quality products and able to penetrate the international market following Japan's success.

Frame Work

In order to analyze the implementation of the cooperation program by looking through hope and reality, the authors will use the theory of Issue Linkage to see the cooperation character between Japan and Indonesia in a macro level and Social Media as a part of globalization to see their hope and the real life of Indonesian trainee itself in reaction or as a feedback to this trainee program in a micro level.

Issue Linkage

To understand how international cooperation can take place, it can use several ways, one of which is the analysis through the concept of Issue Linkage. Here the concept of Issue Linkage used is the concept of Issue Linkage according to E.B. Haas as a conceptual foundation that can explain the dynamics of the implementation of the Technical Internship Program (TIP) between Indonesia and Japan.[20]

Issue linkage is a pattern of cooperation by way of 'barter' issues. A partnership between parties with a conflict of interest (not necessarily in a conflictual context) can be achieved by linking a sphere of issues with other issues so that each party will get what it wants. To analyze the issue of linkage, it is necessary to map out who is the linker, ie the party who offers an aspect of issues to be 'switch' with the realm of issues that are in the interest of the linkee party. Party linkee is the party offered a form of compensation by the linker who generally interests linkee will be reduced and replaced with the compensation. In addition, a clear mapping of the interests of both parties is required.[21]

Japan within the framework of TIP (technical Internship Program) program is a linker that has interests both economic interests and political interests to Indonesia.[22]

While Indonesia is a linkee party of the trainee / TIP program, here Indonesia realizes that this trainee program is an opportunity for Indonesia to get knowledge or technology transfer from Japan which is one of the developed countries in Asia also in the World. Through this partnership Indonesia also expects in addition to the fulfillment of employment opportunities for Indonesia's population of surplus demography, but also the establishment of trained and educated Indonesian workers with new skills and knowledge that can be brought and applied later in Indonesia so that the expectation is that there will be a change that can build nation and state for the better.

Social Media

Social Media is one of the buzzwords that came along the web 2.0 rhetoric, along with some other terms, somewhere around 2005. As such, the concept does not have a strictly defined meaning, but people using the concept want to stress that is a new era.[23]

In social media people voluntarily share content, for example videos, texts, images, music, through online platforms and with the help of applications that are based on social software. The content in social media has its own audience as the traditional media, like TV, radio, magazines and newspapers have, but the biggest difference is that people enjoy sharing the content they have made themselves or maybe copied from others.[24]

In this context to see the image from the trainee program in Japan, I use the netnography methodology to see and gauge what their daily activities which are displayed through their social media such as Facebook, Instagram etc., and how the real conditions of their life as a trainee itself.

History of Relations between Indonesia and Japan Cooperation in Employment

The assistance program of ODA is a technical assistance program between Japan and developing countries. As a developed country, Japan is conditioned to have responsibility in 'human development efforts' that is through the way of providing knowledge and developing the capabilities and quality of human resources of the people of the developing countries. Thus it can be said that the history of Indonesia and Japan cooperation in this trainee program started with the assistance of Japanese ODA in Indonesia which started from 1954, in the form of acceptance of trainees to get training in industry, transportation, agriculture and health communication. This Japanese ODA assistance was created with the aim of contributing through the areas of human resource development, infrastructure and socio-economic development.[25]

Furthermore, Indonesia and Japan have increased their relationship momentum in 2007. On August 20, Indonesia and Japan signed an economic cooperation agreement (IJEPA). The establishment of the EPA itself began when the proposal for the formation of FTA offered by Japanese Prime Minister Junichiro Koizumi to President Megawati who was visiting Tokyo on 22-25 June 2003.[26] Then in a joint announcement made between the Prime Minister of Japan and the President of Indonesia, announced on 8 September 2003 Megawati and Junichiro Koizumi agreed to assign both officials in the two governments to a preliminary meeting to discuss the possibility of establishing an EPA between Indonesia and Japan.[27] The cooperation sectors under the IJEPA agreement between Indonesia and Japan under the White Paper on International Trade in 2001, are described as trade agreements that go beyond the tariff limits in the FTA by reaching areas such as investment, competition, digitizing trade procedures, and harmonizing the system and facilitating the movement of people per person.[28] In the point of people movement per person it can be said that both parties will provide a framework to facilitate human movement in various categories including short-term corporate visitors, intra-business, investors and professional services. In the same context both parties will also provide acceptance for nurses and caregivers. And both sides will also collaborate on an ongoing basis to expand the reach of apprenticeship and engineering programs.

Based on the above explanation, so far, there are two cooperation related to employment that is still on going that is placement of nurse and caregiver of parents from Indonesia in Japan and apprenticeship program or trainee. The placement of nurses and caregivers of parents is in line with the economic cooperation between Japan and Indonesia (The Indonesia-Japan Economic Partnership Agreement / IJEPA) run in 2008. Under the agreement Indonesia promised to send 600 nurses and 400 nannies parents from Indonesia to Japan which will be facilitated by the Japan International Corporation of Welfare Service (JICWELS).[29] The shipment is based on a lack of manpower in the sector despite increasing demand due to the growing number of aging population in Japan.

With regard to the aging population in Japan, 2005 was a turning point for Japan's demographic conditions. According to official Tokyo statistics, the number of deaths in the year is very little compared with the number of births.[30] With the decline in the average number of births, there is a decrease in the number of children's populations and this has resulted in a decrease in the number of productive age populations that will impact on the lack of human resources in Japan. With the condition of the elderly population is more than the young population and productive, this will actually make the level of dependence in Japan to be higher. This problem of population decline is certainly a potential threat to the existence of Japan as a country, because the problem either directly or indirectly will have an impact on other aspects. One of them is the employment aspect that the decrease of the youth population will also decrease the number of productive age population or the worker population, which means the number of human resources in Japan will decrease.

In line with the problem, the population crisis is exacerbating the current condition of Japan, where the rate of productive labor occupation is decreasing. Currently many companies and work sectors in Japan suffer from a severe labor shortage.[31] This can be seen through the following graph 1:

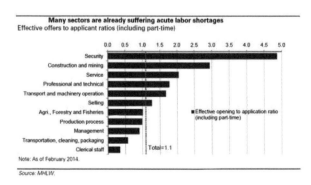

Graph 1. Sectors Experiencing the Disadvantages of Acute Labor Shortages

Sources: Ministry of Health, Labour and Welfare

Through the graph above can be seen that the needs of Japanese productive workforce is very high. And the ongoing demographic crisis condition in Japan has finally caused Japan to open up wide opportunities for foreign workers, especially for nursing staff and industrial sector, which emphasizes on 3K type of work (kitsui, kiken, kitanai).

For nursing workers, although Indonesia has a large supply of nurses and parenting caregivers, in reality the Indonesian government has difficulty recruiting highly qualified and qualified nurses with adequate experience, as well as fluent in Japanese. Furthermore, difficulties with nursing accreditation exams held in Japanese are exactly the same as the tests taken by nurses from Japan themselves who want to obtain accreditation, although nurses from Indonesia are competent and have extensive knowledge in terms of the theory and practice of care but will be difficult to pass the exam when not mastering the Japanese language. It is also seen as an act of the Japanese government that seems to deliberately hinder the entry of Indonesian labor into the Japanese labor market.[32]

Furthermore, to meet the workforce in the field of industry, Indonesia and Japan build cooperation in the field of apprenticeship programs or trainees. As previously mentioned, the trainee program established by the Japanese government since 1954 initially aims to encourage international cooperation and provide assistance to developing countries. This program is formed by the cooperation of Japanese government and business sector in Japan, which is a response from the expansion of post-World War II Japanese economy and post-employment shortage. This led to the influx of newcomers or foreign workers from Korea, Taiwan, Thailand, Malaysia and Indonesia in the 1960s until increasing in the 1980s.[33]

In the new trainee program, the Japanese government also established cooperation with developing countries on the employment sector one of them with Indonesia. As mentioned earlier, Indonesia itself has sent trainees to Japan under a cooperation agreement between the Indonesian Ministry of Manpower and Transmigration with the Association of the Small and Medium Enterprises Japan (IMM Japan) in the year 1993.[34]

Kenshusei acceptance in Japan was started around the end of the 1960s, when many Japanese companies are expanding abroad. However, in the late 1980s, the acceptance of foreign workers who entered work in Japan with the kenshusei system became a major debate in the political, economic, social, and so forth. As a result, the Japanese government in 1990 revised the existing training system by allowing it to receive kenshusei in the broader fields of work, aiming to shift Japan's technology as a contribution to develop human resources in developing countries.[35]

Because the trainee program is established as a program that aims to transfer skills, knowledge and technology to developing countries so that it is expected to improve the quality of its human resources and its opportunities in achieving better job opportunities. So a plan came up to direct the trainees after they had finished their apprenticeship to become entrepreneurs. This is the background of the establishment of the Tokyo Commitment agreement between various government institutions both from Japan and Indonesia in 2007. With the Tokyo Commitment is expected to encourage the development of entrepreneurial spirit through trainee program in Japan, this is done by running training, counseling, and briefing.[36]

The history of the movement of workers in Asia can be traced back to the colonial period in the early nineteenth century, when workers moved from one place to another for construction, agriculture and mining projects. It was not until the 1980s that the Indonesian government decided to start developing programs related to overseas workers by regulating through government regulations and involving the industrial sector. Since then Indonesia has established and submitted the sending of workers abroad as part of the development and development plan.[37]

Currently, of course, as a sovereign country Indonesia must have its own regulation governing Indonesian workers who will be placed abroad, both in terms of rights and obligations, placement, and also of course the protection of labor migrants. The regulation is contained in Law No.39 of 2004 on the placement and protection of Indonesian workers abroad. Within the law there are several articles that are important to be understood contained in chapters 8 and 27. In the law are affirmed the rights and obligations of TKI (Indonesia migrant workers) listed in one of the points in article 8 namely:

"Every prospective migrant worker has the same rights and obligations to obtain the same rights, opportunities,

and treatment obtained by foreign workers."[38]

Under the Indonesian Law, the placement of overseas migrant workers may only be made to a destination country whose government has entered into a written agreement with the Indonesian government or to a destination country that has laws and regulations protecting other foreign workers in accordance with the laws and regulations in country of destination.[39]

There is a special chapter in the Indonesian law covering various articles on the protection of Indonesian workers, namely chapter VI. As Article 77 states that every prospective migrant worker has the right to obtain protection in accordance with legislation starting from pre-placement, placement period, to post-placement. Such protection shall be undertaken by the designated labor attaché the Indonesian government in accordance with the laws and regulations as well as the laws and customs of international supervision, this is as set out in Article 78. Article 79 also said that the representatives of the Republic of Indonesia are required to conduct guidance and supervision over the representatives of private migrant workers and migrant workers placed abroad.[40] Therefore, in relation to the issue of trainees, the Ministry of Manpower and Transmigration as the representative of the Indonesian government should supervise the sending organizations of trainees to Japan from both private and IMM.

Furthermore, in article 80, it is explained that the protection during the period of overseas migrant placement is carried out in accordance with the provisions of laws and regulations in the country of destination and international law and custom, in this case referring to the labor legislation of Japan and the ILO. Where in the regulation the TKI is entitled to obtain defense of the fulfillment of rights in accordance with the work agreement and the laws and regulations in the destination country.[41]

In the rule of labor law of the Republic of Indonesia is also explained about the definition of apprentices. According to the Law of the Republic of Indonesia number 13 of 2003 on Employment, apprenticeship is defined as a system of work training that is organized in an integrated manner between training in training institutions by working directly under the guidance and supervision of instructors or workers who are more experienced, in the process of producing goods and / or services in the company, in order to master certain skills or expertise.[42]

ILO also launched a "discriminatory resistance against migrant workers and minorities in the workplace" project in 1991 as a form of concern for such discrimination cases[43] Japan's labor law rules also have non-discriminatory rules, although they are not described in as much detail as the rules of the ILO, Japanese law also classifies trainees as prohibited from discrimination. However, in reality there is discrimination against trainees in terms of work sector restrictions. The work sector accessible to trainees is limited to sectors such as metal industry, building construction, food, fisheries, and agriculture. And within the already limited work sector, the work to be handled is also limited without the opportunity to move parts during the program.

These jobs can be referred to as manual labor or belonging to 3K jobs. The work undertaken by this factory worker among others includes machine operators, electronic equipment assemblers, packers, food processors from fish, drilling and so on. This, of course, raises the question if the above Japanese employment law prohibits discrimination against trainees, then why only 3K jobs are the type of work performed by the trainees, which is a kind of work that has a history long as a kind of work that is highly avoided by Japanese society.

In JITCO's policy as an organization that oversees the running of trainee programs in Japan itself has actually issued rules that refer to the Japanese Labor Standards Act in various respects, for example in terms of wages. There are, of course, some deductions from the monthly wage to meet operational costs, such as income taxes, housing taxes, social security, employment insurance, and daily and living expenses.[44] In addition to the wages of Japan's labor regulations also regulates the number of working hours referring to ILO regulations.

In the article it appears that in the rules of working hours and public holidays, ILO and Japan labor laws are equally enacting the same rules. Workers will work for approximately 40 minutes to a maximum of 48 working hours in a period of one week, then workers are also entitled to get time off for one day every week. In accordance with the regulations in the JITCO manual, the company where the trainee is employed has an obligation to pay the trainee overtime fee in accordance with the number of hours a trainee is working. To work more than 8 hours a day trainees are entitled to not less than 25 per cent extra wages, as well as overtime work done at night, 22:00 and 05:00 local time, while for overtime work on a trainee's day off entitled to no less 35% extra paid.[45]

> Article 69: *"An employer shall not exploit an apprentice, student, trainee, or other worker, by whatever name such person may be called, by reason of the fact that such person is seeking to acquire a skill"*
>
> Article 69-2: *"An employer shall not employ a worker who is seeking to acquire a skill in domestic work or other work having no relation to acquisition of a skill"*[46]

Yet even so there are still a few companies that employ trainees with unnecessary working hours, this is in line with a quotation from one of the owners of a clothing industry company who says that there are still many factories demanding workers to work from 8 am to 6 pm morning the next morning.[47]

Make Japan Cool For Everybody? An Analysis of Indonesian Trainee In Japan

Japan has been, and remains as one of the most popular destination countries for ASEAN society especially Indonesians in search of employment and a better life. as we know that since the 1990s Japan has been known for its power of soft power through popular culture or "cool Japan" and so on. Of course the success of Japan to be a hegemon country has led to Japanese dream among developing countries. And Indonesia is one of them.

Japan's popularity for the people of Indonesia has started since the era of 1970s, and continues to increase from year to year. Japanese dream emerged after the previous American dreams succeeded successfully spread to various countries including Indonesia. Therefore trainee program cooperation between Japan and Indonesia become easy thing accepted and very much in demand by Indonesian society. It is of course, because being able to work in a country like Japan will give more value.

The positive impression of this trainee program can also be seen clearly from the picture or appearance shown by the trainee participants in Japan through their social media. From the 10 trainees interviewed, 9 of them displayed a very positive impression of the program through their social media. Japan succeeded in giving a wonderfully cool of positive image, and it is seen through anyone who has visited Japan both being studying, tourists and of course for the kenshusei itself.

After doing field observation by following and looking deeper into the activities of these kenshusei, it turns out there are some things that are found contrary to what they display through social media. The photos of happiness taken in every corner of the beauty and sparkling city of Japan is not worth and not as "Cool" as the daily sacrifice of the kenshusei's life. Such is still found a lot of exploitation of working hours, and inadequate facilities from the residence of the kenshusei etc. but the constraints and problems are often reluctant to be expressed by the kenshusei. Besides the reason for language skills, there is also a lack of understanding of the kenshusei regarding the flow of mechanisms related to the rules which applicable in their employment agreement.[48]

However, the difficulties faced by these kenshusei did not stop their hopes. They still hope after returning from Japan they can develop a career and work in a better place in Indonesia and they promise will no longer work on the 3 K type of job (Kitsui, Kiken, Kitanai).[49]

In the scheme of cooperation through the 'Issues Linkage / barter issue' between Japan and Indonesia in the field of employment it can be said that through the Japanese government's immigration policy in this case just looking for a gap to find solutions Japan needs for the entry of non-skill personnel, the Japanese government plays a role in capturing the issues or problems faced by Indonesia as a developing country that is still in need of assistance related to the transfer of knowledge and technology through the development of its human resources, plus the Indonesian government yet to be able to provide employment to meet the number of Indonesians experiencing such demographic bonus . For that cooperation of Indonesia and Japan is a 'barter issue' where in Japanese perspective, Japan has an interest in Indonesia both in terms of politics and also economy. For Japan, it is important that the cooperation of this trainee program is important to position Japan as a developed country in order to be able to say that Japan is taking responsibility and play a role in making progress and progress toward developing countries according to what is stated in Colombo Plan. economic cooperation can certainly fill the shortage or vacancy of the number of productive workers in Japan, especially for the types of jobs that are 3K (kitsui, kiken, kitanai) that is difficult, dangerous and dirty. The vacuum of this productive workforce is important for Japan to cope with, given Japan's economic driving force exists on industrial exports. Furthermore, in terms of its relationship with Indonesia, the cooperation would further legitimize the importance of Japan's position for Indonesia both politically and economically, which, as mentioned earlier, about the features of international cooperation by Robert and Nye, which under international co- operation conditions the pattern of each country that will be mutually dependent on each other.

The dependence then shows that colonialism for developing countries in this case Indonesia to hegemon countries like Japan has not been completed. The form of international cooperation between developed countries and developing countries is a consequence of globalization flow, which between countries will indeed form an unbalanced pattern or a global imbalance. In a report of the world commission on the Social Dimension of Globalization, established in 2001 by the International Labor Organization or ILO (founded in Geneva in 1919 to bring together government, employers and workers). The Commission led by Tanzania Benjamin W.Mkapa and the President of Finland Tarja Kaarina Halonen issued a report containing the issues of skepticism (about globalization) in 2004.

Conclusion

It can be said that Japanese dreams are the result of the success of Japan which established their country as a developed country, the beauty and "cool Japan" is also able to dominate the imagination from the appearance of social media owned by the Indonesian Kenshusei in Japan, although in their daily lives some people (kenshusei) are experiencing contradictory conditions, but for some people (kenshusei), they have to expend their lives for wellbeing.

Acknowledgement

The writer of this study acknowledges and is grateful that this work was supported by The Sumitomo Foundations for "Japan Related Research" for period of 2017 – 2018 and still on-going research.

References

1. ODA

2. Masaaki Shirikawa, The Transition From High Growth to Stable Growth: Japan"s Experience and Implications for Emerging Economies, Bank Of Japan, Accessed on November 2016. At http://www.boj.or.jp/en/announcements/press/koen_2011/data/ko110506a.pdf,

3. Mamoudou Hamidou, the Determinants of the Japanese Economic Growth (1960-1990) and the Causes of Its Recession (1990-2009), Accessed on November 2016 at http://r- cube.ritsumei.ac.jp/bitstream/10367/3665/1/51209659.pdf

4. Soo Im Lee, Japan"s Demographic Revival; Rethinking Migration, Identity and Sociocultural Norms, World Scientific Publishing Co.Pt. Ltd, Singapore, 2016. p. 50-51

5. Zhou Yuan, "The Role of The chinese Labour Agencies in Japanese Foreign Trainee and Technical Intern System" Accessed on November 2016 at http://lup.lub.lu.se/luur/download?func=downloadFile&recordOld=217 5354&fileOld=2175355

6. Chizuko Hayakawa. "Labour Law and Policy Issues Relating to Foreign Workers in Japan, Accessed on November 2016 at i http://web.jil.go.jp/english/JLR/documents/2010/JLR27_hayakawa.pdf   pada November 2016

7. Takeyuki Tsuda, "Reluctant Host: The Future of Japan as a Country of immigration," Accessed on November 2016 at http://migration.ucdavis.edu/rs/more.php?id=39_0_3_0

8. JITCO, Accessed on February 2017 at http://www.jitco.or.jp/english/about/index.html

9. Haning Romdiati "Indonesian Migrant Workers in Japan: Typology and Human Rights," Accessed on December 2016 at http://kyotoreview.cseas.kyoto-u.ac.jp/issue/issue3/article_293.html

10. JITCO, Accessed on February 2017 at http://www.jitco.or.jp/english/about/index.html

11. Haning Romdiati, "Indonesians Migrant Workers In Japan: Typology and Human Rights" Accessed on November 2016 at http://kyotoreview.cseas.kyoto-u.ac.jp/issue/issue3/article_293.html

12. Nana Oishi, Training or Employment? Japanese Immigration Policy in Dilemma, International Labour Office, Accessed on November 2016 at www.smc.org.ph>uploads>apmj_pdf,

13. ODA, Accessed on February 2017 at http://www.id.emb-japan.go.jp/oda/id/whatisoda_02.htm

14. Japan International Cooperation Agency, JICA Profile, Accessed on February 2017 at http://www.jica.go.jp/indonesia/office/others/pdf/brochure01.pdf

15. Pusat Data dan Informasi Ketenagakerjaan RI, "DATA PESERTA PEMAGANGAN LUAR NEGERI TAHUN 1993-2018, Juni 2018 Accessed on November 2018 at www.pemagangan.com

16. Ibid (data center)

17. http://elib.unikom.ac.id/files/disk1/455/jbptunikompp-gdl-nirwanmaul-22713-7-11.bab-i.pdf

18. Cholichul Hadi dan Dodik Kurniawan, Potensi dan Problematik Kenshusei (Pemagang Indonesia di Jepang) Menuju Kemandirian Accessed on February 2017 at http://cholichul-fpsi.web.unair.ac.id/artikel_detail-41301-buku-Potensi%20dan%20Problematika%20KENSHUSEI%20(Pemagang%2 0Indonesia%20di%20Jepang)%20Menuju%20Kemandirian.html

19. BNP2TKI, Accessed on February 2017 at http://bnp2tki.go.id/hasil-penelitian-mainmenu-276/226-permasalahan-pelayanan-dan-

perlindungan-tenaga-kerja-indonesia-di-luar-negeri.html

20 E.B. Haas, "Why Collaborate? Issue Linkage and International Regimes", World Politics, Vol.32. No.3, 1980, p372-373

21 Ibid

22 N.P Mugesejati & A.H. Rais, MPP, IIS Monograph Series- Politik Kerjasama Internasional: Sebuah Pengantar, Institute of International Studies UGM, Yogyakarta, 2011, p. 37-38.

23 Katri Liestala & Esa Sirkkunen, "? Social Media: Introduction to the tools and process of participatory economy", University of Tempere, Finland, 2008, p.17

24 Katri Liestala & Esa Sirkkunen, "? Social Media: Introduction to the tools and process of participatory economy", University of Tempere, Finland, 2008, p.19-20

25 Accessed on August 2017 at http://www.id.emb-japan.go.jp/oda/id/whatisoda_02.htm

26 Yusman L., „After 5 years benefits ijepa less expected", The Jakarta Post, Accessed on August 2017 at http://www.thejakartapost.com/news/2013/03/13/after-5-years-benefits-ij-epa-less-expected.html-0

27 Ministry of Foreign Affairs of Japan, Signing of The Agreement between Japan and the Republic of Indonesia for an Economic Partnership, Accessed on February 2017 at http://www.mofa.go.jp/announce/announce/2007/8/1174856_832.html

28 METI, White Paper on International Trade: Challenge of the Foreign Economic Policy in The 21st Century. Dapat Accessed on January 2017 at http://www.meti.go.jp/English/report/downloadflies/Gwp0140e.pdf

29 ODA official website

30 Nicholas Eberstadt, *Japan Shrinks*, Spring, The Wilson Quarterly, Accessed on 15 March 2016 at http://www.mauldineconomics.com/images/uploads/overmyshoulder/F eat_EberstadtFNL.pdf,

31 Giovanni Ganelli dan Naoko Miake, *Foreign Help Wanted: Easing Japan's Labor Shortages*, IMF Working Paper, Accessed on 4 March 2016 at https://www.imf.org/external/pubs/ft/wp/2015/wp15181.pdf,

32 Chris Maning & Cahyo Aswicahyono, "Perdagangan di Bidang Jasa dan Ketenagakerjaan: Kasus Indonesia" Accessed on 2017 at http://www.ilo.org/wcmsp5/groups/public/---asia/---ro-bangkok/---ilo-jakarta/documents/publication/wcms_185656.pdf

33 Nawawi, "The Dynamics of Indonesian Migrant Workers in Japan Under the Industrial Training and Technical Internship Program", Accessed on 2017 at http//www.mie-u.ac.jp/kokusai/tri/TRIU09PN-08.pdf

34 Ibid

35 JITCO

36 Saputra Wempi, Setiawan Budhi & yandri Erkata, "Indonesian Trainees in Japanese SMEs, Capital Accumulation and Micro-Small Business Development in Indonesia: a Preliminary Study" MPRA Paper, No.11491 (2008)

37 Sylvia Yazid, Global & Strategies *"Indonesian Labour Migration: Identifying the Women"*, Universitas Airlangga, Surabaya, 2015, p.50-51

38 "Undang-undang Republik Indonesia Nomor 39 Tahun 2004 Tentang Penempatan dan Perlindungan Tenaga Kerja Indonesia di Luar Negeri" Accessed on 2017 at www.bpkp.go.id/uu/filedownload/2/39/244.bpkp

39 Ibid hal 6 BPKP

40 Ibid hal.13 BPKP

41 Ibid hal 14 BPKP

42 Cholichul Hadi dan Dodik Kurniawan, Potensi dan Problematik Kenshusei (Pemagang Indonesia di Jepang) Menuju Kemandirian Accessed on February 2017 at http://cholichul-fpsi.web.unair.ac.id/artikel_detail-41301-buku-Potensi%20dan%20Problematika%20KENSHUSEI%20(Pemagang%20Indonesia%20di%20Jepang)%20Menuju%20Kemandirian.html

43 *"Challenging Discrimination in Employment: a Summary of Research and a Typology of Measures"* Accessed on 2017 at http://www.global-migrationpolicy.org/articles/integration/Discrimination%20in%20employment-%20summary%20of%20research%20&%20typology%20of%20measures,%TARAN,%20Zegers%20de%20Beijl,%20McClure%20ILO%2020 04.pdf

44 "Technical Intern Training Guidebook for Technical Intern Trainees" Accessed on March 2016 at http://www.jitco.or.jp/dowlnoad/data/guidebook_english.pdf

45 Accessed on 2017 at http://www.jitco.or.jp/dowlnoad/data/guidebook_english.pdf

46 "Japan Labour Standard Act" Accessed on 2017 at http://ilo.org/dyn/netlex/docs/WEBTEXT/27776/64846/E95JPN01.htm

47 "Kuchikomi, "Black Companies" exploiting foreign trainees" Accessed on 2017 at http://www.japantoday.com/category/kuchikomi/view/black-companies-exploiting-foreign-trainees

48 Intervieweed and Participatory observation with Indonesia Kenshusei in Private Company in Shiga Kyoto, September - October 2016 and May 2017

49 Interviewed and participatory observation with Indonesian Kenshusei in Private Company in Shiga Kyoto, September - October 2016 and May 2017

Urban Heat Island Study Based on LANDSAT Remote Sensing Images: A Case Study of Tokyo

Rui Wang[1], Wangchongyu Peng[2], Wei Chen[2], Weijun Gao[3], Soichiro Kuroki[4]
1 Master Student, Department of Architecture, University of Kitakyushu
2 PhD Student, Department of Architecture, University of Kitakyushu
3 Professor, Department of Architecture, University of Kitakyushu
4 Emeritus Professor, Department of Architecture, University of Kitakyushu

人口過密と産業の集積、そこへ地球温暖化の影響も加わって急速に進む大都市のヒート・アイランド現象。そのメカニズムを、アジアを代表する大都市・東京を例に、LANDSATの観測画像をもとに解明する。

Abstract

The urban is the center of regional society, economy, politics and culture. And the urban is a symbol of human civilization and development. Urbanization is a common trend in many countries. In developing countries, this situation is particularly evident. With rapid urbanization, there are lots of environment problems. Among these environmental problems, the urban heat island effect is the most important. Urban heat island has deep impacts on material cycles and energy transfers within urban ecosystems and has become an important issue in urban climate and environmental research. This paper, based on the Multi-time-phase TM /ETM+ Remote Sensing images, takes Tokyo as an example to contrast four-time inversions results and study the evolution rule and the characteristic of the heat island effect with Single-Channel Algorithm. Through this study, we can find the evolution law of urban heat island in Tokyo. And then for the future development of cities and solutions to the urban heat island effects, it can provide a more effective way of train of thought and methods.

Keywords   Urban Heat Island, ArcGIS; Remote Sensing; Urban Heat Island; Land Surface Temperature

Introduction

With the rapid urbanization, there has been a tremendous growth in population and buildings in the urban. The urbanization has a great impact on the environment in the urban, especially, the thermal environment. It is shown on the rising air-temperature in the center of the urban. And the suburbs air-temperature is at least two degrees lower than the urban. On the spatial distribution of temperature, the urban is like an island. So, we call it the urban heat islands (UHI). (Shown in Fig.1)

The cause of the UHI is wide-ranging. For one thing, it's caused by nature. Such as some special landform condition and climatic condition. For another, the most important is the development of human society. Entering the 21th century, because of urban extension, population concentration, developed industry, traffic jams and air pollution, and most of the buildings in the urban are made of concrete with low heat capacity and high heat

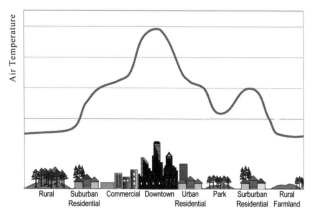

Fig. 1. Diagram of Urban Heat Island

conductivity, at the same time, high-rise building will weaken the wind, the temperature in the urban will be higher. Conversely, in sub-urbans, there aren't so many buildings and population. So, the environment is closer to nature and in stark contrast to that in the urban. It leads to the UHI effect highlighting.

The urban heat island is an important problem for the urban planning because there are many indications that UHIs have several negative impacts on an urban environment. With the air-temperature increasing, air will rise, and there will be a low-pressure vortex at central area of the urban. Then the pollutants, such as sulfur oxides, nitrogen oxides, carbon oxides, hydrocarbons, etc. produced by daily life, vehicles and factory will be gathered in the urban and damage people's health. Next, because of the pollutant, the temperature will rise further. Finally, it will be a vicious cycle, and generate even more serious social problems.

Research Region

Tokyo, officially Tokyo Metropolis, is the capital city of Japan. The mainland portion of Tokyo lies northwest of Tokyo Bay and measures about 90 km east to west and 25 km north to south. Chiba Prefecture borders it to the east, Yamanashi to the west, Kanagawa to the south, and Saitama to the north. Tokyo has an area of about 2188 square kilometers with a population of about 37 million, including urban area of about 621 square kilometers with a population of 13.74 million. The Tokyo Metropolitan Government administers the 23 Special Wards of Tokyo. In addition, Tokyo also includes 26 more cities, 5 towns, and 8 villages, each of which has a local government. (Shown in Fig.2)

The Greater Tokyo Area is the most populous metropolitan area around the world. And at the same time, Tokyo has the largest metropolitan economy in the world. According to a study conducted, the Tokyo urban area had a total GDP of $2 trillion in 2012, that topped in the list. Tokyo is also a major international finance center. About the transportation, Tokyo is Japan's largest domestic and international hub for rail, ground, and air transportation.

Tokyo is a temperate monsoon climate with an annual average air-temperature of 15.6 degrees. It has 4 distinctive seasons with abundant precipitation. There is more precipitation in summer because of the southeastern monsoon. There is less snow in winter.

Considering the characteristics of remote sensing image processing software and corresponding data collection, in this research, we selected The Imperial Palace as the center, and chose a circle area with a radius of 50 kilometers in Tokyo. The total area of research region is about 7853.98 square kilometers, including the most parts of the Tokyo Metropolitan Area. And it can typically reflect the evolution of the urban heat island in Tokyo. The satellite image is shown in Fig.3.

Fig. 3. The Satellite Image of Research Region

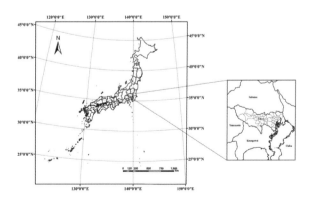

Fig. 2. Research Region

Research Data

The remote sensing data used in this research is Landsat 4-5

TM (Thematic Mapper) and Landsat 8 OLI (Operational Land Imager)/TIRS (Thermal Infrared Sensor) of Tokyo in March from 1985 to 2015 (shown in Table 1). And the orbital number is 107/35.

Table 1. Images used in this research

Sensor	Data
Landsat-5	1985-03-28
Landsat-5	1995-03-08
Landsat-5	2005-03-19
Landsat-8	2015-03-31

The Landsat Thematic Mapper (TM) sensor was carried onboard Landsat 4 and 5 from July 1982 to May 2012 with a 16-day repeat cycle. And the Landsat 5 TM image data files consist of 7 spectral bands. The resolution is 30 meters for Band 1 to 7. Among them, Band 6, the Thermal infrared, was collected at 120 meters, but was resampled to 30 meters. The approximate scene size is 170 kilometers north-south by 183 kilometers east-west.

The Operational Land Imager (OLI) and Thermal Infrared Sensor (TIRS) are instruments onboard the Landsat 8 satellite, which was launched in February of 2013. The satellite collects images of the Earth with a 16-day repeat cycle. And the Landsat 8 OLI/TIRS image data files consist of nine spectral bands with a spatial resolution of 30 meters for Bands 1 to 7 and 9. The ultra-blue Band 1 is useful for coastal and aerosol studies. Band 9 is useful for cirrus cloud detection. The resolution for Band 8 (panchromatic) is 15 meters. Thermal bands 10 and 11 are useful in providing more accurate surface temperatures and are collected at 100 meters. The approximate scene size is 170 km north-south by 183 km east-west.

The weather of data that we selected was sunny. The visibility in the study area is high. And the imaging quality chosen is good. And the software used for the study is ArcGIS 10.3.

Research Method

Land surface temperature is an important parameter for many research applications. And I used Single-Channel Algorithm for automatic retrieval of brightness temperature, land surface emissivity and land surface temperature from Landsat data to estimate land surface temperature.

This method can be used in order to process both Landsat-5 TM and Landsat-8 OLI/TRIS data. It consists of 3 separate steps, namely, NDVI Thresholds, Thermal Band to Brightness Temperature and Retrieve LST (Land Surface Temperature).

1. NDVI Thresholds

This step estimates land surface emissivity employing Normalized Difference Vegetation Index Thresholds Method ($NDVI^{THM}$) to distinguish between soil pixels (NDVI < $NDVI_S$), full vegetation pixels (NDVI > $NDVI_V$) and mixed pixels ($NDVI_S \leq$ NDVI $\leq NDVI_V$). And the threshold values of $NDVI_S = 0.2$ and $NDVI_V = 0.5$ make the method applicable for global conditions. The NDVI can be calculated from Landsat 4, 5 and 7 by equation 1 and Landsat 8 by equation 2. And then Normalized Difference Vegetation Index (NDVI) are converted to Land Surface Emissivity (LSE) using modified $NDVI^{THM}$.

$$NDVI = \frac{Band4 - Band3}{Band4 + Band3} \quad (1)$$

$$NDVI = \frac{Band4 - Band5}{Band4 + Band5} \quad (2)$$

In the conversion, the emissivity (ε) of soil and full vegetation pixels should be used. And the emissivity can be defined by user. In general, the default emissivity values are:

soil pixels:
$\varepsilon = \varepsilon_{S\lambda} = 0.96$

full vegetation pixels:
$\varepsilon = \varepsilon_{V\lambda} + C_\lambda = 0.985 + 0.05 = 0.99$

The emissivity of mixed pixels is calculated by equation 3. Each pixel (P_V) is calculated by equation 4 considering the proportion of vegetation. And the cavity effect (C_λ) that due to surface roughness is calculated by equation 5. In this equation, the geometrical factor (F') is the mean value 0.55.

$$E = E_{V\lambda} \cdot P_V + E_{S\lambda} \cdot (1 - P_V) + C_\lambda \quad (3)$$

$$P_V = \left(\frac{NDVI - NDVI_S}{NDVI_V - NDVI_S} \right)^2 \quad (4)$$

$$C_\lambda = (1 - E_{S\lambda}) \cdot \varepsilon_{V\lambda} \cdot F' \cdot (1 - P_V) \quad (5)$$

Additionally, this step allows the user to define the emissivity for the surface water. Normally, the default emissivity is 0.99. Before then, water bodies mask and the subset area (polygon feature layer) must be defined.

2. Thermal Band DN to Brightness Temperature

The next step is using appropriate conversion coefficients (gain and bias) to convert pixel values of Landsat thermal band (Band 6) to at-sensor spectral radiance in $W \cdot m^{-2} \cdot sr^{-1} \cdot \mu m^{-1}$ according to equation 6 and then transforming L_s to at-sensor brightness temperature (T_s) applying inverted Planck's Law and specific calibration constants (K_1 and K_2) as in the equation 7. And this step can only work with LPGS (Level-1 Product Generation System) data.

$$L_s = gain \cdot DN + bias \quad (6)$$

$$T_s = \frac{K_2}{\ln\left(\frac{K_1}{L_s} + 1\right)} \quad (7)$$

3. Retrieve LST

This step estimates LST (Land Surface Temperature) with S-C (Single-Channel) Algorithm according to equation 8a, 8b and 8c.

$$LST = \gamma \left[\frac{1}{\varepsilon}(\psi_1 L_s + \psi_2) + \psi_3 \right] + \delta \quad (8a)$$

$$\gamma = \left[\frac{c_2 L_s}{T_s^2} \left(\frac{\lambda^4 L_s}{c_1} + \frac{1}{\lambda} \right) \right]^{-1} \quad (8b)$$

$$\delta = -\gamma \cdot L_s + T_s \quad (8c)$$

In these equations, the necessary data are: the calculated brightness temperature (T_s) and the land surface emissivity (ε) datasets as well as some specific atmospheric functions (AF). The AF's (ψ_1, ψ_2 and ψ_3) are used for correction of the atmosphere influence which is very important part of the LST retrieval algorithm. The AF's are computed from atmospheric parameter with equation 9a, 9b and 9c.

$$\psi_1 = \frac{1}{\tau} \quad (9a)$$

$$\psi_2 = -L^{\downarrow} - \frac{L^{\uparrow}}{\tau} \quad (9b)$$

$$\psi_3 = L^{\downarrow} \quad (9c)$$

In these equations, τ is atmospheric transmissivity, $L^{\uparrow}$ is up-welling atmospheric radiance, and $L^{\downarrow}$ is down-welling atmospheric radiance. The site-specific atmospheric parameters can be calculated by means of an atmospheric radiative transfer model, such as ACPC (Atmospheric Correction Parameter Calculator that is a freely accessible web based on MODTRAN interface). The S-C Algorithm uses also Planck's radiation constants ($c_1 = 1.19104 \cdot 10^8 W \cdot \mu m^4 \cdot m^{-2} \cdot sr^{-1}$; $c_2 = 1.43877 \cdot 10^4 \mu m \cdot K$) and the effective wavelength of Landsat-5 TM and Landsat-8 OLI/TRIS Band 6.

These three steps are the whole procedure of land surface temperature retrieval from Landsat data.

Using this method, we can invert the land surface temperature. And then, through ArcGIS, the air temperature pattern of Tokyo can be gotten. The urban heat island effect is obvious in air temperature pattern. And we can find the evolution rule of urban heat island effect in Tokyo in the past several years.

Result and Analysis

According to the above research method, Landsat-5 TM images and Landsat-8 OLI/TRIS images are converted into the distribution maps of Tokyo land surface temperature in March 28th 1985, March 8th 1995, March 19th 2005 and March 31st 2015 (following show with 1985,1995, 2005 and 2015) In the distribution maps, the red area is the high-temperature zone, namely urban heat island area, and the blue area is the low-temperature zone. The more different in color between two regions, the more different in temperature between these regions.

1. Land Surface Temperature and Urban Heat Island Analysis in 1985

Fig.4 shows the distribution of land surface temperature on March 28th 1985.

Fig.5 shows the frequency distribution curve of land surface temperature on March 28th 1985.

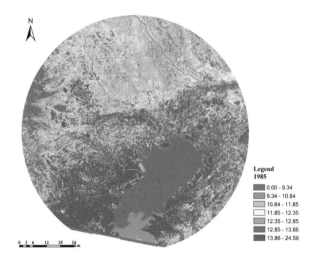

Fig. 4. The Distribution of LST (1985-03-28)

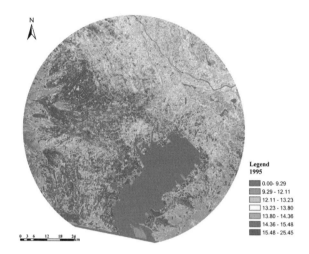

Fig. 6. The Distribution of LST (1995-03-08)

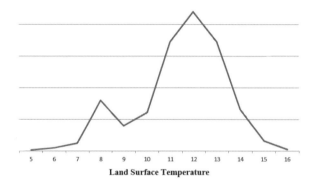

Fig. 5. The Frequency distribution curve of Land Surface Temperature (1985-03-28)

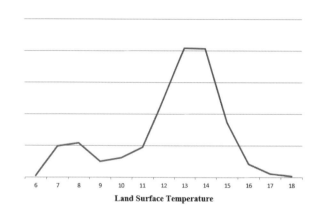

Fig. 7. The Frequency distribution curve of Land Surface Temperature (1995-03-08)

Fig.7 shows the frequency distribution curve of land surface temperature on March 8th 1995.

According to the above two figures, the mean of land surface temperature in 1985 is about 11.44 degrees. The urban heat island is not obvious in the center of Tokyo. And the land surface temperature in the region between Tokyo and Yokohama is commonly higher than that in the other region. And the region with high temperature. The land surface temperature around the Tokyo Bay is higher than that of inland area. Through Fig.5, we can find the temperature is centered on the range of 10 degrees to 11degrees. And the maximum temperature difference is about 4 degrees.

2. Land Surface Temperature and Urban Heat Island Analysis in 1995

Fig.6 shows the distribution of land surface temperature on March 8th 1995.

According to the above two figures, the mean of land surface temperature in 1995 is about 12.39 degrees. The urban heat island is formed in the northwest of the center of Tokyo. But, because of vegetation in The Imperial Palace, comparing to the neighboring regions, the land surface temperature is lower. And at the same time, the region that the land surface temperature was very high in 1985, between Tokyo and Yokohama, is cooling. And the north area is still very cool in 1995. Through Fig.7, the frequency distribution curve of land surface temperature in 1995 is similar to that in 1985. But the temperature is centered on the range of 13 degrees to 14 degrees. And the maximum temperature difference is over 4 degrees. It means that the urban heat island is becoming more serious.

3. Land Surface Temperature and Urban Heat Island Analysis in 2005

Fig.8 shows the distribution of land surface temperature on March 19th 2005.

Fig.9 shows the frequency distribution curve of land surface temperature on March 19th 2005.

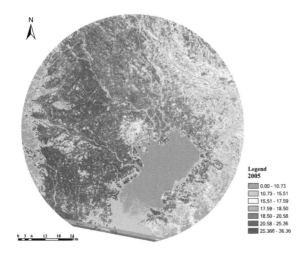

Fig. 8. The Distribution of LST (2005-03-19)

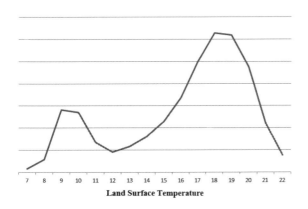

Fig. 9. The Frequency distribution curve of Land Surface Temperature (2005-03-19)

According to the above two figures, the mean of land surface temperature in 2005 is about 16.27 degrees. Comparing to the distribution of land surface temperature in 1995, the area of the region who's the land surface temperature is very high expands obviously, including the north region, the west region and the northwest region. And in these 10 years, the region between Tokyo and Yokohama is warm again. In a word, the whole west region of the Tokyo center is at a high-temperature area. And the east region can still keep cool. And the center of Tokyo always keeps at a relatively low-temperature level. With ten years construction, the land surface temperature of all region is higher. And the temperature is centered on the range of 17 degrees to 19 degrees. And we can also find that the maximum temperature difference is bigger, to about 6 degrees.

4. Land Surface Temperature and Urban Heat Island Analysis in 2015

Fig.10 shows the distribution of land surface temperature on March 31st 2015.

Fig.11 shows the frequency distribution curve of land surface temperature on March 31st 2015.

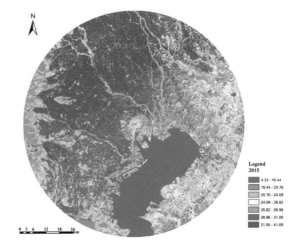

Fig. 10. The Distribution of LST (2015-03-31)

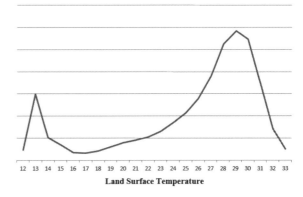

Fig. 11. The Frequency distribution curve of Land Surface Temperature (2015-03-31)

According to the above two figures, the mean of land surface temperature in 2015 is about 25.55 degrees. It's obvious that the mean of land surface temperature is much higher than before. The north region and northwest region of Tokyo center are becoming the central area of the urban heat island. In these regions, high-temperature areas are very intensive, and at the same time, there is a trend towards the east region of Tokyo center. Due to the influence of the marine environment and mainly the vegetation of the Imperial Palace, the center of Tokyo, the Imperial Palace and the surrounding area is still at a low-temperature area. But the mean of land surface temperature rises a lot comparing to 10 years ago. Although the mean temperature of the whole research area has increased a lot, the maximum temperature difference doesn't change too much. It means that the urban heat island is not deteriorated by the rise of land surface temperature in the past ten years.

Conclusion

1) In the thirty years, the urban heat island in Tokyo and the surrounding area is more serious and obvious, especially at the first 20 years. In last 10 years, the urban heat island is relatively controlled effectively.
2) The mean of land surface temperature rose faster and faster, especially after twenty-first century in March.
3) Because of the rapid development of cities and the rapid expansion of population, the area of urban heat island is also expanding. But, at the same time, due to the influence of natural environment, the development speed of urban heat island to east region and west region is slow. And the development speed to north is very fast.
4) The Imperial Palace and surrounding area always stay at a low-temperature area, because of the vegetation in the Imperial Palace and the marine environment.
5) By comparison, it is not difficult to find that the relationship between urban heat island and population activities. The more frequent the population activities are, the more serious the urban heat island effect is. Conversely, the less the population is, the less obvious the urban heat island is.
6) Comparison of actual land use, vegetation can effectively reduce land surface temperature and mitigate the urban heat island.

References

1) Liang Y T, Chen Z H, Xia Z H. Decades Change and Mechanism of the Urban Heat Island Effect in Wuhan Based on RS and GIS. Resources and Environment in the Yangtze Basin. 2010,08: 14-918
2) Fujio K, Shunji T. The Effects of Land-use and anthropogenic Heating on the Surface Temperature in the Tokyo Metropolitan Area: A Numerical Experiment. Atmospheric Environment. 1991,25:155-164
3) Yng Y B, Su W Z, Jiang N. Application of Remote Sensing to Study Urban Heat Island Effect. Geography and Geo-Information Science. 2016,05:36-40
4) S Bonafoni, G Baldinelli, P Verducci. Sustainable strategies for smart cities: Analysis of the town development effect on surface urban heat island through remote sensing methodologies. Sustainable Cities and Society. 2017,29:211-218
5) J P Walawender, M J Hajto, P Iwaniuk. A new ArcGIS toolset for automated mapping of Land Surface Temperature with the use of LANDSAT satellite data. IEEE IGARSS. 2012:4371-4374
6) Hideki Takebayashi, Masashi Senoo. Analysis of the relationship between urban size and heat island intensity using WRF model. Urban Climate. 2017
7) Y. Hirano, T. Fujita. Evaluation of the impact of the urban heat island on residential and commercial energy consumption in Tokyo. Energy. 2012,37:371-383
8) LI Z Q, GONG C L, HU Y, YIN Q, KUANG D B. The Progress of the Remote Sensing Research on Urban Heat Island. Remote Sensing Information.2009,04:100-105
9) D A QUATTROCHI, J C LUVALL. Application of high-resolution thermal infrared remote sensing and GIS to assess the urban heat island effect. Remote Sensing. 1997,18:287-304
10) HU H L, CHEN Y H, GONG A D. A Quantitative Study of the Relationship between Urban Vegetation and Urban Heat Island. Remote Sensing for Land & Resources.2005,03:5-13

Museums and Nationalism: The Political Discourse of the National Palace Museum in Taiwan

Yu-jhen Chen[1]
1 Project Assistant, National Museum of Taiwan History

ミューズ(美神)に捧げた社殿、それがミュージアム(博物館)。しかし近代の国民国家にとって、博物館は民族(国家)意識の醸成に欠かせない政治的装置でもある。とりわけ北京(中国)と台湾にある「故宮」は政治と切っても切り離せない。

Abstract

This paper aims to explore the relationship between museum and nation-state and to examine the political discourses of museums which are utilized to build up nationalism. In the museum study, previous researchers pointed out that, a museum has been considered as a stage of nationalism for the power of exhibition and display. Nevertheless, when it comes to modern China, the development of the nation and national museum seems more convoluted. Therefore, by exploring the case of the National Palace Museum, this paper discusses the relationship between the museum and nation-building in modern China and analyzes the transition of the museum and the political discourse of nations it represents in post-war Taiwan.

Keywords National Palace Museum; Nation-State; Exhibition; Expanding Nationalism

Introduction: Museums and Nation-States

In a brief historical retrospect of the museum, the English "museum" is originally from the Ancient Greek Μουσεῖον (Mouseion), which denotes a temple dedicated to the Muses, who is the patron divinity of the arts and knowledge in Greek mythology. In the fifteenth and sixteenth century, with the geographic development and colonial movement in Europe, collecting exotic artifacts and unusual natural objects had become popular among aristocrats and bourgeoisies. These private collections were often displayed in so-called wonder rooms or Wunderkammer (the cabinet of curiosities) that were precursors to museums.

In his groundbreaking Book, *The Birth of the Museum*, Tony Bennett examines the relation between exhibition and state power by exploring the development of the museum. He points out that the museum is a "distinctive vehicle for the display of power" (1995:94). In the Renaissance period, the aristocrats and the merchant class built private museums that collect rare artifacts and masterpiece to demonstrate the power and distinguish their status from the plebeian. With the emergence of absolutism in the sixteenth century, royal museums came to function mainly as institutions designed to display monarchical power within the limited circles of the aristocracy. Then in the eighteenth century, the outbreak of the French Revolution destroyed the order of old regime and created a condition of emergence for a new institution: the public museum. In the name of popular sovereignty, the collections in royal houses shifted into the hands of all citizens. The museum had migrated from a private and exclusive sphere into the public field (Bennett, 1995: 90-95).

Publicization is regarded as the main characteristic of modern museums. The proliferation of public museums in the eighteenth and nineteenth century is undoubtedly closely connected with the formation of nation-states in Western Europe.

According to Ernest Gellner's definition, the nation-state is the idea that state and nation should be congruent; Nationalism is primarily a political principle, which strives to make culture square with polity, to endow "a culture with its own political roof, and not more than one roof at that." (1983: 39-52) Nation-state became a new political unit and developed the craft of ruling which was different from old regimes. When the cultural border was connected with political boundary, the museum played a more crucial role in the power of the state. As Bennett points out, while the public museum emerged in the republican spirit which indicated the self-rule of people, it functions as an instrument for the reform of public manners on behalf of the ruling class (1995: 99).

Another museologist Eilean Hooper-Greenhill uses the Foucault's concept of the disciplinary society and point outs that the publicization of the museum after the French Revolution created the emergence of new technologies of behavior management. During the modern age, the museum, like the prison and the school in the classical age, became one of the apparatuses that embodies state power and created "docile bodies" through disciplinary technologies (1992: 167). With the new principles of scientific taxonomy and rationality, the museum allowed governors to reorganize and reclassify the collections and to create a new "reason and truth." She notes that the museum functions as an apparatus for the production of knowledge which serves the collective interests of the state rather than the education of people (1992: 174-190).

Also, Simon Knell elaborates the relation between the museum and the nation-state. He analogizes the museum with the theater and considers the national museum as a scenography or a stage for the performance of myth of nationhood. However, he points out that the museum could be a more powerful institute than the theater because people are led to believe that all around them has arrived objectively and all is as it seems to be these things are not merely props (2011: 8). The foundation of the Great British Museum in 1753 is an example of the national museums shaping the nationality. As Flora Kaplan suggests, in the museum, with the trophies from all over the world, the British proudly displayed the spoils of their colonial control of distant trade and markets. The museum could be understood as a place where shows the glory of the great empire on which the sun never sets and where they define and redefine "themselves" as a nation (2011: 164-166).

Another example is the Louvre Museum. In Carol Duncan and Alan Wallach's essay, they discover the profoundly historical and political meaning in the birth of the Louvre Museum. After the French Revolution, the Louvre, which was a Royal Palace, turned into a museum belonging to all French people. As Duncan and Wallach point out, the exhibition in the Louvre subtly embodies the state and the ideology of the state. By categorizing the paintings and arranging artistic genius, the exhibition in the Louvre museum demonstrates a linear evolution of culture, from Greece, Rome and the Renaissance to France. The French grand tradition of paintings was juxtaposed with the Greco-Roman sculptures in the exhibition hall. No one visiting the Louvre Museum can miss the image: France is the true heir of classical civilization (1980: 448-469).

In his classic book, Imagined Communities, Benedict Anderson explores the origin and spread of nationalism. In the additional chapters in 1991, he specifically points out that there are three institutions of power shaping the way in which the colonial state imagined its dominion: the census, the map and the museum. When it comes to the museums, Anderson suggests that the museum and the museumizing imagination are both profoundly political. In the late colonial period in Southeast Asia, instead of the brutal conquest, colonial regimes strives to create alternative legitimacies. Therefore, through colonial archaeology and the "scientific" and "objective" exhibition, colonial rulers were able to classify and display almost everything in the state, including peoples, regions, religions, languages, products, monuments, and so forth, in their own context, to bound the realms and to elaborate the legitimacy of their ancestry (1991: 163-187).

The above remarkable works provide a deep insight into the political function of the museum and its relation between the nation-state. Nevertheless, when it comes to modern China, the development of nation and national museum seems more convoluted and different from the experience of nation-states in the Western. Therefore, this paper examines the development of the National Palace Museum, which is a world-renowned museum with a unique history and profound political meanings. It is worthy to note that there are two museums which have the same name *Gu Gong* (old palace, 故宮) in Chinese-speaking countries. One is the National Palace Museum located in Taipei, Taiwan, and other is the famous Palace Museum in Beijing, China. This peculiar situation reflected the dilemma of the Chinese nation. Therefore, by exploring the case of the National Palace Museum, this paper discusses the relation between the museum and nation-building in China and analyzes the transition of the museum and the political discourse of nations it represents.

Imaging China: the Birth and the Transition of Chinese Nationalism

i. *Constructing China: The birth of the Palace Museum in Beijing*

After the Xinhai Revolution, the Republic of China (hereinafter referred to as "the ROC") was formally established on 1 January 1912. Influenced by the concept of the nation from the Western world, the regime in China shifted from a traditional imperium into a modern "nation-state." As a new nation-state, the ROC inherited the sovereign and the territory from the Qing Dynasty. However, the traditional imperial dynasty consisted of multiple ethnic groups, primarily including Han, Mongol and Muslim Chinese and Tibetan, not to mention the fact that Qing Dynasty was ruled by the Manchu who are the ethnic minority rising from the northeast China.

How to inherit the legacy and borders of the monarchy in the process of modern statization was crucial issues for the new nation-state. Therefore, a political term of *Zhonghua minzu* (Chinese nation, 中華民族) was invented. All the ethnic groups were narrated that they belonged to the *Zhonghua minzu* sharing a common history and destiny. The change of political slogans advocated by the Republicans can be good examples of the nation-building works. During the revolution period, the slogan of the revolutionary was "Expel the Manchus, restore Chinese rule, and establish a federal republic," which regarded the Manchus rulers as invaders and needed to be exiled. However, as soon as the 1911 revolution succeeded in overthrowing the Qing Dynasty, the government of the ROC, composed mostly of the former members of the revolutionary party, converted to the principles of "*Five races under one union*" (五族共和) and emphasized the harmony of the five major ethnic groups in China. The Five-colored flag representing the Han (red), the Manchus (yellow), the Mongols (blue), the "Hui" (Muslim Chinese) (white), and the Tibetans (black) was adopted as the nation flag of the ROC.

In the historical context of nation-building and regime change, Tsai Yuan-Pei and other Chinese intellectuals referring the example of the Louvre in France, the Winter Palace in Russia, and the Royal Museum in German suggested reconstructing the imperial palace into a national museum belonging to the Chinese nation (Song, 2013: 13-14). Therefore, after the expulsion of Pu-yi, the last emperor of China, from the Forbidden City in Bejing, the Committee for the Disposition of Qing Imperial Possessions started to make a comprehensive inventory of the articles in the imperial palaces. On 10th October 1925, the Palace Museum was established in the Forbidden City and opened to the public.

On the opening ceremony of the Palace Museum, Huang Fu, the former Premier of Cabinet, said in his speech:

Today is the Double Tenth Day, the National Day of the Republic of China, and will also become the anniversary day of the Palace Museum. We will celebrate them together. That is, damaging the museum is equal to damaging the Republic. We shall stand up and protect it (quoted in Na, 1966:17).

Huang Fu's speech connected the Palace Museum with the ROC. Those who are against the museum are against the whole nation. He pointed out the foundation of the museum is closely tied to the construction of the ROC. Like the examples of European nation-states, the nationalist government displayed the imperial collections accumulated throughout the *Sung* (宋), *Yuan* (元), *Ming* (明) and *Qing* (清) dynasties. From an imperial legacy to a public asset, the collection of the National Palace Museum created the sharing imagination of Chinese culture and diminished the ethnic variance.

From the administrative level, it also shows the uniqueness of the Palace Museum to the nation. In 1928 after the end of the Northern Expedition, the Nationalist Government officially took over the Palace Museum in Bejing and promulgated the "Palace Museum Organization Statute." In the Article 1, it appointed "The Palace Museum is responsible directly to the National Government." Then in February 1934, after the establishment of the Executive Yuan, highest executive organ of the Nationalist Government, the museum turned into a subordinate of the

Executive Yuan (Na, 1957: 70). Unlike other government-funded museums usually answering to the Ministry of Education, the Palace Museum has been administered directly by the Executive Yuan since 1934; and its director is a cabinet member of the Executive Yuan as same as the Minister of Education. The important role which the Palace Museum plays in the ROC cannot be overestimated.

Furthermore, faced with the threat from foreign intrusions, the Palace Museum started an epic journey and, strengthened its connection with the nation-state as a result. The outbreak of the Manchurian Incident on September 18, 1931, marked the beginning of Japanese military expansion in China. Considering the precarious situation in northern China, the government decided to move the most important collections out of the Forbidden City. Starting from February 1933, those cultural relics traveled over 10,000 miles and almost 14 years before they moved back to Nanjing in 1947 (National Palace Museum, 1995: 140-141). The nationalist government has accomplished the task that the Japanese journalist Nojima Tsuyoshi called "The great relocation of cultural relics in the history of civilization." (2012: 124)

As Nojima Tsuyoshi points out, during the Second Sino-Japanese War, the Palace Museum was sacralized through the toilsome journey (2012:20). Even though faced with the war of "*wang guo*" (lost country, 亡國), the government still spent a significant amount of time and energy moving the collections of the Palace Museum with the headquarters. When the southward plan was announced in the first place, many citizens in Beijing demonstrated against the plan and criticized for abandoning its people (Beiping Morning Post, 8 Feb. 1933). To reduce the rage of citizens, the nationalist government reply: "Those collections are national treasures that represent the cultural essences accumulated for thousands of years. They are vulnerable and unrecoverable. Once our culture destroyed, there is no hope to restore our nation." (quoted in Na, 1966: 60) This government's reply is the debut of the official discourse considering the collections of the Palace Museum as "national treasures." The reply indicates that the collection of the Palace Museum is not only the public asset belonging to the nation but also an essential element for the sustainability of the nation-state. During the war, those relics were symbolized as the nation suffering for survival.

ii. Exhibiting China: The Chinese Art Treasures Exhibition in the United States

In June 1946 the Chinese Civil War began. In 1948 the combat between the Kuomintang (the Nationalist Party, 國民黨) and the Chinese Communist Party (CCP, 中國共產黨) armies took an adverse turn. The Central Government of the ROC which led by Kuomintang decided to transport the collections of the Palace Museum to Taiwan, again, on a top priority over the retreat of the military and officials (Wang, 2004). After shipped to Taiwan, to ensure the safety of the Museum's collections, these artifacts were temporarily stored in the mountain of Wufeng, Taichung County.

After retreating to Taiwan, with military and economic assistance from the U.S., the Kuomintang government had established the "quasi-Leninist authoritarian regime," which is a one-party dictatorship led by Chiang Kai-shek (Cheng, 1989: 471-480.). Although the Chinese Civil War was suspended with the involvement of the US, in the Cold War framework, the civil war did not end for the both parties. As historian Lin Guoxian points out, the Kuomintang government was seeking for opportunities to fight back, so it rule in Taiwan in the 1950s was a "quasi war-time system." (2004, 76) Based on military logic during the civil war, "*Fan gong da lu*" (to retake mainland China, 反攻大陸) became a basic political doctrine and an ultimate goal for the nation. As a result, the collections of the Palace Museum was reinterpreted by the Kuomintang government and was endowed with more political meanings than when they were in Beijing. Beyond Anderson's theory, the museum came to function as an apparatus not only for imaging its dominion in the domestic level but also for demonstrating its legitimacy to others on the international scale. The Kuomintang government constructed a kind of expanding nationalism, which called for international recognition and contest with its rival.

Because of the defeat in the civil war, the Republic of China led by the Kuomintang government lost the main territories of China, and only controlled Taiwan Island and its surroundings. Based on the military forces, the territorial jurisdiction, the size of the population or other material condition, it was difficult for the Kuomintang to claim to be the legitimate government of "China." Also, after the second Taiwan Strait crisis in 1958, under pressure from the US, the Kuomintang was forced to give up its ambition to retake mainland China by military means. Although the Kuomintang did not change its ultimate goal, the principle means shifted from military to political ones (Chang, 2010: 41-42).

In the context of the civil war, the Palace Museum turned into a strong weapon for the Kuomintang to strike the communists and to claim its political legitimacy in China. In May 1961, the Joint Management Office, which was in charge of managing the museum's collections was invited to organize a major exhibition on the theme of "Chinese Art Treasures" in the United States. The Chinese Art Treasures exhibition circulated in Washington, New York, Boston, Chicago and San Francisco in the United States for a year.

When discussing the meaning of exhibition, Yu Jun-zhi, a cultural critic who participated in organizing the exhibition wrote:

Our nation is facing a crisis that has never happened in the past. Shen zhou (the old name for China, 神州) was fallen; the homeland was crumbled to pieces. Only understanding the true spirit of Chinese nation through the historical relics from our ancestors can save this crisis. ....What the totalitarian communist have done is far away from the spirit of "Tian-ren-he-yi" (the unity of heaven and men). They have humiliated our nation and our ancestors! As Sir Percival David said, the great masterpieces of Chinese art can only be bred in the land of freedom and civilization, and will never exist under the gray sky of totalitarianism! (1961:4-5)

Yu Jun-zhi's statement shows the political purpose of the exhibition. Instead of a simple cultural exchange, Yu Jun-zhi saw the exhibition as the only solution for the unprecedented national crisis. By emphasizing the connection between cultural legacy and political succession, he denied the legitimacy of the CCP in China and indicated that the Kuomintang government which possess the relics and antiquities from the ancestors was orthodox successors. Furthermore, Ye Gong-chao, the minister of foreign affairs who negotiated with the U.S. said when asked about the Chinese Art Treasures exhibition:

The president [Chiang Kai-shek] and I are looking forward to achieving this plan......By this exhibition, we will show that not the Communists but we [the Nationalists] are the guardians of the great Chinese cultural heritages (quoted in Nojima, 2012: 158).

What Ye Gong-chao said corroborated Yu Jun-zhi's view and made the official purpose of this exhibition clearer. The Kuomintang called itself as the protector of Chinese culture and considered the CCP as a destroyer. This statement actually inherited from the idea of nation-state since 1912 which considers the cultures relics imply or even equate the nation and its legitimacy. By holding an exhibition in the territory of its supporter, the Kuomintang tried to demonstrate to other countries not only the ownership of cultural relics but also the political legitimacy that those relics symbolized.

Imaging China on the Kuomintang's behalf, the exhibits were selected deliberately. One characteristic of those objects is "systematic." The Committee of Chinese Art Treasures Exhibition chose 253 masterpieces, including famous paintings, calligraphy works, bronze relics, porcelains, jade artifacts, curios, and so on (Central Daily News, 31 Jan.1991). The paintings accounted for the largest proportion. There were 112 traditional Chinese paintings on the exhibiting list. Besides the portability of objects, the reason why the painting was the majority of this exhibition was that paintings could display the Chinese history in a systemic context. The committee explicitly indicated that the collections of *wenrenhua* (literati painting, 文人畫) from the Palace Museum were so abundant that they can be displayed to show the longevity and continuity of Chinses art history (Chuang, 1961: 9).

Another feature of the exhibits is "orthodox." As the member of the exhibition committee, Tan Danjiong, pointed out, the porcelains selected for the were "completely orthodoxy", which means those porcelains were all from *yu yao* (imperial kilns, 御窯) or *guan yao* (official kilns, 官窯) and none of them from *ming yao* (folk kiln, 民窯). These were the collections which represent "the true spirit of our Chinese culture." (Central Daily News, 1 Feb.1991) As the Hooper-Greenhill suggests, those in power create a new truth and reason by reorganizing and reclassifying the collections in the exhibition. While the relics of the Palace Museum origin from the imperial collections, they were chosen and arranged to make a "systematic" and "orthodox" China visible and to support the claim that the Kuomintang was only legitimate government in China.

iii. Building up the Nationalist China: The Rebirth of the National Palace Museum in Taiwan

Inspired by the success of the exhibition tour in the U.S., the Kuomintang government, with the financial support from the U.S., made a decision to move the collections of the Palace Museum from remote mountain area to its temporary capital, Taipei. In 1965 the construction of the National Palace Museum in the Taipei suburb of Waishuanxi was completed. After sixteen years sealed in the mountain, those displaced collections of the Palace Museum finally were settled down and displayed in public again.

The "rebirth" of the National Palace Museum in Taipei has special meanings not only for the Kuomintang government but also for the Chinese nation that they have created since 1911. Although sharing many similarities with the old palace museum in Beijing, the new museum was endowed with different political meanings from the old one. To demonstrate the continuous legitimacy of the ROC, the architecture design of the new museum was in northern Chinese imperial style and referred to the Forbidden City. As Huang Bao-yu (黃寶瑜), the designer of the building, talked about the designing idea of the main hall: "When the sunshine enters the hall, it will create a 45-degree shadow. It will remind visitors of the *Wumen* (Meridian Gate, 午門, the main gate of the Forbidden City) in Peiping." (Huang, 1966) The building of the new museum showed the Kuomintang's ambition to summon the spirit of Chinese nation from the old palace and to claim the Chinese orthodoxy in Taiwan. The symbol of the old building called for the connection with the starting point of the Chinese nation and represented the expansion of the ROC.

However, the Kuomintang added extra elements to the "rebirth" of the Palace Museum in the Taipei. Compared with the image of the Forbidden City, the new museum was equipped with much more symbols of Dr. Sun Yat-sen, the founding father of the ROC. The inauguration ceremony was held on November 12th which was the centenary of Dr. Sun Yat-sen's birthday. Even the name of this new museum site was christened the "Chung-Shan Museum"(中山博物院) by the President Chiang Kai-shek in honor of Dr. Sun Yat-sen's (Chung-Shan is the most popular of his Chinese first names).

In memory of Dr. Sun Yat-sen, there were many facilities relating to Dr. Sun Yat-sen added in the Chung-Shan Museum. A bronze statue of Sun Yat-sen was placed in the great hall of the second floor. Then in 1967 the extension project phase 1 completed a paifang (memorial archway gate, 牌坊) which was identical with the Bo'ai archway gate in the Sun Yat-sen Mausoleum in Nanjing (Song, 2013:113-114). With the hundreds of stairs up to the museum, the spectator seemed to walk through pilgrimage road of the Sun Yat-sen Mausoleu.

The name and design put the new museum in a vague position and caused confusion both to visitors and the original faculty members. As Na Chih-liang, a senior member of the National Palace Museum, pointed out, due to the naming by Chiang Kai-shek, the National Palace Museum changed "from a homeowner to a tenant" (1993:223). However, those symbol of Sun Yat-sen, in fact, reflected the transition of the Kuomintang's discourse of the Palace Museum and the Chinese Nation that the museum represented. Following the strategy of the exhibition tour in the U.S., the Kuomintang had elaborated the discourses of the museum to display its legitimacy and strike the CCP.

One main discourse is about orthodoxy. By combining the image of Dr. Sun Yat-sen with the National Palace Museum, the Kuomintang constructed a new discourse of Chinese nationalism which emphasized the relation between the cultural orthodoxy and political legitimacy. According to Chiang Kai-shek, Dr. Sun Yat-sen, who established the ROC is the true heir of Chinese sages, inheriting from Yao, Shun, Yu, Tang Wang, Yi Yin, Wang Ji, Wen Wang, Wu Wang to Zhou Gong, and he entrusted the ROC to the Kuomintang (1954: 150). Therefore, to construct a linear orthodoxy in China and undergird its legitimacy in China, the commemoration of Dr. Sun Yat-sen become a crucial element in the National Palace Museum.

The other discourse is about the moral dimension of the Chinese nation. The Kuomintang accused the communist's propositions, such as historical materialism and class struggle and proletarian internationalism, of destroying the Chinese traditional ethics and virtue (Hsiau, 1991: 92). In 1966, the Cultural Revolution movement broke out and called to destroy the si jiu (Four Old, 四舊) which were Old Customs, Old Culture, Old Habits, and Old Ideas. The anti-communist war turned into a combat of culture and morality. As a result, when talking about Chinese culture, the Kuomintang emphasized specific moral values. For example, *siwei bade* (Four Anchors and Eight Virtues, 四維八德)[1] became a characteristic of the Chinese nation. What is more, Sun Yat-sen's Three Principles [People's nationalism, People's Democracy, People's Livelihood] was regarded as the core of Chinese culture.

In addition to the architecture symbols, the Kuomintang's discourse and new imagination of Chinese nation were demonstrated in the exhibition of the National Palace Museum. As the director of the National Palace Museum, Chiang Fu-tsung said:

An abstract concept is easily forgotten and ignored, so we need the visible objects or artifacts to testify. The ten thousands of historical relics in the National Palace Museum are the best witnesses and evidence (Chiang, 1977:52-53).

In January 1967 the National Palace Museum hold the "Exhibition of Chinese orthodoxy", exhibiting li dai sheng xian hua xiang (the portraits of sages in Chinese history, 歷代聖賢畫像), ling yan ge er shi si gong chen xiang (the Lingyan Pavilion's portraits of 24 loyal officials, 凌煙閣二十四功臣像)", er shi si xiao tu (24 filial piety, 二十四孝圖) and other collections which represented Chinese orthodoxy and the traditional virtues. The organizer of the exhibition especially pointed out that those relics were displayed on the principle of Dr. Sun Yat-seng's theory (Central Daily News, 1 Jan.1967). By underscoring of the moral dimension of the Chinese nation, the Kuomintang criticized and repudiated the legitimacy of the CCP. Besides, in the exhibition, the manuscript of Chiang Kai-shek was consciously juxtaposed with Dr. Sun Yat-seng's work which was displayed after the portraits of Chinese sages (Central Daily News, 27 Jan.1967). The linear orthodoxy in China which Chiang Kai-shek claimed were clearly presented in the exhibition as real as an undeniable truth.

In the context of anti-communist, the Kuomintang built up a specific nationalism while reconstructing the Palace Museum in Taiwan. The discourse of Chinese nation has added the element of a great person and moral doctrines to demonstrate culture orthodoxy and political legitimacy of the Kuomintang. The relics of the National Palace Museum became more like "nationalist's treasures" than "national treasures."

Conclusion

This paper analyzes the development of the National Palace Museum. From the establishing in Beijing, relocating around the mainland, and finally reconstructing in Taipei, the National Palace Museum represents different political meanings in different periods and demonstrates the transition of the Chinese nation. Following the step of European nation-states, the museum was established as an apparatus for creating the imagination that unifies the different ethnic groups into one "nation." Through museumization, the relics from imperial collections became "national treasures" symbolizing the new nation.

As Anderson suggests, by arranging the exhibits in particular order, the museum assists nations to imagine their dominion and to elaborate the legitimacy of their ancestry. However, he and other scholars above primarily focus on the internal construction of a nation. This case study of the National Palace Museum indicates that the museum can also function as an apparatus for demonstrating nations to other countries. The image of a nation is shaped not only by the domestic rulers but by the international rivals. In the context of anti-communist, the Kuomintang shows the external function of the museum on the exhibition tour in the U.S. By exhibiting the "systematic" and "orthodox" collections, the Kuomintang claim the legitimacy in China to its alliance.

Furthermore, the "rebirth" of the National Palace Museum in Taipei elaborates the transition of the Chinese nation. On the one hand, the new museum emphasizes the linkage with the old palace museum in Beijing to demonstrate the continuity of the ROC. On the other hand, the new museum was endowed with more political meaning in the context of the Kuomintang's rule in Taiwan. In contrast to the old museum in Beijing, the National Palace Museum has added new elements. The symbols of Dr. Sun Yat-sen was coded in the museum to demonstrate the cultural orthodoxy and political legitimacy, and the moral doctrines of the Kuomintang was displayed in the exhibition to undermine the legitimacy of the CCP. By the display in National Palace Museum, the Kuomintang in 1960s created a "nationalist" image of the Chinese nation and an expanding nationalism.

---

1 *Siwei* are propriety(禮), righteousness(義), a sense of honor(廉), and a sense of shame(恥); *bade* are loyalty(忠), filial piety(孝), benevolence(仁), love(愛), faithfulness(信), justice(義), peace(和) and harmony(平).

References

1) Anderson, Benedict (1991) *Imagined Communities: Reflections on the Origin and Spread of Nationalism*. London; New York: Verso Books.

2) Bennett, Tony (1995) *The Birth of the Museum: History, Theory, Politics*. London; New York: Routledge.

3) Chang, Su-ya (2010) The Second Taiwan Strait Crisis and "Return to the Mainland" Propaganda [Chinese]. *Bulletin of the Institute of Modern History*. Taipei: Academia Sinica.

4) Cheng, Tun-jen (1989) Democratizing the quasi-Leninist regime in Taiwan. *World Politics* 41(4): 471-499.

5) Chiang, Fu-tsung (1977) Gu gong bo wu yuan yu zhong hua wen hua fu xing yun dong [*The National Palace Museum and the Chinese Cultural Renaissance Movement*]. Taipei: Taiwan Commercial Press.

6) Chiang, Kai-shek (1954) Zong tong jin nian lai guan yu jiao yu wen hua de xun shi. Taipei: Taiwan Provincial Education Department.

7) Chuang, Shang-yan (1961) Fu mei zhan lan ming hua zhi zhen xuan ji qi yi yi [*The Selecting Process of Renowned Paintings for the U.S. Exhibition and Its Meaning*] Zhongguo gu yi shu pin fu Mei zhan lan zhuan kan. Taipei: Wen xing za zhi she, pp. 9-11.

8) Duncan, Carol, & Wallach, Alan (1980) The universal survey museum. *Art History* 3(4): 448-469.

9) Gellner, Ernest (1983) *Nations and Nationalism*. Ithaca: Cornell University Press.

10) Hooper-Greenhill, Eilean (1992) *Museums and the Shaping of Knowledge*. London; New York: Routledge.

11) Hsiau, A-chin (1991) *The Cultural and Moral Discourses of the Kuomintang Regime(1934-1991): An Analysis of Sociology of Knowledge* [Chinese]. Taipei: National Taiwan University.

12) Huang, Bao-yu (1966) zhong shan bo wu yuan zhi jian zhu [The Architecture of the Chung-Shan Museum]. *National Palace Museum Quarterly* 1(1): 69–78.

13) Kaplan, Flora (2011) Making and Remaking National Identities. In S. Macdonald (Ed.), *A Companion to Museum Studies*. West Sussex: Wiley-Blackwell, pp. 152-169.

14) Knell, Simon (2011) National Museums and the National Imagination. In Knell, Simon e. al (Ed.), *National Museums: New Studies from around the World*. New York: Routledge, pp. 3-28.

15) Lin, Guoxian (2004) Zhan hou tai wan tong zhi ti zhi de zai si kao: Wei quan ti zhi de li lun yu shi yong [Rethink the Ruling System in Post-war Taiwan: Theories and Applications of Authoritarian Regime]. *Formosan Study* (13): 45-88.

16) Na Chih-liang (1993) Dian shou gu gong guo bao qi shi nian [*Seventy Years in the National Palace Museum*]. Taipei: Taiwan Commercial Press.

17) Na Chih-liang (1957) Gu gong bo wu yuan san shi nian zhi jing guo [*Thirty-Year History of the National Palace Museum*]. Taipei: Taiwan Commercial Press.

18) Na Chih-liang (1966) Gu gong si shi nian [*Forty-Year History of the National Palace Museum*]. Taipei: Taiwan Commercial Press.

19) National Palace Museum (1995) Gu gong qi shi nian xing shuang [*Seventy-Year History of the National Palace Museum*]. Taipei: Taiwan Commercial Press.

20) Nojima, Tsuyoshi (2012). *The Separation and Reunion of the Two Palace Museums* [Chinese]. Taipei: Linking Publishing.

21) Song, Zhao-lin (Ed.) (2013) Gu gong yuan shi liu zhen [*The History of the National Palace Museum*]. Taipei: National Palace Museum.

22) Wang, Horng-Luen (2004) National Culture and Its Discontents: The Politics of Heritage and Language in Taiwan, 1949-2003. *Comparative Studies in Society and History* 46(4): 768-815.

23) Yu, Junzhi. 1961. Wen hua jiao liu yu tian ren he yi: Lun zhong guo gu yi shu pin fu mei zhan lan de shi dai yi yi [Cultural Exchange and "Tian-ren-he-yi": On the meanings of the Chinese Art Exhibition Tour in United State]. Zhongguo gu yi shu pin fu Mei zhan lan zhuan kan. Taipei: Wen xing za zhi she, pp. 4-5.

Analysis of Informal Settlements Based on World Bank Guidelines

*Cherry Amor A. del Barrio[1,2], Luis Ma. T. Bo-ot, PhD[3]

1 Instructor, Architecture Department, Technological Institute of the Philippines, Manila
2 Graduate Student, College of Architecture, University of the Philippines, Diliman
3 Associate Professor & Graduate School Director, College of Architecture, University of the Philippines, Diliman

いわゆるスラム街で暮らす人々が建てた非合法の粗末な住居。それは不衛生で災害に弱いと言われているが、調べてみると意外なほど人々の生活の知恵が詰まった安上がりで合理的な建物だった。フィリピンでの貴重なケーススタディ。

Abstract

In 2011, the World Bank, funded by the Trust Fund for Environmentally & Socially Sustainable Development (TFESSD) conducted a research in Mumbai, India with the agenda to address climate change with low cost green housing. This research aimed to make the informal settlements in Mumbai to be both climate resilient and climate responsive.

Slums mostly attract attention towards the economic condition of the people inhabiting such settlements and because of the strong stigma against these marginalized members of the society, significant opportunities to learn and understand unorthodox construction philosophies applied in building these settlements are oftentimes missed-out. However, putting aside the social bias, there are three areas that can be focused on in investigating these settlements, namely, the materials used, its efficiency in terms of cost, and application in building construction.

This study identified the factors that make multi-level informal settlements resilient, and assessed their levels of resiliency by determining the materials and construction methods used in building these self-help dwellings and comparing them to the building guidelines prescribed in World Bank's "Building Guidelines on Informal Housing: Reducing Disaster Vulnerability through Safer Construction". This study found out that, out of the nineteen (19) building guideline requirements, seventeen (17) items or 89% were in compliance with the guidelines or alternative maintenance recommendations specified by the book.

Keywords World Bank, Multi-level Informal Settlements

Introduction: Informal Settlers, and their Past and Current Situations

The phenomenon of informal settlements, contemporary urban vernacular houses, and other poor residential neighborhoods is not new. They exist in urban contexts all over the world in various forms and typologies, dimensions, locations and by a range of names (e.g. squatter settlements, favelas, poblaciones, shacks, barrios bajos, bidonvilles). *(A. Gilbert and J. Gugler, 1992)* Informal settlements manifest on vacant and accessible lands. These are common along city fringes, rivers and seaside, railroad tracks, dump sites and even underneath bridges. The increase in population contributed to the problems of squatting.

According to Icamina and Alcazaren these spontaneous settlements house all demographics, wherein the elderly are not dissociated from the society, and the children dominate the number of population in the community. In these settlements, residents spend most of their time outside their homes and despite the messy surroundings, settlers wear clean clothes. Barbers keep kids and adults well groomed and babies get regular cleansing, which are physical evidence of pride and determination to survive. During the day, the women are the next most visible residents, as men are usually at work, sleeping off a night of hard drinking or just plain sleeping. *(Alcarazen, 2011)*

Appearance, Construction Materials and Perception of Its Stability

Informal architecture addresses the basic need for shelter despite the lack of building materials, utilities and even the land to build on. These unconventional low-tech multi-level residential buildings are usually constructed from standard and/or recycled materials like plywood, corrugated metal sheets, plastic sheets, and cardboard boxes. Its appearance, materials and methods of construction, however, vary according to its environment.

One example is the informal settlements on water villages which uses bamboo as a common material. From above, these settlements present a very striking view as it is perceived as stitched or weaved. However, these settlements are also one of the most fragile and vulnerable types of informal settlements.

Another example is the spontaneous settlements at the main land, which are constructed with lightweight materials, raised floors, and multi-functional spaces, intended for the use of nuclear families, which are not far from the original design and function of the basic nipa hut dwellings. These settlements, due to their location and inability to blend with the generally acceptable urban aesthetics, are oftentimes perceived negatively.

Accurate, localized and available qualitative and quantitative data on the actual structures of informal settlements and associated learning platforms remain limited. Data is often ad hoc and not connected to robust city-wide monitoring and evaluation processes, so the dimensions of inhabitants' lives remain unknown to policy and planning responses. *(Patel, 2012)* Furthermore, as the study of the history and development of vernacular architecture progresses, evolutions of self-help dwellings to multi-level dwelling units are continuing to occur at a much faster rate.

Researches from decades ago up to present are more inclined to the theoretical analysis as to how and why there's been a significant increase in the production of self-built or informal houses rather than the built form and structural design of the housing itself and its evolution. One example is the issue papers presented on the United Nations Conference on Housing and Sustainable Urban Development, Habitat III Quito-2016 about Informal Settlements, which paid more attention to the relationship between the growth of informal settlement and slums, and the lack of adequate housing and land. As a result, only a partial understanding of such settlements has emerged because there has been a virtual absence of empirical data on "squatter" architecture. *(Napier, 1995)* Aside from that, though there have already been published researches on how to improve informal settlers' lives *(III, 2015)*, observers and researchers tend to pay more attention to the negative aspects that these dwellings and dwellers bring. On the same conference, slums are perceived as "degraded environment" where dwellers should be moving out because of absence of legality, substandard in terms of space and infrastructure, absence of permanent materials, etc. By neglecting how industriously-built these settlements are, and how they have achieved their identity through what they are not, or do not have, in comparison with the formally built structures.

Building Guidelines on Informal Housing: Reducing Disaster Vulnerability through Safer Construction

In 2011, the World Bank, funded by the Trust Fund for Environmentally & Socially Sustainable Development or TFESSD, conducted a research in Mumbai, India, in line with the Component 2 of "Addressing Climate Change with Low Cost Green Housing". The book aims to make the informal settlements in Mumbai to be both climate resilient and climate responsive.

Prior to this book, book 1 was published presenting Mumbai's prevalent slum housing which were broadly categorized as wet, dry and hybrid. Such houses are made from recycled or scavenged materials, and are constructed through methods that are lacking in quality and detail. Three reasons that has attributed to these issues were cited, namely, affordability, rapid timeline, and knowledge gap.

The book 2 is a structured manual that provides guidelines for the improvement of informal housing construction. It is also designed to be used as a guide for construction, maintenance, and a reference in the exploration of alternative materials for owners and contractors. It constitutes a four-part manual. The first part provides recommendations on material selection, usage and maintenance through the identification of construction material issues. The second part is focused on the assembly of materials in house construction which covers foundations walls and roofs in consideration of a more climate responsive house through improved light and ventilation. The third part recommends an "ideal" prototype for dry, wet and hybrid housing typology. And finally, part four introduces alternatives to common practices such as existing new low cost construction methods and materials to be explored. This book is used as a guide in the measure of sustainable construction that may be used or are existent in the building of the informal settlements studied in this research.

Statement of the Problem

Slums mostly attract attention towards the economic condition of the people inhabiting such settlements and because of the strong stigma against these marginalized members of the society, significant opportunities to learn and understand unorthodox construction philosophies applied in building these settlements are oftentimes missed-out.

However, putting aside the social bias, and focusing solely on the appreciation of the construction methods and philosophies applied, there are three areas that can be focused on in investigating these settlements, namely, the materials used, its efficiency in terms of cost, and application in building construction.

Objectives of the Study

This paper aims to identify the factors that make multi-level informal settlements resilient or how far it is from being resilient through:

Inventory and Documentation of existing and available materials and methods used in building of these self-help dwellings.

Comparison and Analysis between the gathered data and the Building Guidelines created by the World Bank on Informal Housing focused on reducing disaster vulnerability through safer construction.

Creation of a measure or rating level on informal housing resiliency based on the Building Guidelines of World Bank on Informal Housing focused on reducing disaster vulnerability through safer construction.

Significance of the Study

This study recognizes multi-level informal settlements as adaptive buildings based on responses of the human condition, natural forces and environment; offering good judgement for the creative use of its raw technology on the field of Building Science, by looking at a more comprehensive and balanced understanding of both the product and process dynamics of spontaneous settlements and of the people who create and inhabit them.

Analyzing dimensions of informal dwellings can provide valuable insight into creating viable adaptations for cramped spaces for a better and more appropriate design and guidelines. Moreover, to serve as a resource for donors and policy makers through the presentation of existing approaches from slum building, for a relatively cheaper and sustainable approach to low cost house building improvement and disaster risk reduction.

Study of Related Literature
Common Perceptions towards Informal Settlements

In a paper written by Alex Ray P. Evangelista, titled *"Promoting Awareness and Appreciation of Informal Settlements through Education"*, he reiterated that slums have always been a symbol of a poor economy and is detrimental to one country's progress. Thus, they were labelled as eyesores and are being compared to primitive settlements. In the Philippines, there is an evident stereotyping against informal settlements, as slums are hardly recognized as an effective, affordable, and convenient option for the poor. When in some cases, these dwellings are more liveable than the settlements the government provides.

Contrary to the common residential units offered by the government which are like monotonous series of boxes designed side by side, shanties of informal settlements display innovativeness and ingenuity through the use of recycled materials regardless of the type of land, slope and other environmental hindrances, hazardous or not. These types of structures would usually have one single room with multiple uses, which can be as small as twelve (12) square meters. During the day it serves as the dining, living and kitchen, whereas at night, it is transformed into a bedroom for the whole family – a concept that is very much similar to primitive dwellings.

In conclusion, the research suggests that rather than condemning these informal settlements, the general public should take the opportunity of studying the living conditions of slums along with its physical and social fabric.

In a similar research conducted by Peter Kellett and Mark Napier, titled *"A Critical Examination of Vernacular Theory and Spontaneous Settlements"*, it is stated that for the past three decades, the tradition of study on spontaneous settlements are leaning towards the cause and processes that give rise to informally produced housing rather than the built form of the housing itself. Thus, only a partial understanding of such settlements has emerged due to the virtual absence of empirical data on "squatter" architecture.

Backed up with the 7th Semester Dissertation in Bachelor of Architectural Technology and Construction Management at VIA University College of Natalia Kostelnikova, titled *"Analysis of vernacular architecture in terms of sustainability"*, she discussed vernacular architecture, its sustainable perspective and considerable adaptability in contemporary design. She focused on vernacular architecture along with a few specific kinds of dwellings made by their ancestors. Though there were no exact order or time axes presented, she related her investigations with contemporary buildings, which are connected to traditional principles or local materials.

The Use of Unconventional and Recycled Materials

Using natural or recycled materials, as well as the simple methods of construction execution, is one of the main ideas of sustainable development. *"Unconventional Building Structures in Single Family Social Housing"*, by Magdalena Zalecka Myszkiewicz", focused on the concept of sustainability with regards to unconventional low-tech structures made from natural and/or recycled materials which are believed to be self-sufficient as far as their operation, materials, construction and maintenance cost is concerned. These include off-grid houses making use of used tyres, aluminium tins, glass bottles or plastic containers. However, these unconventional dwellings were commonly associated with weakness and infectivity due to the social stigma on the dwellers and the untypical appearance of their houses, and as such applications require construction parameters on quality control, insulation and installation.

Another paper titled *"Improving Housing Durability in Informal Settlements Using Affordable Building Materials – The Case of Kibera, Nairobi"*, by Ja Walubwa and P Shah" aimed to identify the availability and accessibility of local materials in the construction of durable houses. Stones, used water bottles, corrugated iron sheets and cement are some of the affordable materials that were cited. The respondents also gave special attention to interlocking bricks as it incurs lesser cost in terms of labour and production. Research shows that informal settlers build their house in accordance with their financial capability. A guideline in a Poverty Reduction paper pointed out that in terms of slum upgrading, these dwellers should be involved in the construction and design as they themselves can give solutions to their existing problems. Thus, an effort to make informal settlers intervene and participate in the innovation of building houses was being adopted in Kiberia to ensure that slum dwellers will have a sense of ownership on their homes.

Furthermore, the research concludes that ecological structures, making use of recycled materials, can be an alternative in the construction of sustainable complex buildings and may positively affect social housing since it doesn't require high building skills, nor does it necessitate the use of specialized construction equipments.

Methodology

The study is a mix of comparative analysis and experimental research that is exploratory and interpretative in nature.

Since the type of structure that's being studied is a residential dwelling, the structure, its tenants, users, and builders are the subject of the study. Proper care has been taken on the identification of parts, materials, joints and connections for proper assessment as guided by the Informal Housing Building Guidelines.

The outcome of the study is based on the comparative results of the chosen unit as compared to the Informal Housing Building Guidelines by World Bank. Observation and documentation of the structure, in the form of as-built drawings also took place to supplement the interviews.

It also involved interviews, checking of records or documents, and fieldwork.

Research Findings

The informal housing unit that has been studied is owned by Mrs. Lolita. The building is initially a one (1) storey residence that progressed into a three (3) storey house in a span of two decades, occupying a lot that is roughly around 12.30 sqm, having dimensions of 2.75m (w) x 4.5m (h), less the area of the sidewalk which is about 4.13 sqm.

The residence is occupied by Mrs. Lolita, her husband, her daughter with psychiatric illness, her son and daughter in-law, two (2) grandsons and two (2) house-help.

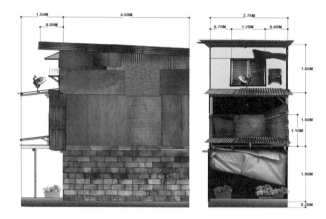

Fig. 2. Elevations

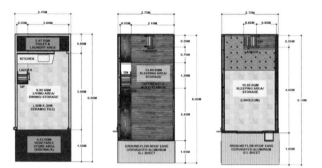

Fig. 1. Floor Plan

Fig. 3. Elevation Details

The ground floor consists of three spaces. First is a space occupying the sidewalk, with an area of around 4.13 sqm, utilized as an open store for vegetables. The interior of the house is divided into two areas. The larger cut is multi-purpose and is roughly around 9.00 sqm, which is used as a living, kitchen and storage area; and the remaining 2.47sqm is used as toilet and laundry area. The second and third floor, on the other hand, serves as an area for storage and sleeping. A ladder-like wooden stairs that is 0.55m wide serves as an access from the ground floor to the second floor. All upper floors are constructed with a roof eave that is 1.00m to 1.50m wide, located at the front part of the house. Floors are made from plywood and lumber scraps with linoleum on top, except for the ground finished floor that is made from slab floor and tiles.

During the day, five (5) persons are simultaneously using the ground floor, three adult females and two children. The second floor is used by a psychiatrically-ill adult female and the third floor is vacant. At night, four (4) female and one (1) male adult occupy the second floor while at a couple and two (2) children occupy the third floor, to rest and sleep.

The average floor to ceiling height is 1.90m. Aside from the timber used in columns, beams, and stairs all other parts of the ground floor were constructed with the use of concrete and steel. The second and third floors, on the other hand, were constructed using segmented coco lumber and plywood in different sizes, with corrugated G.I. sheets on its exterior face as cladding for waterproofing purposes. Both the ground and second floor doesn't have a front wall for ventilation purposes, but uses a polypropylene rice sack and tarpaulin to protect its interior spaces from the rain. From the second floor down, the left and right walls are shared between two housing units.

Furthermore, the chosen subject has three televisions, a refrigerator, an air-conditioning unit, cable television network connection, stereo, stool chairs, foldable tables, beddings and a lot of shelves for storage.

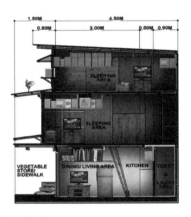
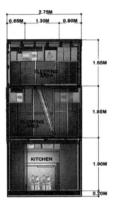
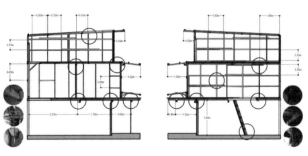

Fig. 6. Longitudinal Section of Structural Framework

Fig. 4. Section

Butt joints, lap joints, dado joints, mitered butt joints, cross-lap joints, and birdsmouth joints were randomly used to join coco lumbers together. A beam or column would usually have three to seven segmented lumbers in varying sizes nailed together or tied using a nylon string or rope.

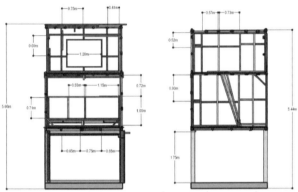

Fig. 5. Cross Section of Structural Framework

Table 1. Comparative Analysis between the Study and the Building Guidelines of World Bank

Existing Conditions	Guidelines Based on Usage and Selection	Maintenance	Remarks
Structural Timber			
→Timber used as beams or columns are mostly free from crack, bend and excessive nail holes. But not all joists are. →Instead of Black Japan, Solignum is used in the Philippines to preserve and protect timber from infestations especially on coco lumbers. →Spanning sections are vertical and adjoining horizontal and vertical joist members are secured with cleats.	→Timber should be free of rot, crack, bends, excessive nail holes and infestations. →A coat of Black Japan should be used for embedded members. →Spanning sections should be used vertically; joists between horizontal and vertical members have to be secured with cleats.	→Wood with infestation, rot, and bends shall be removed.	Three out of the four items were compliant with the guideline as Solignum compensates the loss of Black Japan.
Structural Steel			
→For this specific case study, a C-channel steel was used as a composite column along with concrete mix and reinforcement bars. It is however, embedded into the ground but with red oxide coating.	→Box sections may be used as columns; Channel and I may be used as beams; Angle, T and Pipe section may be used as purlins and joists. →Use all spanning members in vertical sections. →Avoid embedding in to the ground; instead a pedestal should be built.	→Scrub off any minor surface corrosion before use. →Coat all steel with red oxide.	All three items were followed since red oxide coating is used on the structural steel member that is embedded in to the ground.

Structural Bricks

→The counterpart of bricks in the Philippines are concrete hollow blocks (CHB) which are most of the time uniform in color, free from organic matter and salt and are externally plastered.
→The ground floor exterior wall thickness conforms to the 9inch minimum requirement with reinforcement bars and plastering. The succeeding floors on the other hand which is 4.5" thick are made from plywood and lumbers with a G.I. sheet cladding that's used for waterproofing.
→External concrete walls are being shared by two informal housing units for economical purposes.

→Bricks should be uniform in color, free of holes or cracks and the mortar used is free of organic matter and salt. Walls made from used bricks shall be externally plastered.
→External walls shall be at least 4.5" thick. For a two-storey building, the lower floor should be 9" thick. Two to three iron bars should be laid for every 1 meter of the masonry wall.
→External walls should be plastered or covered with plastic/vinyl at a minimum.
→Sharing common external walls is not only economical, but also an efficient way to manage space as well as avoid water seepage.

→Should there be vertical cracks, sinking and tilting, immediate measure should be taken to identify the cause and remedy.
→Fungus shall be removed by scrubbing and application of boric powder dissolved in water.

CHB serves as an alternative to bricks, all other requirement such as wall thickness, wall finish, water proofing for walls, and economical consideration were followed.

Galvanized and Corrugated Sheets

→Corrugations are mostly installed vertically and adjoining sheets are installed with overlaps.
→GI sheets were randomly nailed and bolted at the troughs and not at the crest.
→For every two GI sheets that meet at a corner one sheet is folded over the other.

→Corrugations should always be vertical when GI sheets are used as wall cladding as well as overlaps between adjoining GI sheets.
→GI sheets should be bolted at the crest and never at the troughs.
→Corners where two sheets meet shall be secured by folding the sheet over the other. When folding isn't possible, a ridge piece shall be used.

→Rusts shall be immediately removed by scrubbing off or applying a coat of paint.

Bolts and nails are used to fix the corrugated G.I. sheets at the trough. Hence, only two out of three guidelines were followed.

Plywood

→The plywood used for floors and walls are mostly secondhand and in varying sizes but are not used as a structural member.
→Plywood are used as an exterior wall but are covered with corrugated G.I. Sheets, or just plain G.I. sheets for waterproofing purposes.
→Based on observation, it is not used as a structural member on the subject of the study.

→Second-hand plywood with varying sizes maybe used or reused as cladding for floors and walls.
→Avoid the use of plywood for exterior walls. If it must be, it should be coated with red-oxide and secured with plastic covering.
→Should never be used as a structural member.

→Termite infested and parts with bends and stitch shall be removed and replaced.

Since the use of plywood for exterior walls is not totally prohibited, and the corrugated G.I. sheet compensates the use of plastics for waterproofing, All three requirements were followed.

Plastic/Vinyl Sheets and Tarpaulin

→Tarpaulins are used not just for waterproofing but also as layer of protection from the excessive heat of the sun.
→Since scavenged plastics vary in size, the dimensions are limiting, thus it does not fully cover the roof when used as a waterproofing material. Concrete hollow blocks and car tires are used to secure the plastic in place. When plastics are being fixed into the roof, tire rubbers are used as nailers.

→May be used temporarily for protection against water on roof or walls where plastering is difficult.
→Should be thick enough to withstand weather without any holes and cracks.
→If used, it should cover the entire roof; with secured corners and edges. If using nails, use a wooden pad or folded plastic piece to avoid tearing. Rubber solution may be used as adhesive when joining two sheets.

→Remove sheets after every monsoon to avoid dirt and pest infestation.

Only two out of three guidelines were followed/ applied. However the third instruction is conditional hence the "if used" term.

Conclusion

Out of the nineteen (19) building guideline requirements from the parts 1 and 2 of the book, seventeen (17) items or 89% are in compliance. That is considering the maintenance recommendations when an item or two are not existent or was not followed but has an alternative.

For the structural timber section, since most of the coco lumbers used in the construction of informal settlements are scavenged or are leftovers from a bigger construction, nail holes and cracks cannot be avoided. However, these only apply to joists and purlins. Most of the lumbers used as a beam or column are free of rot, crack, bends, excessive nail holes and infestations, at least for the studied residence. Solignum is also used for preservation purposes.

The Structural Steel section does not have a proper measure since it is not widely used in the building of shanties and from the subject itself, only one member is composed of structural steel.

The Concrete Hollow Blocks took the place of structural bricks in the building guidelines since it is what is widely used in the Philippines. The good compliance result could mean that Filipinos are well versed in the use of concrete in conjunction with hollow blocks and steel.

The guideline does not prohibit the use of plywood on the exterior wall as long as plastics or tarpaulins will be used as waterproofing. With this, galvanized iron sheet plays a great role in the construction of informal settlements. It acts as roofing, an exterior wall, a cladding that waterproofs plywood when used on the exterior walls, among many other uses. However, the proper use of this material is not thoroughly applied on the subject unit. One flaw is that bolts and nails are used to fix the corrugated G.I. sheets at the trough. Another thing is the lack of consistency in the vertical alignments of corrugations in the installation.

Although this research does not assure the resiliency of the structure being studied, 89% is a good percentage to start with.

Recommendation

Since the study is qualitative, a similar study in a quantitative manner would strengthen the findings of this research. The proponent recommends to have an actual as-built in 3D that could be subjected to a simulation of varying live and dead loads with the application of current phenomenon like the wind velocity of Typhoon Haiyan and the expected 7.2 magnitude earthquake called The Big One.

It also recommends having a study that will create a rubric based on the Building Guidelines of World Bank that is applicable to all and may be used to actually measure resilience based on guideline compliance, in consideration of all the recycled and scavenged materials that are used as alternatives in the construction of informal housing.

Lastly, to design a prototype house that is fully in compliant with the guidelines and recommendations of World Bank's Book 2 that is easily adaptable anywhere.

References

1) A. Gilbert and J. Gugler (1992) Squatter Architecture
2) Alex Ray P. Evangelista (2009) Promoting Awareness and Appreciation of Informal Settlements through Education
3) Alcazaren, Benvenuto, Icamina and Paulo (2011) Lungsod Iskwater: The Evolution of Informality as Dominant Pattern in the Philippines
4) Guzman, Sara Soliven De (2014) Green Building 101
5) III, United Nations Task Team Habitat (2015) Habitat III Issue Paper on Informal Settlements
6) Jesus, Amado De (2015) Philippine Green Building Code
7) Francis D.K. Ching (1995) A Visual Dictionary of Architecture
8) Mark Napier, Peter Kellet (1995) Squatter Architecture? A Critical Examination of Vernacular Theory and Spontaneous Settlement with Reference to South America and South Arica
9) Patel, S., Baptist, C., and D. Cruz (2012) Environment and Urbanization
10) Shiro Watanabe, Norihisa Shima and Kaori Fujita (2013) Research on Non-Engineered Housing Construction Based on a Field Investigation in Jakarta
11) Magdalena Zalecka Myszkiewicz (2013) Unconventional Building Structures in Single Family Social Housing
12) Natalia Kostelnikova (2015) Analysis of Vernacular Architecture in Terms of Sustainability
13) Ja Walubwa and P Shah 2014 (2014) Improving Housing Durability in Informal Settlements Using Affordable Building Materials – The Case of Kiberia Nairobi
14) World Bank (2011) Building Guidelines on Informal Housing: Reducing Disaster Vulnerability through Safer Construction.

Under-Resourced Natural Bahasa Indonesia HMM-based Text-To-Speech System

Elok Cahyaningtyas[1], Dhany Arifianto[2]
1 Master student, Institut Teknologi Sepuluh Nopember, Surabaya, Indonesia
2 Associate Professor, Institut Teknologi Sepuluh Nopember, Surabaya, Indonesia

インドネシアは多民族・多言語国家だが、なかでも世界中で2億6000万人以上が使っている言語がバハサ(Bahasa)。しかし、その言語学的な解析は進んでいない。本稿ではHMMをベースに、この知られざる言語の構造解析に取り組んだ。

Abstract

Although Bahasa Indonesia is used by about 263 million people in the world, it is classified as an under-resourced language. In this paper, we outlined the development of casual sentences of Bahasa Indonesia speech corpus which contains speech database and its transcription. Firstly, we selected casual Bahasa Indonesia sentences from movie and drama transcript and formed 1029 declarative sentences and 500 question sentences. We hired six professional radio news readers to utter the sentences to avoid local dialect in a sound-proof booth. Segmentation and labeling were performed to create transcription including the time label of each individual phoneme. Then, we conducted some experiment to develop text-to-speech (TTS) system in Bahasa Indonesia. We do some variation in the number of sentences and the type of sentences which used in the training part. We use 44, 72, 116, 450, 929 and 1379 training data sentences based on the phonetically balance. The goal is to know the speech quality of Bahasa Indonesia TTS system. Besides that, we also compare the method to build the TTS system, which is using HMM-based text-to-speech system (HTS) and CLUSTERGEN (CLS). In the on-going research, we are developing high quality TTS, namely speaker adaptation and speaker averaging.

Keywords Bahasa Indonesia; under-resourced language; speech corpus; TTS; HMM-based speech synthesis

Introduction

Speech synthesis technique has been developed recently. The unit-selection synthesis is a speech synthesis technique which uses database. In this technique, the sub-word unit will be selected automatically from database given [14]. This technique is able to produce synthesized speech which similar as the original speech from the database. However, this technique requires a lot of database to obtain comprehensive data coverage to build the models. So it makes this technique require huge computing load and lacks the flexibility to be modified.

In 1999, Yoshimura, et al., explained the method of modelling the spectral parameter, excitation parameter and duration simultaneously [15]. Then they sparked a speech synthesis technique based on statistical process known as statistical parametric speech synthesis that then began to grow today [15]; [11]; [16]. This technique uses hidden markov model (HMM) to model the probability distribution of speech and linguistic feature. It is called HMM-based speech synthesis system (HTS). Formation of statistical models gives HTS an advantage in flexibility to modify the acoustic models. Some of the advantages that can make the transformation of character voices, speaking styles, speaking adaptation, and supports multilingual speech synthesis.

HTS has evolved in some countries such as Japan [15],

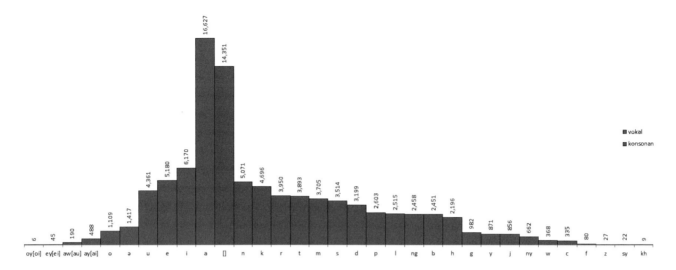

Fig. 1 Phonetical balance of 1529 sentences Bahasa Indonesia speech database [5]

England [3], Chinese (Zen, et al., 2003; Wu and Wang, 2006), Thai (Chomphan and Kobayashi, 2007), Vietnam (Liang, et al., 2008) and other countries. In addition, some modifications for HTS are in style adaptation techniques for speech synthesis using HSMM and features suprasegmental [17], implementation of the algorithm MLLR to sound adaptation of databases bit [19]. While its application in Bahasa Indonesia is still lacking because Bahasa Indonesia is still classified as under-resourced language.

In this paper, we conducted some experiment to develop the speech synthesis system in Bahasa Indonesia. Then we do some variation to know the speech quality and characteristics of Bahasa Indonesia speech synthesis system. Besides that, we also try to compare the method to build the speech synthesis system, which are using HMM-based text to speech system (HTS) and CLUSTERGEN (CLS). To build the speech synthesis system, first we created the Bahasa Indonesia speech corpus [5]. Then applied the HTS demo in Bahasa Indonesia which applied in declarative and question sentences [12]. The implementation of statistical parametric speech synthesis in Bahasa Indonesia by using CLUSTERGEN [8]. Then compare the speech quality of the synthesized speech using subjective and objective measurement [13].

Characteristics of Bahasa Indonesia

Language is an expression of human mind and feeling which using sound as its tool [2]. Every country has a different language with their own characteristics. Bahasa Indonesia is the national language of Indonesia and rooted from the Malay language. Besides Bahasa Indonesia as the main language, most of Indonesians are fluent in their own ethnic language according to the location of their tribe. Some of the ethnic languages such as Javanese, Sundanese, Maduranese, etc. As of 2010 census, Indonesia has 1,340 tribes with each different ethnic language and normally would not be able to understand each other. Then, Bahasa Indonesia is used as national language in order to bridge and bind the Indonesian people together. Bahasa Indonesia has spoken and written system. The spoken system similar to Malay and the written system is referred to Roman alphabet system.

Linguistic studies of Bahasa Indonesia divided in some level, i.e., phonology, morphology, syntax, and lexicon [2]. Phonology explain on how sound produced and its distribution. It is divided in some term i.e. phonetic, phonemic, segmental and suprasegmental sound. Phonetic is a linguistic study of the physical sounds of human speech production. While phonemic is a linguistic study of phonemes and their written representation as the meaning differentiator. A phoneme is the smallest unit of sound which composing a word or phrase. Phonemes is an important role in NLP. Bahasa Indonesia has 32 phonemes and contains of six vocal phonemes, three diphthong phonemes, and 23 consonant phonemes. Table 1 shows the Bahasa Indonesia phonemes based on International Phonetic Alphabet (IPA) excluding a silence character.

Indonesian speech database is the datasets of Indonesian language characteristic in accordance to Indonesian phonology. It consists of phoneme, speech, and transcription. The database contains of 1529 sentences with 1029 of declarative sentences and 500 of question sentences. The sentences sequence is formed from some literature such as novel, book, newspaper and internet which using Indonesian language. Figure 1 shown the phoneme distribution of Indonesian speech database. From the figure, the largest is phonemes "a" with 16.627 phoneme and the smallest is "oi" with 6 phonemes [5].

No	Indonesian	English	Example
1.	/a/	aa	Father
2.	/e/	ah, ae	Ten
3.	/ê/	ah, ax	Learn
4.	/i/	ih, iy, ix	see, happy
5.	/o/	ow, ao	got, saw
6.	/u/	uh, uw	put, too
7.	/ay/	Ay	Five
8.	/aw/	Aw	Now
9.	/ey/	Ey	Say
10.	/oy/	Oy	Boy
11.	/b/	B	Bad
12.	/c/	Ch	Chain
13.	/d/	d, dx, dh	Did
14.	/f/	f, v	fall, van
15.	/g/	G	Got
16.	/h/	Hh	Hat
17.	/j/	Jh	Jam
18.	/k/	k	Keep
19.	/m/	m	Man
20.	/l/	l	Leg
21.	/N/	n	no
22.	/P/	p	pen
23.	/R/	r	red
24.	/S/	s	so
25.	/T/	t, th	tea
26.	/W/	w	wet
27.	/Y/	y	yes
28.	/Z/	z, zh	zoo
29.	/Kh/	—	—
30.	/Ng/	ng	sing
31.	/Ny/	—	—
32.	/Sy/	—	share

Table 1. Indonesian Phonemes based on International Phonetic Alphabet (IPA)

Bahasa Indonesia speech database was recorded by total six speakers with three male speakers (MMHT, MJRA, MEIA) and three female speakers (FENA, FBAP, FALA). Profile of the speakers is shown in Table 2. The two speakers (MMHT and FENA) were recorded firstly in Japan and the others are recorded in Surabaya, Indonesia. The recording process spent approximately 8-10 hours each speaker. The recorded speech duration is 2-5 second for short sentences and 6-9 second for long sentences. The total duration of all recorded Bahasa Indonesia speech database is 10.65 hours with the male voice for around 5.5 hours and for the female voice for around 5.2 hours. The recorded speech was under configuration with the sampling frequency of 44,1 kHz, channel input/output mono, 16 bits/sample and using ".wav" format.

Speaker	Gender	Age	Profession	Length
MMHT	Male	44	Professional announcer	1 h 43 m 50 s
MJRA	Male	22	Professional announcer	1 h 50 m 34 s
MEIA	Male	32	Professional announcer	1 h 52 m 45 s
FENA	Female	26	Professional announcer	1 h 36 m 27 s
FBAP	Female	20	Professional announcer	1 h 44 m 56 s
FALA	Female	21	Professional announcer	1 h 50 m 33 s
Total Duration				10 h 39 m 5 s

Table 2. Profile of Bahasa Indonesia Speech Corpus's Speaker

Statistical Parametric Synthesis

Statistical parametric synthesis expressed the handicraft of expert from rule based model by statistical model. HMM-based Text to Speech System (HTS) is one of statistical parametric synthesis technique which widely known. In the HMM-based speech synthesis, the speech parameters of a speech unit such as fundamental frequency, phoneme duration and spectrum are statistically modeled and generated by using HMMs based on maximum likelihood criterion [4].

A. HMM-based Text-to-Speech System (HTS)

The HMM-based speech synthesis system consists of two main process, that are training and synthesis part which shown in Figure 2 [15]. In the training part, the HMM model represents the excitation source, i.e., F0, the spectrum, and state duration of the context-dependent speech units. Each HMM model has left-to-right state transition with no skip. Acoustic model in HTS is built from the application of maximum likelihood probabilistic equations in the training process (1) and in the synthesis process (2). The optimal model parameter can obtain with maximizing the likelihood of the training data which given in the following equation,

$$\hat{\lambda} = \arg\max_{\lambda} P(O|T,\lambda) \qquad (1)$$

where $\hat{\lambda}$ is the model parameter estimation, O is the training data, T is a word derived from the label (transcription) and λ is a model parameter.

$$\hat{O} = \arg\max_{o} P(O|t,\hat{\lambda}) \qquad (2)$$

where $\hat{O}$ is an estimation model speech, o is the speech parameter, t is the word to be synthesized which derived from the phrase labels, and $\hat{\lambda}$ is the estimation model [15].

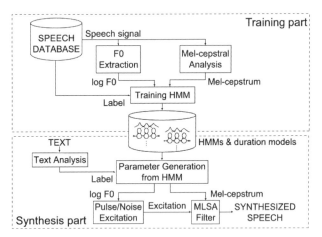

Fig. 2. HMM-based Text-to-Speech System (HTS) [3]

The synthesis part has the inverse operation of speech recognition system. The input system is contextual label sequence of the text which using the same format but different text from the training part. From the context-dependent label of the given text, then an utterance HMM is constructed by concatenating the context-dependent HMMs according to the label. After that, the sequence of spectral and excitation parameter is generated by the speech parameter generation algorithm that maximize their output probabilities. Finally, a speech waveform is synthesized directly from the generated spectral and excitation parameters using the mel log-spectrum approximation (MLSA) filter.

B. CLUSTERGEN

CLUSTERGEN is a method to build synthetic speech with trajectory model. The different way of CLUSTERGEN than HTS model is in trajectory modeling, a setup experiment was set and show trajola, a model trajectory with overlap and add, which is better than other kinds of trajectories model have been build [1]. CLUSTERGEN method predicts vector output in three ways that are previous, current and next. This method is used to get better vector output prediction.

$$S'_t = \frac{S_t - 1 + S_t + S_t + 1}{3} \qquad (3)$$

In equation (3), "s" is a set vector arranged in every word which has been training using HMM. This method actually same with decision tree in HTS, but the selection of the acoustic feature for every phoneme is by considering the previous, current and next phoneme for grouping.

The CLUSTERGEN was included in FesVox [http://festvox.org/] build. The newer version of FestVox not only included CLUSTERGEN but also has been included STRAIGHT [9] and moving segment label [2] technique too. STRAIGHT (Speech Transformation and Representation using Adaptive Interpolation of weiGHTed spectrum) is a procedure to manipulate speech signal based on pitch adaptive spectral smoothing and instantaneous-frequency-based F0 extraction.

Experiments

In this paper, we conducted some experiment to build speech synthesis system by using HMM-based speech synthesis system demo for speaker dependent (HTS-demo-CMU-ARCTIC-SLT). The demo program works with some following software, i.e., SPTK, HMM Toolkit (HTK), HDcode, HTS-2.2, hts-engine API-1.05, festival, ActiveTcl and speech tools. All of them is an open source programs on Linux. The HTS demo is available in English. Then we adapting into Bahasa Indonesia with some modification, that are in the speech corpus which contain of speech unit and its context-label, and the question file to build the decision tree according to the phoneme rule of Bahasa Indonesia [12]. All of them will be used for training part to build the parameter generation of HMM model, then it will be used in synthesis part to generate the speech waveform by Mel log spectral approximation (MLSA) filter.

In this section we will describe our experiment to build synthesized speech of Bahasa Indonesia using HMM-based speech synthesis system. These experiments consist of some variation, first is variation in the number of training sentences, second is variation in the type of sentence using for training process, and third is some comparison of HTS and CLUSTERGEN method.

A. Variation in the Number of Training Sentences

The first experiment is making variation in the number of speech corpus which used in the training part. We are using minimum, maximum and combination number of speech corpus. Such variations are made according to the number of sentences. Declarative sentence has total of 1029 sentences and question sentence has a total 500 sentences. Then we separate the 100 sentences from declarative sentence and 50 sentences from question sentences to be used as synthesized sentences. So we have total 929 and 450 sentences for declarative and question sentences, respectively. This total number of sentences we used as maximum training. While for the minimum training, we construct sentences using the least number of phoneme according to the phonetically balanced of maximum training. So, in the minimum training we have 72 and 44 sentences for declarative and question sentences, respectively. In addition, we also using combination of declarative and question sentences, which was formed from the combination of declarative and question sentences. Thus, obtained combination sentences for minimum and maximum training as many as 116 and 1379 sentences, respectively. The number of speech corpus used in the training can be seen in Table 3. The variation applied to both speaker, mmht and fena.

Training Sentence	Synthesis Sentence	Maximum Training Number	Minimum Training Number	Synthesis Sentences Number
Question	Question	450	44	50
Declarative		929	72	50
Combination		1329	116	50
Question	Declarative	450	44	100
Declarative		929	72	100
Combination		1329	116	100

Table 3. Variation of Training Data Number

Number of Training Data	Time(hours)			
	Question Sentence		Declarative Sentence	
	mmht	*fena*	*mmht*	*fena*
44	1:26:40	0:54:39	0:41:44	0:44:50
72	2:06:26	1:16:33	1:05:16	1:00:05
116	1:25:49	1:25:49	1:16:15	1:11:17
450	2:30:45	2:45:17	2:47:22	2:47:05
929	6:19:38	5:44:14	7:48:42	6:52:31
1329	9:05:05	9:15:15	9:05:05	9:15:15

Table 4. HTS Computation Time

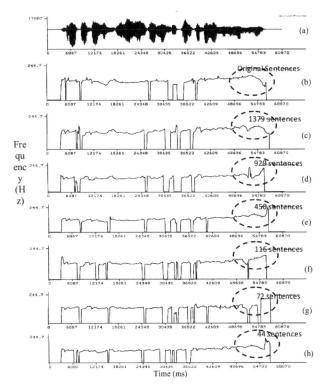

Fig. 3. F_0 Plot of Question Sentence "*Berapa banyak gula yang kau masukkan ke dalam minuman ini?*"

The different training process will give different result in the training models. While variations in the training data number aimed to determine the lower limit of training data to keep produce the natural synthesized speech. The more speech corpus using in the training process, the better acoustic models will be produced. It is because the distribution of phonemes in speech corpus will affect the probability of acoustic model formation. However, with the more speech corpus used in the training part, it will take much computation load and time. In Table 4, shown the computation time while running the HTS demo for Bahasa Indonesia. The computation time varies from the minimum, maximum and combination sentences for both declarative and question sentences. It shows that the increasing number of training sentences, make the computation time longer.

The synthesis process is proceeded after the formation of model training is completed. The step is to combine the acoustics and linguistic features that have been formed in the training part to be desired synthesized speech. From several variations given, it has different synthesized speech quality which located in the level of naturalness. The combination training sentences produced better synthesized speech than maximum and minimum training sentences. It can be seen from the comparison of fundamental frequency plot (excitation parameter) and mel-cepstral plot (spectral parameter) of speech signal.

The fundamental frequency track show how the pitch of speech signal that show an intonation aspect in a sentence change in time. In Fig.2 show F0 plot of question sentence *"Berapa banyak gula yang kau masukkan ke dalam minuman ini?"* in Bahasa Indonesia, if translated in English become "How much sugar you add in this drink?". From that figure can be seen the waveform of speech signal followed by comparison among fundamental frequency (F0) contour of the synthesized speech and original speech. From the F0 contour can be identified the voiced, unvoiced and silence region [6]. Through the dotted line, can be seen the difference of F0 from each synthesized speech.

The F0 extraction is using *pitch* tools from speech signal processing toolkit (SPTK). It done with condition of sampling frequency in 16000 Hz, frame period 80 point (5 ms), minimum F0 80 Hz and maximum F0 165 Hz. Then using fdrw tools to plot the graph. This pitch extraction results still have some lacks in the F0 extractor. They are the F0 contour shape that obtained is not smooth and have many leaps on its surface. That is because the sound is regarded as noise by the extractor, a voiced region which is considered as unvoiced region, and vice versa. Else is because of pitch halving and pitch doubling.

Aside from fundamental frequency plot for extraction parameter, we can see the spectral parameter by using mel-cepstral plot. It can be obtained by converting the speech signal from the time domain to the frequency domain in logarithmic scale (log FFT). MCEP plot for synthesized speech of mmht with question sentence *"Berapa banyak gula yang kau masukkan ke dalam minuman ini?"* can be seen in in Fig.4. Plot MCEP obtained by us sing Speech Signal Processing Toolkit (SPTK) tools *mcep* with condition of sampling frequency 16000 Hz, frame length 400 points (25 ms), frame period 80 points (5 ms), analysis of order 20, frequency warping parameter FFT size of 0.42 and 512 points, then stored in the file *.mcep*. Afterward plotted in MCEP graph using tools *glogsp* and *mgc2sp*.

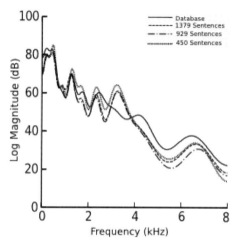

Fig. 4. Mel-cepstral Plot of Question Sentence *"Berapa banyak gula yang kau masukkan ke dalam minuman ini?"*

Mel-cepstrum plot has two main information, that are cepstral and cepstral envelope. Both of which will provide information of location, magnitude, and the characteristics of speech signal including duration, formant frequency (F1-F5), delta (the speed of speech, derived from the difference between the cepstrum peaks), delta-delta (the speech acceleration, derived from derivative of delta cepstrum).

For voiced speech at cepstrum plot will have more energy at lower frequency and have lower energy at high frequency (cepstral tilt). Whereas for the unvoiced speech will have the energy that is almost evenly on each frequency. When compared based on MCEP plot of each synthesized speech both for mmht or fena, and for declarative or question sentences, it appears that between original speech and synthesized speech with maximum training data have less distortion than synthesized speech with minimum training data. This is because of the increasing number of training data that be used, the more acoustics model will be generated. So the probability of the system to generate synthesized speech will be even greater by maximizing the acoustics model of speech which will be synthesized with the acoustics model that generated in training process.

B. Variation in Type of Sentences

The second experiment is to make training using variation in the type of sentences, which are declarative and question sentences. The scheme is we do training using declarative sentences then make the synthesized speech for question sentences, and vice versa. The goal is to see the changes of declarative sentences into question sentence, and vice versa. In the end of question sentence is followed by the rising intonation. While in declarative sentence has flat and decrease intonation in the end of the sentence.

Type of Training Sentence	Number of Training Data	Question		Declarative	
		mmht	fena	mmht	fena
Question	44	100%	100%	40%	20%
Declarative	72	0%	0%	80%	40%
Combination	116	20%	40%	40%	20%
Question	450	100%	100%	0%	20%
Declarative	929	0%	0%	100%	60%
Combination	1329	80%	20%	100%	100%

Table 5. Synthesized Speech Identification

For this purpose, we try to conduct synthesized speech identification with using subjective test evaluation. The evaluation is done with total 20 respondents of male and female whose have healthy hearing. Respondent will be heard the result of synthesized speech randomly, then will try to guess whether the synthesized speech categorized as declarative or question sentence. The result of the test is shown in the Table 5. In the table can be seen the identification result of question and declarative sentences separately both for minimum and maximum training. For the question sentences identification, the respondents were able to identify overall by 50% for mmht voice and 43% for fena voice.

So, to produce synthesized speech with the same training sentences (question to question sentences or declarative to declarative sentences) have higher percentage compared to synthesized speech with combination training sentences. However, the formation of declarative synthesized speech was able to produce transformation to question sentences with a small percentage of between 20 - 40%. But it cannot be achieved from question to declarative synthesized speech. This is because of the original speech that used has different characteristic with synthesized speech. Therefore, it should be given an additional parameter to be able to change the synthesized speech from question to declarative sentences, respectively.

In addition, while looking at the excitation parameter by fundamental frequency shown in Fig. 3 can be seen the difference. The figure shows the variation in training number and also in the type of training sentences to synthesized question sentence. When compared with the original speech, the best result is provided by 1379 and 450 sentences, which have almost the similar pattern. It means that the declarative sentence still not able to produce question sentences, and only can produce better with question and combination sentence.

C. HTS vs CLUSTERGEN

The third experiment aims to compare the HTS and CLUSTERGEN method [13]. In TTS system with CLUSTERGEN for Indonesian language was built by Evan [8], using EHMM [9] as a technique for obtaining label files from each database, it creates label from estimate phoneme based on fully connected state models and forward connected state model of HMM. This technique is shown a number of log likelihood better than technique is use 5 state sequence of HMM. Training part is done with CLUSTERGEN method, this method essentially contains some part, the first step is an extraction of F0 from the audio file in the database with Speech Tools [11]. Then, the next step is combines 24 MFCCs with F0 which have been extracted, as the result is given 25 vectors for every 5ms [11]. The last part of training process is clustering the MFCCs from every sample, this part is used wagon tool which contains in Edinburg Speech Tools CART tree builder [11]. The result of training part is to obtain model parameter which used in synthesis part [8].

The spectral parameter for synthesized speech male and female voice with HTS and CLUSTERGEN shown in Fig. 5. The full line represented the original speech, the dash-line is the synthesized speech of CLUSTERGEN, while the dotted-line is the result of HTS synthesized speech. From the spectral plot, we can see in the male voice shows that the lower frequency of synthesized speech is having almost the similar pattern with the original speech. The CLUSTERGEN give better result than the HTS. While in the female voice do not have significant differences.

In Fig. 6 and Fig 7. can be seen the waveform of speech

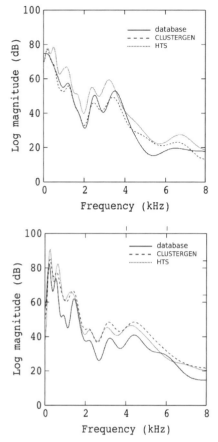

Fig. 5. MCEP plot of male (a), female (b) synthesized speech with HTS and CLS

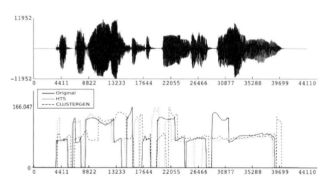

Fig. 6. F₀ Plot of female synthesized speech with HTS and CLS

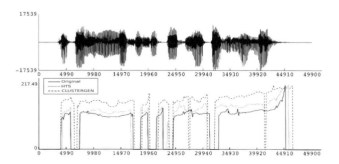

Fig. 7. F₀ Plot of male synthesized speech with HTS and CLS

signal followed by comparison among fundamental frequency contour of the synthesized speech. Fig. 6 is for male voice mmht, and Fig. 7 is for female voice fena. The full line represented the original speech, the dash-line is the synthesized speech of CLUSTERGEN, while the dotted-line is the result of HTS synthesized speech. From the F0 track, can be seen that there is some distortion between the original speech and the synthesized speech. The distortion is quite big and it is the reason why the synthesized speech still has robotic sound and noise. From the male voice, the F0 track has almost the same pattern with the original speech both for the HTS and CLUSTERGEN, but the HTS give the better result. While the result of female voice is far from the original speech for both methods.

Evaluation and Discussion

In this paper, we are using two kinds of test to measure the quality of synthesized speech. First is using objective test, which using mel-cepstral distortion (MCD) method. Second is using subjective test with degradation mean opinion score (DMOS) method.

The objective test is intended to assess the speech quality of the synthesized speech by analyzing mel-cepstrum distortion value from the original speech. The smaller MCD value indicate the closer synthesized speech to produce the natural speech. Fig. 8 and Fig. 9 is the objective test result of synthesized speech for male voice and female voice, respectively.

Based on the results indicate that the speech quality of synthesized speech is still not enough. The smallest distortion value on mmht voice for question sentence is on 450 training data with score 4.32 and for declaration sentence have 5.13 score with 929 training data. Based on these data, can be concluded that the distortion of mel-cepstral will be smaller as the higher number of database which being used. That is because of the more probabilities of the appearance phonemes when using the maximum training data.

Then the objective result for the comparison of HTS and CLUSTERGEN is shown in Fig. 10. From the graphic, the synthesized speech with CLS give better result than HTS for the male voice, while for female voice the HTS produce better synthesized speech. From the result, we can see that the speech quality is still not enough to produce natural voice, it because the distortion of the original and the synthesized speech is too big. It probably caused from extraction feature process which not perfect.

The subjective test aimed to measure the naturalness of synthesized speech by using DMOS method. It consists of two parts for each session that are training part and test part. The training part intend to familiarize the respondent to assess but not include in the assessment. Then the test part is a section that will be used as the assessment.

Fig.11 and Fig.12 show the result of subjective test for mmht voice and fena voice, respectively. From this graphic, can be seen that the highest value for mmht voice in declarative and question sentences are obtained with 1379 data training with score 3.53 / 5.00 and 3.36 / 5.00, respectively. Then for fena voice, the highest value for question sentence is obtained in 450 training data with score 2.98 / 5.00 and for declarative sentence is obtained in 1379 training data with score 3.04 / 5.00. That score means that "degradation speech is slightly annoying".

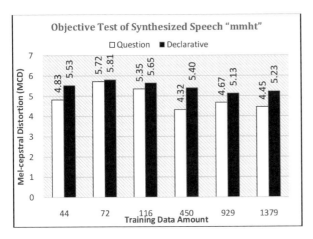

Fig. 8. Objective Test of Synthesized Speech of Male Voice

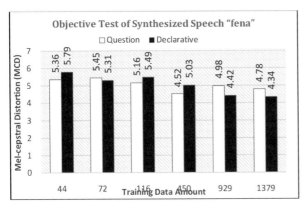

Fig. 9. Objective Test of Synthesized Speech of Female Voice

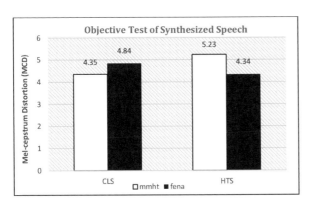

Fig. 10. Objective Test of Synthesized speech with HTS and CLS

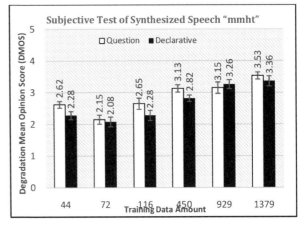

Fig. 11. Subjective Test of Synthesized Speech of Male Voice

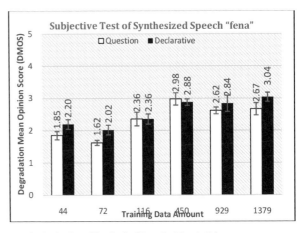

Fig. 12. Subjective Test of Synthesized Speech of Female Voice

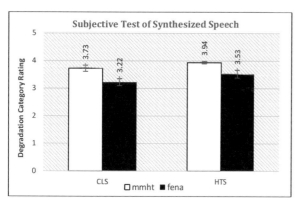

Fig. 13. Subjective Test of Synthesized speech with HTS and CLS

In addition, the comparison result of speech quality in HTS and CLS by subjective evaluation can be seen in Fig.13. It shows that there is no big difference between the synthesized speech of CLUSTERGEN and HTS. But still, HTS who produce the better-synthesized speech with score 3.94/5.00 for mmht and 3.53/5.00 for fena which means that *"degradation speech is slightly annoying"*.

Conclusion

Based on the explanation above, it can be concluded that speech synthesis system for Bahasa Indonesia has been built. The system built by statistical parametric speech synthesis system which using statistical model to run the mapping between the speech and linguistic information. Some variation has been applied to the system and achieved the speech quality which measured by objective and subjective test. The speech quality by objective test result is acquire the best value for question sentences is 4.32 using 450 training sentences and for declarative sentences is 5.13 using 929 training sentences. Based on subjective test, acquire the highest value for question and declarative sentences using 1379 training sentences with score 3,53/5.00 and 3,36/5.00 respectively which mean *degradation speech is slightly annoying.*

Beside that also has been compare the HMM based text to speech (HTS) method and the CLUSTERGEN method. This method has difference in the trajectory model which provided by CLUSTERGEN method. From the evaluation acquired that the speech quality result of the synthesized speech by using CLUSTERGEN and HTS are not having big different. The subjective test has shown that both produce the synthesized speech with degradation speech is slightly annoying. The objective test has shown that the synthesized speech still produces big distortion.

That result possibly because of poor F0 estimates. In the future work, should be improved to increase the synthesized speech quality by modifying the system drawback, especially in HTS, by using better vocoder like STRAIGHT (Speech Transformation and Representation using Adaptive Interpolation of weiGHTed spectrum), make better acoustic model and reduce post filtering. The others future work is to build the speaker adaptation of Indonesian TTS with only using small adaptation data, and also build expressive Indonesian TTS.

References

[1] G. K. Anumanchipalli and A. Black, "Adaptation Techniques for Speech Synthesis in Under-resourced", SLTU 2010, Penang, Malaysia, 2010.

[2] A. Black and J. Konimek "Optimizing Segment Label Boundaries for Statistical Speech Synthesis" ICASSP 2009, Taipei, Taiwan. 2009

[3] K. Tokuda, H.Zen and A. BLack "An HMM-based Speech Synthesis System Applied to English", Proc. of 2002 IEEE SSW, Sept. 2002.

[4] K. Tokuda, T. Yoshimura, T. Masuko, T. Kobayashi, T. Kitamura, "Speech parameter generation algorithms for HMM-based speech synthesis". In Proceeding of ICASSP, p. 1315-1318, 2000.

[5] A. Elok. "Pembuatan Perangkat Basis Data Untuk Sintesis Ucapan (Natural Speech Synthesis) Berbahasa Indonesia Berbasis Hidden Markov Model (HMM)". Jurnal Teknik POMITS Vol. 2, No. 2, (2013) ISSN: 2337-3539, hal. A 443-A 447

[6] K. Tokuda, T. Mausko, N. Miyazaki, T. Kobayashi, "Multi-space probability distribution HMM". IEICE Transactions on Information and Systems, E85-D(3), p. 455-464, 2002.

[7] Muslich, Masnur, "Fonologi Bahasa Indonesia Tinjauan Deskriptif Sistem Bunyi Bahasa Indonesia", Jakarta: PT Bumi Aksara, 2009.

[8] E. Tysmayudanto G and D. Arifianto, "Natural Indonesia Speech Synthesis by using CLUSTERGEN", International Conference on Information, Communication Technology and System, 2014 (ISSN: 978-1-4799-6858-9/14)

[9] K. Prahallad, A. Black, and R. Mosur, "Sub-phonetic modeling for capturing pronunciation variation in conversational speech synthesis," in Proceedings of ICASSP 2005, Toulouse, France, 2006

[10] H. Kawahara, I. Masuda-Katsuse, and A. Cheveigne, "Restructuring speech representations using a pitchadaptive time-frequency smoothing and an instantaneous frequency based f0 extraction: possible role of a repetitive structure in sounds, "Speech Communications, vol. 27, pp. 187–207, 1999.

[11] A. Black. "CLUSTERGEN: A Statistical Parametric Synthesizer Using Trajectory Modeling", in Interspeech 2006, Pittsburgh,PA., 2006

[12] Cahyaningtyas, E., Arifianto, D., "HMM-based Indonesian Speech Synthesis System with Declarative and Question Sentences Intonation". Proc. IEEE 2015 International Symposium on Intelligent Signal Processing and Communication Systems (ISPACS) November

9-12, 2015, 1E -7 (pp.153–158).

[13] E. Cahyaningtyas and D. Arifianto, "Synthesized speech quality of Indonesian natural text-to-speech by using HTS and CLUSTERGEN," 2016 Conference of The Oriental Chapter of International Committee for Coordination and Standardization of Speech Databases and Assessment Techniques (O-COCOSDA), Bali, 2016, pp. 110-115.doi: 10.1109/ICSDA.2016.7918994

[14] A. J. Hunt and A. W. Black. 1996. Unit selection in a concatenative speech synthesis system using a large speech database. In Proceedings of the Acoustics, Speech, and Signal Processing, 1996. on Conference Proceedings., 1996 IEEE International Conference - Volume 01 (ICASSP '96), Vol. 1. IEEE Computer Society, Washington, DC, USA, 373-376. DOI=http://dx.doi.org/10.1109/ICASSP.1996.541110

[15] T. Yoshimura, K. Tokuda, T. Masuko, T. Kobayashi, T. Kitamura, Simultaneous modeling of spectrum, pitch and duration in HMM-based speech synthesis, Proc. of Eurospeech, pp.2347-2350, Sept. 1999.

[16] H. Zen, T. Nose, J. Yamagishi, S. Sako, T. Masuko, A.W. Black, K. Tokuda, The HMM-based speech synthesis system version 2.0, Proc. of ISCA SSW6, Bonn, Germany, Aug. 2007.

[17] Makoto Tachibana, Junichi Yamagishi, Takashi Masuko, and Takao Kobayashi. 2006. A Style Adaptation Technique for Speech Synthesis Using HSMM and Suprasegmental Features. IEICE - Trans. Inf. Syst. E89-D, 3 (March 2006), 1092-1099. DOI=http://dx.doi.org/10.1093/ietisy/e89-d.3.1092

[18] ITU-T, "Methods for Objective and Subjective Assessment of Quality", http://www.itu.int/rec/T-REC-P.800-199608-I/en.

[19] J. Yamagishi, T. Kobayashi, Y. Nakano, K. Ogata, and J. Isogai. Analysis of Speaker Adaptation Algorihms for HMM-based Speech Synthesis and a Constrained SMAPLR Adaptation Algorithm, IEEE Audio, Speech, and Language Processing vol.17 issue 1, pp.66-83, January 2009.

[20] E. Cahyaningtyas and D. Arifianto, "Development of under-resourced Bahasa Indonesia speech corpus," 2017 Asia-Pacific Signal and Information Processing Association Annual Summit and Conference (APSIPA ASC), Kuala Lumpur, Malaysia, 2017, pp. 1097-1101. doi: 10.1109/APSIPA.2017.8282191

Erosion Mitigation Based on the Geographic Information System (GIS) With Agroforestry for Water Conservation Concept

M. Adhitya Arjanggi[1], Bachtiar Rifa'i Idris[2]
1 Researcher of Urban and Regional Planning Department, Engineering Faculty, Brawijaya University
2 Researcher of Urban and Regional Planning Department, Engineering Faculty, Brawijaya University

開発と地球温暖化による豪雨などの影響でインドネシアの河川流域では土壌の浸食が急速に進んでいる。土地を守るための森林再生事業も一貫性を欠く。森林保護と農業生産の持続可能な共存に向けた施策をGISのデータに基づき考察する。

Abstract

The lack condition of upper Bango watershed happened due to the average erosion rate that reaches 126.81 ton/ha/year. The gap is significantly huge compared to the tolerance threshold of 12.5 ton/ ha/ year. Actually, the management of Bango upstream is directed to the protected areas, but its development towards protected areas tend to be less effective because sustainability management also ended after the reforestation program. In addition, the land acquisition increasingly forces the function of the existence of the upstream area. Therefore, it needs a reforestation model that could empower public life, also sustainable, economically valuable and is able to maintain the environmental quality of the catchment area. Thus, the expected agroforestry planning concept can help solving the problem of protected areas in upper Bango watershed areas. Management model that will be applied to the upper Bango watershed is reforestation. Reforestation is one action in watershed management as resource land. It should be related to other relevant measures to obtain optimum results. Reforestation aims to regulate or control the direction of the desired watershed in order to avoid undesirable things (ex. floods and landslides). Utilization of GIS (Geographical Information System) as a research tool will be able to facilitate the identification of threatened watershed areas that need a priority handling.

Keywords Erosion, Agroforestry, Reforestation

Introduction

Watershed management plan is a comprehensive approach that encapsulates all the aspects related to the water resources, which in turn affects water quality and quantity aspects (Tejo Yuwono, 2006). The case study of this paper is appointed upper Bango watershed, which is one of the main basins in East Java. Nature and existence are considered to be important on existing ecological systems. Bango River spring water is sourced from the Brantas river with an average depth of 12-20 meters and has a current speed of 0.3 to 0.4 m/sec (dry season) or 2 to 2.2 meters/second (the rainy season).

On 2003, Bango upper watershed has an average erosion rate of 126.81 ton/ha/year (BP DAS Brantas, Engineering, and Field Plan rehabilitation and Soil Conservation, 2003) that is significantly different from the tolerance threshold of 12.5 ton/ha/yr. The river lies in Malang district and Pasuruan. Bango watershed, as one of primary drainage channel that exists in Malang, makes the role of conservation areas deemed vital and requires special attention, especially upstream. Upland conservation areas have to be protected in order to maintain a stable water cycle and secure the presence of groundwater.

The watershed management model that will be applied to

upper Bango watershed is reforestation. Reforestation is one of the actions in the watershed management as the land resource. Reforestation should be related to other relevant actions to obtain the adequate result. Reforestation and its supporting actions aim to control the direction of the desired watershed so that it can avoid undesirable things (such as floods and landslides) (Tejo Yuwono, 2006). According to the general sense, the 'greening' and 'reforestation' are not essentially different. The difference lies only in the state where both types of activities are performed. Greening worked on farms, especially smallholder agriculture, meanwhile reforestation is being done in the forest area (Notohadiprawiro, 1980).

Agroforestry is a good land management system by improving crop yields cropping land through the merger of income, including the trees plantation, forests and crops or livestock in cropping or rotating on the same plot of land, and management procedures implementation is normally done in harmony with the local (King, 1970). Agroforestry management system has two main objectives that have a synergy; the preservation and improvement of the location and at the same time optimize the joint production of crops agriculture and forestry. Agroforestry which aims to exploit land can provide the best result. This system has two main targets: the principal agricultural yields, as well as forestry that creates a harmonious environment while earning extra yield.

Agroforestry development of Bango watershed is directed to the upstream region, because it is vital area and has special character as 'land degradation'. Bango watershed conditions also on less than ideal level because the average erosion rate is 126.81 tons/ha/year (BP DS Brantas, Engineering and Field Plan Rehabilitation and Soil Conservation, 2003) that is far above the tolerance threshold of 12,5 ton/ha/yr.

Generally, the management of the upstream is directed to protected areas (including Bango watershed). However, the development towards protected areas tends to be less effective because, after the reforestation program, sustainability management is also ended. In addition, the land acquisition increasingly forces the function of the existence of the upstream area. Therefore, it needs a model of reforestation that is good for the society, can sustain economic values and maintain the environmental quality of the catchment area that makes up the 'river head area'. Finally, the concept of planning agroforestry can help resolve the complexity of protected areas in the upper Bango watershed areas.

Literature Review
Definition of watershed

The river is one of the water resources that has an important function to life and human life. According to Soejono Sosrodarsono (1985), the river is a combination of river flow and streams, that river flow is a long flow into earth's surface from rainwater. The river consists of watersheds, the basin, river border, and riverbanks which is an integral ecosystem.

According to Asdak (2002:4), A watershed is a geographic area that drains to a common point, which makes it an attractive unit for technical efforts to conserve soil and maximize the utilization of surface and subsurface water for crop production, and farmers whose actions may affect each other's interest.

Definition by the function is divided into several sections, first is watershed upstream, have functions to keep watershed environment condition that not degraded. Conservation functions indicated on the condition of watershed land vegetation cover, water quality, the ability to store water (debit) and rainfall. Second, the center of the watershed based on the function as river water can manage to benefits of social and economic thing. That indicates water quantity, water quality, the ability to deliver water, groundwater levels, management of water infrastructures such as rivers, reservoirs, and lakes. Third, watershed downstream as river water has benefits to social and economic, that indicated from quantity and quality of water, the ability to deliver water, the height of rainfall, and related to the needs of agriculture, water supply, and water management waste.

Definition and classification of Erosion

Erosion is the event of lost or eroded land or parts of land from a place which is transported to another place, either caused by the movement of water from a place that is transported to another place, or wind (Arsyad, 1989).

Two causes of the erosion are natural erosion and erosion because of human activity. Natural erosion can happen because the process of soil formation and its process to maintain the natural balance of the land and usually still supply media for ongoing

Source	Type of erosion or degradation process
Water	Raindrop Splash
	Sheet Erosion
	Rilling
	Gullying
	Stream/Channel Erosion
	Wave Action
	Piping dan sapping
Ice	Solifluction
	Glacial Scour
	Ice Plucking
Wind	Wind erosion cannot be classified by "type" but have various of degree
Gravitation	Creep
	Earth Flow
	Avalanche
	Debris Slide

Table 1. Causes and types of erosion (Gray and Sotir, 1996)

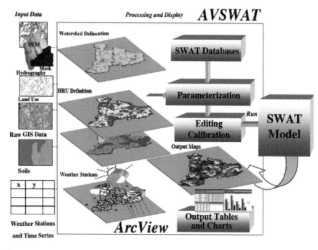

Figure 1. Model data structures in AVSWAT
(Source: https://geo.arc.nasa.gov/sge/casa/hydrologic/swat.html)

growth of most plants and medium erosion happen because of human activities that by peeling surface of the land, because ways of farming that not heed the rules of land conservation.

As for erosion control, in principle, can be managed with:

- Reducing thrust or traction, with reducing flow velocity of water on the soil surface, or with reducing the energy of water flow in the affected area
- Raising erosion resistance to protect or strengthen the soil surface with a suitable cover, or by increasing the strength of the bonds between soil particles.
- Enlarging soil infiltration capacity, so that the speed can be reduced runoff.

Research Method

AVSWAT 2000 (Arc View Soil and Water Assessment Tool)

AVSWAT 2000 (Arc View Soil and Water Assessment Tool) is a software-based Geographic Information System (GIS) ArcView 3.2 or 3.3 (ESRI) as an extension (graphical user interface). The program issued by Texas Water Resources Institute, College Station, Texas, USA. ArcView is one of many programs based Geographic Information System (GIS).

AVSWAT 2000 program is development program from an earlier version, SWAT (Soil and Water Assessment Tool), that not work in ArcView software. AVSWAT designed to predict the effects of land management on the flowing water, sediment, and agricultural land in complex components of watershed like soil type, land use, and land management conditions periodically. For modeling purposes, AVSWAT program enables users to divide a large watershed area into several parts of subwatershed to simplify the calculation.

The data structure used as a representation of original condition the appearance objects on earth. In database processing, AVSWAT 2000 divided into two groups: the type of spatial data that the database structure and database vectors in the structure of the grid/ raster.

Agroforstry Concept

Agroforestry is a collective name for technology systems and technology of land use in which woody plants seasonal (*trees, shrubs, palms, bamboo, etc.*) and food plants seasonal or livestock has grown on the same land in some form of arrangement space and time (Nair, 1993).

Characteristic of agroforestry is having interaction between the components of ecology and economy. Michon and de Foresta (1995) said Agroforestry subdivided based its complexity elements, simple agroforestry, and complex agroforestry.

Simple agroforestry is farming system that combine elements of a tree that has economic importance (such as *coconut, rubber, clove, teak*) or has ecological importance (*dadap, Gamal, petai china*) with element of seasonal plants (*rice, corn, vegetables*) or other crops such as *bananas, coffee, cocoa* that has economic value too.

Complex agroforestry is a system that consists of elements

trees, shrubs, seasonal crops, and grasses. Physical appearance and dynamics in complex agroforestry are similar to the forest ecosystem.

Based on a combination of agricultural crops and forestry crops, agroforestry can divide into several forms, (Vergara, 1982b):

1) Silviagricultur

    Silviagricultur is a form of agroforestry that mix between food crops (rice, corn, vegetables, etc.) with forest trees on the same land.

2) Silvipastura

    Silvopastura is a combination of planting trees with forage crops on the same land.

3) Silviofishery

    Silvofishery is a combination of planting forestry to fisheries on the same land.

4) Silviagripastura

    Silviagripastura is a combination of components forestry, agriculture, and livestock on the same land. The results obtained are food, fodder and forest products.

5) Silviagrifiseri

    Silviagrifiseri is agroforestry form that mix forestry, agriculture, and fisheries on the same land. The results obtained are food, forest products, and fish.

Results of Research

Analysis with GIS (AVSWAT 2000)

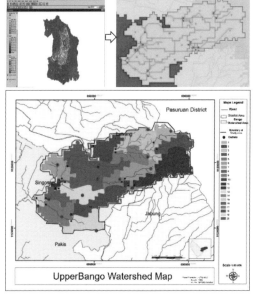

Figure 2. 20 outlets of the sub on Bango watershed

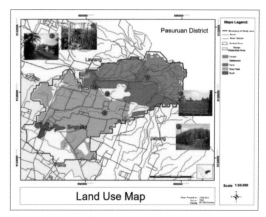

Figure 3. Land use of Malang Regency district

For make delineation, several data needed is stream river, slope, and Bango watershed catchment area. Results of delineation obtained that upper Bango watershed area has 20 outlets and 20 sub-watersheds with each character. The end result of the analysis will develop to make zoning of capabilities and compatibility land. Then that zoning areas will plan with agroforestry concept.

Analysis of Erosion with USLE (Universal Soil Loss Equation)

After analyzing data using AVSWAT program, the delineation data reanalyzed to determine the level of erosion in the studied area using the analysis of *Universal Soil Loss Equation* (USLE) calculation. The USLE equation is a tool used to estimate average annual soil loss caused by sheet and rill erosion). The USLE Equation is:

$$A = R \times K \times LS \times C \times P$$

With:

A   = Predicted soil loss (tons per acre per year)

R   = Rainfall and runoff factor by geographic location (mm per acre per year)

K   = Soil erodibility factor,

LS = Slope length-gradient factor (length and steepness)

C   = Crop/vegetation and cover management factor

P   = Conservation practice factor

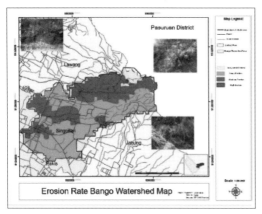

Figure 4. Rate of upper Bango watershed erosion

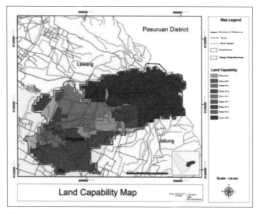

Figure 5. Analysis of land capability of upper Bango watershed which uses overlay model (Arc-GIS)

Based on the USLE calculation, the average rate of erosion in the upper Bango watershed is 62.3581974 ton/ha/year, it's classified in the 'medium erosion'. The classification level of erosion divided into four classifications: very small, small, medium and high.

Agroforestry concept is a method that can reduce the rate of erosion at upper Bango watershed. Agroforestry-based regional planning effort requires an analysis of land (both the ability and compatibility of land) by 'overlay' method of the data (soil type, slope, erosion, effective depth, drainage and rock) thus its purpose to suppressor of the rate of erosion in the area upper Bango watershed can be actualized optimally.

Analysis of Land Capability

Evaluation of land capability is a way to use land according to its potential. Assessment of the potential land is needed for policy making, utilization, and sustainable land management. To develop it, required land capability map. Analysis and evaluation of capability land supporting the process of preparation land use planning in a region that is arranged quickly and precisely as the foundation in overcoming conflicts of land use or utilization of natural resources (Suratman et al, 1993).

Analysis of land capability used the Ministerial Environment Decree No. 17 2009 on Guidelines for Determining Environmental Carrying Capacity in Regional Spatial Planning. In this case, will be analyzed 7 variables of capability land that is: soil texture, slope surface, effective depth, drainage, erosion, gravel, and flooding in the area of the upper Bango watersheds.

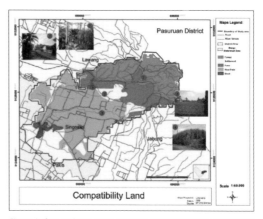

Figure 6. Compatibility land analysis of upper Bango watershed which uses Overlay Technique (SK, Minister of Agriculture No. 837 / Kpts / UM / II / 1980 and No. 683 / Kpts / UM / II / 1981)

Land capability analysis is divided into several capability land classifications with its limiting factor. The Result of upper Bango watershed capability analysis classes ranges from class III to class VII. The inhibiting factors at each grade level include slope, erosion, depth, drainage and soil texture. The final results in determining the sub-watersheds that are appropriate (based on the overlay area along the existing policies) to developed with agroforestry concept resulted in 10 sub-watersheds that suitable. Sub-watershed that suitable for use with the agroforestry concept is sub-watershed 2, 9, 10, 13, 14, 15, 16, 17, 18 and 19.

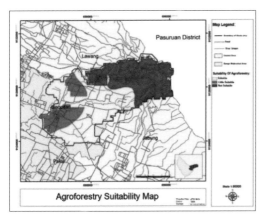

Figure 7. Result of Analysis of agroforestry suitability land of upper Bango watershed which uses overlay model (Arc-GIS)

Agroforestry Landscape Concepts and Management in Upper Bango Watershed

Landscape management by empowering upstream catchment area is expected to improve the productivity of the region and the downstream relationship with harmony and sustainable. As for regional, land-use diversity, beauty, culture, and landscape agroforestry potential eco-village are seen as a variable that has potential to develop eco-tourism in addition to the conservation area (Arifin et al, 2009).

Triple Bottom Line Benefit management is a system that implemented on the Bango upper watershed. Which based on the *Agroforestry* concept, that output target is harmonization of agroforestry development based on landscape watershed from upstream to downstream.

1) Conservation of the environment

The level of erosion in the upper Bango watershed has an average erosion 62.3581974 tonnes/ha/ year, then the rate of erosion in the upper Bango watershed is classified as 'medium erosion'. Therefore, the upper Bango watershed feasible to developed into environmental conservation.

2) Increased public welfare

The base concept that will use in upper bango watershed is agroforestry system. A concept that combines an element of agroforestry and agriculture as the cornerstone of development in the upper Bango watershed areas and economically valuable.

3) Preservation of cultural and social

In addition, the economic sector of the target implementation, other targets are sociocultural preservation that implemented by involving the community as the main subject of the program. Then its emerge a sense of belonging and the creation of the character building for the ecological environment.

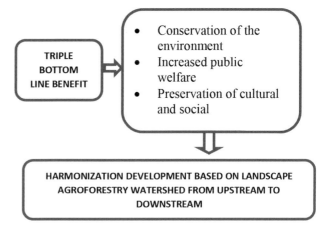

Figure 8. Integrated area management in the upper Bango watershed with agroforestry concepts

No.	Pattern Classification Crops
1	**Basic Corps;** forestry plants intended for wood production, the determination of rotations for 5 years. Types of plants selected are the type sengon (Faraserianthes falcataria). Besides sengon plant species that has great potential to be used is bamboo. Where bamboo can absorb rainwater up to 90% compared to the rainwater that ranges from 35-40% (Wahyuddin, 2008).
2	**Seasonal Corps (Step I);** short rotation crops were planted among the main crop with a minimum distance of 30 cm from the main plant stem. Timely planting carried out in the first year / before the main crop one year of age, the type of plants that have fruit trees such as bark, mango, and sapodilla. It is intended to obtain non-timber products (fruit)
3	**Seasonal Corps (Steps II);** short rotation crops that can be grown with/without shade, harvesting seasonal crops planted after first stage (fruit trees) until the time limit of staple crop was two years old. Types of plants selected food crops (horticulture) such as corn, tomatoes, eggplant, peanuts, and soybeans.

Table 2. Planting pattern classification based on agroforestry concepts

Pre-Implementation

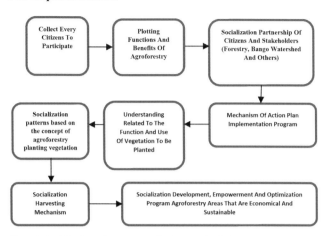

Figure 9. Socialization referral program implementation in the upper Bango watershed agroforestry

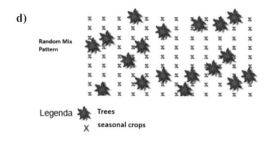

Implementation

Based on a combination of agricultural crops and forestry crops cultivated, agroforestry can be divided into several forms, namely silviagrikultur, silvipastura, silvifishery and silviagripastura (Vergara, 1982b). The type of agroforestry that can be applied to the upstream watershed is silviagricultur. A form of agroforestry that is a mix of business between food crops (rice, corn, vegetables, etc.) with plant forestry on the same land. The combination of these efforts can be carried out by way of setting.

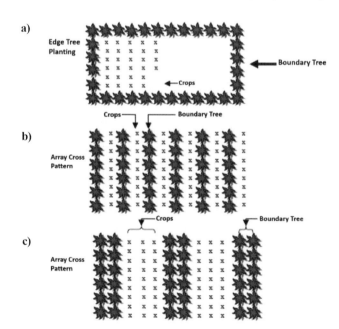

Function	Jenis Tanaman
Control Erotion	Sengon Sea, Waru Mountains, Marmoyo, Giyanti, Hope, Kemlandingan, Johar, Mindi, Balsa, Bungur, Alingsem, Eucalyps, Laban, Pecan and Damar
Controlling Landslides	Tekik, Pilang, Asem, Tanjuman, Trengguli, Sono Keling, Sisso Sono, Sono Kembang, Mahogany broad leaves, Rengas, Kesambi and Teak
Crops fruit trees - fruit / advocated for the preservation of agricultural land and water	Cloves, Cashew, guava, rambutan, soursop, avocado, jackfruit, and Aren
For the purpose of providing forage	Elephant Grass, Sentro, Stilo, king grass, Setaria grass, Bahia grass
Crops riverbank reinforcement and retaining landslides	Aren, Bamboo, Kaliandra, Gamal, Salak, Rattan

Table 3. Recommended crop types based on land function

Figure 10. Recommendation of crops for medium erosion

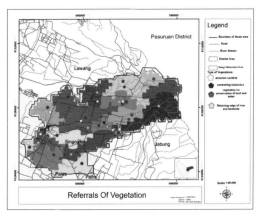

Figure 11. Referrals of vegetation on upper Bango watershed

Monitoring and evaluation

With the monitoring and evaluation on a regular basis, it is expected that an execution error will not be protracted and could be corrected immediately. The objectives of this monitoring are:
1) To control the implementation of activities and use of natural resources in upstream Bango watershed with agroforestry concept.
2) To push the mechanism of self-control of the perpetrator program management of natural resources in the upstream Bango watershed with agroforestry system.
3) To monitor the activities of the stakeholders in upper Bango watershed condition against reform-purpose resources primarily managed with agroforestry techniques.

Parameter monitoring and evaluation (including criteria and indicators) must be relevant to methods or tools that used in research or the results of the development program. For tools that used in monitoring and evaluation are:
1) To know the role of trees that used in Farming system analysis in the upper Bango watershed.
2) To determine the role of trees in agricultural landscapes using agroecosystem on upper Bango watershed.
3) To determine the impact of the tree-based system on the diversity and sustainability of results towards improving the socio-economic and environmentally beneficial on upper Bango watershed.

Conclusion

Based on the calculation, the limit of acceptable erosion rate is 12.5 tonnes/ha/year. Based on the USLE calculations, the average rate of erosion in Bango upper watershed is 62.3581974 ton/ha/year, the rate of erosion in the upper watershed is classified as 'medium erosion'. With high erosion rate and compared with the tolerance limit allowed erosion (12.5 tonnes/ha/year) will require special conservation to control erosion.

Land ability analysis is divided into several classes of land capability with some limiting factors. The result of the analysis, the capability of upper Bango watershed classes from class III to class VII. The limiting factors at each grade level include slope, erosion, depth, drainage and soil texture. The land compatibility analysis resulted that in the Bango Upper Watershed the study area divided into 4 areas: the protected areas, buffer zones, and the cultivation of annual crops cultivated area year. In determining the sub-watersheds, that is appropriate (based on the overlay area along the existing policies), to develop the concept of agroforestry there are 10 sub-watersheds that suitable. Sub-watershed that suitable for use with the concept of agroforestry is: sub-watershed 2, 9, 10, 13, 14, 15, 16, 17, 18 and 19.

The concept of agroforestry is a method that can reduce the rate of erosion in the upper Bango watershed. Planning program based Agroforestry later divided into two stages are implementation and monitoring-evaluation. For implementation phase, that includes 5 stages are Determination of vegetation will be planted, empowerment and optimization program agroforestry, determining the planting pattern to be used in the upper Bango watershed, briefing and dissemination of program implementation, team building (concept, implementing, monitoring and evaluation).

Monitoring and evaluation, the tools used that farming system analysis (monitoring and evaluating the role of trees in upper Bango watershed), agroecosystem analysis (monitoring and evaluating the role of trees in the landscape of and tree-based system (monitoring the impact of the tree-based system the diversity and sustainability.

References

[1] Arifin, HS., Munandar, A., Arifin N.H.S, and Kaswanto. 2009. Harmonization of DAS-Based Agricultural Development in Rural Landscape-City Region Bogor-Puncak-Cianjur (Bopunjur). Proceedings of the National Seminar on Indonesian Network for Agroforestry

Education (INAFE) in UNILA Bandar Lampung on May 7, 2009. ISBN 978-979-18755-6-1Arsyad, S. (1989). Konservasi Tanah dan Air. Bogor: IPB Press

[2] Asdak, C. 2002. Hydrology and Watershed Management. Gajah Mada University Press. Yogyakarta.

[3] Bannet, H.H. 1939. Element of Soil Conservation. Mc. Graw Hill. New York.

[4] BP DAS Brantas. 2003. Technical Plan and land rehabilitation Field and Soil Conservation. BP DAS Brantas: Surabaya

[5] Gintings, A.N et al. 1995. Guidelines for Selection Type Trees Planted Forests and Suitability Lahan.Jakarta

[6] HU Wani. 1989. Soil Conservation in Indonesia. Rajawali Press: Malang

[7] Notohadiprawiro, T.1980. Greening: Prolonged controversy. Greening Seminar P.P.I.R./R.S.D.C. Yogyakarta

[8] Soewarno. 1991. Hydrology. Publisher: Nova.

[9] Sosrodarsono, S. 1985. Hydrology for Irrigation. Pradnya Paramitha: Jakarta

[10] Suhartanto, Ary. 2008. Free AVSWAT 2000 and Its Application in the Field of Water Resources. Malang: CV: Asrori Malang

[11] Susilo, HS. Landscape Analysis Agroforestri.2009.IPB Press: Bogor

[12] Tejo Wiyono. 2006. Watershed Management and Greening Program. UGM: Yogyakarta

[13] Thompson.L.M, 1957.Soil and Fertility.New York: Mc.Graw Hill Bosk Co.

Developing Alternative Temporary Shelter (ATS) Solutions as Interim Coping Mechanism for the Displaced among Urban Poor Communities

Geomilie S. Tumamao-Guittap[1,2], Ansherina Grace Talavera[3]
1 University Researcher 2, School of Urban and Regional Planning, University of the Philippines
2 Capacity Building Cluster Head, Emergency Architects, United Architects of the Philippines
3 Program Director, Assistance and Cooperation for Community Resilience and Development Inc.

紛争や大規模災害によって長期にわたる避難生活を強いられる人は世界中で膨大な数にのぼり、2016年だけで3000万人も増えた。彼らが安心して暮らせる避難所や仮設住宅の建設はどうあるべきかを、都市・地域計画の観点から探る。

Abstract

Each year, floods force thousands of urban poor families living in informal settlements along the Tullahan River into the role of internally displaced persons (IDPs) evacuating in covered courts, community halls, churches and schools. Oftentimes, these places lack the space and facilities needed by the evacuees, which lead to significant health, privacy, and safety issues.

To help communities and local government units address these issues, contingency plans and emergency evacuation centers of twelve partner communities in Malabon, Valenzuela, and Quezon City were assessed along with local capacities through a combination of scientific and participatory approaches including: focus group discussions, interviews, community surveys, and ocular inspections. The study yielded the need to develop context- appropriate alternative temporary shelter (ATS) models to address the massive supply-demand gap. Collaboration between stakeholders from public-private-people sectors facilitated the development of home-grown ATS solutions to meet these needs.

This paper focuses on the process by which the "ATS menu of options" was conceptualized and developed by combining local technical expertise with community-based knowledge and capacities in a bid to uphold human dignity during disasters. It also points toward strategies that will significantly improve evacuation shelter planning in urban areas where there is scarcity of space.

Keywords disaster response; evacuation; temporary shelter; community-based disaster management, participatory design and development

Introduction

The Global Report on Internal Displacement (GRID) 2017 indicates that 31.1 million new displacements were recorded in 125 countries and territories in 2016. Majority of these take place in environments characterized by high exposure to natural and human-made hazards, high levels of socioeconomic vulnerability, and low coping capacity of both institutions and infrastructure. Of this number, 24.2 million is brought about by sudden onset natural hazards while 6.9 million forced displacements were triggered by armed conflicts. With displacement due to sudden-onset natural hazards outnumbering displacements associated with conflict and violence by more than three to one, climate and weather-related disasters account for 97 per cent; roughly 23.5 million, of all disaster-related displacements. Majority of these reported weather-related displacements is related to flooding (Norwegian Refugee Council and IDMC, 2017).

The GRID 2017 report also noted that East Asia and the Pacific accounted for 68 per cent of the global total with 16.4 million incidents disaster-related displacements. China and the Philippines account for a disproportionate share of the world's disaster-related displacement. In 2016 alone, around 7.4 million Chinese IDPs and 5.9 million Filipino IDPs were added owing to the flooding of the Yangtze and as a result of typhoons Nock-Ten *(Nina)* and Haima *(Lawin)* respectively.

Probabilistic risk models for disasters indicate that nine of the ten countries with the highest displacement risk are in South and Southeast Asia. Astride both the Typhoon Belt and the Asia-Pacific Ring of Fire, the Philippines feature a "high degree of ecological degradation and socio-economic vulnerability due to the large number of people and economic assets exposed to multiple recurring hazards such as cyclones, floods, earthquakes and landslides," making it among the most-vulnerable to climate change (IDCM, 2013 p.7). Based on an analysis of more than 40 social, economic, and environmental factors, the country ranked fifth among countries with largest modeled Average Annual Displacement. Over half a million Filipinos are at risk of displacement. The capital metropolis of Manila is ranked by the Climate Change Vulnerability Index (CCVI) as the second-most vulnerable to climate change of the world's 20 "high growth cities" (Maplecroft 2013 quoted in IDMC 2014, p.42).

Of the world's 31 megacities (that is, cities with 10 million inhabitants or more), the urban agglomeration of Metro Manila ranked fourth largest in terms of population with an estimate of 24.3 million in an area of 690 square miles (1,790 square kilometers) and a population density of 35,100 per square mile (13,600 per square kilometer); the highest density among the top six built-up urban areas (Demographia, 2018). According to the National Economic Development Authority (2017), as of 2015, three out of the 33 highly-urbanized cities (cities having a population of more than one million) in the country, are located in Metro Manila; namely: (a) Quezon City (2.94 million), (b) Manila City (1.78 million); and Caloocan City (1.58 million). More than 20 per cent of its population is either under or near the poverty line (PSA, 2015), with an estimated one-third of its population living in slums.

This area, which now constitutes a vast urbanized drainage basin formed atop a semi-alluvial floodplain formed by sediment flow from the Meycauayan and Malabon-Tullahan river basins in the north and the Marikina river basin in the east (Bankoff, 2003), Metro Manila has also experienced catastrophic disasters in recent times– Typhoon Ketsana (Ondoy) in 2009 with $11 billion damage/ 464 deaths, Habagat in 2012 (monsoon rains enhanced by Typhoon Haikui) with $3 billion damage/ 109 deaths to wit (Rappler, 2013). Bankoff (2003) attributed flooding in Metro Manila as a result of natural causes such as flat terrain, rainfall intensity and high tides in Manila Bay compounded with the unintended consequences of rapid urbanization that led to the encroachment of structures along the banks of waterways that lace its way around the plains, along with the reduction of the capacity of rivers and streams to hold runoff due to siltation from denuded watersheds, as well as the gradual disappearance of *esteros* which severely impacted the area's natural ability to dissipate floodwaters.

Since the 1990s, floodwater depths continued to rise especially in the northern cities of Caloocan, Malabon, Navotas and Valenzuela. Collectively referred to as CAMANAVA, with its flat lands ranging 0.3 to 3 meters above sea level, the area is considered one of the most flood-prone in Metro Manila. Rising floodwater depths in these areas have resulted to hundreds of thousands of families regularly requiring evacuation to higher ground (Bankoff, 2003). In 2014, Pornasdoro et al. conducted a GIS-based flood-risk assessment of barangays in Metro Manila and found that, by 2020, half of the barangays in Malabon and Navotas cities, 28 per cent of barangays in Valenzuela, 11.3 per cent of barangays in Quezon City, and 23.3 per cent of barangays in Caloocan are potentially at high risk of flooding. Most of these high-risk barangays are situated along creeks, rivers and waterways.

Situationer

The Philippine Disaster Risk Reduction Law (R.A.10121) mandates local government units (LGUs) to lead disaster risk reduction and management (DRRM) planning as well as the resilience building of communities in their respective jurisdiction. Past events have indicated vast discrepancies in their ability to fulfill this mandate as limited by various constraints in terms of resources, manpower, and capacities.

The study conducted a rapid needs assessment in targeted cities which straddle the banks of the 15-kilometer stretch of the Tullahan River from the La Mesa Reservoir to Manila Bay that forms part of the larger Malabon-Navotas-Tullahan-Tinajeros River System; namely: Malabon, Valenzuela and Quezon City.

Fig. 1. Partner Cities along Tullahan River
(Source: *Google Earth 2018, processed by ACCORD, Inc.*)

Fig. 2. Typical housing units along Tullahan River
(Source: *ACCORD, Inc.*)

This river is home to a sizable number of informal settler families spread across various barangays. Through focus group discussions and key informant interviews of DRRM officials in these select barangays and cities, it became evident that the urban poor are seen as factors that aggravate risks. Local authorities reveal that hazard events are seen as providential in removing urban poor communities from high-risk zones. DRR and basic services are also withheld in order to discourage settlement in these zones. In effect, inhabitants in these informal settlements are constrained into the role of internally displaced persons (IDPs) every monsoon season and during typhoon events as they are "forced to flee their homes or places of habitual residence…as a result of, or in order to avoid the effects of… natural or human-made disasters" (UNCHR, 1998 p.5).

Among the key challenges in addressing urban disaster risk in Metro Manila is the lack of safe and adequate space for shelter. The assessment found this to be consistent among the twelve communities included in the study. Urban poor shelters are often located in high risk areas prone to flooding, earthquake, and fire. Construction is patchy at best; utilizing substandard housing materials and non-engineered construction methods. In addition, existing systems on disaster preparedness, response, and evacuation center management are insufficient. Evacuees are exposed to a plethora of other risks such as health, security, protection, and gender-based violence. These issues, including safeguarding their properties and livelihood, are the leading reasons why at-risk households refuse to evacuate preemptively, placing them and their rescuers in grave danger during disasters.

Methodology

Prior to developing the alternative temporary shelter "menu of options", a detailed needs assessment was carried out in the following barangays:

Table 1. Partner Communities

City	Barangay Name
Malabon City	Catmon, Hulong Duhat, Panghulo, and Potrero
Quezon City	Bagong Silangan, Batasan Hills, Roxas, and Tatalon
Valenzuela City	Arkong Bato, General T de Leon, Punturin, and Ugong

Specifically, the assessment:

○ Determined current practice in evacuation planning of these barangays,

○ Identified the gaps in the provision of temporary emergency shelter services involving inventory of safe spaces and existing evacuation centers;

○ Quantified the number of families that will sustain significant damage to their houses, or whose location would put them in harm's way, and therefore would require safe temporary shelter assistance;

○ Determined potential temporary shelter needs based on worst-case scenarios for flood and typhoon and earthquake event; and

○ Provided information inputs to the development of alternative temporary shelter solutions for adoption by local government units and communities.

Necessarily, the methodologies employed scientific and participatory approaches that are cost-efficient to enable communities and local governments to sustain, replicate, and scale up the practice.

Primary Data Collection

Focus Group Discussion (FGD) and Key Informant Interviews (KII) –A total of 24 FGDs were conducted in the twelve partner communities. Separate FGDs between barangay leaders and community members were done to encourage better sharing of experiences amongst the participants. Community members selected to participate in the FGDs live in high-risk, urban poor communities who experienced flooding or evacuation in the past. Local barangay officials who were selected for the FGDs are key personnel in disaster risk reduction, with prior experience handling small to large-scale emergency situations. The FGDs looked into the worst disaster experiences including data on the characteristics and number of affected populations, extent of urban poor areas, and actual flood height experienced. In addition, existing evacuation planning process and systems, evacuation center conditions, factors affecting evacuation, and duration of displacement were also discussed.

Household survey– A combination of stratified and random sampling methods was employed for the representation of the surveyed households. At-risk and flood-affected households in urban poor settlements were determined first through the FGD, from which the sample population and number of respondents was computed. The survey was designed to complement available information from official sources, such as disaggregated information on housing from NSO.

To validate the assumptions drawn from MMEIRS (2004), the survey adopted the PHIVOLCS "Self-Check for Earthquake Safety of Concrete Hollow Block Houses in the Philippines" as a component. While this tool is designed only for houses made with concrete hollow blocks, houses made of concrete and a mix of concrete and wood make up 60 per cent of all residential houses in Malabon, 76 per cent in Quezon City, and 78 per cent in Valenzuela City. Nonetheless, the use of the self-assessment tool on a more significant portion of the total population strengthens the findings from the table exercise on estimating the damage potential.

For the *analysis of ATS gaps*, an inventory of available space in existing evacuation centers was conducted through ocular inspections of identified evacuation facilities. As-built plans of these structures were requested for reference purposes where available. The total amount of space needed for the potentially displaced population was compared with the available space in existing evacuation facilities to compute the gaps in alternative temporary shelters.

Secondary Data Collection

Review of related literature on risks and hazards such as City Risk Atlas, CDRRMP and BDRRMP plans were conducted. Other thematic data such as population and poverty were obtained from the Philippine Statistics Authority. Various humanitarian aid manuals such as the "Sphere Handbook and the Humanitarian Charter and Minimum Standards in Humanitarian Response" as well as some Federal Emergency Management Agency (FEMA) guides were consulted in conjunction with local laws and standards.

Needs Assessment Findings

In all of the partner communities assessed in the study, the following common features emerged in the survey (Table 2):

○ The household size in these communities exceed the national average of 4.4 person per household in 2015 (PSA, 2016) at six to seven members per household
○ Prevalence of two or more households occupying a single structure (100 per cent)
○ Prevalence of female-headed households (48 to 84 per cent)
○ Close to or more than half of the families have minors (46 to 85 per cent)
○ The percentage of families that have members with disabilities in all of these communities exceed national average of 1.57 per cent in 2005 (PSA, 2013) at 8-14 per cent
○ While persons aged 60 years old and above constitutes 6.8 percent of the household population in 2010 (PSA, 2012), the percentage of families having members aged 60 years old and above in these communities from 7 to 20 per cent

The 12-question survey on "Self-Check for Earthquake Safety of Concrete Hollow Block Houses in the Philippines"

Table 2. Profile of Partner Communities

	MALABON CITY				QUEZON CITY				VALENZUELA CITY			
	Panghulo	Hulong Duhat	Catmon	Potrero	Tatalon	Bagong Silangan	Batasan Hills	Roxas	Punturin	Arkong Bato	Gen T. de Leon	Ugong
Flood affected population	1,110	718	13,085	3,267	33,320	32,000	5,840	9,320	1,340	8,500	7,880	1,504
Average number of families per structure	2	2	3	2	2	2	2	2	2	2	2	2
Average number of persons per structure	6	7	6	6	7	7	6	7	6	6	6	6
Percentage of families with minors	84%	69%	72%	65%	84%	85%	46%	56%	55%	77%	71%	72%
Percentage of families that have members with disabilities	9%	14%	11%	9%	11%	7%	8%	10%	20%	13%	12%	8%
Percentage of families that have members aged 60 years old and above	22%	38%	24%	33%	24%	20%	13%	27%	32%	33%	28%	34%
Percentage of female-headed households	62%	51%	79%	51%	84%	73%	73%	61%	48%	54%	70%	49%

provided the following score interpretations: (a) *11 to 12 points out of 12 possible points* - this seems safe for now, please consult an expert for confirmation, (b) *8-10 points out of 12 possible points* - This requires strengthening, please consult experts; and (c) *0-7 points out of 12 possible points*-this is disturbing, please consult experts soon. The questionnaire was adopted in the study in order to determine the worst-case scenario number of potential IDPs in these barangays – the magnitude 7.2 generated by the nearby West Valley Fault (MMEIRS, 2004).

With 65 to 76 per cent surveyed of the households in partner communities garnering scores of 7 points or less, self-reported perception of house safety among residents reveal widespread awareness of unsafe conditions of their dwelling units (Table 3). Anecdotal evidence relate the "self-build" nature of houses in these communities using salvaged materials and non-engineered construction methods to the large number of families needing pre-emptive evacuation as their houses are easily damaged by the strong winds and torrential rains.

Given the magnitude of households that will require evacuation during disasters, the total amount of space needed was computed using the Sphere Standard of 3.50 square meters (sq.m.) per person. Estimates revealed severe deficit in the space available to meet each communities' evacuation needs.

Compared with the amount of space available in identified

Table 3. Summary of Household Safety Survey Results

The house we live in is:	MALABON CITY				QUEZON CITY				VALENZUELA CITY			
	Panghulo	Hulong Duhat	Catmon	Potrero	Tatalon	Bagong Silangan	Batasan Hills	Roxas	Punturin	Arkong Bato	Gen T. de Leon	Ugong
Safe	1%	2%	1%	1%	1%	1%	2%	1%	3%	4%	1%	0%
Needs strengthening	29%	23%	23%	34%	29%	33%	23%	23%	22%	31%	29%	24%
Disturbing/ not safe	70%	75%	76%	65%	70%	65%	75%	76%	75%	65%	70%	76%

Table 4. Gaps in terms of Evacuation Spaces/ Temporary Shelter

City	Percentage of Potential Evacuees that can be Accommodated in Existing Evacuation Spaces at 3.50 sq.m. per person
Malabon City	3% - 6% *based on SPHERE and PHIVOLCS standards
Quezon City	5% - 6% *based on SPHERE and PHIVOLCS standards
Valenzuela City	7% - 12% *based on SPHERE and PHIVOLCS standards

Table 5. Previous Disaster Experience

City	Barangay's Previous Disaster Experience
Malabon City	1992 (Hulong Duhat - Fire), 1993 (Panghulo - Fire), 2006 Milenyo, 2009 Ondoy, 2011 Fire, 2012 Habagat, 2017 Fire (Catmon); Barangays: Hulong Duhat, Catmon, Panghulo, Potrero
Quezon City	2006 Milenyo, 2009 Ondoy, 2012 Habagat; Barangays: Tatalon, Batasan Hills, Bagong Silangan, Roxas
Valenzuela City	2006 Milenyo, 2009 Ondoy, 2012 Habagat; Barangays: Ugong, Arkong Bato, Punturin, GTDL
Legend:	Fire / Strong winds / Strong winds and flooding / Flooding

evacuation spaces in each community such as barangay halls, covered or open courts, schools, and churches, FGD participants agreed that the 3.50 sq.m./ person requirement will mean less people will be accommodated in these shelters. In most of the communities, the shortfall ranges anywhere from 88 to 94 per cent.

Majority of the respondents in these barangays have experienced a number of disasters. All twelve barangays were severely affected by three hydro-meteorological events, namely: (1) Typhoon Xangsane *(Milenyo)* in 2006, (2) Typhoon Ketsana *(Ondoy)* in 2009, and (3) Monsoon rains enhanced by Typhoon Haikui *(Habagat)* in 2012. Fire outbreaks have also featured in some barangays in Malabon, particularly: (a) Panghulo in 1993, and (b) Catmon in 1992 and in 2017. In the unaided recall of events among FGD and survey participants, earthquake and other geological hazards did not figure in the discussion.

Design Considerations

Recognizing that "people, even the poorest and most marginalized, have capacities that they can put to work in order to prevent, resist, cope with, and recover from stresses and shocks" (Wisner, et al., 2014) is a central concept in CDRRM. Framed as a self-help solution whereby partner communities will be involved in varying capacities during the design, fabrication and integration of the ATS solutions into community-based contingency plans, the focus of the intervention is on bridging design-engineering knowledge among building professionals with local knowledge and capacities available in the community as enabled by partners from local government units, non-government and humanitarian organizations and the academia. In line with the findings from the needs assessment, additional site visits; this time with volunteer planning, architecture and engineering professionals, in the twelve partner communities were conducted in order to fully understand the evacuation site conditions, potentials and challenges that are specific to each locale from a technical standpoint. Parallel series of stakeholder engagements were conducted in order to refine the design criteria which will guide the development of the alternative temporary shelter model designs (see Table 6) along with the following considerations:

Space per occupant

In the subsequent discussions, DRRM officials and community members recognize that evacuation spaces must be augmented given the large number of potential IDPs in each community. However, since resources and land available for the construction of additional evacuation facilities are severely constrained, the interim strategy adopted is to reduce the amount of space each person will occupy in the evacuation center without compromising dignity and privacy.

Aside from SPHERE standard of 3.50 sq.m./person, the FEMA guidelines (2010) recommend 1.86 sq.m./person for short-term evacuation and up to 3.72 sq.m./person for sheltering longer than 72 hours. People who use wheelchairs, lift equipment, a service animal, and personal assistance services can require up to 9.30 sq.m./person. While these are ideal, the stakeholders noted that anthropometrics vary depending on ethnicity, biological factors, context and culture; and that the international standards may not reflect the tight-knit Filipino culture where the concept of personal space is smaller compared to Western cultures. FGD participants further suggested patterning the module after the area occupied by a sleeping bag. From 1.44 sq.m./person (1.80m x 0.80m), the size was reduced further to a bare minimum of 1.20 sq.m./person (+/- 1.70m x 0.70m) for the project since the average height among adult Filipinos 20 yrs and older is 1.63m for males and 1.51m for females (FNRI- DOST, 2014).

Capturing additional space

Besides the existing spaces identified by the barangays for evacuation, external and internal capacities of communities and cities could be tapped to fill in the huge gap for space where temporary shelters may be set up. Private establishments, parking lots, open grounds in schools and other public institutions, vacant lots and other alternative spaces may be considered as potential locations for temporary shelters.

Considering the limited area available where temporary shelters can be set up, vertical space should also be maximized, whenever possible.

Context-rooted designing

Considering the profile of the potentially displaced population with high number of women-headed households, children per family, and persons with disability, evacuation centers and alternative temporary shelter solutions should consider at least the following factors: accessibility, ease of deployment, and privacy.

In addition to this, according to anecdotal evidence, the duration of stay under evacuation situations may vary anywhere from: (a) 2-3 days for monsoon rains, typhoons and flood events, (b) 7 days or more for storm surges and tropical cyclones; and (c) 14 days or more in case of fire and earthquake events. Duration of stay has a large bearing on the durability; and in turn, the cost of production of the ATS solutions that will be developed.

Table 6. ATS Design Criteria

Design Criteria	Weight	Points
ROBUSTNESS	*22%*	
Design should be robust enough to be re-used many times instead of "disposable" solutions. This reduces wastage and allows for buildup of assets for the community		10
Design should consider means to sanitize and clean the unit after each use to ensure hygiene		5
As much as possible, materials used should prevent or deter the spread of fire		7
AFFORDABILITY	*21%*	
Design should be fabricated using locally available materials and, as much as possible, incorporate reused/ recycle materials / and/ or utilize rented/ leased/ sub-contracted materials to lower production cost		9
Design should consider possibility of using local labor or sweat equity to lower production cost		5
Design should also consider the cost of transporting and setup/ dismantling of ATS		7
SCALABILITY	*21%*	
Design should be modular to facilitate ease of deployment		8
Design should be versatile in terms of application and configuration		5
Design should be gender-sensitive as well as provide access to persons with disabilities		8
RANGE OF APPLICATION	*15%*	
Outdoor open space (parking lots, parks, open lots)		5
Covered court/ multipurpose halls, ware house, multi-level parking buildings		5
Classrooms and chapels		5
SPEED OF CONSTRUCTION	*21%*	
Should be easy to construct or fabricate		7
Connections are easy to understand and can be made using simple tools		7
Design can be easily assembled and dismantled		7
Total	*100%*	**100**

Developing the ATS Menu of Options

A range of possible alternative temporary shelter solutions that takes into account varying timeframes of occupancy, availability and configuration of space, as well as deployment conditions were developed resulting from these participatory engagements.

Lightweight Indoor Solutions

These options were developed to manage enclosed or semi-enclosed spaces used as evacuation shelters such as community halls, covered courts, schools and churches. These spaces are often used not only because it can provide much needed shelter from the elements but also because of the availability of large floor areas which can accommodate a sizeable number of people. Since these spaces are designed to provide unobstructed visual from end to end, families evacuating in these facilities commonly complain about lack of privacy aside from cramped conditions. In covered courts, families located at the periphery of the enclosure are exposed to the elements if screens are not provided.

Fig. 3. Lack of privacy as well as exposure to the elements for families located at the periphery of the enclosure is commonly observed in covered courts used for emergency evacuation.

(Source: *ACCORD, Inc.*)

Since these spaces are already provided with a shell, the ATS are primarily designed to provide some form of enclosure to maintain privacy. The Foldable Sleeping Module (Figs. 4a and 4b), made up of tubular pipe framing, plyboard panels for bed base and opaque plastic sheet privacy panels, was designed for use in covered courts, municipal halls, and churches in order to maximize vertical space. Once connected side by side, it can provide some level of privacy for four occupants per module.

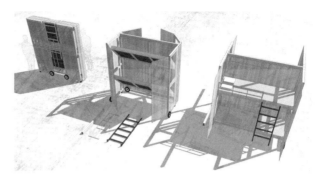

Fig. 4a. Foldable Sleeping Module (single unit) which can be wheeled into place, unfolded and setup in minutes.

(Source: *UAP-EA*)

A Temporary Classroom Partition System (Figs. 5a and 5b) using threaded pipes and fixtures to form the frame on which tarpaulin or fabric sheets can be stretched was conceived to partition a typical 56 sq.m. (7.00m x 8.00m) classroom into four modules that can fit six persons each.

Fig. 4b. Multiple unit Foldable Sleeping Module placed back to back, side by side to form an enclosure for four people per module

(Source: *UAP-EA*)

Fig. 5a Artist's rendering of the Temporary Classroom Partition System (3D model) of the design to provide some privacy for sleeping spaces in classrooms and other enclosed spaces.

(Source: *UAP-EA*)

Fig. 5b Mockup model being inspected by social workers.
(Source: *ACCORD, Inc.*)

Lightweight Outdoor Solutions

These options were developed to take advantage of open spaces found in school yards, parks, parking lots and vacant lots as infill solution to augment spaces for evacuation. The modules are lightweight, easy to store and assemble by women or in some cases, even adolescents. These options were deemed advantageous in communities where families prefer some level of autonomy in their evacuation and where warehousing of temporary shelter solutions cannot be done en masse due to space limitations. While many tent solutions are readily available for purchase, partner communities see the advantage of being coached to fabricate their own ATS units as it allows for some level of customization to better accommodate larger family sizes. Aside from savings accrued through a communal "do-it-yourself" approach, this also has the potential of providing another income stream for urban poor families.

The Barrel Vault Tent (Fig. 6), which can fit four adults and two children for sleeping, makes use of pre-fabricated metal tubes with snap-in-place connections to provide a sturdy frame on which tent fabric can be stretched and fastened in place using hook-and-pile fastening fabric strips. The units can be connected end to end with metal plate connectors to enlarge available space. Organized side by side, rows can be reinforced with metal plate connections to increase wind resistance.

The Folding Tent (Fig. 7) is made of similar materials and provided with a pivot hinge connection which allows the tent to be folded in a nested manner similar to a fan. An option to further lighten the frame using PVC pipes was piloted successfully. Each unit can fit four adults and two children for sleeping.

In both above mentioned designs, the openings that will

Fig. 6 Barrel Vault Tent prototype features being discussed with stakeholders.
(Source: *ACCORD, Inc.*)

Fig. 7 Folding Tent prototype on exhibit during the MOVE UP National Resilience Conference
(Source: *ACCORD, Inc.*)

serve as the door and windows are provided with a layer of mesh to keep insects out while cover flaps are typically rolled up and secured with a strap.

The Snail *(Kuhol)* Tent (Fig. 8) features a structure made up of a series of elliptical frames made up of PVC pipes across which tarpaulin material is stretched. The design allows for better air circulation during hot or humid periods. Ad hoc, the tarpaulin sheets can be secured in place using duct tape. For ease of assembly, a heat-sealed sleeve located at the edge of each tarpaulin panel where PVC pipe frames can be slipped through can be incorporated in the design. Eyelets and snaps may be provided in strategic areas to secure the tarpaulin panels in place. Each unit has an enclose-able space at the rear that can fit seven individuals for sleeping which can be fitted with mesh and fabric privacy panel. Unlike the first two designs which will require a separate communal setup for meals and other activities, the front portion of the Snail Tent provides a shaded area that can accommodate a table and some chairs to serve as living and dining space for families.

Along with waterproof membrane to prevent ground moisture infiltration, other accessories to be included in the kit are guy wires, ropes, pegs and other fasteners in sufficient quantities to anchor the tent firmly onto the ground. Ideally, an additional tarpaulin sheet can be anchored on pipes raised at least 6 inches from the ground as flashing to provide a second barrier against the entry of mud and water within the units.

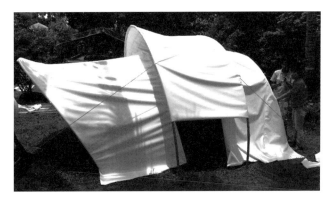

Fig. 8 Snail Tent prototype inspection
(Source: *ACCORD, Inc.*)

Durable Outdoor Solutions

These options were developed bearing in mind protracted evacuation periods which will require shelters that are fairly durable. The design took into account the possibility that some open lots will be exposed to the elements; needing sturdier construction to ensure occupant safety. Another consideration is the ubiquity of concrete surfaces which will make tent pitching difficult. For instance, in Malabon, where almost every nook and cranny is already built-up, closing off some road sections to provide additional area for the setup of temporary shelters in order to augment evacuation spaces is being explored. These options were designed to make full use of ordinary building materials that can be easily found in neighborhood hardware stores that are familiar to community members, as some of them work in various capacities in the construction sector.

The Slotted Steel Angle-framed Shelter (Fig. 9) is clad in 18mm marine plywood fastened with Tek® screws onto a balloon frame composed of 3mm x 50mm x 50mm slotted angle steel. The roof is made up of corrugated GI sheets on slotted steel angle frames. Spaced every 0.60m and bolted back-to-back, the slotted steel angle provides a robust structure take can accommodate significant vertical and lateral forces. A single module of 2.40m x 2.40m, the size of two boards joined side-by-side, can fit four individuals in two customized bunk beds. Units can be joined to fit more people, and arrayed in a line or back to back in order to maximize space. A stacked version of the design, which can support over 1,000 kilograms, was piloted.

Fig. 9 BDRRM officers from partner communities inspected a two-storey prototype of the Slotted Angle Steel-framed Shelter for the community feedback session.
(Source: *ACCORD, Inc.*)

The Urcia Street Shelter (Fig.10) works on a similar principle; however, structural support is provided by scaffolding frames and the cladding material is made out of lightweight concrete panels. Each 3.60m x 4.80m module can be fitted with two double deck bunk beds and provided with a tiny common living-dining area to accommodate 5-7 individuals.

Fig. 10 Artist's impression of the Urcia Street Shelter which was designed for deployment in parking lots and streets.
(Source: *UAP-EA*)

Fig. 11 The lightweight concrete panel has a sturdy clean, smooth, water-resistant surface
(Source: *UAP-EA*)

Fig. 12 A cross-section of the panel shows the cardboard core assembly reinforced by wire mesh
(Source: *UAP-EA*)

Fig. 13 Salient features of the prototype Container Van Shelter were discussed during the the community feedback session.
(Source: *ACCORD, Inc.*)

The cladding panel (Fig. 11) is a wire mesh-reinforced assembly with cylindrical cardboard core covered in thin lightweight concrete that is finished to a water-resistant semi-gloss sheen.

To improve thermal comfort, the core assembly recycles discarded toilet paper cores to serve as spacer and insulating material for the panel (Fig. 12). This panel, which requires production in advance, is envisaged as a potential source of additional livelihood for the community through an LGU or private sector sponsored capacity building program.

Built for rough conditions at sea, retired container van units were explored for modification into mobile emergency shelter (Fig. 13) suited for protracted evacuation situations in open spaces and parks. This model is envisioned to form part of a fleet composed of mobile kitchen, showers and lockers that can and portable toilet system for a total mobile solution that can be deployed and transported where needed. Each 20-foot container van is divided into two sleeping capsules, each with two levels on which three individual sleeping mats are provided to fit a family of six. Chequered plate set on metal frames that form the second sleeping level of the capsule can be slid into place through angle bars provided on three sides of the cabin. By simply removing the flooring, one can use the capsule's full height. A roof assembly consists of tarpaulin material stretched on tubular frames that provide shade for an outdoor lanai which may be used as living-dining space. For ventilation, louvered windows and doors made with recycled pallet wood were set onto the walls of the sleeping capsules.

Conclusion and Recommendations

Past experiences have shown that access to materials and supplies can be challenging during disasters. As such, materials for these shelters may be acquired, stored and distributed by the LGU at the city or barangay level, or through a community-based cooperative/enterprise ahead of time using any of the following modalities: (a) outright purchase of materials and stockpiling, (b) rental arrangement with suppliers, (c) retainer arrangement with suppliers, (d) a combination of any of the suggested modalities.

Despite efforts to: (a) reduce the minimum space allotment per person, (b) create modular units that are relatively easily to assemble and expand as needs arise, (c) manage and stack units vertically to maximize space available, and (d) explore usage of car parks, streets and other open spaces to increase the evacuation area, the demand for space is still too large to be met. Since community members vary in adaptive capacities, increasing their coping mechanisms may effectively reduce the potential number of displaced persons. The researchers recognize that moving urban poor families out of harm's way is still the best option, but this will take much time and resources. In the meantime, community members with the least capacity to move him or herself to safety may be identified and prioritized in LGU-provided evacuation spaces through an ID system which can be matched with an inventory of safe evacuation spaces.

Having an "ATS Menu of Options" is not enough. It can only work effectively in conjunction with appropriate local contingency plans that are matched with detailed, responsive community-based operation plans. Understanding how many units and what options to be deployed, when, where, and how to lay them out is crucial in ensuring that ATS deployment will support and enhance disaster response efforts.

Creating an enabling environment for partnerships to flourish through innovative and progressive use of local incentives will help in the buildup of capital or assets, technology, and skills that will make these communities resilient. Leveraging idle land tax regulations along with fiscal incentives for land owners may facilitate access to unused private land. LGUs may also explore the possibility of approaching mall or shopping center owners to partner with the government in its emergency response efforts by allowing the use of their parking space/ building for temporary evacuation. Tapping into Corporate Social Responsibility (CSR) initiatives may also assist urban poor communities in sourcing out funds for the acquisition, development, construction and stockpiling of their ATS solutions.

Finally, participating in hazard assessment and workshops in reducing risks and managing disasters empowers the marginalized, restores their dignity and upholds their rights as human beings. Building the resilience of the urban poor should anchor into a wider, comprehensive suite of urban management and development plans consistent with provincial, regional and national planning and development frameworks.

Acknowledgement:

This work is part of the Moving Urban Poor Communities towards Resilience (MOVE-UP) Project, a European Commission - Civil Protection & Humanitarian Aid Operations (ECHO)-funded project being implemented by Action Against Hunger (ACF) together with CARE Philippines, local partner Assistance and Cooperation for Community Resilience and Development (ACCORD Inc.) and Plan International with technical assistance from the United Architects of the Philippines-Emergency Architects. The authors acknowledge the support of all the partners and their generous contributions.

References

1) Bankoff, G. (2003) "Constructing Vulnerability: The Historical, Natural and Social Generation of Flooding in Metropolitan Manila" Disasters, 2003, 27(3): 95–109. Retrieved from https://pdfs.semanticscholar.org/3ddd/92a1a264effa32af884596c42f7226d46b17.pdf Date accessed: 25 Mar 2018

2) Demographia (2018) Demographia World Urban Areas (Built-Up Urban Areas or Urban Agglomerations) 14th Annual Edition: March 2018. Retrieved from http://demographia.com/db-worldua.pdf> Date accessed: 26 Mar 2018

3) Department of Science and Technology – Philippine Institute of Volcanology and Seismology (2014) HOW SAFE IS MY HOUSE? Self-check for Earthquake Safety of Concrete Hollow Block (CHB) Houses in the Philippines. retrieved from http://www.phivolcs.dost.gov.ph/images/Flyer-How-Safe-Is-Your-House.pdf Date accessed: 28 Mar 2018

4) Federal Emergency Management Agency (2010) Guidance on Planning for Integration of Functional Needs Support Services in General Population Shelters. Retrieved fromhttps://www.fema.gov/pdf/about/odic/fnss_guidance.pdf Date accessed: 26 Mar 2018

5) Food and Nutrition Research Institute of the Department of Science and Technology (2014) 8th National Nutrition Survey (NNS). Retrieved fromhttp://122.53.86.125/NNS/8thNNS.pdf Date accessed: 22 Mar 2018

6) Internal Displacement Monitoring Centre (2013) Disaster-induced internal displacement in the Philippines: The case of Tropical Storm Washi/Sendong Retrieved from https://pdfdokument.com/disaster-induced-internal-displacement-in-the-philippines_59e475361723d-da21fd491c9.html Date accessed: 31 Oct 2018

7) Internal Displacement Monitoring Centre (2014) The risk of disaster-induced displacement in south-east Asia and China. Retrieved from http://www.internal-displacement.org/library/publications/2014/the-risk-of-disaster-induced-displacement-in-south-east-asia-and-china Date accessed: 22 Mar 2018

8) Internal Displacement Monitoring Centre (2017) Country Profile | Philippines | Mid-Year-update-2017 Retrieved from http://www.internal-displacement.org/assets/country-profiles/Mid-Year-update-2017/PHL-disaster.pdf Date accessed: 18 Mar 2018

9) National Economic Development Authority (2017) Philippine Development Plan 2017-2022. Retrieved from http://pdp.neda.gov.ph/wp-content/uploads/2017/01/PDP-2017-2022-07-20-2017.pdf

10) Norwegian Refugee Council and the Internal Displacement Monitoring

Centre (2017) Global Report on Internal Displacement (https://reliefweb.int/sites/reliefweb.int/files/resources/2017-GRID.pdf)

11) Pornasdoro, Karlo P.; Silva, L., Munárriz, M. L., Estepa, B and Capaque, C (2014) Flood Risk of Metro Manila Barangays: A GIS Based Risk Assessment Using Multi-Criteria Techniques. Journal in Urban and Regional Planning 1:1 (p. 51-72) ISSN 2362-9487 retrieved from http://journals.upd.edu.ph/19May2014_surp/article/view/4207>. Date accessed: 27 Mar 2018.

12) Philippine Statistics Authority (2017) poverty statistics for the basic sectors for 2015 Retrieved from http://psa.gov.ph/poverty-press-releases Date accessed: 27 Mar 2018.

13) Rappler (2013) BY THE NUMBERS: Ondoy, Habagat 2012, Habagat 2013 Published 10:58 PM, September 26, 2013 Updated 6:10 PM, July 11, 2014. Retrieved from https://www.rappler.com/newsbreak/39948-by-the-numbers-ondoy-habagat-2012-2013 Date accessed: 18 Mar 2018.

14) United Nations Commission on Human Rights (1998) Guiding Principles on Internal Displacement retrieved from https://documents-dds-ny.un.org/doc/UNDOC/GEN/G98/104/93/PDF/G9810493.pdf?OpenElement Date accessed: 30 Oct 2018

15) United Nations Office for the Coordination of Humanitarian Affairs (2018) Philippines: 2017 Key Displacements and Responses Snapshot retrieved from https://www.humanitarianresponse.info/sites/www.humanitarianresponse.info/files/documents/files/180202_ocha_phl_2017_events_snapshot_0.pdf Date accessed: 16 Mar 2018.

16) Wisner, B.; Kelman, I and Gillard, JC (2014) Hazard, vulnerability, capacity and participation in Alejandro Lopez-Carresi , Maureen Fordham , Ben Wisner , Ilan Kelman , J. C. Gaillard (Eds.), Disaster Management : International Lessons in Risk Reduction, Response and Recovery (pp. 13-22) Oxon, London: Routledge

17) Persons with Disability in the Philippines (Results from the 2010 Census) (2013 January 10). Retrieved from https://psa.gov.ph/content/persons-disability-philippines-results-2010-census Date Accessed 19 Mar 2018

18) The Age and Sex Structure of the Philippine Population: (Facts from the 2010 Census) (2012 August 30). Retrieved from https://psa.gov.ph/content/age-and-sex-structure-philippine-population-facts-2010-census Date Accessed 19 Mar 2018

19) Highlights on Household Population, Number of Households, and Average Household Size of the Philippines (2015 Census of Population) (2016 December 29). Retrieved from https://www.psa.gov.ph/content/highlights-household-population-number-households-and-average-household-size-philippines Date Accessed 19 Mar 2018

20) Japan International Cooperation Agency, Metropolitan Manila Development Authority and Philippine Institute of Volcanology and Seismology (2004) Metro Manila Earthquake Impact Reduction Study. Retrieved at: http://www.phivolcs.dost.gov.ph/index.php?option=com_content&view=article&id=419:mmeirs&catid=66 Date Accessed 02 Feb 2018

An Investigation on Coconut-timber Waste as Construction Material for Earthquake Resistant Wooden House in North Sulawesi, Indonesia

Rilya Rumbayan[1], Donny Taju[2], Rudolf Mait[3]
1, 2, 3 Senior Lecturer, Department of Civil Engineering, Manado State Polytechnic, Indonesia

インドネシアで大量に栽培されているココヤシ。生産力を維持するため、その木は定期的に植え替えられる。伐採された木は、そのままなら大量の廃棄物となるが、建材として利用すれば地震に強い木造住宅の普及につなげることができる。

Abstract

This paper presents a current study into the use of coconut-timber waste as an alternative construction material to build earthquake-resistant timber house in North Sulawesi, Indonesia. The objectives of this research are: to obtain the physical and mechanical properties of coconut-timber, to identify the strength classification of coconut-timber, to design a model of earthquake-resistant house made of coconut-timber, and to perform structural analysis of the house under earthquake load. Research methods include: (1) Laboratory testing of the physical and mechanical properties comprising of moisture content test, density test, tensile test parallel to grain, compression test parallel to grain, compression test perpendicular to grain, shear strength parallel to grain, flexural test, and toughness. All tests were performed according to the American Standard Testing Material (ASTM) D143-09; (2) Identification of strength classification of coconut-timber based on the Indonesian Standard (SNI) 03-3527-1994; (3) Design of an earthquake-resistant coconut-timber house; (4) Calculation of the dimensions of structural elements of earthquake-resistant coconut-timber house; and (5) Testing of the performance of the coconut-timber house under earthquake load with ETABS software. Results from this research are expected to support the beneficial usage of local coconut-timber waste as construction material for timber house in an effort to mitigate the risk of earthquake hazard in North Sulawesi.

Keywords Coconut-timber; timber strength class; physical properties; mechanical properties; earthquake-resistant

Introduction

North Sulawesi Province is one of the regions in Indonesia that has a high risk of earthquake because it is geologically located in one of the path of the Pacific Rim. Based on the map of earthquake regions used as a reference for structural building design, the province of North Sulawesi in Indonesia is located in Earthquake Region 5 which is categorized as a high-risk zone with earthquake scale between 5-7 Richter.

Building construction made of timber offers many benefits such as relatively higher structural stability and integration. This is due to the fact that timber has higher strength-to-weight ratio compared to steel and concrete. This weight or mass of construction has a linear correlation to the lateral force (inertia) sustained by the construction. These properties have caused timber to become an alternative building material for earthquake prone areas such as North Sulawesi.

Coconut (*Cocos nucifera Linn*) is one of the many potential plantation crops commodity grown in North Sulawesi with a total area of 277.649 Ha in 2015, covering 15 districts. The total area is comprised of 37.675 Ha of coconut tree plantation that are not yet productive, 225.003 Ha of coconut tree plantation that are productive and 17.259 Ha of coconut tree plantation with coconut trees aged over 50 years and needed rejuvenation because of their declining fruit productivity (Data from Dinas Perkebunan Prov. Sulut, 2015). This rejuvenation is needed to allow more space for new coconut plantation. The largest waste from the rejuvenation of coconut trees are the trunks from old coconut trees. If the trunks are left unprocessed, they can become breeding places for diseases that could strike coconut seedlings, which in turn will bring disadvantages to the local farming communities. Processing and utilization of the unproductive coconut trees as a construction material for timber house can be an alternative solution to the handling of coconut tree trunks after the rejuvenation, which will be beneficial to the local communities.

In general, the anatomical structure of a coconut tree consists of vascular bundle and ground tissue in the form of parenchyma. Macroscopically, there are differences in the density (distribution) of vascular bundle based on its location (height and depth) in the coconut tree trunk. More toward the center, the density of vascular bundle decreases, while toward the vertical the density of vascular bundle increases (Sudarna, 1990). The ability of vascular bundle as a support for timber strength is closely related to the thickness of fibre cell wall and silica content in the cell (Rahayu, 2001).

Density of coconut-timber varies depending on depth and height of the trunk. The density decreases with increasing trunk height and increases from the central part to the edge of the trunk. More toward the center of the trunk, coconut-timber is softer. Moreover, the density of coconut-timber also varies according to variety, location and age of the coconut tree (Polomar, 1990). Density of coconut-timber can be categorized into three based on the thickness of timber starting from the part closest to the bark. High density wood (>0.6 g/cm^3) covers 53% of the trunk, generally located closest to the bark with thickness from 7.5 cm to 12.5 cm, having characteristic of very resistant to scratches; medium density wood (0.4-0.6 g/cm^3) covers 25% of the trunk, is in the thickness from 5 cm to 10 cm after the high-density-wood part, having characteristics of slightly resistant to scratches and cannot withstand humid weather; and low density wood (<0.4 g/cm^3) covers 22% of the trunk, located in the center, quite soft, quickly weathered, cannot withstand scratches and humid weather.

The Indonesian standard about the quality and dimensions of construction timber, SNI 03-3527-1994, uses the physical properties (Air-dry Density) to classify timber into 5 strength classes (**Table 1**).

Table 1. Mechanical properties of timber

Strength Class	Air-dry Density	Absolute Flexural Strength (Kg/cm^2)	Absolute Compressive Strength (Kg/cm^2)
I	≥ 0.90	≥ 1100	≥ 650
II	0.90 – 0.60	1100 – 725	650 – 425
III	0.60 -0.40	725 – 500	425 – 300
IV	0.40 – 0.30	500 -360	300 – 215
V	≤ 0.30	≤ 360	≤ 215

Source: SNI 03-3527-1994.

The specific objectives of this research are: (1) To obtain the physical and mechanical properties of coconut-timber as a construction material for timber house and to identify the strength class of coconut-timber; (2) To design a earthquake-resistant timber house model made of coconut-timber; and (3) To test the performance of the coconut-timber house under earthquake load.

This research is one of the applications of building construction engineering to mitigate earthquake disaster through the design of timber house that is safe for earthquake prone areas. This research is important as an effort to utilize and to increase the value of local coconut-timber waste from unproductive coconut trees to be used as a construction material to build earthquake-resistant timber house. Moreover, results of this research are expected to support the empowerment of local economy by utilization of potential sustainable local natural resources.

Research Method

Research methods (**Figure 1**) comprise of laboratory tests, design of coconut-timber house prototype that is resistant to earthquake and performance test of the prototype of coconut-timber house under earthquake load.

The experimental stage in the laboratory consists of physical and mechanical properties tests which cover moisture content test, density test, tensile test parallel to grain, compression test parallel to grain, compression test perpendicular to grain, shear strength parallel to grain, flexural test, and toughness (**Figure 2**). Samples for the tests were obtained from unproductive coconut trees from Minahasa Selatan region in North Sulawesi. Total numbers of samples were 791. Experimental tests were performed at the Civil Engineering Material Testing Laboratory and Mechanical Engineering Material Testing Laboratory, Manado State Polytechnic. Test methods were based on the American Standard Testing Material (ASTM) D143-09. Results from this experimental stage were used as references in design stage of a 6m x 6m model of coconut-timber house.

The design stage of the prototype includes the drawing of design plan of the timber house and calculation of coconut-timber structural elements. The design stage was performed in accordance to design principles and standards of building model by considering earthquake load. Preparation of dimensions of structural elements which consist of beam, column, floor panel, wall panel and roof was performed after the structural analysis calculation.

The next stage was testing of the performance of coconut-timber house prototype. Performance test of structure was done by analysis of the structure under earthquake load with simulation of structural model. The software used for the simulation was ETABS (Structural software for building analysis and design).

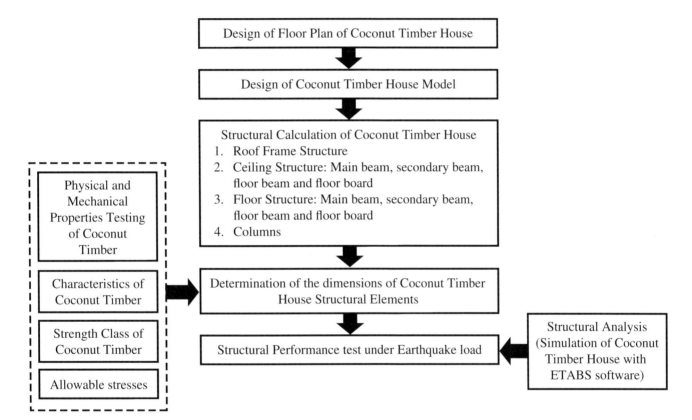

Fig. 1. Research Method

Fig. 2. Mechanical properties tests of coconut-timber at the Material Testing Laboratory, Manado State Polytechnic

Results

A. Characteristics of coconut-timber as timber house construction material.

The experimental test results are presented in **Table 2**.

According to the categories of timber strength classification in SNI 03-3527-1994, the strength class of coconut-timber is as follow:

- The air-dry density is in the range of strength class I and II, therefore can be used as structural timber, which usage requires calculation of load.
- The compressive strength parallel to grain is in the range of strength class III, therefore can be used as non-structural timber, which usage does not require calculation of load.
- The flexural strength is in the range of strength class III to IV, therefore can be used as auxiliary building material or temporary building.

Table 2. Test results from the mechanical properties tests in the laboratory

No.	Characteristics of coconut-timber	Test result
1	Modulus of Elasticity (kg/cm^2)	67000
2	Flexural strength (kg/cm^2)	458.66
3	Compressive strength parallel to grain (kg/cm^2)	399.3
4	Compressive strength perpendicular to grain (kg/cm^2)	179.79
5	Shear strength parallel to grain (kg/cm^2)	65.13
6	Density (gr/cm^3)	0.9
7	Moisture content (%)	15.95
8	Tensile strength – parallel to the grain (kg/cm^2)	44760.1
9	Toughness (kgf)	424.74

B. Structural Design and Floor Plan of Coconut-timber House.

Results of structural design of a coconut-timber house with a floor plan size of 6 m x 6 m are shown in **Figure 3**.

The result of the design of a coconut-timber house model is shown in **Figure 4**.

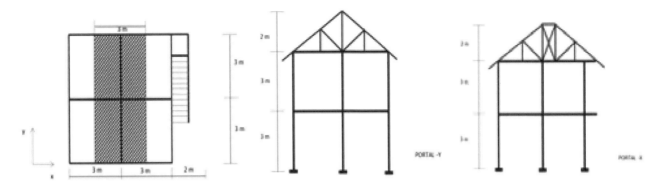

Fig. 3. Design of coconut-timber house: (A). Floor Plan; (B). Portal Frame X-axis; and (C). Portal Frame Y-axis.

Fig. 4. Design drawing and model of coconut-timber house.

C. Calculation of the dimensions of Structural Elements of Coconut-timber House

Structural calculation of coconut-timber house includes roof frame structure, ceiling structure: main beam, secondary beam, floor beam and floor board, floor structure: main beam, secondary beam, floor beam and floor board, and columns. Determination of the dimensions of coconut-timber house structural elements was performed in accordance to design principles, standards and implementation methods building model construction by considering earthquake load. Design results of dimensions of the coconut-timber house structural elements are presented in **Table 3**.

D. Structural Analysis of coconut-timber house structure under earthquake load.

Structural performance test is done by analysis of structure under earthquake load with simulation of structural model. The software used for this simulation process is ETABS (Structural software for building analysis and design). The sway mode caused by earthquake on the frame structure of coconut-timber house generated by ETABS software can be seen in **Figure 5**. Result from the structural analysis of the frame structure of coconut-timber house under earthquake load with ETABS software shows that the construction is safe under earthquake load.

Table 3. Calculation result of the dimensions of coconut-timber house structural elements

No.	Construction	Element	Dimension
1	Roof truss	Compression	b=8 cm and h=12 cm
		Tension	b=8 cm and h=12 cm
2	Ceiling	Main beam	b=10 cm and h=18 cm
		Secondary beam	b=10 cm and h=18 cm
		Floor beam	b=5 cm and h=10 cm
		Floor boards	b=25 cm and h=2,5 cm
3	Floor	Main beam	b=15 cm and h=20 cm
		Secondary beam	b=15 cm and h=20 cm
		Floor beam	b=5 cm and h=10 cm
		Floor boards	b=25 cm and h=2,5 cm
4	Upper columns		b=15 cm and h=15 cm
5	Lower columns		b=15 cm and h=15 cm

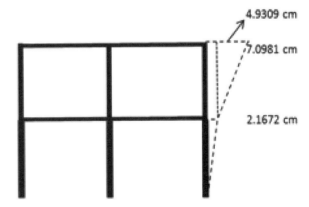

Fig. 5. Sway mode due to earthquake load acting on the frame structure of coconut-timber house (generated with ETABS)

Conclusions and Expected Outcomes

Results of laboratory testing that conform the SNI 03-3527-1994 classification, the strength class of coconut-timber can be used as structural construction timber, of which usage requires the calculation of load; as a non-structural construction timber, of which usage does not require the calculation of load; and as a temporary construction material.

The determination of the dimensions of coconut-timber house structural elements was performed based on the experimental results from the laboratory tests of the physical and mechanical properties of coconut-timber. The prototype of coconut-timber house was built based on the design and structural analysis followed by structural performance test against earthquake load using ETABS software. Results from the structural analysis of the coconut-timber house frame structure under earthquake loading using ETABS software show that the house is safe.

Results from this research are expected to support the beneficial usage of the potentiality of coconut-timber as a construction material for timber house in an effort to mitigate the risk of earthquake hazard in North Sulawesi.

References

1) ASTM Standard Methods for Testing Small Clear Specimens of Timber. ASTM Designation D143 – 09. Annual Book of ASTM Standards, Vol. 04.10. ASTM, West Conshohoken, PA, 2009.
2) Killmann W. dan F. Fink. 1996. Coconut Palm Stem Processing Technical Handbook. Protrade: Depart. Furniture and Wooden Products Deutche Gesellschaft. Federal Republic of Germany.
3) Polomar, R.N. 1990. State of the Art: Coconut Utilization Asia and Pasific Coconut Community. Jakarta.
4) Rahayu, I. S. 2001. Sifat Dasar Vascular Bundle dan Parenkim Batang Kelapa Sawit Dalam Kaitannya dengan Sifat Fisis, Mekanis serta Keawetan. Thesis Program Studi Ilmu Pengetahuan Kehutanan, Fakultas Pascasarjana. Institute Pertanian Bogor.
5) SNI 03-3527-1994. Mutu Kayu Bangunan. Badan Standarisasi National.
6) Sudarna, N. S. 1990. Anatomi Batang Kelapa. Jurnal Penelitian Hasil Hutan. Vol 7, No 3 hal 111-117.

Women as Victims of the Conflict in North Aceh (A Study about the Resiliency through Local Wisdom Perspective)

Winda Putri Diah Restya[1], Ika Rahmadani[2]
1 Lecturer, Psychology Faculty, University of Muhammadiyah Aceh
2 Lecturer, Economic Faculty, University of Teuku Umar

長年にわたるインドネシア国軍との紛争で疲弊し、2005年に和平合意ができた後も多くの人が避難生活を続けているアチェ。生活基盤や家族を失いながらもたくましく生きる女性たちの強さの秘密を探ると、昔ながらの生活の知恵があった。

Abstract

This study focuses on the resilience of women victims of the Aceh conflict based on a local wisdom perspective. The discussion on how the victims cope with the conflict is worth to be studied, because the Aceh conflict has been one of the longest running in Asia. Aceh is also the best example in Asia of the transformation of a violent into an enduring peace. The concept of resiliency refers to the five characteristics of resiliency from Wagnild (2010) namely meaningfulness, perseverance, equanimity, self-reliance and existential aloneness. The subjects in this research are chosen by using a purposive technique, by choosing women who were victims of the conflict and already risen up without showing any traumatic signs. Picture of resilience and Acehnese cultural studies was obtained using qualitative research method through in-depth interview method and non-participant observation. Data were collected in North Aceh in three different villages which are Gedong – Sawang, Matang Kuli, as well as Lhok Sukon which were suffered most during the conflict era. The results show that the participants are already in a good state of resiliency, furthermore the Acehnese cultural aspects that associated with resiliency ability among the conflict's victims are Islamic value as the way of life for people in Aceh, grateful value, and some of the Aceh proverbs that passed down from generation to generation such us *"Udep Beusare Mate Syahid"* and *'Geut Tapubut, Geut Geubalah. Jeuheut Geukubah lam Nuraka"*. Therefore, it is important for the society to retain the values of local wisdom as it can be one of the supporting factors which can help the conflict's victims cope with their unpleasant situations. This study is a preliminary research on how resilience can be done through a local wisdom approach.

Keywords *Conflict, Resiliency, Local Wisdom*

Introduction

The conflict is the friction that occurs between the two camps or more caused by the difference in value, status, power, resource scarcity, as well as uneven distribution, which can give rise to relative deprivation in the community. According to Soderberg (2005) horizontal violence in the third world countries is usually due to two elements, which often join and eventually become a trigger of a continuing conflict. The first element is called "identity element", namely people mobilization in communal identity group based on race, religion, culture, language differences and the second is called "distribution" element that is mainly caused by the issues of economic resources distribution, social jealousy and political conditions in the society. Horizontal conflicts in Indonesia are, as matter of fact, mostly caused by social and economic gaps or social jealousy but it will be embarrassing for the conflicting parties to show that such reasons are to be the causes of their anger and aggression.

One of the conflicts that took place in Indonesia was the conflict in Aceh. The Aceh conflict has been the longest running in Asia. Conflict or insurgency in Aceh between the years 1976 up to the year 2005 was waged by the Free Aceh Movement (GAM) to be independent from Indonesia (Putranto, 2006). The Free Aceh Movement or GAM was a separatist organization which has stood in Aceh since 1976 (Putranto, 2009). The purpose of the establishment of GAM was to be separated from the sovereignty of Indonesian Republic. This movement is also known as the Aceh Sumatra National Liberation Front (ASNLF). One of the things that led to the conflict in Aceh is Aceh people's disappointment against the Central Government, namely when the Government revoked special autonomy rights of the Acehnese. The next conflict resolution in Aceh that tends to be the militarization by applying Aceh as a Military Operation Region (DOM) has worsened the State as many human rights violations occurred during the enforcement of this thing and increasingly encouraged people to be more supportive of the GAM on the Central Government.

When the memorandum of understanding between the Government of Indonesia (GoI) and GAM (Free Aceh Movement) was finally signed on August 15, 2005, in Helsinki, Finland, the agreement brought an end to the nearly thirty years of bloody armed conflict that claimed 15,000 lives, displaced tens of thousands and impacted the whole country, economically as well as politically (Putranto, 2009). This conflict leaves a profound suffering for those who experienced it as well as for the families of the victims are left out, the long-term psychological impact may continue to haunt the victims of conflict in a relatively long after the conflict occurred, the victims conflict suffer from death, injuries – cuts and from the aspect of feeling will arise out of fear, anxiety, guilt, anger, grief, and loss. Whereas in the aspect of the mind people become confused and frantically (Foundation recovers & JICA, 2006). The ability to bounce back after experiencing the unpleasant event is called resiliency.

Since the last 30 years resiliency has become a concept in psychology that are increasingly being explored (Wagnild, 2009). Resiliency means a concept that relates to the ability to adapt positively in the face of pressure or difficulty to be able to return to the original state (Mastern & Gerwirtz 2006).

According to Neil (2006) resiliency is not a coincidence but it appears in people who have trained hard, had a special attitude of good cognitive ability, emotions and an unwavering heart to overcome challenges.

Some of the factors that play a role in the development of it among others are personal support or social support. Besides, the culture and the community in which one lives also affects the ability of the person's resilience. Individuals are aware of the importance of culture as a benchmark against the behavior of his own. Culture is something that complex includes knowledge, belief, art, morals, law, custom, and any other capabilities and habits acquired by man as a member of the community. Cultural influence is the developmental aspect of the individual. In turn different individuals whose behavior patterns are different – between one community with other communities (Holaday and McPhearson in Santrock, 2002). Similar to that, Beuf in Holaday (1997) expressed resilience is influenced strongly by culture, good attitude – attitude that believed in a culture value – the value of the good in a society, the same thing also mentioned by Delgado (in LaFromboise, Hoyt, Whitbeck & Oliver, 2006) which is local wisdom is necessary in terms of understanding the capability of individual resilience. The Acehnese known as the community who value the culture most. For Acehnese, culture and religion are two things that cannot be separated in their everyday lives, therefore, this research was conducted to obtain an overview of resilience among women as a victims of Aceh's conflict through the local wisdom perspective. The sense of resiliency which is used on this research refers to the five characteristics from Wagnild (2010) namely: meaningfulness, perseverance, self-reliance, equanimity, and existential aloneness.

Literature Reviews

Resiliency

Grotberg (2001) defined resiliency as the individual's capacity to handle, eliminate, even change unpleasant experience including natural disasters as well as man-made. Resiliency help individuals who are living in conditions or bad experience by increasing expectations and beliefs sufficient to social function. Resiliency is a capability that must be owned by a person to rise from the problems in some productive and healthy ways that is productive without doing violent. And also it is very important to be able to control the pressure in life when being under the pressure (Reivich & Shatte, 2002).

The characteristics of resilient people, according to Grotberg (1999), consist of these following things:
1. Have the ability to control a wide range of thrust that emerged from inside a person.
2. Have the ability to be able to rise from the issue and trying to resolve it.
3. Independent and can take decisions based on the thinking and the initiative itself, has the attitude of empathy and concern to fellow.

According to Young & Wagnild (1993) there are five characteristic among resilient people which are:
1. *Meaningfulness*, has a purpose in life
2. *Perseverance*, has the desire to forge ahead despite difficulties
3. *Self-reliance*, believing in their self by understanding the deficiency and excess.
4. *Equanimity*, the ability to remain optimistic even faced by the difficult situations and has a sense of humor.
5. *Existential aloneness* i.e. someone accept him/her self for what it is, has a strong establishment and has no desire to contrast with the environment.

Although the concept of resiliency is universal, but humans are living in a different culture, so in reality, the difficulties faced by someone else will be varied. Communities who are not from the West will adapt in different ways from those of who lives in the West. And most of the cultural differences are hardly touched by studies that discuss about the resiliency (Young & Wagnild, 1993 in Xiaonan & Zhang, 2007).

Conflict

The conflict is a social sympthom which present in social life, so conflicts are inherently means that conflict will always exist in any space and time, anywhere and anytime. The term of "conflict" is etymologically derived from the Latin "con" which means "together" and "fligere" which means the collision or collisions (Setiadi & Kolip, 2011). In general term of social conflict contains a series of phenomena of contention and interpersonal disputes from class conflict to the international wars.

According to Coser (in Jameson, conflict can be defined as struggle over values and status claims, power and resources in which the aims of the opponents are to neutralize, injure or eliminate their rivals. In another sense, the conflict is a social process which takes place by involving persons or groups who are challenging each other with threats of violence (Soekanto, 1993). Conflict can be interpreted as a clash of power and interests among a group with other groups in the process of seizure societal resources (economic, political, social and cultural) which relatively limited (Lawang, 1994).

Lauer (2001) divides the conflict based on the perpetrator into 3 cathegories:
1. A vertical Conflict is a conflict between components of the community in a structure that has a hierarchy. For example, a conflict between a boss with a subordinate in the Office.
2. Horizontal Conflict is a conflict between individuals or groups that have the same relative position. For example a conflict between the mass and the organizations
3. A Diagonal Conflict is a conflict which caused by inequality of resources allocation between the central government and the local. For example a conflict in Aceh.

Understanding the Aceh War

Aceh is one of the provinces of the Republic of Indonesia located in the Northern of Sumatra Island. It is close to the Andaman and Nicobar Islands of India and separated from them by the Andaman Sea. Its population has the highest percentage of Muslims in Indonesia, who mostly live according to Sharia customs and laws. Aceh has substantial natural resources of oil and natural gas with some estimates that Aceh gas reserves are one of the largest in the world. Relative to most of Indonesia, it is a religiously conservative area. During the 1970s, under an agreement with the Indonesian central government, American oil and gas companies began exploitation of Aceh's natural resources. Alleged unequal distribution of profits between the central government and the native people of Aceh induced Dr. Muhammad Hasan Tiro, former ambassador of Darul Islam to call for an independent of Aceh.

He proclaimed independence in 1976. During the late 1980s, several security incidents prompted the Indonesian central government to take repressive measures and to send troops to Aceh. Human rights abuse was rampant for the next decade, resulting in many grievances on the part of the Acehnese toward the Indonesian central government. In 1990, the Indonesian government through military operations sent more than 12,000 Indonesian army in the region to fight againts GAM.

During the late 1990s, chaos in Java and an ineffective central government gave an advantage to the Free Aceh Movement (GAM) and resulted in the second phase of the rebellion, this time with large support from the Acehnese people.

This support was demonstrated during the 1999 plebiscite in Banda Aceh which was attended by nearly half a million people (of the four million population of the province). The Indonesian central government responded in 2001 by broadening Aceh's autonomy, giving its government the right to apply Sharia law more broadly and the right to receive direct foreign investment. This was again accompanied by repressive measures, however, and in 2003 an offensive began and a state of emergency was proclaimed in the Province. The war was still going on when the tsunami disaster of 2004 struck the province.

Culture, Resiliency and Conflict

Culture has a very large function for human beings and society. Therefore man cannot be separated from religion and culture, one part of the culture is local wisdom.

Local wisdom can be interpreted as a whole views or teachings alive, tip, adage, and values a living tradition and practiced by the society are respected, both of which have indigenous or sanctions that have no sanctions (Sanusi, 2005:24). The local wisdom can serve as mechanisms of socio-cultural traditions which is believed to be and has been proven as a powerful means of fraternity and solidarity between citizens who have work in the social and cultural order. Cultural approach by involving local wisdom is strategic and effective because in the community legal system has been living, known as customary law. For example, there is a local wisdom in Maluku which called *Pela* and *Gandong*. Pela was born based on a Treaty of friendship and fraternal bonding between two or more villages, and while *Gandong* was formed due to an awareness of the genealogical (Aditjondro, 2007; 310-311). Furthermore, in Sulawesi especially in Poso (Central Sulawesi) there is a similar local wisdoms called *Pekasiwia*, means the degree of equalization. While in Aceh, there are Di'iet, Sayam, Suloh, and Peusijuk, this tradition has been long entrenched and practiced in the society till this day. Local wisdom preserved in order to resolve conflicts that occur in the community. As an example of conflict resolution processes that develop in the community are resolved within the framework of indigenous laden with religious values. This tradition is the process of conflict resolution which are very democratic without the occurrence of bloodshed and revenge between the two parties in conflict, either vertically or horizontally.

Local wisdom is viewed as customary law by Acehnese, therefore, it is very timely to understand resiliency through local wisdom perspective because it is already widespread in the community. Local wisdom is something that was already rooted and usually is not only oriented to profane, but also sacred oriented so that its implementation can be more quickly and easily accepted by the society. As revealed by Beuf (in Holaday 1997) resiliency is strongly influenced by culture and good attitude which is believed in society With local customary conflict resolution is expected to be quickly realized, could be accepted all groups so that there is no longer a hidden latent conflicts in the community (Sriyanto, 2007).

Research Methodology

To execute this study, the author of this paper used qualitative approach. Qualitative approach is conducted to obtain the description of social phenomena in a more natural environment (Hancock, 1998). Due to its specific terms then this research used purposive sampling method which means the samples in this research are determined based on certain specific criteria which are:

1. Women aged 30 – 50 years
2. Still living in conflict areas (North Aceh)
3. The direct or indirect victims of Aceh's conflict
4. Experience loss of one or all family members

The research sample was selected based on these selection criteria that has been mentioned above, Three major conflict areas in North Aceh namely Ulee Geudong-Sawang, Matang

Kuli, and Lhok Sukon has been chosen to represent Aceh's conflict area. The data obtained from the authorities, showed that there are at least five subjects who meet the research criteria, one of the subject had moved to another cities while the other one is not willing to be the participant on this research project, therefore there are only three participants available on this research.

Methods of Data Collection

Data collection procedure in this study using the method of observation, interviews, and documentation. With each explanation as follows:

1. Observation Method

The observation method was used in this research was a direct observation. Direct observation enables researchers to felt, seen and lived within the subject. In this study, researchers used a non – participant observation i.e. in this technique researchers were the outsider and not participate in subject activities.

2. In-depth Interview Method

The process of obtaining information for research purposes is done by face-to-face interview between the interviewer and the interviewee using a tool called the interview guide (Guide interview). In this study the approach chosen is unstructured interview instructions. The reason for using this method is to locate and uncover the profuse and gather so as much as possible data by using the guidelines of the interview which has been made. Interview guidelines drawn up based on five resiliency characteristics expressed by Wagnild (2010) which are the meaningfulness, perseverance, equanimity, self-reliance, and existential aloneness, as well as some questions related to the local culture in Aceh.

Data Analysis

Means giving the meaning to analysis, describes a pattern or a category, look for the relationships between the various concepts. Based on explanation above, then the data analysis techniques used in this research are:

1. Reduction and Elimination

The raw data or material which had been collected from the field are summarized then selected. Furthermore, it is later can be categorized based on the same theme or the same issues.

2. Display and Data Clustering

The results of the reduction necessary in particular-display in each pattern, the category, the focus, the theme of which was about to be understood and to understand the issue is sitting together. The data display can help researchers to be able to see the whole or certain parts of the research results.

3. Conclusion

The estuary from the conclusions of the qualitative data analysis are located on how the researcher represent the research result to the reader so that it can be understood with regardless an issue which is examined.

Research Results

The implementation of this research study was conducted on January 10th – 27th 2018, starting by looking for the information of demographic data from the office of Village chief in North Aceh. Basically there are three regencies which experiencing severe conflict in Aceh i.e., Bireun, Pidie, North Aceh. However, this study only focused on the area of North Aceh, especially at the village or subdistrict namely Ulee Geudong – Sawang, Matang Kuli and Lhok Sukon, because these areas are the most numerous population of women as a victims when conflict was happened in Aceh several years ago. In some aspects of the analysis is also presented according to age, not only because of the age of predicting the risk of some form of illness, but also because of the age and gender are jointly associated with traumatic events experience certain as part from the conflict. The data base of three participants can be found in this following table:

	Subject 1	Subject 2	Subject 3
Name/ Initial	HH	NH	SS
Sex	Female	Female	Female
Age	38	50	31
Address	Rangkileh	Mencat	Karing
Educational Status	Junior High	Elementry	Senior High
Occupation	Farmer	Housewife	Housewife
Number of Siblings	7	5	5
Number of Children	2	5	—
Number of Family Lost	1	2	3
Duration of Conflict	16 years	12 years	6 years

The informed-concern sheet was given to the three participants in order to express their approval in involving in the research process. Resilience measurement was begin with a general question such as "over the last year have you ever encountered problems with mood and how is your feeling? (e.g., feels sad or depressed, anxious, scared, or could you control your anger)?" If Yes, do you think the problem is caused by stress or trauma related to the conflict in Aceh in the past?". Two of the three subject assumes that anxiety that had happened today could be caused by the conflicts from the past. Measurement of resiliency was done using a semi structured interview questionnaire drawn up based on the resiliency aspects expressed by Wagnild (2010) namely the Meaningfulness, Perseverance, Self-reliance, Equanimity, and Existential aloneness. Summary of interview guideline can be seen in the following list:

1. Experience in facing conflict Aceh
   - Any losses incurred when conflicts occur? (lost property/family?
   - Can you tell what things you are experienced at the time
   - At the onset of the conflict, do you evacuate?
   - What do you do when faced with unpleasant situations such as that?
2. Perseverance: "capability continue to face life despite the decline"
   - Is there the time when you got to feel hopeless, why?
   - What makes you possible to raise from that unpleasant situation?
3. Equanimity: "inner balance"
   - What is the insight from that situation?
   - What is the plus side of experiencing that kind of incident?
   - Is there the time when you feel self-pity?
4. Meaningfulness: "Life meaningfulness"
   - What is the purpose of your life when the conflict was happened?
   - Are there certain people who were strengthen you when the conflict happened?
   - What do you do in order to get out of the problems that you face?
5. Self-reliance: "Confidence"
   - What is your biggest motivation which makes you survived?
   - Are you confident that you can survive the hard timed?
6. Existential Aloneness: "Accepting yourself"
   - Did the conflict makes you feel alone?
   - Do you think you can adjust to the unpleasant situation?
   - Are you able to make a decision in that kind of situation? Or did you had someone help you in decision making?
7. Local wisdom and Resiliency
   - To what principles you hold when you are experiencing the conflict?
   - What is the Aceh proverbial you recall when severe the conflict?
   - What is philosophy which derived (hand downed) by your family that you hold steadfast to this day?
   - How do you see the Aceh cultures and its effects on the ability of Acehness in the face of prolonged the conflict?

The research finding shows some interesting facts which will be delivered briefly in this paper namely about forms of the violence, the natural causes of the trauma of these three participants, how it affect the social life of the subjects, and how the process of resiliency was achieved, as well as how local cultural factors can help the process of resiliency on the subject of research. Discussion of deeper against the findings will be explained as follows:

Forms of violence and implications on the subjects

There are some traumatic experiences which were experienced by the participant during the conflict era such as beaten on the head, strangulation, being drowned, be electrocuted, etc. In accordance with what is expressed by the subject of the respondents reported that they have been struck on the head with the heavy wood, then got the serious head injuries, two out of three respondents claimed had a memory lost, confusion, difficulty in thinking, wheezing breath, pain and a prolonged headache after experienced the conflict.

Physical violence then promoted the psychic health of the participants, as for the psychic symptoms of post conflict felt by participants are the thoughts or memories that go back about the most painful or scary, feeling as if the event is happening again, the nightmare that reappear, physical or emotional reactions unexpectedly when admonished about events the most painful or traumatic, even further in social living subjects feel away from the people, unable to feel emotions, as well as declining interest in daily activities, feeling as if they don't have a future.

Other interesting finding regarding the participants experienced was the term of *"Nafsi- nafsi"* which mentioned several times during the interview process by the three of participants. *Nafsi – nafsi* here means "being individualistic" to describe the impact of conflict in society, i.e. to ensure their own safety people at that time did not thing about anyone else beside their selves as long as they are safe. At its worst, *"Nafsi – nafsi"* implies a selfish individualism without attention to other people, but if further reviewed of the transcript interview indicated that *nafsi – nafsi* is appeared as a consequence of the unfortunate situation.

Resiliency of the Participants
1. Meaningfulness

For the participants, the most important thing in life is the quality of life itself, trying to take the wisdom and learning to be grateful to each unpleasant situation in life. Each incident in life is a small step to become even better.

"I told myself that I ought to have a life purpose. I should not continue to grieve" (the subject of the SS, line 10).

Any event that is experienced when a conflict is meant as a valuable life lesson and be a turning point in deciding the destination of the next life

"The purpose of my life is to be a better person in the future" (the subject of NH, line 92).

In addition the surviving family members became the biggest reason for the subject researches to continue to persist in living life. The subject feels they need to keep unruly for the sake of family members who were still there than on lamenting the family members who are already gone. Furthermore, through the experience of the conflict in the past, the subject can take the wisdom and making it a springboard to progress his life forward. The participants reach their life goal by having positive thought.

2. Perseverance

In cope with the prolonged conflict, it is common for the subjects to feel that the conflict might be the hardest problem in their life, that kind of feeling might encourages the subject to feel desperate and want to give up with the existing situation. That such feelings can be overcome by belief in God Almighty. They belief that a person should not despair at his Lord.

"I surrender myself to God. We should be able to receive God's trial/test" (The subject of HH, line 211).

In addition, other findings in this study also shows that the mandate or messages infused by both parents also taught the subject to avoid the attitude of despair when overridden a disaster.

"My father is a tough and a strong man, I wonder why I cannot be as strong as he is. My father passed away when I was a little but his mandate always remained in my mind. My father ever said to me that do not take revenge of others who disturb or doing something bad to us. Give your forgiveness if that person apologize to you. "(The subject of the SS, line 109).

So it can be inferred that the two things that make the subject can rise from the feeling of despair is the beliefs in God's Providence and advices from parent which instilled since their childhood.

3. Equanimity

Those three subject is an open minded people, they can take insight in any event of their life and they are not giving up on achieving their life's goal. The subjects see the problems as a challenge which should be faced to be a better person. The subject didn't take a much time to be fully recovered from their despair because they are having a positive spirit, they also get so much attentions and assistance from their neighbors as well as the participants were able to receive everything gracefully.

"I intend to live further away then the past. I don't want to live in such desolation. I want to rise from the deterioration. I should be strong for people that I loved. "(Subject initialed HH, line 224).

"My neighbors are always happy to help" (Subject initialled HH, line 265).

4. Self-reliance

Two of the three research subjects were capable of assess themselves, especially regarding to their strength point and their weakness. The second subject is even able to make a decision of what is considered the best for herself, advice from their closet people were listened in order to help them in making the decision.

"Follow your heart carefully that's how you should live" (Subject initialed SS, line 89).

"By making a decision for myself, people even respect me more, furthermore, I feel more appreciated and preferred by the community particularly the village where I live" (Subject initialed SS, line 109).

5. Existential Aloneness

In addressing their opinion toward the communities, the participant confessed that they did not have any courage to be indifferent with their communities. The third subject looks scared to be in contrast with her group. This situation happened due to the conflict its self, the conflict situation lead the subject to hide their opinions, because it might harm themselves, thus follow the public opinion are quite the best option at that time.

Description of local culture

It was noticeable through the interview that when the conflict was happened the religiosity of the society increased. Also from interview result, it was noted that the subjects faced the conflicts by sticking to religious thing, which is basically the Aceh's culture itself. Aceh's culture cannot be separated from Islamic religion. Women's of conflict victim always try to cope with the religion in order to face that miserable situation.

"More thankful, more prostrate to Allah almighty, ask Allah to thus He give you the best solution". (Subject initialed SS, line 233).

"Whatever happens I keep praying to God. Sometimes it was flashed to my head I could be shot when I was praying, but I tend to ignore that feeling and my goal was to remain praying to God whatever happens ". (Subject initialed HH, line145).

From the statement above it can be concluded that all the participants consistently declare that being close to God is the only way of surviving the conflict and makes them able to went through a tough situation especially when the conflicts occured. Cultures and religion has been assimilated and interact simultaneously in Aceh throughout the community for a decades. The concrete of customs and culture of Acehnese has been applied in their daily life, in many sectors such as social, economic or political, and law. Islam religion has become the way of life of Acehnese people. This view of life later affects the entire community including in cultural activities. Because a person's outlook on life will affect how they think and how they behave and interact with their society, all of which are part of the culture. Local wisdom is something that was already rooted and usually is not only oriented to profane, but also sacred oriented so that its implementation can be more quickly and easily accepted by the society. Another thing that is revealed in this study is about the character of the people of Aceh. One of the latent character of Acehnese is they have been known since long ago as stubborn people. Stubborn character has become a value or cultural community is trained to make Aceh ready to face any bad circumstances.

"The area we've been living are a war zone since the very long time ago, and we never prepare something to face it, so if the war are going to happen, we must be ready anytime, anywhere" (Subject initialed NH, line 208).

This specific characteristic helped the community to rise quickly from adversity. In addition to that when they were asked about life philosophical quotation that hold by the family and delivered through generation to generation, the subjects said that:

"Geut tapubut, geut geubalah. Jeuhet geukubah in nuraka" means if we are good to people then we people will be good to us, the bad behavior will be rewarded in the underworld"

(Subject initialed NH, line 201).

Almost similiar to that, one subject said that her family holding to this proverbial *"Udep beusare Matee Syahid"* which means *Life safely in the world and died martyred.*

The diversity of Aceh culture as expressed by the participants is a reflection of the Acehnese society itself. Some of Aceh's arts contain religious teachings that convey the message of life, so it can be concluded that if talking about the customs and culture of Aceh, then almost all the customs of Aceh refers to Islamic religion. People in Aceh overcome their problems by caring for worship and praying because they believe in the power of prayer. This is in line with Bergin's, Gartner's and Meichenbaum's (2005) notions that observe the North Americans' main way of overcoming traumatic events is through faith and prayer. Talsya (1994) says that Islam is the basis of their lives so that everything should be based on the religion of Islam. Thus, it can be concluded that religion becomes a support factor against the capabilities of the resilience of Acehnese in the face of hardship.

Conclusion

The Aceh conflicts are the only one example of many regions of Indonesia which have potentials of social conflict. In fact, each region has its respective local wisdoms related to the terms of living together in harmony. By elaborating Aceh as a sample areas, it is expected to provide a brief overview on how local culture can be a supporting factor for the victims of conflict achieving the state of resilience. Although the concept of resiliency is one and universal, but humans are living in a different culture, so in reality, the difficulties faced by someone else will vary depending on where their lives and what culture they absorb.

Communities which come from East-cultural societies will adapt differently from people who come from West cultural society. And most of the cultural differences are hardly touched by studies that discuss about the resiliency (Young & Wagnild, 1993 in Xiaonan & Zhang, 2007).

Almost every community has its own local wisdom in resolving conflicts. Local wisdom can serve as a socio-cultural mechanisms contained in the tradition of Indonesia society. The tradition is believed to be and has been proven as a powerful means of rallying fraternity and solidarity between citizens who have worked and solidified in the social and cultural order.

There are some cultural values which associated with the resiliency process, which are Islamic values that well believed by the Acehnese, the character of Acehnese and, the last one is the life philosophy that hand-downed from generation to generation.

References

1) Bengt Save Soderberg, in Peter Harris and Ben Reilly, (ed.), 2005, Democracy and Deep-Rooted Conflict: Options for Negosiators, Sweden: IDEA, p.v.

2) David c. Korten, People-centered Development (Jakarta: Yayasan Obor Indonesia, 1985), p. 14

3) Elly m. Setiadi and Usman Kolip, an introduction to the sociology of Understanding facts and symptoms of social problems: theory, applications, and possible solution (Jakarta: Kencana Prenada Media Group, 2011), p. 345

4) Holaday, m. (1997). Resilience and Severe Burns. Journal of Counseling and Development, 75, 346 – 357

5) Hancock, b. (1998). An Introduction to Qualitative Resarch Trent Focus for Research and Development in Primary Health Care. Downloaded from http://faculty.cbu.ca/prnacintyre/course_pages/MBA603/_file/IntroQualitativeResearch.pdf

6) Irving m. Zeitlin, grasp the Back of sociology, (Yogyakarta: Gadjah Mada University Press, 1998), p. 156

7) Jameson, S.H. 2011. "Lewis a. Coser, The Function of Social Conflict" – the Annals of the American Acedemy of Politics and Social Science, vol. 310. Current Issues Grotberg, e. (1999a). The International Resilience Research Project. In r. Roswith (ed.), Psychologists/acing the challenge of a global culture with human rights and mental health (pp. 239-256)

8) Grotberg, E.H. 2001. Resilience Programs for Children in Disaster. Ambulatory Child Health. 7:75

9) LaFromboise, T.D., Hoyt, D.R., Oliver, L & Whitbeck., Benny (2006). Family, community and School Influences on Resilience among American Indian Adolescent in the Upper Midwest. Journal of Community Psychology, 34 (2), 193 – 209

10) Lawang, R. 1994. *Teori Sosiologi Klasik dan Modern.* Jakarta : Gramedia Pustaka Utama

11) Masten, A & Gewirtz, A.H. (2006). Resilience in Development: The Importance of Early Childhood. Encyclopedia Earky on Childhood Development, 1 – 6 Neil, j. (2006). What is Psychological Resilience. Downloaded from http://www.wilderdom.com/psychology/resilience/PscyhologicalResilience.html

12) Putranto, JP. 2009. Aceh Conflict Resolution: Lesson Learned and The Future of Aceh. Thesis. California: Naval Postgraduate School

13) Setiadi, E and Kolip, E. Introduction to the sociology of Understanding facts and symptoms of social problems: theory, applications, and possible solution (Jakarta: Kencana Prenada Media Group, 2011), p. 345

14) Soekanto, s. Sociology: an introduction (Jakarta: Eagle Press, 2005), p. 172.

15) Soerjono Soekanto, dictionary of sociology, (Jakarta: PT Raja Grafindo Persada, 1993), p. 99.
Robert Mace, the book Introduction to the subject matter of sociology,

(Jakarta: Open University, 1994) p. 53

16) Masten, A & Gewirtz, A.H. (2006). Resilience in Development: The Importance of Early Childhood. Encyclopedia Earky on Childhood Development, 1 – 6 Reivich, k. and Shatte, a. 2002. The Resiliency Factor: 7 Keys to Finding Your Inner Strength and Overcoming life's Hurdles. New York: Three Rivers Press.

17) Sanusi. 2005. Local wisdom and the role of the Commander in the process of settlement and Laot realignment of Coastal Aceh Post Tsunami, Banda Aceh, Research Reports: Research Center for social sciences and Culture University of Syiah Kuala.

18) Santrock, J.W. (1995). Life-Span Development. Volume II, translated by Chusairi, vol 2. Jakarta: Eason

19) Santrock, j. w. (2002). Life-Span Development: The Development Of Life. The 5th Edition of Jakarta: Eason

20) Lauer, R. 2001. Perspective On Social Change. Jakarta: Pt. Rineka Copyright

21) Wagnild, GM & Young, H.N. (1993). Development and Psychometric Validation of the Resilience Scale. Journal of Nursing Measurement, 1, 1165 – 178.

22) The Foundation recovers & JICA (2006). Together Reaching For Hope. The Center Of The Crisis Psychology: University Of Indonesia

Optimization of Potential Asset of Waqf Land as a Market to Prevent Poverty and Promote Prosperity

Alifya Zahra[1], Ajeng Safitri[2], Nailun Najla[3]
1,2 Industrial Engineering, Faculty of Engineering, UPN "Veteran" Jakarta
3 Arabic Studies, Faculty of Humanity, Universitas Indonesia

動産・不動産を公平に分配し、かつ有効に活用するためにイスラム法で定められた仕組みの1つが"waqf"。現状ではモスクや学校などの建設に土地を無償提供する例が多いが、そうした土地を市場に組み込んで貧困解消につなげる道を探る。

Abstract

Waqf is one of the instruments in Islamic finance that emphasize the value of social and economic justice. In Indonesia, waqf has been developed by a state institution named Badan Waqf Indonesia (BWI). Based on data collected by the Ministry of Religious Affairs of Indonesia, 2017, Indonesia has a potential waqf land with a total area of 4.3 billion square meters. More than 90% of proven waqf land is only used for non-productive purposes such as mosques, cemeteries, school, and orphanages. Therefore we propose the optimization of waqf land through building a market. As a market, waqf land opens wide-opportunity for people to earn a living income without illegal levies. Besides, any nation, including Indonesia, can get some benefits through declining of unemployment rate, rising prosperity in its society, and more dynamic economic activities. Actually anyone who owns waqf land does not take any profits. Although waqf is an institutionalized form of charity, its beneficial effects may well be common to all, irrespective of one's belief system, which may be characterized by the creation of peaceful and mutually beneficial conditions. The psychological condition of a giver who gladly give without expecting any reward is usually called altruism. This research uses method of literature review which is taken from literature sources related to waqf issues in Indonesia. Afterwards, this current study also attempt to provide an alternative way of waqf land development which can be applied in the field as an effort to improve the productive management of waqf land for social welfare.

Keywords waqf land; optimization; market; prosperity

Introduction

Waqf is one of the instruments in Islam to achieve the economic goals of Islam manifesting prosperous life in the world and in the afterlife. Muslim countries such as Egypt, Saudi Arabia, Jordan, Turkey, Bangladesh, Egypt and Malaysia, develop and implement endowments as a tool to assist various activities of people and address the problems of people like poverty. [1]

Waqf can be in the form of immovable and movable property, one of them is waqf land. Waqf land has very high potential to be developed, as its wide availability in Indonesia. Based on data obtained from the Badan Waqf Indonesia (BWI) in March 2016, there are 435,768 land listed waqf with total area of 435,944.317 acres throughout Indonesia.

Here is the data we get from the Directorate of Waqf Empowerment of the Ministry of Religious Affairs of the Republic of Indonesia:

Table 1. Utilization of Waqf Land Data in Indonesia

Utilization	Percentage
Mosque	44.90%
Musholla	28.40%
School	10.57%
Other Social	8.37%
Graveyard	4.61%
Pesantren	3.15%

Based on these data, more than 90% of the land use of waqf is used to develop non-productive sectors. The use of waqf land in Indonesia is still synonymous with mosques or tombs. In fact, waqf can be managed into economic assets that generate financial benefits. In New Zealand for example, the land of waqf is managed as a sheep farm that the results can be enjoyed by the community. Regardless of one's belief, this waqf system becomes one of the interesting and unique potential solutions to fulfill the society's economy.

But there are some obstacles in the development of waqf land into the market, because only 65% of waqf land in Indonesia are certified (only 287,160 of the total 435,768). So feared the occurrence of land disputes, besides the existence of irresponsible elements who blackmail and do illegal levies to market traders.

Since the enactment of Law no. 5 of 1960 on Basic Regulation of Agriculture and Government Regulation No.28/1977 on Land Owned Donation, Law no. 41 of 2004 on Waqf and Government Regulation No.42 of 2006 on the Implementation of Waqf, donation ranging continue to be addressed by the reforms in the field of management and understand the general waqf (Directorate of Waqf, 2008). [2]

Regardless of the theory of belief, the reason someone donates the land they have for free to the state is for their own happiness that they will feel psychological. This theory is one of the psychological theories called altruism.

Based on the above explanation, this research tries to discuss Implementation of waqf land potential to be developed into a productive sector in the form of market. The scope of the discussion consists of supporting theories, the flow of thought along with the system schemes related to referring to the development of waqf land existing and in the future.

Definition of Waqf

Waqf is a word from Arabic وَقَفَ – يَقِفُ – وقفًا which means hold, confinement, prohibition. It is issued in the Islamic Law in the meaning of holding certain property and preserving it for the confined benefit of certain philanthropy and prohibiting any use or disposition of it outside its specific objective. Usually, waqf relates to land and buildings. And sometimes there are books, agricultural machinery, cash money, etc. [3] From the history of Islam, we can know how the concept of waqf has evolved. Long time ago, in Madinah, Muhammad SAW asked for someone to buy the well of Bayruha' and designated it as free public utility for drinking water. Waqf in that case serve the welfare of the society in all and their different aspects. One day, Umar, as a friend of Muhammad SAW asked him how he has to manage his land in Khaibar. Then Muhammad SAW advised Umar to assign his land in Khaibar as a waqf for the poor and needy. [4]

Encyclopedia Britannica described waqf as a peculiarly Islamic institution whereby the founder relinquishes his ownership of real property, which belongs henceforth to Allah, and dedicates the income or usufruct of the property in perpetuity to some charitable purposes, which may include settlement in favour of the founder's own family. Also, the ownership of waqf cannot be transferred. Only its benefits are to be used for the specific purposes which are maintained as charitable in nature. Waqf is a voluntary charity characterized by perpetuity. The institution of waqf may be usefully utilized in an organized and deliberate manner to provide education, health care, and physical facilities to the target groups of people in a poverty-alleviation program.

According to Rifyal Ka'bah, waqf is one of Islamic Law that requires state power for its implementation. Without any implementation rules, will not receive proper and effective acceptance in the community. The state can regulate this waqf through legislation to be managed and developed productively, so that waqf is not only useful for worship activities to God, but also as an alternative to tackling poverty. [5]

Waqf in Islam has the pillars and the conditions. The first pillar is there must be a person who provided waqf (*al-Waqif*), the second one is the property represented (*al-Mawquf*), the third is the receiver of the property or the benefit of the waqf (*al-Mawquf 'alaih*), the fourth is that the handover of the waqf must use lafaz akad through words or writing (*al-Sighah*). Then the conditions applicable to those who provide waqf are free (not slave), adults, have a conscious mind, worthy of providing waqf, and voluntary (not forced). [6]

Altruism Effect Cause of Giving

Happiness is not a thing that can be defined. Every person has their own definition of happiness. Because the thing called happiness has no numerical measurement, and there is no certain standard can determine if the person happy or not, and which level someone's happiness on. There is a research in the field of positive psychology about happiness. That thing, happiness, well often define a happy person as someone who experiences frequent positive emotions, such as joy, interest, pride, and infrequent negative emotions, such as sadness, anxiety, and anger. Happiness has also been said to relate to life satisfaction, appreciation of life, moments of pleasure, but overall it has to do with the positive experience of emotions. [7]

Philosophers sometimes use 'happiness' differently, notably to denote the kind of well-being or flourishing that in the ancient Greek of Aristotle and Plato went by the name of eudaimonia. [8] Aristotle defined that "happiness is a final end or goal that encompasses the totality of one's life. It is not something that can be gained or lost in a few hours, like pleasurable sensations. It is more like the ultimate value of your life as lived up to this moment, measuring how well you have lived up to your full potential as a human being." [9] People who evaluate their lives negatively would likely be motivated to improve the conditions of their lives, and those who evaluate their lives positively would be motivated to maintain or further improve these conditions. Thus, happiness and related constructs are thought to signal how well a person's life is going, which should mean that as a person's life improves, so should the happiness that person reports.

Again, happiness is a thing that we can't count and define how it works in every person. Because Happiness can change, and happiness does change — during a single day and during a lifetime. What makes happiness interesting is genetic and environmental factors. Genetic factors contribute primarily to stability in happiness; environmental factors predominantly contribute to short- and long-term change. Social contexts that are consistently thwarting of our needs can greatly limit our ability to be fully functioning and well and thus expectably are also associated with less positive and more negative affect. [10]

Market as a Place of Productive Waqf

Market is a place where goods and services exchange as a result of buyers and sellers being in contact with one another. According to Kotler, "the Market is made up of all customers potentials that possess the same specific needs or wants, which are may be willing and able to execute an exchange to satisfy needs and wants".

Sudarman said the market has five main functions; a.) the market sets the value (sets value). In the market economy, the price is size of value, b.) markets organize production. Factor price of production at market will encourage the producer (entrepreneur) to choose the efficient-method production, c.) the market distributes goods. The ability of a person to buy goods depending on their income, d.) market has a function to organize rationing. Allotment is the point of the price, e.) the market maintains and prepares the necessities in the future come. [11]

Problems faced by developing country are quite the same, namely poverty, unemployment, abandoned children. In Indonesia those problems also exist, including poverty, and the saddest part is there are still large number of poor people in Indonesia, the following data on the number of poor people from 2013 to 2017:

Table 2. Number of Poor People in Indonesia (2013-2017)

Year	Number of Poor People
2013	28,553.93
2014	27,727.78
2015	28,513.57
2016	27,764.32
2017	26,582.99

In the year of 2017 Statistic Central Bureau data shows that 26.58 million Indonesian still live in poverty. On the other hand, the government keeps trying to alleviate poverty. Indonesia is a country with a majority Muslim population and the largest in the world, poverty is still the case that we see in this country. Reflecting from the history, to create social and economic justice in the society, waqf instrument is one of the solution that considered able to answer all of social economic problem faced by Indonesia, that poverty alleviation.

Waqf can act as a tool to support the economic development of society. Waqf is one of the instruments in Islam to achieve the economic goals of Islam manifesting prosperous life in the world and in the afterlife. Muslim countries such as Egypt, Saudi Arabia, Jordan, Turkey, Bangladesh, Egypt and Malaysia, develop and implement endowments as a tool to assist various activities of people and address the problems of people like poverty. [12]

Waqf can be in the form of immovable and movable property, one of them is waqf land. Waqf land has very high potential to be developed, as its wide availability in Indonesia.

Table 3. Waqf Land in March 2016

Waqf Land	Area
Total	435,768
Certified Waqf	287,160
Not Yet Certified Waqf	148,447
Total Area (acres)	435,994.317

Based on data obtained from the Badan Waqf Indonesia (BWI) in March 2016, there are 435,768 land listed waqf with total area of 435,944.317 acres throughout Indonesia.

Table 4. Utilization of Waqf Land Data in Indonesia

Utilization	Percentage
Mosque	44.90%
Musholla	28.40%
School	10.57%
Other Social	8.37%
Graveyard	4.61%
Pesantren	3.15%

Based on these data, more than 90% of the land use of waqf is used to develop nonproductive sectors. The use of waqf land in Indonesia is still synonymous with mosques or tombs. In fact, waqf can also and can be managed into economic assets that generate financial benefits. In New Zealand for example, the land of waqf is managed as a sheep farm that the results can be enjoyed by the community. Regardless of one's belief, this waqf system becomes one of the interesting and unique potential solutions to fulfill the society's economy.

But there are some obstacles in the development of waqf land into the market, of which is only 65% of waqf land in Indonesia which is certified1 of 435,768 waqf land, only 287,160 are certified. So feared the occurrence of land disputes, besides the existence of irresponsible elements who blackmail and do illegal levies to market traders.

Regardless of the theory of belief, the reason someone donates the land he has for free to the state is for his own happiness that he will feel psychological. This theory is one of the psychological theories called altruism.

Based on the above explanation, this research tries to discuss Implementation of waqf land potential to be developed into a productive sector in the form of market. The scope of the discussion consists of supporting theories, the flow of thought along with the system schemes related to referring to the development of waqf land existing and in the future.

Land Market

A land market is said to exist when land rights are exchanged for consideration (Robert Mahoney et al, 2007). A land market can be basic, advanced and highly advanced. It can be formal and informal. The formal land market is one that is incorporated by the government in the Land Administration System, a legal framework and a financial system. The Land Administration System will manage property rights, the legal systems will define them, and the property institution will generally measure market operations (see Williamson et al, 2007).

A waqf property not only needs advanced land market but also formalized. At the moment, it is questionable whether or not waqf lands are fully capable to be offered in the basic land market, as the main infrastructure of land administration i.e. the National Land Code, excludes waqf law, the legal framework provided by the State laws for the waqf land indicate only that it can be used and enjoyed, leased and rented and put to crop sharing.

Other forms of dealings such as disposal by sale, charge and bequeath, are not applicable, for they will not be registered, and recognized by courts. As such one may even discount the possibility of an informal land market, for a land market to exist there must be a legal framework to define the rights of parties and a land administration to recognize them. Only then the land market can function with confidence and security (Williamson, 2000).

A market confidence in waqf properties is possible when the land administration system is capable to fully protect the rights of landholders and the landholders have the freedom to enter transactions. Less than that a reform is needed (See Malcolm Childress et al, 2004). It is clear that the Malaysian legal framework does not give such freedom to waqf landholders and does not protect them if such a transaction is ever entered.

Waqf land is not a commodity in sale and purchase land market, while in leasing and rental markets, it is treated discriminatively; they are rented often below market price (Jasni, M.Z, 2006).

Research Method

Type and Objective of Research

The type of research used in this research is literature study and quantitative descriptive. Descriptive research can be done in a quantitative way, so that statistical analysis can be performed (Sulistyo-Basuki, 2006). The object of research can be expressed as the social situation of research to know and what happens in it. In the research object, the researchers were able to observe in depth activity people as actors that existed at the specific place (Sugiyono, Educational Research Methods [Quantitative Approach, Qualitative, and R&D], 2007). Object of this study is the management of Productive Waqf. [13]

Data

i. Primary Data

According to Umar (2003), primary data is data obtained directly in the field by researchers as the object of writing. Interviews conducted by researchers is the use of the interview guide, intended for a more in-depth interviews with focus on issues that will be examined. [14]

ii. Secondary Data

According to Sugiyono (2005), secondary data is data that does not directly provide data to researchers, such as research should be through another person or looking through documents. [15]

Technical Analysis

To analyze the data collected in this study using descriptive analysis techniques Data derived from the quantitative data in the form of collection and fund distribution of financial statements then analyzed which describe the reality of the phenomenon, as it is, apart from a subjective perspective. [16]

Table 5. The Different Concepts of Waqf Between Traditional and Productive

No	Concept	Traditional	Productive
1	Object of Waqf	Pledge (still) limited to fixed assets such as land, buildings, and other.	Manqul (moving) not only fix assets but other/ moving assets used as an object Waqf, such as Waqf of money, securities and other.
2	Allocation	For social, such as education, health, etc.	Not only the social side but a greater focus and effort directed at the welfare of the people, such as working, capital, investment, construction of business center and so on.
3	Development of Object	Management is static without any attempt to develop further.	Managers want growth, not only in terms of asset waqf but expansion of the value of benefits to be received by the community is expected to continue to be sustainable.

Result

Sticking to the waqf management objectives above, nadzir and wakif also need to consider the impact of each selected management alternatives in order to maintain the existence of waqf assets and improve the outcome of these arrangements, which include Directorate General of Islamic Community Guidance and Implementation Hajj (2003):

1. Effect "Good Deed".

    Waqf management should refer to the order of priorities and benefits for many parties. This is not only empowering, but also pay attention to the impact on the expected goals.

2. Effect "Free Rider".

    According to Islamic economic theory, this "free rider" effect will occur when the initial donation worth Rp. 100.000, -for example, it decreases in value when utilized. This condition should be avoided, because that will lower motivation to contribute.

3. Effect "Income Redistribution".

    Waqf management should be done carefully with attention by using the operation to provide significant income distribution from one group to the other income.

Simply, the process of utilizing waqf land for market management as the central of people's economy is as follows in Figure 1.

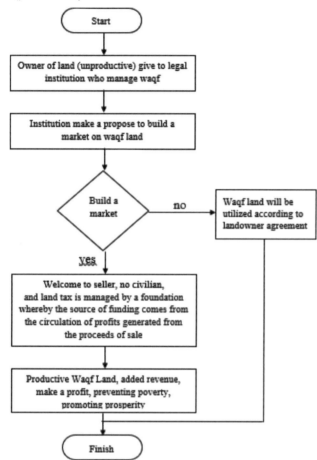

Fig. 1. Flow of Waqf Land Process

Conclusion

We should pay more attention to waqf assets by making regulations that can minimize risks or issues that may cause problems. Because as we all know that the regulations of the government is not specific enough to support the productive waqf, so we need to review the regulation.

This paper argued for inclusion of waqf lands in Land Administration System, and to treat them equal to any other land in the sense of formalization, marketability, valuation, and collateralization, as far as such is in accordance to the principles of Islamic law. To support this idea the legal framework must be revised and accordingly both State and Federal laws need to be amended. This current study also attempt to provide the alternative way of waqf land development which expected to apply it in the field as an effort to improve the management of productive waqf for social welfare.

These efforts are still relevant as the institution of waqf is rich and promising aiding us to reach the Promised Land of a sustainable community.

References

1) Prihatini, F. et. al. (2005) Hukum Islam Zakat dan Waqaf. Jakarta: Kerjasama Penerbit Papas Sinar Mentari dengan Badan Penerbit Fakultas Hukum Universitas Indonesia, 131

2) Direktorat Pemberdayaan Wakaf. (2008). Paradigma Baru Wakaf di Indonesia. Jakarta: Departemen Agama RI.

3) Kahf, Monzer. (2003) The Role of Waqf in Improving the Ummah Welfare, presented to the International Seminar "Waqf as a Private Legal Body" organized by Islamic University of the North Sumatera, Medan, Indonesia.

4) Sadeq, Abul Hasan M. (2002) Waqf, Perpetual Charity and Poverty Alleviation, Malaysia: International Journal of Social Economics, Vol. 29, No. 1/2, 2002, pp. 135-151.

5) Ka'bah, Rifyal. (2004) Penegakan Syariat Islam di Indonesia. Jakarta: Khairul Bayan.

6) Direktorat Pemberdayaan Wakaf. (2006). Fiqih Wakaf. Jakarta: Direktorat Pemberdayaan Wakaf.

7) Sheldon, Kennon M. and Richard E. Lucas (2014) Stability of Happiness Theories and Evidence on Whether Happiness Can Change. USA: Elsevier Inc.

8) Haybron, Daniel M. (2003). What Do We Want from a Theory of Happines. USA: Blackwell Publishing, Vol. 34, No. 3.

9) Aristotle, Nichomachean Ethics (2004),ed. Hugh Treddenick. London: Penguin. The main source for Aristotle's ethics

10) Sosis, Clifford L. (2012). Happiness: The Potential Power Of Environment. The Baltic International Yearbook of Cognition, Logic and Communication

11) Sudarman, Ari. (2011). Teori Ekonomi Mikro 1. Jakarta: Universitas Terbuka.

12) Prihatini, F. et. al. (2005) Hukum Islam Zakat dan Waqaf. Jakarta: Kerjasama Penerbit Papas Sinar Mentari dengan Badan Penerbit Fakultas Hukum Universitas Indonesia, 131

13) Sugiyono. (2007). Metode Penelitian Pendidikan (Pendekatan Kuantitatif, Kualitatif, dan R&D). Bandung: Alfabeta.

14) Umar, H. (2003). Metode Riset Komunikasi Organisasi. Jakarta: PT Gramedia Pustaka Utama.

15) Sugiyono. (2005). Memahami Penelitian Kualitatif. Bandung: Alfabeta.

16) Ai Nur Bayinah (2010) Analysis of Alternative Models of Productive Investment Management of Endowments

List of Hosts, Supporters and Collaborators

主催・後援・協力者等一覧

Hearty Thanks to All

The 4th Asia Future Conference was hosted by Atsumi International Foundation, co-hosted by Korean Social Science Research Council and Center for Future Human Resource Study, and was supported by many institutions, foundations and companies listed below. We would also like to express our heartfelt gratitude to some 400 participants, to those who supported the holding of the conference, and to volunteers who cooperated in many ways, for the success of our Conference.

ご協力、ありがとうございました

第4回アジア未来会議は渥美国際交流財団の主催、韓国社会科学協議会および未来人力研究院(韓国)の共催で開催され、下記のとおりたくさんの団体・機関・企業からご支援をいただきました。また約400名の参加者の皆様、円滑な運営のために尽力くださった皆様、さまざまな面でご協力くださったボランティアの皆様にも、この場を借りて心より感謝申し上げます。

List of Hosts, Supporters and Collaborators

Host	Atsumi International Foundation Sekiguchi Global Research Association (SGRA)
Co-hosts	Korean Social Science Research Council Center for Future Human Resource Studies
Supporters	Japanese Ministry of Education, Culture, Sports, Science and Technology Embassy of Japan in Korea Seoul Japan Club
Grants	Tokyo Club
Collaborators	CISV Korea Honjo International Scholarship Foundation Doalltec Inc. Global BIM Inc.
Sponsors	POSCO E&C HAEAHN Architecture, Inc N. I Steel Co., Ltd. Chugai Pharmaceutical Co., Ltd. Mitsubishi Corporation Tokio Marine Holdings, Inc. Kokuyo co., Ltd. Kajima Road Co., Ltd. Taiko Trading Co., Ltd. Kajima Tatemono Sogo Kanri Co., Ltd. East Real Estate Kajima Oversea Asia PTE Ltd. Kajima Corporation

主催者・支援者・協力者リスト

主催	(公財)渥美国際交流財団関口グローバル研究会(SGRA)
共催	韓国社会科学協議会 (財)未来人力研究院
後援	文部科学省 在韓国日本大使館 ソウルジャパンクラブ
助成	(一社)東京倶楽部
協力	CISV Korea (公財)本庄国際奨学財団 Doalltec (株) グローバルBIM(株)
協賛	POSCO建設(株) HAEAHN Architecture(株) (株)NIスティール 中外製薬(株) 三菱商事(株) 東京海上ホールディングス(株) コクヨ(株) 鹿島道路(株) 大興物産(株) 鹿島建物総合管理(株) イースト不動産(株) Kajima Overseas Asia(株) 鹿島建設(株)

第4回アジア未来会議
運営組織

【大会委員会】
会長	明石 康	元国連事務次長
副会長	渥美伊都子	渥美国際交流財団理事長
副会長	李 鎮奎	(韓国)未来人力研究院理事長
副会長	朴 贊郁	韓国社会科学協議会会長

【第4回アジア未来会議韓国実行委員会】
実行委員	李 元徳	国民大学
	金 雄熙	仁荷大学
	南 基正	ソウル大学
	朴 栄濬	国防大学校
	金 賢旭	国民大学
	梁 明玉	建国大学
	韓 京子	慶熙大
	李 垠庚	ソウル大学
	金 崇培	延世大学
	李 孝庭	世宗大学
	呉 正根	国立環境科学院
	李 Saebom	ソウル大学
	金 律里	東京大学
	Cho Ahra	ソウル大学

【事務局】未来人力研究院

【実行委員会】
委員長	今西淳子	渥美国際交流財団
副委員長	金 雄熙	仁荷大学
実行委員	全 振煥	鹿島建設
	Cakir, Murat	関西外語大
	楊昱 Gloria	九州大学
	全 相律	神田外国語大学
	Lamsal, Bikash	鹿島建設
	李 志炯	第一工業大学
	盧 Jooeun	東京大学
	沈 雨香	早稲田大学
	江 永博	早稲田大学
	金 Boram	東京大学
運営企画	基調講演・シンポジウム・歓迎会	
	南 基正	ソウル大学
	李 周浩	立命館大学
	金 賢旭	国民大学
	円卓会議A	国史たちの対話
	劉 傑	早稲田大学
	三谷 博	跡見学園女子大学
	葛 兆光	復旦大学
	趙 珖	高麗大学名誉教授
	村 和明	三井文庫
	徐 静波	復旦大学
	李 恩民	桜美林大学
	金 範洙	東京学芸大学
	孫 軍悦	東京大学
	金 凰泰	高麗大
	彭 浩	大阪市立大学
	鄭 淳一	高麗大学
	円卓会議B	東南アジア宗教間の対話
	島薗 進	上智大学
	小川 忠	跡見学園大学
	Maquito, Ferdinand	フィリピン大学ロスバニョス校(UPLB)
	Mukhopadhyaya, Ranjana	デリー大学
	Sonntag, Mira	立教大学
	Tenegra, Brenda	LINGO 24
	Rostika, Mya Dwi	国士舘大学
	Mohammad, Jakfar Idrus	国士舘大学
	歓送会・授賞式	
	Napoleon	SMBC日興証券
	Dale, Sonja	一橋大学
	Rio, Aaron	ミネアポリス美術館
	呉 正根	(韓国)国立環境科学院
特別補助金	Maquito, Ferdinand	フィリピン大学ロスバニョス校(UPLB)
	片桐 Kanokwan	チュラロンコン大学
	Vu Thi Minh Chi	ベトナム社会科学院
	Iko Pramudiono	インドネシア三井物産
	張 桂娥	東呉大学
【事務局】	角田英一	渥美国際交流財団
	船橋 博	渥美国際交流財団
	石井慶子	渥美国際交流財団
	本多康子	渥美国際交流財団
	辰馬夏実	渥美国際交流財団
	長井亜弓	編集者
	今西 Kittiwan	IBC Travel
	今西勇人	IBC Travel
	Wachirasak Maneewatnaperk	IBC Travel

【学術委員会】
委員長	平川 均	国士舘大学
副委員長	高 偉俊	北九州市立大学
副委員長	金 外淑	兵庫県立大学
副委員長	李 恩民	桜美林大学
	Maquito, Ferdinand	フィリピン大学ロスバニョス校(UPLB)
	朴 哲主	三育大学
	施 建明	東京理科大学
	金 雄熙	仁荷大学
	李 來賛	漢城大学
	南 基正	ソウル大学
	張 紹敏	涅盤会館
	李 周浩	立命館大学
	孫 艶萍	コロンビア大学
	許 暁原	コロンビア大学
	葉 文昌	島根大学
	林 泉忠	台湾中央研究院
	Iko Pramudiono	インドネシア三井物産
	Mukhopadhyaya, Ranjana	デリー大学
	孫 建軍	北京大学
	張 桂娥	東呉大学
	李 済宇	(豪)AECOM
	Napoleon	SMBC日興証券
	王 健歓	Citizens Bank
	Sim Choon Kiat	昭和女子大学

【査読委員】
Alfonso, Mynn	サント・トーマス大学
Arcenas, Joy	フィリピン大学ロスバニョス校(UPLB)
Baconguis, Rowena	フィリピン大学ロスバニョス校(UPLB)
Bello, Rolando Trinidad	フィリピン大学ロスバニョス校(UPLB)
陳 姿菁	(台湾)開南大学
Dacanay, Jovi	(フィリピン)アジア太平洋大学(UAP)
Dale, Sonja	一橋大学
De Maio, Silvana	ナポリ東洋大学
Gilles, Stephanie	(フィリピン)SNGデザイン
何 祖源	上海交通大学
鄭 成春	(韓国)対外経済政策研究院
川崎 剛	津田塾大学
Khomenko, Olga	キエフモヒラアカデミー国立大学
高 煕卓	(韓国)グローカル・ニュース
李 香哲	光云大学
李 鋼哲	北陸大学
梁 興国	中国海洋大学
Mateo, Antonio Francisco	(フィリピン)AMECOS
Musikasinthorn, Prachya	カセサート大学
沼田貞昭	鹿島建設
小川 忠	跡見学園女子大学
奇 錦峰	広州中医薬大学
Rio, Aaron	ミネアポリス美術館
Sapuay, Grace	フィリピン廃棄物管理協会
Sonntag, Mira	立教大学
Tan, Rosalina	アテネオ大学
Tenegra, Brenda	(フィリピン)LINGO 24
Tomeldan, Michael Velasco	フィリピン大学ディリマン校
Toribio, Jane	(フィリピン)農地改革省
上野 宏	村田製作所
Wachirasak Maneewatnaperk	IBC Travel
武 玉萍	理化学研究所
楊 接期	(台湾)国立中央大学
朱 庭耀	日本海事協会

今西淳子　Junko Imanishi

学習院大学文学部卒。コロンビア大学大学院美術史考古学学科修士。1994年に家族で設立した渥美国際交流財団に設立時から常務理事として関わる。留学生の経済的支援だけでなく、知日派外国人研究者のネットワークの構築を目指す。2000年に「関口グローバル研究会（SGRA）」を設立。また、1997年より異文化理解と平和教育のグローバル組織であるCISVの運営に加わり、現在CISV日本協会理事。

B.A. Gakushuin University. M.A. Columbia University. Since 1994, Managing Director of Atsumi International Foundation, which aims not only to support international students financially, but also to build a network of Japan specialists around the world. In 2000, established Sekiguchi Global Research Association (SGRA). Since 1997, Board Member of CISV Japan, a global organization for cross-cultural and peace education.

公益財団法人
渥美国際交流財団
関口グローバル研究会
Sekiguchi Global Research Association
Atsumi International Foundation
〒112-0014　東京都文京区関口3-5-8
3-5-8 Sekiguchi, Bunkyo-ku, Tokyo 112-0014, Japan
Tel: +81-3-3943-7612　　FAX: +81-3-3943-1512
Email: office@aisf.or.jp

アジアの未来へ―私の提案 4
Toward the Future of Asia: My Proposal Vol.4

2019年4月5日　初刷発行	
編　者	今西淳子
発行者	堤　丈晴
発行所	株式会社ジャパンタイムズ
	〒102-0082　東京都千代田区一番町2-2
	一番町第二TGビル2F
	電話　050-3646-9500（出版営業部）
ウェブサイト	https://bookclub.japantimes.co.jp/
印刷所	株式会社シナノパブリッシングプレス

定価はカバーに表示してあります。
万一、乱丁落丁のある場合は、送料当社負担でお取り替えいたします。
本書のコピー、スキャン、デジタル化等の無断複製は、著作権法上での例外である私的利用を除き禁じられています。

Copyright ⓒ 2019 by Junko Imanishi　Printed in Japan
ISBN978-4-7890-1721-3